The Archaeology of Nucleation in the Old World

The Archaeology of Nucleation in the Old World: Spatiality, Community, and Identity

edited by

Attila Gyucha and Roderick B. Salisbury

ARCHAEOPRESS ARCHAEOLOGY

ARCHAEOPRESS PUBLISHING LTD
Summertown Pavilion
18-24 Middle Way
Summertown
Oxford OX2 7LG

www.archaeopress.com

ISBN 978-1-80327-090-6
ISBN 978-1-80327-091-3 (e-Pdf)

Cover: Ruins of a town, Mut, Dakhla Oasis, Egypt.
Image: Attila Gyucha.
Cover design: Mátyás Rózsavölgyi

This book is available direct from Archaeopress or from our website www.archaeopress.com

Contents

List of Figures iii

List of Tables v

List of Authors vi

Chapter 1: Nucleation as Social Process: Built Environment, Community Organization, and Identity.
An Introduction to the Volume 1
Attila Gyucha and Roderick B. Salisbury

Chapter 2: What Does Settlement Layout Tell Us About the Community?
An Ethnoarchaeological Study 14
E. Nurcan Yalman

Chapter 3: From Sanctuaries to Towns: The Role of Religion in Early Urbanization 32
Manuel Fernández-Götz

Chapter 4: Activity Zones and Community Formation: The Role of Spatial Structure in
Early Nucleated Villages 43
Roderick B. Salisbury

Chapter 5: Population Aggregation and Social Transformations in Middle-Range Societies:
A Comparative Study of Neolithic Nucleated Settlements on the Great Hungarian Plain 62
Attila Gyucha

Chapter 6: Large Settlements of the Funnel Beaker Culture in Lesser Poland: Instruments of
Social Cohesion and Cultural Conversion 82
Marek Nowak, Klaus Cappenberg, Marta Korczyńska and Magdalena Moskal-del Hoyo

Chapter 7: Spatio-Demographic Structure and Social Organization: A Linear Trajectory or
Overlapping Trends? 99
Aleksandr Diachenko and Ezra B.W. Zubrow

Chapter 8: Sanctuaries and Settlements: Spatial Organization in the Nuragic Landscapes of
Sardinia 115
Ruth Beusing

Chapter 9: Settlement Mounds, Identity, and Continuity in the Settlement Organization of
Iron Age Jutland 131
Niels Haue

Chapter 10: Multilinear Settlement Development and Nucleation during the Early Iron Age in
Southwestern Jutland, Denmark 142
Niels Algreen Møller and Scott Robert Dollar

Chapter 11: Nucleated Settlements as Assemblages: A Regional Network Approach to
Built Environments 157
Francesca Fulminante

Chapter 12: Landscape as Metaphor: Burial Monuments and 'Landscapes of Power' in Late Iron Age Britain..173
Karolis Minkevičius

Chapter 13: Kernavė Town in the 13th and 14th Centuries: Social and Cultural Patterns of Community 186
Rokas Vengalis and Gintautas Vėlius

Chapter 14: The Creation and Maintenance of Powerful Places in Etruria 200
Simon Stoddart

Index..212

List of Figures

Chapter 1
Figure 1.1. A street in the ancient Greek city of Selinus 1
Figure 1.2. Mosaic on the building of the National Museum of History in Tirana 4
Figure 1.3. The Baiterek Tower in Astana 6
Figure 1.4. Manhole cover, depicting the Aztec Sun Stone in the Pilsen neighborhood of Chicago 7

Chapter 2
Figure 2.1. House plan at the Akşehir Settlement 17
Figure 2.2. House plan at the Çumra Settlement 18
Figure 2.3. The Çumra Settlement, Upper Quarter 22
Figure 2.4. A household's spatial distribution within the Akşehir Settlement 23
Figure 2.5. The herd/flock gathering around wells, the routes from settlement to pastureland, and the distribution
    of threshing floors at the Upper Quarter of the Çumra Settlement 25
Figure 2.6. The herd/flock gathering in the center and the route from settlement to pastureland at the Akşehir Settlement.... 26

Chapter 3
Figure 3.1. Ruins of the ceremonial center of Göbekli Tepe 33
Figure 3.2. Burial mounds at Gamla Uppsala 34
Figure 3.3. Distribution map of Late Iron Age *oppida* between the Atlantic and East Europe 35
Figure 3.4. Recreation of the center of the *oppidum* of Corent 35
Figure 3.5. Plan of the Titelberg *oppidum* 36
Figure 3.6. Plan of Temple A at Manching 38
Figure 3.7. Location of the central temple and visual axes with the southern and the eastern gates at Manching 38
Figure 3.8. Late Iron Age public space of 'La Terrasse' and the nearby Gallo-Roman temple at Bibracte 39
Figure 3.9. Aerial view of the *oppidum* of San Cibrán de Las 39

Chapter 4
Figure 4.1. Case study area in the eastern Carpathian Basin within Hungary, with locations of major settlements
    mentioned in the text 47
Figure 4.2. Interpretation of the magnetic anomalies at the Late Neolithic settlement of Csárdaszállás-Félhalomdűlő 49
Figure 4.3. The household cluster activity zones model 53

Chapter 5
Figure 5.1. Sites, archaeological groups, and regions mentioned in the text 63
Figure 5.2. Szeghalom microregion: Middle Neolithic and Late Neolithic settlements in 5- and 10-km radius
    around Szeghalom-Kovácshalom 65
Figure 5.3. Öcsöd microregion: Middle Neolithic and Late Neolithic settlements in 5- and 10-km radius
    around Öcsöd-Kováshalom 65
Figure 5.4. Polgár Island: Middle Neolithic and Late Neolithic settlements in 5- and 10-km radius
    around Polgár-Csőszhalom 66
Figure 5.5. The Szeghalom-Kovácshalom settlement complex 67
Figure 5.6. The Öcsöd-Kováshalom settlement complex 68
Figure 5.7. The Polgár-Csőszhalom settlement complex 69

Chapter 6
Figure 6.1. Location of SE TRB 83
Figure 6.2. Distributions of Early and Middle Neolithic sites in the Bronocice microregion 84
Figure 6.3. Results of geomagnetic prospection in the southeastern part of Mozgawa 85
Figure 6.4. Reconstructed density of anthropogenic features at Mozgawa 86
Figure 6.5. Development of the Bronocice site 87
Figure 6.6. 'Fuzzy' chronology of Funnel Beaker culture surface findings at Mozgawa 88

Chapter 7
Figure 7.1. Tripolye sites in the Southern Bug and Dnieper Interfluve and neighboring regions 102
Figure 7.2. Settlement clusters, with the centers at Nebelevka and Maidanetske 103
Figure 7.3. Graphs showing the weak and strong Allee-effect 106
Figure 7.4. Mortality pulses impacting lower cohorts and then moving upward through the pyramid 108
Figure 7.5. The number of survivors at the end of each cohort 109

Chapter 8
Figure 8.1. Distribution of *nuraghi–tombe dei giganti* and *nuraghi–*water-temples in Sardinia 119
Figure 8.2. Voronoi-partitioning into regions 123

Figure 8.3. Intervisibility of *nuraghi* and water-temples..124
Figure 8.4. Voronoi-partitioning of Class 3 *nuraghi* and surrounding *nuraghi* in the test area.........................125
Figure 8.5. Cumulative viewshed and intervisibility of water-temples and *nuraghi* and Class 3 *nuraghi* and
        surrounding *nuraghi*...126

Chapter 9
Figure 9.1. Jutland and the Limfjord region...132
Figure 9.2. Diagram showing the length of Iron Age longhouses at Nørre Tranders.....................................134
Figure 9.3. Simplified ground plans of two longhouses at Nørre Tranders...135
Figure 9.4. Burned House A371 seen from the east..135
Figure 9.5. The excavated area at Nørre Tranders, with longhouses..138

Chapter 10
Figure 10.1. Map of southwestern Jutland, with the sites mentioned in the text..144
Figure 10.2. Nucleated common-fenced villages from Jutland..144
Figure 10.3. Result of point-pattern analysis..146
Figure 10.4. Development of clustered villages in the Oksbøl settlement cell...148
Figure 10.5. ERIA row-village at Vejen Vestermark..151

Chapter 11
Figure 11.1. Southern Etruria and *Latium vetus* in Central Italy...158
Figure 11.2. Etruscan and Latin networks of Orientalizing bronze ribbed bowls..164
Figure 11.3. Orientalizing Age Latin network...165
Figure 11.4. Characteristic measures of southern Etruria and *Latium vetus* cultural networks from the Final Bronze Age
        to the Archaic Period...166
Figure 11.5. Efficiency measures calculated on fluvial and terrestrial routes networks in Etruria and *Latium vetus*....................166
Figure 11.6. Comparison between the Latin empirical network models..168

Chapter 12
Figure 12.1. Viewshed analysis, with areas intervisible with the Folly Lane..177
Figure 12.2. Viewshed analysis from five points along the Gorhambury Lane...179
Figure 12.3. Viewshed analysis, with areas intervisible with the Stanway complex..180
Figure 12.4. Viewshed analysis, with areas intervisible with the Lexden tumulus..181
Figure 12.5. Viewshed analysis from five points along the Gosbecks Road...182

Chapter 13
Figure 13.1. The territory of the Grand Duchy of Lithuania during the reign of Grand Duke Gediminas......................188
Figure 13.2. The hillforts of Kernavė..190
Figure 13.3. Kernavė in the 13th and 14th centuries..191
Figure 13.4. Buildings and fences in the excavated area of Lower Town I..193

Chapter 14
Figure 14.1. Etruria and the major nucleated centers..202
Figure 14.2. A comparison of three nucleated centers...204
Figure 14.3. A comparison of relationships between five nucleated centers and their countryside..........................205
Figure 14.4. Three phases of development in Veii...207
Figure 14.5. The layout of nucleation in Perugia..208

List of Tables

Chapter 2
Table 2.1. Comparison of the two settlements in terms of collective versus close family-based activities 25

Chapter 7
Table 7.1. Settlement cluster with a 'center' at Nebelevka 104
Table 7.2. Settlement cluster with a 'center' at Maidanetske 104
Table 7.3. *K*-values dependent upon spatial hierarchy 104
Table 7.4. Density of dwellings at the largest Tripolye settlements of the SV1 in the Southern Bug and Dnieper Interfluve 106
Table 7.5. Small villages that were branched-off from the largest settlements 107
Table 7.6. Summary results from simulations of the demographic structure of prehistoric villages 110

Chapter 8
Table 8.1. Chronology of Sardinian archaeology from the Eneolithic to the Late Iron Age 116
Table 8.2. Number of monuments utilized in the analysis 118
Table 8.3. Sanctuaries with more than one water-temples 120
Table 8.4. Supralocal or 'federal' sanctuaries 120
Table 8.5. Intervisibility matches *nuraghi* Class 3 and Class 2 with water-temples 123

Chapter 11
Table 11.1. Settlement dynamics in Central Italy between the end of the Final Bronze Age and the end of
 the Archaic Period 160
Table 11.2. Social dynamics as mirrored by the funerary evidence in Central Italy between the end of
 the Final Bronze Age and the end of the Archaic Period. 160
Table 11.3. Measures selected to characterize the empirical networks 161
Table 11.4. Pottery production from the Final Bronze Age to the end of the Archaic Period, and luxury items and
 architectural decorations of the Orientalizing Age and Archaic Period considered in this study 163
Table 11.5. Metal production from the Final Bronze Age to the end of the Archaic Period considered
 in this study 163

List of Authors

Ruth Beusing, Landesamt für Bodendenkmalpflege Hessen, Wiesbaden, Germany

Klaus Cappenberg, Landesamt für Archäologie Sachsen, Dresden, Germany

Aleksandr Diachenko, Institute of Archaeology of the National Academy of Sciences of Ukraine, Kiev, Ukraine

Scott Robert Dollar, Sønderskov Museum, Brørup, Denmark

Manuel Fernández-Götz, School of History, Classics and Archaeology, University of Edinburgh, Edinburgh, UK

Francesca Fulminante, Department of Anthropology and Archaeology, University of Bristol, UK, and Department of Humanities, University Roma Tre, Italy

Attila Gyucha, Department of Anthropology, University of Georgia, Athens, GA, USA

Niels Haue, Historical Museum of Northern Jutland, Aalborg, Denmark

Marta Korczyńska, W. Szafer Institute of Botany, Polish Academy of Sciences, Kraków, Poland

Karolis Minkevičius, Vilnius University, Vilnius, Lithuania

Niels Algreen Møller, Museum Thy, Thisted, Denmark

Magdalena Moskal-del Hoyo, W. Szafer Institute of Botany, Polish Academy of Sciences, Kraków, Poland

Marek Nowak, Institute of Archaeology, Jagiellonian University, Kraków, Poland

Roderick B. Salisbury, Austrian Archaeological Institute (ÖAI), Austrian Academy of Sciences, Vienna, Austria

Simon Stoddart, McDonald Institute for Archaeological Research, University of Cambridge, Cambridge, UK

Gintautas Vélius, Administration of the State Cultural Reserve of Kernavė, and Department of Archaeology, Faculty of History, Vilnius University, Lithuania

Rokas Vengalis, Department of Archaeology, Lithuanian Institute of History, Lithuania

Emine Nurcan Yalman, Department of History, Nişantaşı University, Istanbul, Turkey

Ezra B.W. Zubrow, Department of Anthropology, University at Buffalo, Buffalo, USA, and Department of Anthropology, University of Toronto, Canada

Chapter 1

Nucleation as Social Process:
Built Environment, Community Organization, and Identity.
An Introduction to the Volume

Attila Gyucha and Roderick B. Salisbury

The relationship between community formation and physical settlement configurations has been the subject of scrutiny and design since Antiquity. From Plato to Thomas More, thinkers of social utopias emphasized habitation areas, and particularly cities, and have proposed markedly different ideas for organizing space to ensure livability and well-being (Baker-Smith 2000; Charbit 2002; for a summary of utopias, see Rosenau 1983). Ancient and historic architects and architectural manuals, including the Hindu vaastu shastras (Sinha 1998) and Joseph Smith's *Plat of the City of Zion* for Mormon communities (Hamilton 1995), also reflected the principal role of ideological agendas in settlement planning.

Some early efforts, such as those promoted by the Greek architect Hippodamus of Miletus, were explicit in aspiring to substitute organic spatial arrangements for regular, linear structure. In his famous and still relevant book *Town Planning in Practice*, Unwin (1909) presents the gridded layouts of the Greek city of Selinus and Roman Pompeii as examples of the early influence of this style (Figure 1.1). Regularity and administrative efficiency triumphed over human social interactions and natural landforms. Similar to these early works, social aspects were of central importance in settlement design manuals compiled for colonial settings from the 16th century onward, such as those issued by the Spanish Crown for its colonies in the Americas and the Philippines (Mundigo and Crouch 1977).

More recently, urban planners seeking recipes to achieve social unity and betterment have reconsidered the cities' built environment as a key determinant. In contrast to the classical approaches to urban planning, Fredrick Law Olmstead's plan for the Riverside suburb of Chicago followed natural contours and deliberately avoided right angles (Beveridge *et al.* 1998). As the well-known modernist examples of Le Corbusier's Ville Radieuse (The Radiant City; Le Corbusier 1935),

Figure 1.1. A street in the ancient Greek city of Selinus (Selinunte) on the southwest coast of Sicily, showing the linear alignment of buildings and walls, facing south (photo by R. Salisbury).

Frank Lloyd Wright's Broadacre City (Wright 1932), and Ebenezer Howard's Garden Cities (Howard 1902) demonstrate profound differences remain in how scholars view the role of the organization of the built form in shaping societies and what mechanisms facilitate community formation (see also Fishman 1982). Moreover, despite the millennia-long history of urban planning ideas, until recently, advanced theories rarely have been formulated concerning how and why the spatial organization of cities develops. The increasingly growing trend of urbanization in the past several decades, however, has resulted in an overall shift, and the principles, processes, and aftermaths of the evolution of city shapes and forms have become focal themes in urban theories (Batty 2005; Marshall 2008; Taylor 1998).

What these approaches have frequently in common is an assumption that spatial organization should be imposed on a community. Nevertheless, the history of urban spatial design indicates that universally optimal plans do not exist. Furthermore, tracking such approaches frequently imposes an archaeology of elites while ignoring the earliest, formative stages of settlement organization before the formalization of spatial structure (Stoddart and Malone 2002); this latter point being a key strength of archaeology. Moreover, some very successful urban plans, such as that of Teotihuacán in the Valley of Mexico, may have developed through collective action (Manzanilla 2017b). By concentrating on the origins and outcomes of variation in human settlement behavior, and those initiated at the community level, in particular, we will have a better chance to achieve and maintain resilience and sustainability in our present and future cities. Exploring the underpinning principles and trajectories in the formation of built forms as they relate to social developments over space and time should be an essential part of this process.

This volume aims to contribute to this body of scholarship from a cross-cultural and cross-temporal perspective. The diversity of methodological and conceptual approaches used by the authors, in conjunction with the breadth of historical contexts being analyzed, makes comparison both challenging and rewarding. Archaeology is, of course, comparative at its roots, whether we compare ceramic vessels to identify 'cultural' affiliation (e.g., Nelson 1985), or social responses to climate change (e.g., Fagan 2008), or examine diachronically the roles of motherhood (e.g., Romero and López 2018). With a particular focus on prehistoric and historic Old World, the authors of this volume explore the role of the built environment in expressing and shaping community organization and identity. Not all of the chapters are comparative by design, but the contributions provide theory-driven and data-rich case studies to interpret organizational

variability in the archaeological record. When taken as a whole, these contributions enable the analysis of archaeological data at multiple spatial and social scales. Comparing like to like produces little new information—comparative analyses of multiple cultures, times, and spatial scales can reveal the many ways how communities can structure their settlements and social life, get along, and deal with environmental, social, and economic stressors. This variability in past human responses has particular relevance to present, pressing issues in our rapidly urbanizing world (e.g., Smith 2010).

Recent advances in theory, as well as field and analytical methods in archaeology, allow investigations of nucleated settlements to an extent and depth of detail that was previously impossible. Taking advantage of these improvements, in particular related to the interplay between the spatial and social organization of communities, this volume addresses a few specific topics. Among these are how the built environment and location of activity zones can be used to understand social configurations, how various scales of social units can be identified and the resulting patterns interpreted, how collective actions contributed to settlement organization and community integrity, how changes in social relations are reflected in the development of the built environment, how cooperation, competition, and measures to decrease social and communication stress can be identified in the archaeological record, and how the built environment was used to express or manipulate identity.

Most papers in this volume focus on large, nucleated settlements, and many of the contributors employ a multiscalar perspective. Throughout history, large settlements developed via the process of population aggregation, and co-dependency typified the relations of these settlements with their hinterlands in pre-industrial societies (e.g., Fox 1977; Hall 1998; Mumford 1961). Thus, the formation and evolution of nucleated settlements cannot be explored productively without shifting back and forth between various geographic scales, from local to microregional to regional. This multiscalar perspective, however, must be paired with a systemic approach to address the social, ecological, economic, and cultural dynamics that governed the development of nucleated settlements. Finally, these studies ideally are conducted in a diachronic framework that permits exploration of the temporal aspects of systemic transformations at these sites as well as in their hinterlands.

In the rest of this introductory chapter, we reflect on this complex approach and utilize historic and modern examples to demonstrate the reflexive relationship between the built environment, and social organization and identity formation.

Community and Space

Representing various conceptual approaches and perspectives, an array of definitions has been created by social scientists to describe the term 'community' (for summaries, see Canuto and Yaeger 2000; Mac Sweeney 2011; Salisbury 2012). However, it is widely accepted that shared social experiences, practices, and traditions generate a sense of community (Yaeger and Canuto 2000).

For this volume, the geographical community approach is particularly relevant. Mac Sweeney defined a geographical community as '*an identity-bearing social group whose conscious sense of collective belonging is rooted in the experience of residential proximity and shared space*' (2011: 32). Salisbury (2012) emphasizes that the community of space can develop not only at the settlement level but at any spatial scale that people recognize as their own geographic area. Thus, communities are not necessarily based on everyday face-to-face interactions, practices, and experiences (Anderson 1991), and this is manifested particularly well at large, nucleated settlements as geographical communities.

Young's (1990) community approach for cities is another conceptual framework that facilitates understanding not only the development and operation of modern cities but also those of ancient nucleated settlements. She views the city as the social construction of many small communities that do not constitute a community as defined by mutual identification and reciprocity. Instead, to satisfy their various needs and demands, mediation among these small communities and institutions is necessitated, and over the course of these processes, a single polity comes into being. Batty and Marshall share a similar notion, stating that the '*city is not conceived of as a unified whole following a developmental program, but is more usefully seen as a collection of inter-dependent, co-evolving parts*' (2009: 552).

Therefore, we find it useful to distinguish communities as social units and communities as identity units. Communities as social units develop through the organization of individuals and groups into an integrated, operative whole to meet existential needs as they relate to human existence and well-being, such as the provisioning of basic goods and services. Shared laws and norms, and their active enforcement, as well as social and economic agendas, are instrumental to achieve and maintain communities as social units. The construction of communities as identity units requires different and/or additional measures in order to create a sense of unity. From this perspective, the community is '*a mental construct rather than a natural or structural phenomenon*' (Mac Sweeney 2011: 35). Communities as identity units develop through the integration of individuals and groups by way of shared values and ideological agendas. Some measures taken to generate communities as social units and as identity units might correspond, and the built environment is one of the mediums that has played a major role in their creations throughout history.

Built Environment and Community Organization

The transformation of the physical environment has always been an essential means to bring order to societies (Bogucki 1999; Hodder 1990; Renfrew 2007). The construction and reconstruction of architectural features and their spatial configurations, together constituting the built environment, are instrumental measures to establish, maintain, and renew social order, and the built form embodies clues to identify laws and rules that operated in past societies.

Therefore, the built environment is a commonly used source to scrutinize the origins and trajectories of various developments in past societies (Kostof 1991; Pauknerová *et al.* 2013; Vis 2009). Regardless of scale, the architectural features and their spatial configurations testify to the interplay between social, cultural, and economic principles and dynamics, and changes in the built form and organization indicate shifts in one or multiple subsystems. We illustrate the timeless nature of these premises by a modern example. After World War II, East European countries became part of the Communist Bloc, resulting in fundamental and abrupt transformations in these societies. Settlement patterns across entire regions were profoundly altered in only a few years due to forced collectivization and a rapid pace of industrialization. Masses of people lost their lands, abandoned their farms or villages, and migrated to cities, several of which were built from scratch (Fallenbuchl 1970; Iordachi and Bauerkamper 2014). In many cases, the historic urban fabric also was dramatically reconfigured. Large factories were established and complete neighborhoods with apartment blocks housing tens of thousands of people were rapidly built (Popescu 2009). Furthermore, strikingly different architectural styles spread across the region, with civic and residential buildings erected using a constructivist approach as well as with central, monumental structures of so-called Stalinist style typically built in capital cities (Figure 1.2; Kelleher 2009; Moravčíková 2009). From an anthropological point of view, this example illustrates that highly centralized political control tends to bring about similar, groundbreaking, and expeditious developments, as well as overall standardization in the built form over large areas and at many different scales. These top-down processes are certainly not limited to the post-industrial era, as similar advancements occurred in pre-industrial contexts too (e.g., Yegül and Favro 2019).

Figure 1.2. Mosaic on the building of the National Museum of History in Tirana, Albania
(photo by A. Gyucha).

Many papers in this volume, however, substantiate the generative force of bottom-up processes in the development of built forms throughout history. Demonstrating the instrumental role of local needs and challenges, a high degree of variability may occur in the layout and organization of nucleated settlements within even the same sociopolitical units. When strong, centralized planning is not implemented, the spatial arrangement and architectural properties of the built environment primarily developed through the interplay of local social dynamics and cultural preferences (Kostof 1991; Sjoberg 1960; Storey 2006).

The built environment not only reflects but also structures sociocultural dynamics and processes, and its reconfiguration is a productive mechanism to achieve major sociocultural transformations. A historic example from the Medieval Age properly illustrates this process at the regional scale. At the beginning of the 11th century AD, the establishment of the Hungarian Kingdom coincided with the systematic introduction of Christianity to the pagan Hungarians. In addition to bishoprics, dioceses, and monasteries, King Stephen I ordered that every ten villages had to build a church across his kingdom (Kosztolnyik 2002). This measure produced fundamental modifications in the physical landscape and was a major tool to exert political control and impose an ideological shift throughout the realm.

Spatial and architectural reconfigurations in the context of nucleated settlements and cities even more apparently testify to the profound role of the built environment in sociocultural transformations. According to Giddens (1979, 1984), individual behaviors and interactions create social organization, and social reproduction is the process of reconfiguration of social relations through regular and ordinary practices and actions. Throughout history, the built form has been an arena, as well as a productive tool, for social reproduction, as practices and actions both occur in the physical landscape and transform it as an integrated, spatial component of these processes (see Lawrence and Low 1990).

As the application of constructivism in the cities of the Communist Bloc shows, changes in the built form are frequently utilized to engineer overall social shifts. Resonating with the physicalism perspective in urban theory, Batty and Marshall note in their paper on city evolution that *'changing the physical form of cities to meet social goals is a somewhat more effective way than broaching social change directly: that controls and instruments to engender physical change are somewhat less intrusive than the more direct forms of action'* (2009: 567). This approach is remarkably attested in ancient city planning as well, particularly when urban open spaces are concerned. For example, in Rome, through the implementation of architectural alterations, the fora shifted from places that encouraged the free flow of people to places where a greater degree of control over movement and interaction could be imposed, and these transformations coincided with an increasing degree of centralized political control in the empire (Perring 1991).

By assuming that social challenges in urban contexts may be resolved through the manipulation of the built environment, physicalism is a useful approach to understanding the morphological development of nucleated settlements also in pre-industrial and stateless societies (Batty and Marshall 2009). As growth in population and density occurs at large sites, rules and orders to tackle organizational challenges and scalar stress must be introduced. Architectural planning, including the spatial configuration, and reconfiguration, of the built environment, is a widely used adaptive response to these problems. Similar to the communicative planning approach, where modern urban design is viewed as a form of communicative action (Healey 1996; Innes 1995), ancient societies might have incorporated a wide variety of stakeholders in decision-making processes. In all probability, these constituted the generative base for collective action more often than we previously thought (Blanton and Fargher 2016; Carballo 2013). The socio-spatial significance of clustering, boundary making, and the creation of public spaces and places is worth mentioning in this context (Carballo and Fortenberry 2015; Vis 2018; York et al. 2011).

The built environment is charged with messages regarding rules of conduct and behavior (Bradley 1998; Fletcher 1981; Rapoport 1994). These rules are particularly associated with interactions among community members, the scales, forms, locations, and timing of which unfold through the application of cultural and social norms, as well as everyday practices, to develop and sustain order and organization. Many elements of the built environment, from roads to homes and from fortifications to religious and civic structures, are specifically designed to promote and regulate the movements and encounters of people, and thus to shape human interactions. These interactions occur at many different social scales, from families to entire communities to societies, of which the architectural contexts vary. During the past decades, the introduction of new approaches has paved the way for a better understanding of interactions between people and the built environment in urban contexts, and environmental psychological studies have been proved to be particularly useful for anthropologists (Hillier and Hanson 1984; Lawrence and Low 1990). These studies address the important question of how variations in physical properties and configurations in the built environment influence the movement and interactions of people. For archaeologists, these investigations highlight the significance of considering

psychological factors and agency in the study of the development and use of built forms in order to get a more nuanced understanding of organization and order in past societies.

The subtitle of this volume refers to the complexity of relational systems in the evolution of the built environment. Changes in the physical landscape at any scale, from scattered residential structures to nucleated settlements, to fortifications, to sanctuaries and monuments, occur in the context of individual communities with their own histories and sociopolitical dynamics. Builders must consider these social and cultural contexts, just as they must acknowledge their physical and environmental settings. Thus, analyzing spatial layouts at various scales provide hints at the environmental, cultural, social, and political configurations of ancient communities.

Built Environment and Community Identity

The concept of collective identity as it relates to community building is paramount to understand the development of the built environment in past societies. We define collective identity as a shared consciousness of belonging to a group—a consciousness that originates from the recognition of the importance of one or more actual or imaginary commonalities and is sustained through recurring social practices by the members. As opposed to personal and social identities, the latter based on social roles and categories, such as age, gender, religion, or ethnicity in a society, collective identities are more elastic and transient, not a priori associated with or deriving from other forms of group identities (Melucci 1995; Snow 2001). Therefore, the formation and maintenance of collective identity require cognizant, active, and lasting work.

A collective entity of sets of individuals and groups commonly develops at and sustains close emotional ties to specific spaces in the physical landscape. The experience of shared locale may generate the sense of connectedness and is a major source for the creation and affirmation of place-based communities of identity (Furholt et al. 2012; Neustupný 1991; Tönnies 1963). However, at large nucleated settlements, residential proximity does not necessarily correspond to the formation of community identity (Mac Sweeney 2011). Similar to entire societies (see Castells 1997), large settlements tend to exhibit a higher degree of organizational complexity and diversity. Rather than facilitating shared identity, these factors can render the development of collective identity remarkably challenging. Conscious measures, incorporating primarily inclusive social practices and activities, are a prerequisite to an evolving sense of unity among occupants at these sites. These measures have spatial components that become charged with social significance for the community members. Thus, when collective identity emerges at any scale, from settlements to entire societies, the process is embedded in the development of the built environment.

Group cohesion is a fundamental goal to sustain large settlements that typically form through the aggregation of multiple social groups. At these sites, the co-residence of corporate groups, corresponding to a plethora of social and organizational identities based on gender, kinship, origin, or ethnicity (Tajfel and Turner 1979; Tönnies 1963), is common. In the built environment and the associated material culture, lower-order group identities may manifest themselves by distinctive attributes spatially bound to specific territories within the confines of the settlements (Hegmon 1992; Manzanilla 2017a; Rapoport 1994). Physical and psychological boundaries may differentiate these subgroups within the fabric of these sites (Vis 2017).

The construction of collective identity and community rationale at large, nucleated settlements facilitate in overcoming social stress and conflicts among lower-order identity groups to ensure and sustain cohesion and commitment (Keller 1968; Simmel 1955; Young 1990). The identity work toward a collective entity can unfold through various processes, including mechanisms to complement, repress, and eliminate other, lower-order identities through social and political measures. Over the course of these developments, the major integrative role of the built environment at nucleated sites primarily occurs through its capability to evoke associations with shared ideology, including collective identity. Resources to recall, and disclose, collective identity incorporate an array of potential attributes, such as architectural features, including monumental structures, special building materials, color, decorations, and symbols, as well as the consciously configured spatial arrangements of these features. Thus, these attributes are proxies for identity and convey nonverbal messages for the community members who could decipher and perceive them as markers to incite a sense of connection (Cohen 1985; Fisher 2009). Moreover, the more inclusive and highly standardized performances at these integrative architectural features also are identity resources. The enactments of community aim to counteract differences between individuals and subgroups by accentuating and reiterating commonalities, such as the shared experience of co-residence and the formation of shared beliefs, among the occupants (Mac Sweeney 2011: 57).

Ideological agendas to foster the formation of collective identity have always impacted urban design and planning principles and remain important during the modern era as well (see Dibble et al. 2017: 18). A timeless instance of the interplay between spatial and ideological concepts of identity is the representation of worldviews in the layout and architectural features of settlements. Although the interpretation of ancient cities as cosmograms is frequently debated (e.g., Baines et al. 2017; Carl et al. 2000; Smith 2007), there are many cases through the ages where cosmological principles are evident in urban designs (Janusek 2004; Landau 2015; Stencel et al. 1976). These principles unfolded to various spatial extents and through specific architectural elements and configurations, particularly in relation to communal performances in urban cores. Similar to ancient cities, architectural elements that suggest stability and convey the message of potential for future collective identity through their scale, materials, symbols, directionality, and centrality also are evident in modern urban contexts. In Astana, the new capital of Kazakhstan designed in 1997 and built from scratch, the central, 97-m-high Baiterek Tower is an outstanding example of imposed collective identity (Figure 1.3; Johnson 2014). The tower is one of the structures in the city that represent Kazakh history, myths, and symbols. Baiterek embodies a local origin myth and cosmology of the tree of life. Located at the top of the tree are the sacred bird and its golden egg, and at the bottom, there is a dragon who seeks to consume the egg. The golden egg symbolizes the Sun as the source of life and hope. Similar to other, ancient examples, such as the Forbidden City, this religious content of Baiterek was linked to the legitimization of political

Figure 1.3. The Baiterek Tower in Astana, Kazakhstan. The inset shows the gilded handprint of the country's former president in the tower (photo by D. Pugh).

power. In the egg, thus with the Sun as the center of the universe, the gilded handprint of the former president of the country, the commissioner of the construction of Astana, Nursultan Nazarbayev is found. Visitors are encouraged to place their hands in the handprint to make a wish, and through this act, the monument subversively suggests that the source of life and hope resides in the president. Astana's construction was a major part of a nation-building project consciously using the built form to reinforce collective identity via symbols that evoke deeply-rooted narratives and traditions (Anacker 2004; Schatz 2003).

Large settlements are dynamic entities, and transformations in the built environment are fundamental mechanisms in the creation of not only collective identities but also new group identities throughout their history. The historic Pilsen neighborhood in Chicago, for example, originally was established and inhabited predominantly by Bohemians in the early 1870s, and they expressed their ethnic identity through buildings constructed in the styles of and with decorations from their homeland (Pero 2011). In the 1960s and 1970s, a demographic shift occurred with increased migration of Mexicans from other neighborhoods of Chicago and elsewhere. Although Pilsen has largely retained its late nineteenth- and early twentieth-century character, public spaces have gradually and profoundly changed. In addition to the establishment of the National Museum of Mexican Art, symbols of Mexican heritage have been incorporated throughout the neighborhood, including a monument in Pilsen's central square, a park with prominent Mexican heroes, hundreds of murals featuring Mexican mythology and history, as well as manhole covers on the main street decorated with the Aztec Sun Stone (Figure 1.4). Although similar transformations are difficult to identify archaeologically at the neighborhood level, they might have occurred commonly in ancient and pre-industrial nucleated settlements.

The sense of unity, rooted either in spatial and/or social commonalities, is the most powerful force to trigger collective action and solidarity. There is a reflexive relation between collective identity and collective action (Carballo *et al.* 2014). The formation and maintenance of collective identities allow and inspire the group members to engage in collective actions, and these collective actions are generative forces during the establishment and reinforcement of collective entity as well as of individual group membership (Calhoun 1991). Throughout history, major, labor-intensive construction projects are frequently spectacular manifestations of resource mobilization strategies to achieve a shared goal and collective experiences as well as to build and sustain community identities. These collective projects, such as the above-mentioned construction of early Christian churches across the Hungarian Kingdom,

Figure 1.4. Manhole cover, depicting the Aztec Sun Stone in the Pilsen neighborhood of Chicago (photo by A. Gyucha).

created identity anchors in the social landscape and the associated, repeated activities, frequently at these focal venues of interactions, resulted in the development and regular re-enactment of positive emotional experiences and emotional unity (Bradley 1993; Pauketat 2009). Studies on relations between modern social movements and identity production indicate the marked importance of emotional involvement to bolster collective entities (Adams 2003; Fominaya 2010), and the emotional component of the sense of we-ness encourages solidarity in geographical identity groups as well.

Over the course of major sociopolitical shifts in societies, collective identities are regularly reshaped. This process commonly develops through the devaluation and replacement of principles and attributes of previous collective identities. Similar to horizontal self-definition processes to accentuate differences between coexisting groups (e.g., We and the Others), the built environment and the embedded symbols are principal targets during these advancements. At large settlements, the establishment of new and/or the reconfiguration of existing open public spaces to incorporate cues about new values and norms through alterations in architectural features, symbols, and their spatial arrangements play critical roles in this process. Redundancy in these cues, such as the Lenin statues and Soviet war memorials across the countries of the

Communist Bloc (Kelleher 2009), is a productive tool to 'ensure that social actors recognize the signs that remind them of "proper" or expected behavior' (Fisher 2009: 455).

The Sections of the Book

The chapters in this book present a range of geographic, methodological, and theoretical approaches to investigating the role of the built environment in the formation of nucleated settlements. The contributions cover the Old World, from the first large, Neolithic sites to Medieval cities and present-day communities, providing a solid basis for cross-cultural comparisons. Moreover, many contributions are explicitly or implicitly multiscalar, providing greater depth to both data and conclusions.

E. Nurcan Yalman's chapter *What Does Settlement Layout Tell Us About the Community? An Ethnoarchaeological Study* opens with an ethnoarchaeological investigation into the relationship between the structure of human communities and settlement layout, with a case study from Central Anatolia. This chapter fundamentally challenges archaeological assumptions about 'culture groups' and common-sense similarities between settlements of the same culture in the same region. It turns out that in the absence of top-down sociopolitical structures, different groups of the 'same people'— sharing basic modes of subsistence, production, ethnicity, and ideology—can develop particular local modes of social organization, leading to quite different spatial organization. This research further demonstrates how important group identity is for structuring social space and social interactions.

The role of religion and sacred places in nucleation processes for early urban centers is the subject of *From Sanctuaries to Towns: The Role of Religion in Early Urbanization* by Manuel Fernández-Götz. Sacred or ritual sites are key attractors for social aggregation and important contributors to spatial patterning. In this chapter, the author examines Late Iron Age *oppida* of temperate Europe, with cult or ritual locations within many of them. When these contexts were present prior to the construction of these fortified urban centers, the most likely conclusion is that they served as focal points for population aggregation, regularly visited by people from the surrounding rural landscape. He contrasts these arguments with examples of other early aggregation centers, such as Göbekli Tepe. During the process of regional demographic centralization, these places provided a point of collective identity as well as being an accepted social meeting point.

The following chapters, drawing their data from prehistoric and historic landscapes and settlement contexts in Europe, are organized broadly chronologically. In the first of several papers focusing

on the Neolithic of Central and East Europe, Roderick B. Salisbury's chapter *Activity Zones and Community Formation: The Role of Spatial Structure in Early Nucleated Villages* examines the role of spatial organization in early nucleated villages. Taking a cross-cultural comparison of settlement structure from several Late Neolithic cultures in the eastern Carpathian Basin, Salisbury looks for evidence of integrative mechanisms during this period of settlement and population aggregation. By contrasting the Hungarian data with comparative examples from North America, he presents significant differences in the use of space at fortified settlement mounds and flat, extended settlements. He concludes that there is little evidence for settlement-wide integration and that discrete communities lived close to each other, presumably interacting but never completely integrating.

Attila Gyucha employs a multiscalar approach in *Population Aggregation and Social Transformations in Middle-Range Societies: A Comparative Study of Neolithic Nucleated Settlements on the Great Hungarian Plain*. In a comparative framework, he elucidates the demographic and social development of three Late Neolithic nucleated villages on the Great Hungarian Plain. The author sees overall similarities in the origins and processes of population aggregation and emphasizes the importance of social behavioral drivers as pull factors in the evolution of these large sites. Based on settlement layout and integrative architectural features, Gyucha identifies a high degree of variability in the sociopolitical organization of the studied villages and argues that these differences emerged due to site-specific challenges related to population growth, density, and heterogeneity. The author concludes that these diverging local trajectories played a vital role in the dissolution of the Neolithic worldview across the region.

In *Large Settlements of the Funnel Beaker Culture in Lesser Poland: Instruments of Social Cohesion and Cultural Conversion*, Marek Nowak, Magdalena Moskal-del Hoyo, Marta Korczyńska, Klaus Cappenberg, and Jakob Ociepka investigate a process of settlement aggregation wherein some sites grew to be microregional centers, while many smaller sites were abandoned. Describing the sociopolitical organization as transegalitarian, the authors see evidence for nominal or incipient leaders who attempted to both control the distribution of certain goods and materials and exert decision-making authority over the nucleated settlements and neighboring satellite sites. The authors posit that the formation of a new identity— archaeologically 'Funnel Beaker'—was an essential component of the successful integration of people into these new social structures.

Cucuteni–Tripolye settlement systems are the subject of an analysis of the relationship between demographic and economic factors and the spatial layout of large settlements in Aleksandr Diachenko and Ezra Zubrow's *Spatio-Demographic Structure and Social Organization: A Linear Trajectory or Overlapping Trends?* This paper deals with superficially similar settlement structures to those observed by Nowak and colleagues but takes a very different analytical approach. Applying Central Place Theory and computer simulations, Diachenko and Zubrow found that archaeologists likely underestimate the impact of random mortality factors on the size and duration of mega-sites. Results suggest that population growth leads to increased variability in social organization, similar in some respects to the variability observed by Salisbury and Gyucha in their chapters. Within an overall settlement system, satellite sites that branched off from large, aggregated settlements served as a mechanism of demographic self-regulation.

The contribution by Ruth Beusing, *Sanctuaries and Settlements: Spatial Organization in the Nuragic Landscapes of Sardinia*, takes us from the Middle Bronze Age to the Early Iron Age in Sardinia. This is the first paper in the volume to examine the role of monumental architecture in facilitating social integration and political manipulation, in this case, the Sardinian cultural landscapes of *nuraghi*, tombs, and sanctuaries. Beusing conducted intervisibility analyses between the buildings at two analytical scales—the entire island and a mesoregion—to address the changing relations between profane and religious architecture. This approach enables the assessment of the reciprocal relationship between different classes of monuments in their cultural and environmental contexts at two spatial scales. The author evaluates architectural inclusiveness and exclusiveness, as well as transformations in the social meaning of *nuraghi* over a millennium.

Two papers examine Early Iron Age settlements in Jutland, Denmark, where settlement aggregation occurred at the end of the Bronze Age. In *Settlement Mounds, Identity, and Continuity in the Settlement Organization of Iron Age Jutland*, Niels Haue elucidates the use of architecture to express and manipulate identity within societies commonly considered egalitarian. Despite the absence of archaeologically typical wealth indicators, such as weapons and imported goods in burials, Haue identifies indications of socioeconomic inequality, particularly in terms of the 'best addresses,' in a comparison of two, newly excavated villages and two other datasets from northern Jutland. In an excellent archaeological example of the ethnographic phenomenon presented by Yalman in Chapter 2, Haue notes that in each of the four villages, community organization, longhouse number, and longhouse occupational continuity varied based on local responses to sociopolitical, economic, or environmental stress. He adds that by the end of the pre-Roman Iron Age,

prestige goods began to appear in burials, and evidence for economic inequality became more marked.

Niels Algreen Møller and Scott Robert Dollar also investigate this period of aggregation in *Multilinear Settlement Development and Nucleation during the Early Iron Age in Southwestern Jutland, Denmark*. Møller and Dollar question unilinear evolutionary models of settlement nucleation, using distribution analysis and detailed microregional studies. Although employing a different methodological approach in a different landscape, their results indicate developments that were very similar to those observed by Haue—there was no single, traditional process for Early Iron Age nucleation. Rather, communities followed their own trajectories informed by local conditions and social configurations.

Francesca Fulminante discusses Etrurian population aggregation and the relative success of different centralization processes in her chapter *Nucleated Settlements as Assemblages: A Regional Network Approach to Built Environments*. Fulminante compares terrestrial and riverine networks in the Final Bronze Age and Archaic Era in Etruria and *Latium vetus* diachronically and at a regional scale. By examining networks of communication and transportation systems, the author concludes that the more nucleated settlement pattern of *Latium vetus*, with its consolidated political structure, enabled Rome to overcome the more dispersed and politically fragmented structure of the Etruscans.

Karolis Minkevičius explores the landscape context of Late Iron Age cremation burial monuments in East and Southeast Britain in his chapter of *Landscape as Metaphor: Burial Monuments and 'Landscapes of Power' in Late Iron Age Britain*. Similar to Beusing, Minkevičius conducted a GIS-based viewshed and spatial analysis of burial mounds in relation to other monuments (earthworks) and roads. He concludes that the burial monuments served as identity markers that helped to validate political power and demonstrated continuity of control. Further, the reuse of these sites for Roman temples and sanctuaries following the Claudian conquest suggests a deep history of place, which could have been manipulated by outsiders seeking to legitimize a new political structure.

Rokas Vengalis and Gintautas Vėlius detail the relationship between spatial layout and social dynamics in the unique setting of *Kernavė Town in Thirteenth and Fourteenth Centuries: Social and Cultural Patterns of Community*. Kernavė was one of the most significant economic centers in Medieval Lithuania and is notable for having distinctive quarters shaped by various social groups. The authors describe cultural differences between the Upper and Lower Towns, including both socioeconomic stratification and the importance of pagan and Christian identities. Archaeological research indicates that the quarters retained their distinctive identities, although there is no record of this in historical documents.

In the final chapter, *The Creation and Maintenance of Powerful Places in Etruria*, Simon Stoddart summarizes the various challenges inherent in reconstructing nucleation processes from the built environment. Then, he demonstrates that the Etruscans successfully balanced opposing forces of dispersed political lineages, as indicated by burial evidence, and burgeoning centralization of power seen in the spatial organization of settlements. Stoddart offers a cautionary note, emphasizing that apparent uniformity in the built environment might mask significant differences in relationships between urban centers and their surrounding countryside, on the one hand, and with Rome, on the other. These differing relationships generated 'divergent patterns of nucleation' in Etruria, comparable to examples drawn from Mayan political centralization in Mesoamerica. As the final chapter in this volume, this paper exemplifies the rewards of comparative research and reflects our opening chapters.

Concluding Remarks

In this book, we collected papers about the role of the built environment in expressing and shaping community organization and identity in different times and places in the Old World, with particular attention to nucleated settlements. The contributors apply various methodological and theoretical frameworks, and, in some cases, started with rather different questions within a single region (e.g., chapters by Haue, and Møller and Dollar).

Several papers employ multiscalar analyses, with authors focusing on different aspects of cultural landscapes, including settlement patterns (e.g., Gyucha, and Diachenko and Zubrow), the role of monuments (e.g., Beusing and Minkevičius), and communication routes (Fulminante). Contrasts between macroregional descriptions of archaeological patterns and detailed local, or microregional, case studies provide not only a greater depth of understanding but also raise important questions. When we know that the processes of nucleation varied for nearly all settlements within a given region (e.g., Nowak and colleagues for TRB and Haue for Iron Age Jutland), we can challenge unilinear evolutionary models (e.g., Møller and Dollar).

Cross-cultural comparisons form a second analytical trend, with authors drawing from neighboring groups, as in Fulminante's evaluation of networks in Etruria and *Latium vetus*, or looking further afield, such as Salisbury's comparison of settlement spatial patterning in the Carpathian Basin and North America and

Fernández-Götz's comparison of Iron Age *oppida* across Europe with other early urban centers. Taken as a whole, papers in this book offer a cross-cultural examination of trajectories of settlement and demographic nucleation.

The overarching theme, with ramifications for all European archaeological research, is of similar culture groups, even within a given region displaying quite different processes of nucleation and aggregation (e.g., Møller and Dollar in southern Jutland and Haue in northern Jutland). Demonstrated ethnoarchaeologically by Yalman, and succinctly summarized in the chapter by Stoddart, this is more than a European phenomenon. As the papers in this volume amply demonstrate, variability arising from bottom-up processes of aggregation is not limited by time, space, or cultural group. One lesson to be learned for future archaeological studies is to take each research case as potentially unique, without imposing preconceived notions of how nucleation should occur, and then compare these to regional patterns and other archaeological or ethnographic examples. Nevertheless, the comparative approach produces positive results as well. Similar processes in action, such as the role of ritual architecture in providing an attraction point for creating nucleation (Fernández-Götz's cult sanctuaries, Beusing's *nuraghi* and water temples, and the burial mounds presented by Minkevičius, in this volume), or the localization of sub-communities within a nucleated settlement to maintain community (e.g., Salisbury, Vengalis and Vélius). In comparing case studies from a range of cultural contexts across the Old World and across time, we found commonalities in the human reasons for and responses to moving together.

Acknowledgments

We are grateful to Daniel Pugh to provide us with photos of the Baiterek Tower in Astana. Two anonymous reviewers helped us to focus our objectives and highlight the advantages of a broadly comparative approach to the diversity of nucleation processes.

References Cited

Adams, J. 2003. The Bitter End: Emotions at a Movement's Conclusion. *Sociological Inquiry* 73(1): 84–113.

Anacker, S. 2004. Geographies of Power in Nazarbayev's Astana. *Eurasian Geography and Economics* 45(7): 515–533.

Anderson, B. 1991. *Imagined Communities. Reflections on the Origin and Spread of Nationalism*. London: Verso.

Baines, J., M.T. Stark, T.G. Garrison and S. Houston 2017. Cities as performance arenas, in N. Yoffee (ed.) *Early Cities in Comparative Perspective, 4000BCE–1200BCE* (Cambridge World History 3): 94–109. Cambridge: Cambridge University Press.

Baker-Smith, D. 2000. *More's Utopia*. Toronto: University of Toronto Press.

Batty, M. 2005. *Cities and Complexity: Understanding Cities with Cellular Automata, Agent- Based Models, and Fractals*. Cambridge (MA): MIT Press.

Batty, M. and S. Marshall 2009. The evolution of cities: Geddes, Abercrombie and the new physicalism. *The Town Planning Review* 80(6): 551–574.

Beveridge, C.E., P. Rocheleau and D. Larkin 1998. *Frederick Law Olmsted: Designing the American Landscape*. New York: Universe.

Blanton, R.E. and L.F. Fargher 2016. *How Humans Cooperate: Confronting the Challenges of Collective Action*. Boulder: University Press of Colorado.

Bogucki, P. 1999. *The Origins of Human Society*. Malden (MA): Blackwell.

Bradley, R. 1993. *Altering the Earth: The Origins of Monuments in Britain and Continental Europe*. Edinburgh: Society of Antiquaries of Scotland.

Bradley, R. 1998. *The Significance of Monuments: On the Shaping of Human Experience in Neolithic and Bronze Age Europe*. New York: Routledge.

Calhoun, C. 1991. The Problem of Identity in Collective Action, in J. Huber (ed.) *Macro-Micro Linkages in Sociology*: 51–75. Newbury Park (CA): Sage.

Canuto, M.A. and J. Yaeger (eds) 2000. *The Archaeology of Communities: A New World Perspective*. London: Routledge.

Carballo, D.M. (ed.) 2013. *Cooperation and Collective Action: Archaeological Perspectives*. Boulder: University of Colorado Press.

Carballo, D.M. and B. Fortenberry 2015. Bridging Prehistory and History in the Archaeology of Cities. *Journal of Field Archaeology* 40(5): 542–559.

Carballo, D.M., P. Roscoe and G.M. Feinman 2014. Cooperation and Collective Action in the Cultural Evolution of Complex Societies. *Journal of Archaeological Method and Theory* 21(1): 98–133.

Carl, P., B. Kemp, R. Laurence, R. Coningham, C. Higham and G.L. Cowgill 2000. Were Cities Built as Images? *Cambridge Archaeological Journal* 10(2): 327–365.

Castells, M. 1997. *The Power of Identity*. Oxford: Blackwell.

Charbit, Y. 2002. The Platonic City: History and Utopia. *Population* 57: 207–235.

Cohen, A.P. 1985. *The Symbolic Construction of Community*. London: Routledge.

Dibble, J., A. Prelorendjos, O. Romice, M. Zanella, E. Strano, M. Pagel and S. Porta 2017. On the origin of spaces: Morphometric foundations of urban form evolution. *Environment and Planning B: Urban Analytics and City Science* 46(4): 707–730.

Fagan, B. 2008. *The Great Warming: Climate Change and the Rise and Fall of Civilizations*. New York: Bloomsbury.

Fallenbuchl, Z.M. 1970. The Communist Pattern of Industrialization. *Soviet Studies* 21(4): 458–484.

Fisher, K.D. 2009. Placing social interaction: An integrative approach to analyzing past built environments. *Journal of Anthropological Archaeology* 28(4): 439–457.

Fishman, R. 1982. *Urban Utopias in the Twentieth Century: Ebenezer Howard, Frank Lloyd Wright, and Le Corbusier*. Cambridge (MA): MIT Press.

Fletcher, R. 1981. Space and Community Behaviour: A Discussion of the Form and Function of Spatial Order in Settlements, in B.B. Lloyd and J. Gay (eds) *Universals of Human Thought*: 71–110. Cambridge: Cambridge University Press.

Fominaya, C.F. 2010. Collective Identity in Social Movements: Central Concepts and Debates. *Sociology Compass* 4(6): 393–404.

Fox, R.G. 1977. *Urban Anthropology. Cities in Their Cultural Settings*. Englewood Cliffs (NJ): Prentice-Hall.

Furholt, M., M. Hinz and D. Mischka (eds) 2012. *'As time goes by'? Monumentality, Landscapes and the Temporal Perspective* (Universitätsforschungen zur prähistorischen Archäologie 206). Bonn: Dr. Rudolf Habelt.

Giddens, A. 1979. *Central Problems in Social Theory: Action, Structure and Contradiction in Social Analysis*. Berkeley: University of California Press.

Giddens, A. 1984. *The Constitution of Society: Outline of the Theory of Structuration*. Berkeley: University of California Press.

Hall, P. 1998. *Cities in Civilization*. New York: Pantheon.

Hamilton, C.M. 1995. *Nineteenth-Century Mormon Architecture and City Planning*. New York: Oxford University Press.

Healey, P. 1996. The Communicative Turn in Planning Theory and Its Implications for Spatial Strategy Formation. *Environment and Planning B: Planning and Design* 23(2): 217–234.

Hegmon, M. 1992. Archaeological Research on Style. *Annual Review of Anthropology* 21: 517–536.

Hillier, B. and J. Hanson 1984. *The Social Logic of Space*. Cambridge: Cambridge University Press.

Hodder, I. 1990. *The Domestication of Europe: Structure and Contingency in Neolithic Europe*. Cambridge: Blackwell.

Howard, E. 1902. *Garden Cities of To-Morrow*. 2nd ed. London: S. Sonnenschein & Co.

Innes, J. 1995. Planning Theory's Emerging Paradigm: Communicative Action and Interactive Practice. *Journal of Planning Education and Research* 14(3): 183–189.

Iordachi, C. and A. Bauerkamper (eds) 2014. *The Collectivization of Agriculture in Communist Eastern Europe: Comparison and Entanglements*. Budapest and New York: Central European University Press.

Janusek, J.W. 2004. *Identity and Power in the Ancient Andes: Tiwanaku Cities Through Time*. New York: Routledge.

Johnson, H. 2014. Bringing theory into practice: seeking constitutive utopian potential in Astana, in *ARCC/ EAAE 2014. Beyond Architecture: New Intersections & Connections Ends: The Dystopia in Utopia and the Final Cause. Forces, Causality, Ideology, Values, Myth*: 493–502. Electronic document: https://www.arcc-journal.

org/index.php/repository/article/view/303/239, accessed on August 2, 2021.

Kelleher, M. 2009. Bulgaria's Communist-Era Landscape. *The Public Historian* 31(3): 39–72.

Keller, S. 1968. *The Urban Neighborhood: A sociological perspective*. New York: Random House.

Kostof, S. 1991. *The City Shaped: Urban Patterns and Meanings Through History*. London: Thames and Hudson.

Kosztolnyik, Z.J. 2002. *Hungary Under the Early Arpads, 890s to 1063*. Boulder (CO): East European Monographs.

Landau, K. 2015. Spatial Logic and Maya City Planning: The Case for Cosmology. *Cambridge Archaeological Journal* 25(1): 275–292.

Lawrence, D.L. and S.M. Low 1990. The Built Environment and Spatial Form. *Annual Review of Anthropology* 19: 453–505.

Le Corbusier 1935. *La Ville Radieuse*. Boulogne: Editions de l'Architecture d'Aujourd'hui.

Mac Sweeney, N. 2011. *Community Identity and Archaeology: Dynamic Communities at Aphrodisias and Beycesultan*. Ann Arbor: University of Michigan Press.

Manzanilla, L.R. 2017a. *Multiethnicity and Migration at Teopancazco: Investigations of a Teotihuacan Neighborhood Center*. Gainesville: University Press of Florida.

Manzanilla, L.R. 2017b. *Teotihuacan. Ciudad Excepcional de Mesoamérica*. Mexico City: El Colegio Nacional.

Marshall, S. 2008. *Cities, Design and Evolution*. London: Routledge.

Melucci, A. 1995. The Process of Collective Identity, in H. Johnston and B. Klandermans (eds) *Social Movements and Culture*: 41–63. Minneapolis: University of Minnesota Press.

Moravčíková, H. 2009. Monumentality in Slovak architecture of the 1960s and 1970s: authoritarian, national, great and abstract. *The Journal of Architecture* 14(1): 45–65.

Mumford, L. 1961. *The City in History: Its Origins, Its Transformations, and Its Prospects*. San Diego (CA): A Harvest Book Harcourt.

Mundigo, A.I. and D.P. Crouch 1977. The City Planning Ordinances of the Laws of the Indies Revisited. Part I: Their Philosophy and Implications. *The Town Planning Review* 48(3): 247–268.

Nelson, B.A. (ed.) 1985. *Decoding Prehistoric Ceramics*. Carbondale: Southern Illinois University Press.

Neustupný, E. 1991. Community areas of prehistoric farmers in Bohemia. *Antiquity* 65(247): 326–331.

Pauketat, T. 2009. *Cahokia: Ancient America's Great City on the Mississippi*. New York: Viking.

Pauknerová, K., R.B. Salisbury and M. Baumanová 2013. Human-landscape interaction in prehistoric Central Europe: analysis of natural and built environments. *Anthropologie* 51(2): 131–142.

Pero, P.N. 2011. *Chicago's Pilsen Neighborhood*. Charleston (SC): Arcadia.

Perring, D. 1991. Spatial organization and social change in Roman towns, in J. Rich and A. Wallace-Hadrill (eds) *City and Country in the Ancient World*: 273–293. London and New York: Routledge.

Popescu, C. 2009. Introductory argument: architecture of the Communist Bloc in the mirror. *The Journal of Architecture* 14(1): 1–6.

Rapoport, A. 1994. Spatial Organization and the Built Environment, in T. Ingold (ed.) *Companion Encyclopedia of Anthropology: Humanity, Culture and Social Life*: 460–502. London: Routledge.

Renfrew, C. 2007. *Prehistory: The Making of the Human Mind*. London: Weidenfeld & Nicolson.

Romero, M. and R. López (eds) 2018. *Motherhood and Infancies in the Mediterranean in Antiquity*. Oxford and Philadelphia: Oxbow Books.

Rosenau, H. 1983. *The Ideal City. Its Architectural Evolution in Europe*. London and New York: Methuen & Co.

Salisbury, R.B. 2012. Place and identity: networks of Neolithic communities in Central Europe. *Documenta Praehistorica* 39: 203–213.

Schatz, E. 2003. What Capital Cities Say About State and Nation Building. *Nationalism & Ethnic Politics* 9(4): 111–140.

Simmel, G. 1955. *Conflict and The Web of Group Affiliations*. Glencoe (IL): Free Press.

Sinha, A. 1998. Design of Settlements in the Vaastu Shastras. *Journal of Cultural Geography* 17(2): 27–41.

Sjoberg, G. 1960. *The Preindustrial City. Past and Present*. New York: Free Press.

Smith, M.E. 2007. Form and Meaning in the Earliest Cities: A New Approach to Ancient Urban Planning. *Journal of Planning History* 6(1): 3–47.

Smith, M.E. 2010. Sprawl, Squatters and Sustainable Cities: Can Archaeological Data Shed Light on Modern Urban Issues? *Cambridge Archaeological Journal* 20: 229–253.

Snow, D.A. 2001. Collective Identity and Expressive Forms, in N.J. Smelser and P.B. Baltes (eds) *International Encyclopedia of the Social & Behavioral Sciences*: 2212–2219. Oxford: Pergamon.

Stencel, R., F. Gifford and E. Morón 1976. Astronomy and Cosmology at Angkor Wat. *Science* 193(4250): 281–287.

Stoddart, S. and C. Malone 2002. Editorial. *Antiquity* 76(291): 1–14.

Storey, G.R. (ed.) 2006. *Urbanism in the Preindustrial World: Cross-Cultural Perspectives*. Tuscaloosa: University of Alabama Press.

Tajfel, H. and J.C. Turner 1979. An integrative theory of intergroup conflict, in W.G. Austin and S. Worchel (eds) *The social psychology of intergroup relations*: 33–37. Monterey (CA): Brooks/Cole.

Taylor, N. 1998. *Urban Planning Theory Since 1949*. London: Sage.

Tönnies, F. 1963. *Community and Society (Gemeinschaft und Gesellschaft)*. London and New York: Harper & Row.

Unwin, R. 1909. *Town Planning in Practice: An Introduction to the Art of Designing Cities and Suburbs*. Reprint 1994. New York: Princeton Architectural Press.

Vis, B.N. 2009. *Built Environments, Constructed Societies. Inverting Spatial Analysis*. Leiden: Sidestone.

Vis, B.N. 2017. Understanding by the Lines We Map: Material Boundaries and the Social Interpretation of Archaeological Built Space, in C. Siart, M. Forbriger and O. Bubenzer (eds) *Digital Geoarchaeology: New Techniques for Interdisciplinary Human-Environmental Research*: 81–105. Cham: Springer.

Vis, B.N. 2018. *Cities Made of Boundaries. Mapping Social Life in Urban Form*. London: UCL Press.

Wright, F.L. 1932. *The Disappearing City*. New York: W.F. Payson.

Yaeger, J. and Canuto M.A. 2000. Introducing an archaeology of communities, in M.A. Canuto and J. Yaeger (eds) *The Archaeology of Communities: A New World Perspective*: 1–15. London: Routledge.

Yegül, F. and D. Favro 2019. *Roman Architecture and Urbanism: From the Origins to Late Antiquity*. Cambridge: Cambridge University Press.

York, A., M.E. Smith, B. Stanley, B.L. Stark, J. Novic, S.L. Harlan, G.L. Cowgill and C. Boone 2011. Ethnic and Class-Based Clustering through the Ages: A Transdisciplinary Approach to Urban Social Patterns. *Urban Studies* 48(11): 2399–2415.

Young, I.M. 1990. *City Life and Difference*. Princeton (NJ): Princeton University Press.

Chapter 2

What Does Settlement Layout Tell Us About the Community?
An Ethnoarchaeological Study

E. Nurcan Yalman

Abstract

The layout of a settlement reflects long-term processes and mutual interactions that occur among many variables. Sometimes, the factors that shape a settlement are the result of various deliberate decisions, but indirect effects also play a role in these processes. At an archaeological site, we usually excavate only parts of a settlement and can observe only those parts that have been preserved. Therefore, we accept that many of the components are missing. Because of this, and especially for prehistoric settlements, it can be difficult to interpret the community by exploring only the site plans. Through an ethnoarchaeological study from Central Anatolia, this paper will discuss the relationship between the structure of a community and the settlement layout, and address the factors that make a settlement nucleated, dispersed, or agglomerated.

Introduction

The past 50 years have witnessed intensive debate about the most appropriate theoretical and methodological approaches to interpreting archaeological sites and the people who inhabited them. The tendency toward more holistic approaches led to the establishment of ethnoarchaeology—systematic observations of present societies—as an important tool for interpretation (Binford 1967, 1978a, 1978b; David and Kramer 2001; Edgeworth 2003). In time, direct analogy from ethnoarchaeological data, as used in early interpretations based on ethnoarchaeology, was heavily criticized, and relational analogy was found to be a better approach for interpreting archaeological data (David and Kramer 2001; Hodder 1982). Furthermore, various academic schools have developed different methods according to their theoretical perspectives (see Marciniak and Yalman 2013). Despite early and recent criticism (Hamon 2016; Wylie 2002), ethnoarchaeology remains an irreplaceable method for understanding past cultures as long as researchers remain aware of its limitations. Ethnoarchaeology gives us an important opportunity to evaluate the whole site with its activity zones and extensive area of interaction, together with its community. By comparing and contrasting entire occupied settlements, this ethnoarchaeological study aims to give colleagues awareness of a variety of possibilities available during the interpretation of archaeological data.

Among various other different types of *in situ* finds in archaeology, the built environment (i.e., architectural remains and spaces left intentionally among structures) provides direct information about the community and the reciprocal relationships between the community, the site, and the outside world. However, it is uncommon to be able to conduct comparative analyses of complete settlement plans; in many archaeological excavations, only some portions of the settlements are unearthed for various reasons, such as limited budget, specific goals, or lack of time. As a result, research on the spatial organization of entire settlements remains underdeveloped, both theoretically and methodologically, in comparison, for example, to the relatively well-developed landscape and household archaeologies (Creese 2014: 2).

In archaeological studies, scholars have developed different approaches to understand social organization by using the settlement's built environment. Consequently, understanding related concepts, such as household (Allison 1999; Hendon 1996; Steere 2017), neighborhood (Smith 2010; Smith and Novic 2012), space left between and among buildings, as well as territoriality (Osborne and Van Valkenburg 2013), any decision made by preferences or obligations became important topics on the way to identifying the characteristics of a society. This paper aims to bring an ethnographic approach to those issues from the points of socioeconomic and cooperative practices in the process of generating units, such as households, neighborhoods, and quarters, as well as provides some hints about the concepts of territoriality and internal (community) politics that reflect on the settlement layout.

The relationship between the community and the built environment, together with its activity zones, will be examined by comparing two communities living in two differently formed modern village settlements in Central Anatolia. In the first phase of this ethnoarchaeological research, 22 settlements were visited to understand the variability of rural architecture and settlement formation. Later, eight villages were revisited and five were selected for this research; three of them are located in the Akşehir region and two of them are found in the Çumra region. While two of these five villages were examined in detail, the other three were used for comparisons and validations (Yalman 2005: 52–56). These two villages are selected for this comparison, in part, because they have clearer characteristics than the others, and are better suited to refine the data and focus on variability.

The studied settlements were evaluated at three different scales. The small scale is the generation, by the household, of a compound or residential unit with all its components. The medium scale is the groupings of these units and the mode of creating neighborhoods, and the large scale is the overall settlement and the formation of quarters.

In this paper, I will primarily focus on three questions: 1) Why settlement layouts are the way they are?; 2) What are the factors that give a settlement its form?; and 3) How can we get insights about a community and materialization of its identity by looking at its settlement? I will examine these questions by comparing two villages with different layouts—nucleated versus dispersed—in terms of their community, environment, subsistence economy, and local histories. The two selected settlements will be referred to by their regions (Akşehir Settlement and Çumra Settlement); the actual names of the villages are not given in order to help protect the rights of particular individuals and residents. In the course of this examination, I will explore cause and effect relations by following three scales of analysis and by comparing the two sites to see variations in each part.

Regional, Social, and Historical Background Characteristics in Relation

To be able to address the Akşehir Settlement and the Çumra Settlement in their regional context, it is useful to clarify regional similarities and differences. Of particular interest for this paper is the appearance of more differences than similarities in this small part of Central Anatolia. Both settlements are located at about 1000–1200 m in altitude (Bozyiğit and Güngör 2011: 175; Roberts *et al.* 1996: 19), and on the historical passageway from west to east. Historically, these communities lived under the same rulers. Both villages, settled by Turkish-speaking, Sunni Muslim communities, consist of patriarchal families mainly originated from central Asian Turks (Türkmens and Yörüks). These basic ethnic and denomination-based similarities are considered important in order to discern reasons for dissimilarities in settlement form. One of the villages is located on the

Çumra Plain and the other is on the Akşehir Plain; the distance between these two regions is approximately 180 km. The reasons for their differences start from the regional level and include a wide range of features, from environmental to social characteristics.

Although both the Akşehir and Çumra settlements are located on high plains, the topography of these two regions varies slightly. The Akşehir region is surrounded by shallow hills and the Akşehir Settlement is situated 3 km from the Sultan Mountains. The Çumra Settlement is located on a large, flat plain and the nearest hilly area, the Karadağ Mountain, is located about 40 km away. The dimensions of these two plains are also different, with the Akşehir Plain covering 950 km² and the Çumra Plain covering 4000 km² (Karabayır 2001: 35).

The Akşehir Plain has fertile alluvial soils and an average annual rainfall between 700–900 mm³, which is conducive to cultivating various agricultural products. In the Çumra Plain, however, the average rainfall is about 250–300 mm³, and the agricultural soil in this arid land is not deeper than 30–40 cm; this area is much more suitable to be used for grazing than farming (Diyarı and Derneği 1956: 12).

The Konya Plain is a closed basin, and after the Salt Lake (Tuz Gölü) Plain, it is the largest lacustrine depression of the central Anatolian high plateaus (Naruse *et al.* 1997: 175). The altitude of its flat bottom is 1000 m (Kuzucuoğlu *et al.* 1998: 258). During the Late Pleistocene, the Konya Plain was occupied by a 20-m-deep freshwater lake (Kuzucuoğlu *et al.* 1998: 258). The Salt Lake and the Konya Basin do not have any direct outlet toward a sea, but the presence of some sinkholes (*obruks:* surface depression created by underground collapse) prevented the Konya Basin from becoming an enormous salt lake (Naruse *et al.* 1997: 175). The Çumra Plain is the southern sub-basin of the Konya Plain, and until quite recent times, the region had some marshy areas (such as Lake Hotamış) and *obruk* lakes (Bozyiğit and Güngör 2011: 179–180; Erol 1985). The Çumra Plain lacks river systems except for the Çarşamba River. Although this river has little influence as a source of natural watering for the arid plain today, yet the region became suitable for industrial-scale agriculture after irrigation and drainage management was established (Bahçeci *et al.* 2006: 262; Şeker *et al.* 2017: 585). Efforts to establish irrigation farming in the region go back to 1915–1918 (Altuntaş 2001: 151; Konukçu and Akbuğa 2006: 106). Due to the existence of an underground aquifer, many wells can be seen across the Çumra Plain. These wells had great importance for both agriculture and livestock before the construction of concrete water channels and a modern irrigation system. Prior to large-scale irrigation, the natural vegetation in the region was steppe. The mountain slopes are usually bare, with the exception of juniper, oak, and almond trees on the northern slopes of the volcanic Karadağ (Kuzucuoğlu *et al.* 1998: 260).

The Akşehir Plain is one of the most fertile agricultural areas of Anatolia. This relatively small plain is covered with alluvial and colluvial soils featured by significant farming potential. The region is watered by various springs—with the biggest being the Adıyan and Ilgın streams flowing from the Sultan Mountains—and an underground water network. In addition, Lake Akşehir eases agricultural activities and the growth of vegetation. The Akşehir Settlement in this research is located where soils accumulated from the mountains by alluvial activities (Sargın and Akengin 2009: 149–153). There are also many fountains for communal use within and outside the settlements of the Akşehir Plain.

Due to its fertile nature, population density in Akşehir has been high throughout history (Sargın and Akengin 2009: 153). Moreover, because of its geopolitical importance, the region became a target to be conquered in many periods and by numerous historic political powers, including the Byzantine period, Islamic states, such as the Umayyad State, the Crusades period, and different Turkish principalities until the establishment of the Republic of Turkey (İnalcık 2009: 7–8; Konyalı 1945: 67–88). The villages were often attacked, plundered, and dispersed, but afterward, individual families founded new settlements together in the same area. Most of the populations have not migrated out of the region, and therefore, the residential history of the settlements on the Akşehir Plain goes back at least 500 years (Konyalı 1945: 135). Nevertheless, a major increase in population occurred on the plain in the 19th century, when Yörük nomadic groups settled here, and then toward the end of that century when people arrived from the Balkans and Crimea (Sargın and Akengin 2009: 153). As the major part of the plain was reserved for agricultural purposes, the villages on the Akşehir Plain were compact, and had limited space for expansion and new buildings. Over time, farmlands took place of pasturelands around the settlements, causing a decrease in small livestock (i.e., sheep and goat) production.

Conversely, the environmental history of the Çumra Plain has resulted in it being a rather barren grassland. One of the most significant problems for agricultural activities in the Konya Basin, where the Çumra Plain is located, is insufficient water resources (Bahçeci *et al.* 2008: 436). The Konya Basin is the most arid zone of Anatolia (Bozyiğit and Güngör 2011: 177), therefore, the land was almost exclusively suitable for grazing and pasture until the establishment of irrigation and drainage management (Bahar and Koçak 2004: 6; Yücel 1987: 161). Until the end of the 1950s, animal husbandry, with goats, camels, and horses, and migrations from the southern slopes of the Taurus Mountains resulted in many flocks of sheep grazing on the inner plateaus

of Anatolia (Kuzucuoğlu *et al.* 1998: 260). Advancements in agriculture eventually caused a rapid decline in small livestock herding of sheep and goats in the region (Yalman 2005).

While the wide grasslands in many parts of the Konya Plain offered favorable conditions for pastorage, they also were used as transit areas by caravans rather than for permanent settlements, as indicated by the high number of caravanserais in this region (Demirkent 2002: 2; Keleş 2002: 27; Ödekan 1995: 432). During intensive conflict periods, especially in the Principalities period from around the 11th century until times of stability in the mid-20th century, the plain was not favored as a residential area for security reasons either. The communities that relied on animal husbandry started to show interest in the region around the end of the 19th and the beginning of the 20th century (Hütteroth 1974: 22). The current Çumra Settlement has a very recent past, as it was founded about 1919–1920. As did many others, this Turkmen group—as they name themselves Şefaatli Kabilesi (Şefaatli Tribe)—moved from their origins in Central Asia to Syria, near Damascus, around the 11th century (Sümer 1972: 101, 133), then arrived in Hatay on the southeastern coast of Anatolia before moving to their final destination in Central Anatolia. It is possible to say with some certainty that the community of the Çumra Settlement maintained its original, semi-nomadic lifestyle. As far as is known, they settled no longer than 45–50 years in any one settlement until they arrived in Çumra. The previous village of the same community is about a walking distance away from where they live now, and their movement was caused by a rapid rise in groundwater level. Even during the time of this research, when the plain underwent a serious drought, the old people of the village started to talk about moving somewhere else; however, because of restrictive modern laws, this was no longer an option. Eventually, moving and establishing a new settlement means an advantage of a large tract of available land where there is no limitation for residential expansion, but these processes also bring about social impacts that will be discussed later in this paper.

The differences summarized above have had important influences on regional geopolitics and human mobility, as well as have impacted long-term demography, and these factors all combined to affect the formation of settlements.

Basic Formal Characteristics of the Two Settlements

The Akşehir Settlement

This settlement is nucleated and compact in form, as the whole site surrounds a communal center with village cafés, two small shops, and a mosque. Around this center, the settlement is located on the two sides

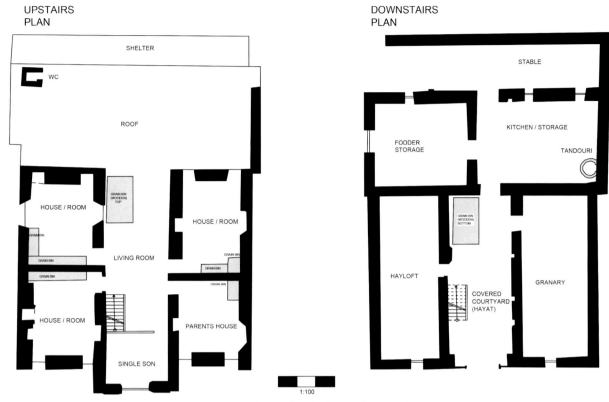

Figure 2.1. House plan at the Akşehir Settlement, showing an economically dependent household (figure by the author).

of a spring coming down from Sultan Mountains, and consists of mostly adjacent buildings along the streets. The residential buildings are two-storied, where the first floor is used for stables, fodder, and grain storage facilities. Food was traditionally stored in a huge wooden box, called *sarpın* in the past, on the first floor. It had small openings to get the grain out, with large lids on the upper floor to fill in. In this research, we only recorded *sarpın*s in one of the oldest houses. Apart from this main storage facility, each room may have smaller versions of *sapın*s to store durable food supply for common use, but this was not always the case.

A covered courtyard, *hayat*, was constructed at the entrance of each building. This space is designed as a hall and a workshop and is surrounded by storage rooms, although people prefer to sit in front of the main entrance during favorable weather conditions to do some dirty and collective tasks, such as sorting, sieving, and peeling. There are usually gardens in the front or at the back of the houses for planting vegetables and fruits. In the past, the backyard and some of the buildings around the *hayat* functioned as sheep and goat barns. With the removal of small livestock production, these spaces were utilized as gardens for vegetables and fruits, and the *hayat* was partially incorporated into the residential space (Yalman 2005).

There is only one fire pit, *tandır*, for each house, where women cook weekly or monthly stocks of loaf-bread

and *yufka* (phyllo-thin bread). This is an important place for socializing, and it is situated usually outside of the main building, under a flimsy shelter or in a shed, either at the front or at the rear garden.

The upper floors of residential buildings are for accommodating extended families, and traditionally each room belongs to a nuclear family. Because of this, they name each room as *ev* (house). The buildings typically have four rooms/houses, incorporating four nuclear families. Sometimes, some of the rooms are reserved for bachelors and/or single daughters who still live with their family (Figure 2.1). Females are not supposed to continue to be a part of the household once they get married, but the household expands around males and their core families.

The Çumra Settlement

This settlement has a dispersed form, consisting of three discrete quarters, spread approximately 1 km apart over the plain. In each quarter, residences in separate compounds are surrounded by high, mudbrick walls. Usually, there are two building groups constructed around two courtyards within these enclosure walls: one is for people and the other is for animals, and these are connected via internal access. The former one is named as 'clean courtyard' and the latter is called 'dirty courtyard' or 'animal courtyard.' While there are multiple houses and kitchen/storage

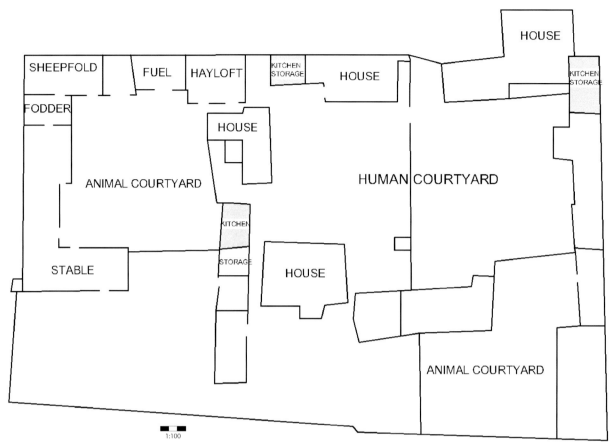

Figure 2.2. House plan at the Çumra Settlement. Note the number of kitchens, indicating the number of families economically independent in the same compound (figure by the author).

buildings arranged around the 'clean courtyard,' a storehouse (for crops and fuel), haylofts, sheepfolds, and stables are placed around the 'animal courtyard' (Figure 2.2). Activities, such as dung production, occur either in this dirty courtyard or along the outside of the wall. There is always an additional, outward-facing building in the compound used as a guest room for foreign and/or male visitors. Generally, all the buildings are single-story. The most important structure of the clean courtyard is the *ekmek mutfağı* (bread-kitchen), with a small room for food storage for daily use, the *kiler*, attached to it. Much like the *tandır* at the Akşehir Settlement, the *ekmek mutfağı* is a significant place for women to socialize while they prepare the monthly supply of bread and *yufka*. At the Çumra Settlement, however, this unit is also an important indicator of economic independence within the household, because the number of the bread-kitchen and daily storage room within a compound indicates the number of households featured by independent economic activities.

The Reciprocal Relation of Regional and Historical Backgrounds on the Community Structure and Its Effects on Variability in the Forms of Settlements

The preference of a geographical region with fertile soils and/or geopolitical advantages has a direct impact on the communities both in the short and long terms because favorable locations often bring conflict. This situation has led the people of Akşehir to focus on their own safety, and therefore, their priority has become survival rather than the development of internal social and settlement organizations. The communities of the region tend to resist unstable political environments by developing solidarity among their members, without caring about the fact that they have the same kin or tribal origin. This condition reflects itself in spatial layouts, with settlements shaped around a center (i.e., nucleated settlements) being the most convenient forms against any danger from outside. Furthermore, nucleated settlements promote a sense of community. In the Akşehir region, both mountain and plain settlements have similar sociohistorical backgrounds, and therefore, apart from topographical differences, their communities have shared characteristics.

The situation is quite different in the Çumra region. Most of the groups used this plain only for grazing their animals and seasonal settlement (Kuzucuoğlu et al. 1998: 260), and their permanent villages were located on the higher parts of the region, such as Karadağ, the Bozdağ Mountains, or places very close to the mountains, such as at Lake Hotamış. According to interviews conducted during this research, it is understood that the Çumra Plain was relatively empty in terms of permanent settlement almost until the foundation of the Republic of Turkey (Yalman 2005). While one of the reasons that the communities of this region preferred to settle higher areas was security against brigands, another reason was poor soil quality. To come down to the plain with their large herds then return to their upland settlements was a better solution than trying to farm the plain. Additionally, it seems like the population was not living under intense pressure and fear as the Akşehir people did, which resulted in community behavior different from that of the Akşehir people. One relevant example is the development of strong solidarity among different lineage groups living in compact and nucleated settlements (Yalman 2005).

It is important to identify how regional features became major factors in settlement formation. For instance, while the Çumra Settlement community kept its kin-based structure[1] to be continued through time, the Akşehir Settlement seems to represent a community of mixed families. This important knowledge has a key role to play in gaining insights about differences in the behavior of these two communities within the settlement and in their relations within the society.

The Process of Formation at Three Scales

Formation of Houses/Compounds in Relation to the Economic Structure of the Household: Different Practices in Two Villages

In this part of the paper, the focus is placed on the household concept. The smallest unit, the household, has become of common interest in archaeology and other social sciences (Düring and Marciniak 2005; Hendon 1996; Matthews 2012; Wilk and Rathje 1982). A household, in its most general definition, is a social unit based on production and consumption (Netting *et al.* 1984: xix–xx). Some researchers with a focus on household archaeology perceive societies as a combination of multiple households (Yaeger and Canuto 2000: 4).

The tendency to live physically close for kin-based groups likely applies to anywhere in the world, including all of rural Anatolia. Although the term 'household archaeology' refers to various studies in archaeology, the household is a research topic in anthropology and ethnography. As Allison stressed in her book, '*Archaeologists do not dig up households. They dig up dwellings and domestic artefacts but not social units (Wilk and Rathje 1982:618). A household is an ethnographic phenomenon, not an archaeological one*' (1999: 2). The difficulty in identifying household

units using archaeological methods is underlined here because, although a household can be described, every variation in household practices reflects on the material environment very differently; thus, it is important to observe and understand households in living communities.

Indeed, there are different practices in daily life, and these practices are related to the local cultural background in our research area as well. The different perceptions and practices around a household and their effect on the built environment for the Akşehir and Çumra settlements create the variability. In all of the 22 villages in Central Anatolia originally considered for this study (see above), the household represents either a nuclear or an extended family. Each adult member of a household has particular tasks in production processes, and, as typically happens in patriarchal families, the products and cash earnings are always managed by the father of the family (Yalman 2005).

The process of multiplication and division of a household may occur as a response to an increase in population when the number of people reaches a level that creates administrative difficulties and inhibits the comfort of living together. A nuclear family that breaks away from a household must become economically independent when launching a new household unit. Therefore, the most important rule is to 'produce together and consume together.' Interestingly, this rule is one of the main factors to have direct effects on settlement formation. Nevertheless, it is more important that this system of shared economic relations shows variation from one settlement to another in the process of settlement construction.

At the Çumra Settlement, where this phenomenon can clearly be observed, people have large lands as they engage in industrial-scale agricultural production (wheat, sugar beets, beans, etc.) based on irrigation and mechanized farming. Therefore, households frequently possess sufficient land as capital to share among multiple sons. Although living together as an extended family is important for the Çumra Settlement people, followed through male members (females move to their husband's compound when they get married), three resolutions may appear when the household needs to expand by dividing because of population increase:

1. The most common case happens when the family has more than one son and has enough space within their residential area and enough agricultural land to free the eldest son economically. In this instance, they usually continue to live in the same compound but with separate kitchen/food storage buildings. This separation is often clearly visible in the material evidence; multiple family residences

---

[1] The Çumra Settlement people describe themselves as a tribal group, *kabile* in Turkish.

with only one kitchen/food storage structure indicate an economically dependent extended family. The economically dependent households are expected to share the same kitchen/food storage facilities and eat together.

2. On the other hand, if multiple kitchen/food storage units are present in the same compound, the number of these units is indicative of the number of economically independent core families who live together. In time, the stables, fodder storage buildings, and others will multiply, but the multiplication of the kitchen/food storage facilities is the first and immediate indicator of division (see Figure 2.2).

3. A less common situation occurs when the lack of space is the principal reason for expansion, but the main household continues to be in an economic relationship with the new household. In this case, two spatially separate compounds are present, but the new one does not have its own kitchen/food storage structure and continues to share the same dining table by joining the main family for meals.

Economic dependence of extended families also occurs at the Akşehir Settlement, but the built environment reflects this dependency differently compared to the Çumra Settlement. As mentioned above, the Akşehir Settlement is a village of at least 500 years old and is surrounded by fertile fields. The inhabitants are small-scale agriculturalists who sell their products at local markets, the lands owned by families are typically patchy and scattered around the village, but this system is not sufficient to support multiple families. Therefore, the economy is still based on subsistence farming rather than a cash economy. Additionally, households do not have large lands to share easily among their sons. For this reason, the households tend to keep the labor power together as long as possible rather than being split up. When the daughters get married, they leave for their new home, and the only change in the house is having more space. When a son gets married, the new family occupies one of the rooms in the house. Consequently, unlike the Çumra compounds, not much physical alteration takes place in the Akşehir residential buildings (see Figure 2.1). This situation manifests itself in the design of a residential unit. Because it is difficult to add new rooms or buildings to two-story, compact structures, when they need to expand, another structure is built wherever space is available in the settlement. Therefore, close kin groups are scattered in different parts of the settlement.

Defining the household as a center for production also implies its characterization as an economically interdependent social unit with shared residence and economic tasks, usually bound by kinship (Byrd 2000: 66; Wilk and Rathje 1982: 621). According to

our research in Central Anatolia, living in the same structure indicates the continuation of economic ties. When the structure is dissolved, the economic ties also are dissolved; this is valid for both of the studied settlements. On the other hand, the Çumra Settlement offers a different example for the material reflection of economic interdependency among household members. As explained above, although economically independent families exist, they might continue to live in the same compound, but one can only see the duplication or multiplication of specific architectural units that symbolically and practically represent the economic assets of one family.

Distinguishing individual architectural units is therefore important for making assertions about relative household autonomy. Matthews (2012: 187) addressed how to identify individual architectural units, particularly in the early levels of archaeological sites. She considers the repeated occurrence of features, such as ovens, storage bins, and grinding stone installations, across aggregated clusters of rooms, based on which the presence of individual units of food production and consumption, as well as residence, can be reconstructed for the Neolithic period of the Near East. Byrd (2000: 87) sees evidence for the degree of household economic autonomy in the location of storage facilities, processing areas, and production areas. He also argues that if the nuclear family was the primary social unit during the Neolithic of the Levant, then these activities should have occurred in each household in a redundant manner. On this subject, two Neolithic tells in Central Anatolia, Aşıklı Höyük and Çatalhöyük, can be taken as the best archaeological examples. Because the overall layout of these sites is quite similar, they have been compared by a number of scholars (e.g., Cutting 2006; Düring 2006; Düring and Marciniak 2005). For instance, architectural continuity was observed through several hundred years of occupation at both Aşıklı Höyük and Çatalhöyük, and both settlements comprise agglomerated mudbrick structures to which the entrances were located on the roof. However, the archaeological evidence suggests that the organization of daily activities and the use of space were quite different (Cutting 2006: 92). Among many other differences, such as the size and elaboration of houses, elements like fire installations and storage facilities indicate significant variations in household organization and daily practices in these communities. My concern here is the repetitive existence versus rarity or lack of storage areas, such as bins and rooms, because they signify a very important point about the economic structure of these communities at the household level and the communal versus individual perception of various subgroups at the sites (households, household clusters, etc.). At Çatalhöyük, nearly all buildings have a standard pattern of platforms, benches, pillars, ovens or hearths, and storage areas to make it a 'Catalhoyuk building' (Cutting 2006: 94). On the other hand, buildings at Aşıklı Höyük display the clear scarcity of features related to domestic production, consumption, and storage, such as bins and grinding stones in interior spaces, but middens occurred in open areas, which seems to suggest a communal nature (Düring 2006: 92; Steadman 2015: 179).

Although I do not intend to open a way to a direct analogy, two of the ethnographic settlements in this study facilitate in defining indicators concerning economic relations within household residential units. At this point, small-scale indicators are the most important parts of the definition because they determine all the activities, decisions, and responses that shaped the rest of the built environment. The core concept of settlement and community is rooted in that small-scale establishment, as explained above.

Formation of Neighborhoods and Diversity in Speed of Settlement Growth in Relation to Regional History and Social Grouping

The multiplication of households by generating new compounds/houses corresponds with the process of neighborhood formation, and the frequency of these building activities determines the speed in village growth. According to Smith (2010: 137), although neighborhoods are cross-temporal and cross-cultural phenomena, and have remarkable importance to understand social units in the past, they only recently attracted the attention of historians and archaeologists (Arnauld *et al.* 2012). Neighborhoods are defined by Smith and Novic (2012: 4) as residential zones that have both considerable face-to-face interactions and distinctive physical or social characteristics. In recent research, neighborhoods usually are considered as a unit in an urban settlement (pre-industrial or industrial), however here, a neighborhood is defined as clusters of compounds or, as mentioned by Smith and Novic (2012: 2), clusters of houses.

The creation of new compounds/houses in accordance with the rest of the built environment is a process that directly affects the general layout of any settlement. The positioning of the compounds or house clusters is influenced by various factors, and this becomes more complicated in the studied sites of this paper as the scale gets larger. During the process of multiplication, the availability of space and settlement history both prove to be important determinants. It is more feasible to design clusters according to one's social and economic preferences on a scarcely inhabited, large space than it is in a relatively small, congested, and old settlement.

The occupants of the Çumra Settlement never settled around a central space, and this conceptual approach gave them an additional dimension of freedom to spread over the plain. The Akşehir Settlement, on the other hand, nucleated around a center, and the growth pattern has unfolded from the center to the periphery, indicating a common interest to live as close as possible to the center. The general layout in the Akşehir Settlement consists of densely arranged buildings that do not allow the easy addition of new structures to the old sections of the village. Nevertheless, although the spatial characteristics are important, social decisions and preferences also have played a crucial role here. In other words, none of the factors could remain unaffected by others during settlement formation; at this point, the significance of social preferences and settlement age requires a more detailed discussion.

Although archaeologists have addressed the concept of 'living well together' (e.g., Bailey *et al.* 2008), the same concept must be considered at the middle scale, relating to the creation of compounds/house clusters. Below, however, it is not the 'togetherness' of economically dependent households but rather the economically and physically independent households that will be taken into account. The three Çumra Settlement quarters were established by closely related, kin-based households (Figure 2.3). In the Akşehir Settlement, new houses are constructed wherever there is available space, however, the obvious first choice would be adjacent to the family's main house (Figure 2.4). In comparison, the Çumra Settlement community seriously insists that new compounds be in close proximity. Here, in the 1980s, at the cost of breaking laws and risking severe punishment, people did not give up on being spatially close to their relatives. Therefore, settlement arrangement seems to be more important than legal sanctions for the Çumra community (Village Law 1987, Articles 9–15).

Chesson's (2003: 87) study on southern Levant Early Bronze Age settlement organization, interpreted as heterarchical, shows domestic compounds, combining roofed and unroofed spaces, as the arena of many daily activities. This pattern suggests a logic of compound formation physically comparable to the Çumra Settlement, as a group of structures surrounded, or was erected next to, an open workspace or courtyard. Chesson (2003: 85–86) also argued that people living in walled compounds formed and maintained neighborhood groups and networks. In the present ethnographic case study, living next to the close kin group in the Çumra Settlement does not only take advantage of the abundance of space—which is a diminishing resource after the initial establishment of the site—but also of a cooperation system among these kin-based, independent households. Cooperative activities include rotating milk production, *öndüç*,[2]

---

[2] According to this system, the women of economically independent households collect daily milk and give it to one member, the collector, so that the quantity of milk is sufficient to be processed

21

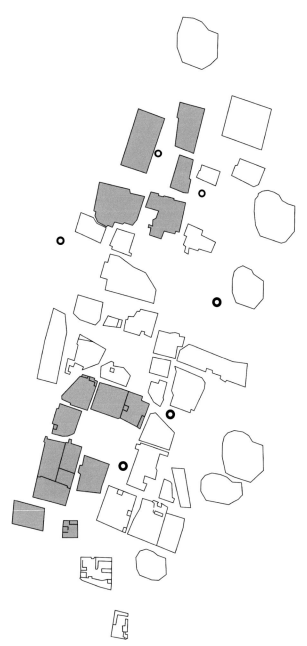

Figure 2.3. The Çumra Settlement, Upper Quarter.
Two of the household clusters are highlighted
(figure by the author).

making monthly bread stock, sharing the same shepherd to send animals to graze, using shared wells to water herds, sharing agricultural equipment, and sharing common trash areas. While these cooperative activities are restricted to close relatives in the Çumra

Settlement, there is no such rule in the Akşehir Settlement.

The other reason for the focus of Çumra residents on keeping the close kin group together is the importance of the size of the occupied land. A larger family is more powerful, and the best visual expression of this is the large size of the house cluster that corresponds with the extended household and kin-based neighborhood. While attempts by other families to settle in between kin-based households are frowned upon by the community, it is also inappropriate for members of other families to wander without reason in and around these house clusters. Thus, when a household multiplies, it is preferred to leave as wide a distance as possible between the compounds to reserve empty space for the next family compound. This facilitates keeping close kin households together for a longer period of time. This attitude was not observed in the Akşehir Settlement community, where cooperative activities are implemented by neighbors that are not necessarily relatives, and there is access for everyone to walk anywhere in the settlement area.

Behavioral aspects in the creation of new compounds/ houses also determine settlement growth rate. It is already evident that the growth rate of the Akşehir Settlement is lower than that of the Çumra Settlement, and this process, along with its causes, has been discussed above. However, a similar variation was observed between two quarters at the Çumra Settlement: the growth rate in the Lower Quarter is higher than that of the Upper Quarter.[3] When questioned, the reason given was that only one or two different surnames occur in the Upper Quarter, and there is more variation in families in the area of the Lower Quarter.

Another point of interest is that when the two studied settlements are compared at the middle scale, two, opposing attitudes appear to be present. On the one hand, there is a tendency to rapid separation of households but also an emphasis on keeping the household clusters intact (Çumra Settlement), as opposed to the slow separation of households without a strong tendency to create household clusters within the site (Akşehir Settlement). As was discussed above, household clustering was crucial for the Çumra community because of their well-developed cooperation system. Cooperation is a necessity for communities who live together, but there is a marked difference in how cooperation was operationalized at the studied settlements. These differences are associated with the characteristics and backgrounds of the communities as well as the internal spatial organization of the settlements. At this point, the

as dairy products (butter, cream, yogurt, and cheese). The women take the collector role in turns and reserve a day for this task, although a woman whose household has more animals becomes collector more frequently. This system was established in the past when there was no refrigeration to preserve milk until enough was collected for processing. The women who participate in this system must be reliable and trustworthy, and therefore, öndüç can only be applied amongst close relatives. Moreover, the women must carry milk buckets, and so, must live close to one another for this to be a practical system.

[3] Lower and Upper terms for the quarters of the Çumra settlement is given by its residences, it does not indicate a difference in elevation.

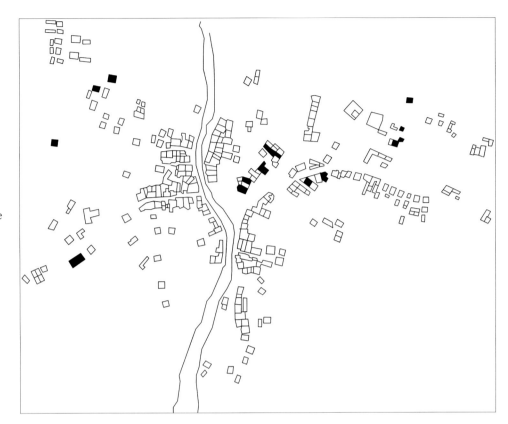

Figure 2.4. The Akşehir Settlement. A household's spatial distribution within the site after economic separation (figure by the author).

large-scale factors in relation to the backgrounds of the studied communities must be examined as they relate to the formation of these villages.

Formation of Quarters and the Entire Settlement

For the large-scale analysis of the present paper, it is important to note that the reconfiguration of social layout by displacement and territoriality plays an important role in overall settlement formation. Although traditional archaeological interpretations often associate territoriality with political boundaries between communities or settlements, there can be other causes. Bintliff (2013: 28–29; see also Whittle 1996) pointed out that the settlement patterns of farming communities in Europe from *c.* 7500 to 2000 BC tend to include dispersed, small, and short-lived sites, with movements of families around the landscape every few generations. This contrasts with several large settlements established as early as the Linearbandkeramik period in Central Europe, including Eythra in Germany (Stäuble and Veit 2016), Bylany in the Czech Republic (Květina and Končelová 2013), Vráble in Slovakia (Furholt *et al.* 2020), and Ludwinowo in Poland (Pyzel 2012). Nevertheless, the value of this observation in terms of the reconfiguration of social layouts is in Bintliff's (2013: 30) conclusion that the distinctive web of small settlements was created as a response to defuse social tensions and not to wall off discrete communities and their possessions. Bintliff's emphasis on the reorganization of the settlement

layout to reduce social tension mirrors observations in my research.

The social layout of the Çumra Settlement—by means of positioning of specific household clusters according to other household clusters—represents a solution to tackle internal social tensions. The current layout of the village is different from the community's previous one, and the relocation of lineage groupings was actually a resetting of the social layout in response to social stress. In the former Çumra Settlement, many households were tethered to the most powerful family whom they worked for in a type of feudal relationship. Over time, some of these 'satellite' families prospered, causing a power struggle among families. The new village structure was established in accordance with the new power relations, with the aim of diminishing social stress in the community.

Territoriality is also related to new power relations at the Çumra Settlement. While still living in the previous site, the villagers collectively utilized the current settlement area as a pastureland and built several water wells as the first structures. Each extended family group constructed their own well because multiple families possessed large herds and they would not prefer their animals to graze in close distance to each other. When power struggle intensified, families started to move and establish their residences where their wells were located. Therefore, the new social layout formed around the wells, which symbolically represent family/lineage identifiers on the empty plain. The symbolic meaning of these wells for the family/lineage groups is still very important, evidenced by an attitude toward their protection even today, although almost all of them are dry and no longer functioning as water sources.

The effort to occupy as large a parcel of land as possible in the process of creating lineage- or family-based neighborhoods is related to the same territoriality perception, which explains the villagers' concerns about the remains of the initial settlers and intracommunity competition. In the process of movement, the TKE family group, who gained new social power in the settlement, established their own quarter (Lower Quarter), and all the other families positioned themselves around TKE and away from CRT, the former leading family.[4] CRT created its own cluster, the Upper Quarter, on its own. Thus, the initial stage of the Çumra Settlement in its current location consisted of the Lower and Upper Quarters, and the Middle Quarter was formed as a respond to rising groundwater level. Unfortunately, the conflict between the TKE and CRT families intensified over time and ended up with human death. As a result, the CRT families had to abandon the village and moved to a city, and the Upper Quarter of the Çumra Settlement was left deserted for several years. During the time of our research, some families from the CRT lineage began to return.

Another identifier of wealth and power is also hidden in the layout of the Çumra Settlement, although understanding them within the Çumra community was difficult. Ethnoarchaeologists have tried to account for social hierarchy and differences in wealth by utilizing house sizes. However, building size itself is not a consistent reflection of those factors (Chesson 2003: 87; see also Horne 1994; Kramer 1982; Watson 1979). At this point, it is necessary to address the socioeconomic organization during the initial establishment of the Çumra Settlement. The longitudinal overall layout of this site is related to the practicality of the departure of flocks/herds, and it is important to stress that departing order was arranged according to the level of wealth among the family groups. Possessing animal flocks/herds means wealth in the Çumra Settlement, and the number of animals owned by a family group is an indication of the level of wealth and power in the community. This information allows us to learn more about socioeconomically different groups in villages by studying settlement layouts alone because families with large flocks/herds tend to occupy areas toward the edges of longitudinal-shaped settlements, while families with no animals or fewer animals dwell in the internal sections.

When diachronic settlement growth pattern is concerned, it is clearly seen that the Akşehir Settlement households tend to create their own close kin-based clusters at the very beginning of village formation, but over time, the problem of limitation of space caused newly established households to be placed more distant from their main house. Today, the village has started to effuse toward the agricultural fields and new household clusters have appeared there, although the main settlement has mixed-family neighborhoods.

In the Çumra Settlement, increased communication with the outside world brought the idea of core family concept. New couples tend to immediately move out to their own compound, although space is still available within the village to build a new compound adjacent to the main one. In addition, the development of mechanized agriculture in large, irrigated lands has resulted in the introduction of the concept of cash economy and a reduction of security issues. These processes are gradually overriding traditional household solidarity, and have profound impacts on the formation and speed of settlement growth.

Analyzing Variation Types and Scales of Behavior at the Two Case-Study Communities

In this section, it is argued that while most of the variations in behavior, attitude, and activities in the Çumra and Akşehir communities are archaeologically invisible, those that are visible, including some daily basic activities, strategies, and approaches to various problems, provide crucial hints to understand the relations between community and settlement structure.

Behavioral Variation in the Use of Activity Spaces: Kin-Based Activities Versus Communal Activities

Many behavioral attitudes of the Çumra and Akşehir communities are as different from each other as it was previously seen concerning variations in the processes of creating compounds and neighborhoods. While the Çumra Settlement shows a closed, exclusive concept in every detail of acting in the community in regard to attitudes toward other village members and the outside world (other than the close kin-based households), the Akşehir Settlement represents an open, inclusive, communal system, which is clearly collective in nature. It is quite informative to study these completely opposite behavioral approaches as they manifest themselves in the daily life and use of activity spaces—processes that are difficult to investigate in archaeology—at the two villages. The most relevant differences in kin-based (exclusive) versus communal (inclusive) activities in the Çumra and Akşehir villages are summarized in Table 2.1.

---

[4] CRT and TKE are used in reference to specific family groups. Their full name is not given here to protect their personal rights.

Feature	Çumra Settlement	Akşehir Settlement
Wells/Fountains	Lineage-based	Common use
Threshing floors	Lineage-based	Common use
Number of mosques	3	1
Guest houses	Lineage-based	Common use
Herd/Flock grazing	Lineage-based	Common use
Drovers/Shepherd	Lineage-based	Common use
Seasonal festival celebrations	None	Communal activity
Weddings/Funerals	Restricted	Communal activity
Village cafés	None until 1994	In the center (2)

Table 2.1. Comparison of the two settlements in terms of collective versus close family-based activities.

The Çumra Settlement has a dispersed structure and a slightly longitudinal overall layout to render specific, kin-based activities possible. For instance, the layout of the settlement facilitates the departure of animal herds from stables to grazing lands separately, without crossing the internal parts of the village. Every herd has its own route, and watering the animals takes place at the lineage-specific wells. The family residential clusters and their agricultural fields are closely located to one another, or situated in a way that the landowners do not need to cross the whole village to reach their fields. Because the sons of the families share their father's land once they become adults, the household clusters can be considered as an echo of the agricultural land division and sharing order. A situation similar to herd routes occurs concerning threshing fields in post-harvest periods; the route from the agricultural field to the lineage-based threshing field is different for each family group.

In the Çumra Settlement, every compound consists of a guest room, and it is also used for social gatherings among close kin-based male members. Therefore, family group members do not utilize a village café or any other communal place, that is inclusive for other villagers, rather they prefer to remain exclusive even in their socializing times.

The occupants of the Çumra Settlement perform all their daily or seasonal activities without walking into the rest of the village (Figure 2.5). Even the places of worship are separated. There are three religious structures in the Çumra Settlement—two mosques and one *mescid* (small mosque)—therefore, every quarter has its own venue. The villagers do not have any cross-communal festivals, celebrations, or other activities. Since 1992, there has been an intent to establish a center around the village school, a small café, and a small shop. Today, cafés and other socializing spaces are more in use in the settlement, but these places were founded by the community as necessities in the process of being a municipality.

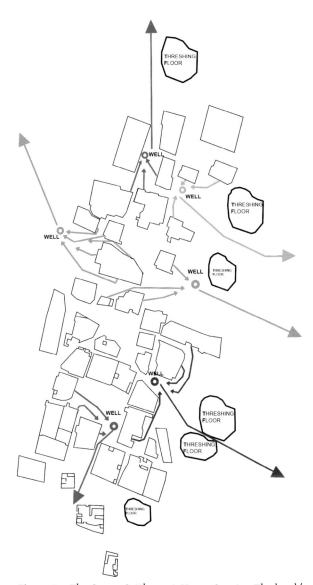

Figure 2.5. The Çumra Settlement, Upper Quarter. The herd/flock gathering around wells, the routes from settlement to pastureland, and the distribution of threshing floors (figure by the author).

In contrast, the Akşehir Settlement community gathers their herds in the village square, and the animals are driven off to the pastureland together by one shared

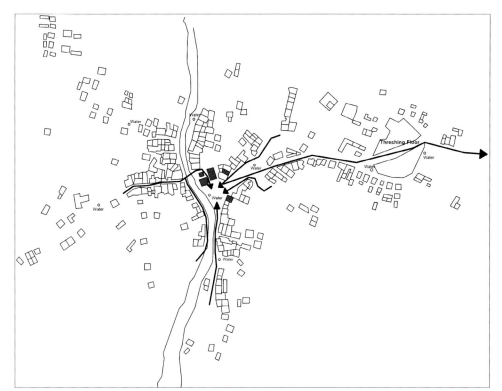

Figure 2.6. The Akşehir Settlement. The herd/flock gathering in the center and the route from settlement to pastureland (figure by the author).

drover or shepherd. There are a couple of fountains for watering the animals and one threshing area for common use (Figure 2.6). Because the agricultural lands are dispersed all around the village, bringing the harvest to a common threshing field is practical.

Although there are a couple of guesthouses in the village for foreigners, people usually invite guests into their own houses. The community celebrates not only seasonal festivals but also organizes special events for religious or national holidays. All the weddings, circumcision feasts, important anniversaries' ceremonies are announced to the whole village from the minaret of the mosque. The mosque is shared by all the members of the Akşehir Settlement.

Profound differences between the Çumra and Akşehir settlements also are reflected in the movement of people within the villages. While the streets of the Çumra Settlement are usually empty, they always are active in the Akşehir Settlement where men and women visit their close relatives who usually live in distance from each other. The exclusiveness and inclusiveness in attitude can be identified at various scales. For instance, at the Çumra Settlement, exclusivity occurs from small to large scale:

1. Exclusivity within the economically dependent household when it comes to other, economically independent core families.
2. Exclusivity among kin-based relatives when it comes to other families in a neighborhood.

3. Exclusivity within the Çumra Settlement community when it comes to outsiders, such as other villagers and foreigners.

Concerning these scales, apart from the economically independent core families, the Akşehir Settlement is featured by inclusiveness.

The two central Anatolian Neolithic sites mentioned above, Aşıklı Höyük and Çatalhöyük, represent a similar kind of contrast. Aşıklı Höyük is inclusive, with open, communal midden areas, implying that the production and consumption of foodstuffs, as well as craft production, occurred in the communal sphere (Düring 2006: 92)—in a 'pebble paved street' and two, large, probably communal buildings located southwest of this street (Esin and Harmankaya 1999: 124, 2007: 269). In contrast, Çatalhöyük is exclusive. At that site, each typical 'house' had storage facilities, and there is no evidence for public buildings, ceremonial centers, or communal production areas (Hodder 2013: 304). The different perceptions of individualism versus communalism must be taken as an important indicator to characterize a community. These attitudes or behaviors should not be understood as intentional decisions made by individual community members. Instead, they are a consequence of the long-term accumulation of traditions transferred through generations. Furthermore, these behaviors may have been, at least in part, rooted in the origin stories of the communities.

Variation in the Perception of 'Community Past' and the Depth of Shared Memory

Another striking difference between the Çumra and Akşehir communities lies in their origin histories, including where they came from and how and why they built their villages. The story of the Çumra Settlement in the living memory starts with migration from Central Asia to Anatolia via Syria. Almost every family knows this shared history, and in addition, they have their own family histories. Demonstrating its importance for the community, the origin story is always proudly shared with others; in fact, one of the community members has published a book about it (Özüdoğru 1997).

On the other hand, the Akşehir community members tend to recall a few stories about two friends or brothers who came to the current village location from Central Asia and built their houses on the two opposite sides of the river. When the reason for this poor and short memory was questioned, it appeared that it is directly related to the community structure.

These data on community origins are consistent with other differences between the Çumra and Akşehir communities, and imply remarkable organizational differences; that is, a kin-based structure versus a community of mixed families. Reasons for differences regarding origin stories include:

1. Shared history is inherited by and transferred to more people in the kin-based structure. Regarding the community of mixed families, the Akşehir people came from different groups to the current settlement in the past. Therefore, the Akşehir villagers do not have a holistic, shared history, and even though each family has its own history, the transmission of knowledge regarding common history is weak because it has never been considered important.
2. More importantly, in contrast to the attitude of the Çumra community, the Akşehir people do not seem to prefer to remember the history of their small family group. Judging from interviews and friendly chats conducted during the fieldwork of this study, it appears that remembering versus forgetting the past is closely linked to the perception of community identity.

Therefore, the Çumra community does not need to underline their unity because they are a kin-based group, with a shared tradition of living as a community. On the other hand, the Akşehir people need to have measures to keep their community together because they do not tend to highlight their tradition of being a mixed but integrated community.

Variation in the Concept of Unity (Togetherness) Dependently or Independently from the Settlement as Place

The concept of 'being together' independently from the settlement is also linked to the community structure. Çumra Settlement people identify themselves as a group that had already existed before they settled at the current site, as opposed to the Akşehir people, whose integration fully depended on their settlement. This self-perception influences settlement formation in various ways that is very similar to the concepts of the 'depth of historical knowledge' discussed above.

The duration of settlements is affected by this self-perception of the residents. The Çumra community moved from their previous settlement to the current one quickly and in a very organized manner. The transportation of entire household groups was completed within approximately 3–5 years. According to the interviews, the reason for this relocation was the rapid rise of groundwater at the previous site. It is difficult to tell whether it was possible to solve this environmental problem in a way other than abandoning the land completely. For the time being, that land is occupied by another group, and a 98–100-year-old village still exists almost at the same location. Thus, the history of the Çumra community suggests that leaving a settlement should be understood in the framework of the repetitive action of settling a new one. Being a community independently from a settlement place increases potential mobility. For the Akşehir people, however, leaving the settlement means the dissolution of the community because these people create their community where they settle.

Consequently, the Çumra Settlement community has its own identity independent of the settlement, while the Akşehir Settlement community's social identity is attached to their physical settlement. This perspective of the Akşehir Settlement is discussed in more detail below.

Variation in the Attitude and Capacity of Resolving Environmental Problems and Social Conflicts

Similar to the previous Çumra Settlement, the Akşehir Settlement also has encountered environmental problems. In that village, a river passes through the center that occasionally overflows its banks, causing serious problems, including human death. Despite financial support provided by state authorities to relocate the village to a higher location, the community has rejected this opportunity; only houses by the river have moved for a very short time. Instead, the problem was resolved through other measures, such as deepening the riverbed and repairing buildings and gardens destroyed by the flood.

Efforts associated with intending to remain at the same place are not only related to environmental issues but also we see a similar attitude toward the resolution of social problems. The Akşehir Settlement community has a great concern to settle even the most trivial conflict among people immediately. They explain this effort by asking 'Otherwise how could we continue to live together?' In contrast, there are many unresolved conflicts among the Çumra people; even a long-lasting feud among lineages has occurred, causing human death in the past. The Çumra community does not feel that this could cause the dissolution or collapse of their settlement. Instead, as a response, they live in discrete, walled, close kin-based neighborhoods, and keep themselves not only physically but also socially distant from other families. For them, the spatial rearrangement of residences is the solution, and settlement dissolution perhaps never has been considered as an option to deal with conflicts. In fact, the Çumra community may have used recurrent settlement relocations as a way to reorganize their social layout when social stress occurred.

Discussion and Conclusions

The dwellers of the two central Anatolian villages presented in this paper are both Turkish, both practice the same religion and sect, and both originate in Central Asia from nomadic backgrounds. The most important result of this study is that although the communities of the Çumra and Akşehir settlements share similar basic characteristics, they structure their space in different ways to accommodate their very particular social organization.

Based on formal differences between these villages, various concepts have been discussed relative to their economic, environmental, historical, sociostructural, and behavioral characteristics, all of which exist in cause and effect relations. What we have seen is that household economic relations and their reflections in the built environment are the keystones of the development of entire settlements. Furthermore, it is not a standardized phenomenon, as it varies within the same region, among communities of the same ethnic and religious background.

Agricultural land ownership—in other words, the economic wealth of the family—has an important impact on the development of a compound as it relates to the multiplication of bread-kitchens and storage buildings. This material manifestation of household intraeconomic relations can be observed in compound (Çumra) or house (Akşehir) structures, and it also reveals production and consumption practices among household members (i.e., core families).

By generating neighborhoods, the physical multiplication of a household unit determines the speed of settlement growth. However, the actual contents of socioeconomic relations play a very important role in this growing process. The formation process of compact versus dispersed/low-density settlements has been discussed by Feinman and Nicholas (2012). They explored the interrelationship between settlement form and land use at Classic Maya sites as well as neighborhood collective action in the contexts of compact and dispersed settlements for the pre-Hispanic Mesoamerican period (Feinman and Nicholas 2012: 134–139; see also Drennan 1988). Feinman and Nicholas also concluded that growing patterns are strongly linked to subsistence economies at the household level because economic independence is an essential condition for a household to separate from the main one; sometimes, separation starts from the kitchen/storage building, and sometimes, bigger steps are taken to multiply the whole compound.

The structure of household clusters or neighborhoods within settlements is again related to socioeconomic organization. The Çumra Settlement's dispersed household clusters were established relative to the distance and direction of their agricultural lands and herd routes, while the compact Akşehir Settlement did not follow the same pattern, as the farming fields of its inhabitants are located in patchy distribution around the village.

Contrasting behavioral approaches, individualism (exclusiveness) versus collectivism (inclusiveness) seem to be a crucial ingredient that accounts for variation between settlement forms at the Çumra and Akşehir sites. The identification of concrete elements in association with these conceptual variations, including the location of wells, multiplication of mosques, threshing areas, etc., is one of the most important contributions of this paper. This analysis also highlighted other reasons for the formation process of dispersed settlements, such as social stress and intracommunity competition caused by a kin-based social configuration.

Consequently, this research provides an opportunity to consider important anthropological concepts, such as intracommunity competition, as they relate to the speed of settlement growth via multiplication of economically independent household clusters, the interrelation between increasing social stress and territoriality, and the connection between the rearrangement of settlement layout and the mobility of a community to maintain peace among people. During this study, the reasons for variability in self-perception also were traced, such as the opposing concepts of 'being a community in the context of a settlement' versus 'being a community independently from a settlement' and the relationship between depth of historical memory and preferred social identity, which all are difficult to detect at an archaeological site. It also was important to observe how factors like the background story of a community and the structure of the society worked along with the environment, geography, topography, subsistence economy, and local histories in the process of settlement formation.

Avoiding direct analogy and focusing instead on surprising inferences should be taken as an advantage of ethnoarchaeological research. Archaeology deals with physically or contextually differentiated finds and data over time. As mentioned briefly in the introduction, the study of past communities within their complete environmental, demographic, economic, and historical contexts is extremely difficult in archaeology. In the process of interpreting settlement sites, we should take into account that a community with a common background, shared ethnicity, religion, etc. does not necessarily share facilities and activity areas. Conversely, family clustering of specific activity areas or the existence of recurring activity spaces, such as threshing fields, wells, and guestrooms, does not necessarily indicate an integrated community of people from different backgrounds. Additionally, the cumulative knowledge and variations in values and perceptions among communities represent the greatest challenges in the process of understanding past societies.

The Çumra and Akşehir case studies, when placed in the larger context of Central Anatolia, provide insights into the interplay between opposing concepts, such as interpersonal relationships in kin-based tribal (*kabile*) communities versus those in mixed communities. When compared with developments in other regions of the world, the examples presented here call into question archaeological assumptions about how physical structures of the archaeological record are related to past social structures. Other issues also were investigated in this research, including active usage (daily routes) of compounds/houses by its members, territoriality within a single unit, shifts in settlement forms due to recent changes, modern technologies, and adaptations of city life in these rural sites, and the application of ethnoarchaeological results in archaeological interpretations. These lie outside the scope of this paper, but they may be equally valuable for refining both the questions and the assumptions concerning interpretations regarding social and spatial organization.

This ethnoarchaeological study of contemporary settlement communities cannot answer all related archaeological questions. Nevertheless, similar studies have enormous potential to open wider perspectives and trigger alternative approaches in the way we interpret the past. Moreover, studies like this might provoke broader and more holistic archaeological work by revealing the complexity of social processes involved in settlement formation.

Acknowledgments

I would like to thank Prof. Dr. Ian Hodder and the Çatalhöyük Excavation and Research Project, where my research was based, for all their support. I am grateful to Dr. Todd Whitelaw (UCL) for helping me to analyze my raw data, and I thank my doctoral thesis supervisor Prof. Dr. Mihriban Özbaşaran (İstanbul University). Also special thanks to all the village communities for their hospitality and patience to my endless questions, to Kunter Kınacı for his help digitizing the illustrations for this paper, and to Faik Karaaba for reading and checking my text.

References Cited

Allison, P.M. 1999. *The Archaeology of Household Activities*. London and New York: Routledge.

Altuntaş, A. 2001. Geçmişten Günümüze Sulamanın Tarihi Seyri ve Kuru Kafa Mehmet Efendi, in H. Karpuz, A. Baş and R. Duran (eds) *I. Uluslararası Çatalhöyük'ten Günümüze Çumra Kongresi. Bildiriler. 15-16 Eylül 2000*: 149–160. Çumra: Çumra Belediyesi.

Arnauld, M.C., M.E. Smith and L.R. Manzanilla (eds) 2012. *The Neighborhood as a Social and Spatial Unit in Mesoamerican Cities*. Tucson: University of Arizona Press.

Bahar, H. and Ö. Koçak 2004. *Eskiçağ Konya Araştırmaları 2: Neolitik Çağ'dan Roma Dönemi Sonuna Kadar*. Konya: Kömen Yayınları.

Bahçeci, İ., N. Dinç, A.F. Tarı, A.İ. Ağar and B. Sönmez 2006. Water and salt balance studies, using SaltMod, to improve subsurface drainage design in the Konya-Çumra Plain, Turkey. *Agricultural Water Management* 85(3): 261–271.

Bahçeci, İ., A.F Tarı, N. Dinç and P. Bahçeci 2008. Performance Analysis of Collective Set-Move Lateral Sprinkler Irrigation Systems Used in Central Anatolia. *Turkish Journal of Agriculture and Forestry* 32: 435–449.

Bailey, D., A. Whittle and D. Hofmann (eds) 2008. *Living Well Together? Settlement and Materiality in the Neolithic of South-East and Central Europe*. Oxford: Oxbow Books.

Binford, L. 1967. Smudge Pits and Hide Smoking: The Use of Analogy in Archaeological Reasoning. *American Antiquity* 32(1): 1–12.

Binford, L. 1978a. Dimensional Analysis of Behavior and Site Structure: Learning from an Eskimo Hunting Stand. *American Antiquity* 43(3): 330–361.

Binford, L. 1978b. *Nunamiut Ethnoarchaeology*. New York: Academic Press.

Bintliff, J.L. 2013. Territoriality and Politics in the Prehistoric and Classical Aegean. *Archaeological Papers of the American Anthropological Association* 22(1): 28–38.

Bozyiğit, R. and Ş. Güngör 2011. Konya Ovasının Toprakları ve Sorunları (Soils and Problems of Konya Plain). *Marmara Coğrafya Dergisi Sayı 24 – Temmuz 2011*: 169–200.

Byrd, B.F. 2000. Households in Transition: Neolithic Social Organization within Southwest Asia, in I. Kuijt (ed.) *Life in Neolithic Farming Communities: Social Organization, Identity, and Differentiation*: 63–98. New York: Kluwer Academic/Plenum.

Chesson, M. 2003. Households, Houses, Neighborhoods and Corporate Villages: Modeling Early Bronze Age as a House Society. *Journal of Mediterranean Archaeology* 16(1): 79–102.

Creese, J.L. 2014. Village Layout and Social Experience: A Comparative Study from the Northeast Woodlands. *Midcontinental Journal of Archaeology* 39(1): 1–29.

Cutting, M. 2006. Traditional architecture and social organization: The agglomerated buildings of Aşıklı Höyük and Çatalhöyük in Neolithic Central Anatolia, in E.B. Banning and M. Chazan (eds) *Domesticating Space: Construction, Community, and Cosmology in the Late Prehistoric Near East* (Studies in Early Near Eastern Production, Subsistence, and Environment 6): 91–102. Berlin: Freie Universität.

David, N. and C. Kramer 2001. *Ethnoarchaeology in Action*. Cambridge: Cambridge University Press.

Demirkent, I. 2002. XII. Yüzyılda Bizans'ın Ege Bölgesinden Güneye İnen Yolları Hakkında, in *Anadolu'da Tarihi Yollar ve Şehirler Semineri Bildirileri*: 1–14. İstanbul: İÜ Edebiyat Fakültesi Tarih Araştırma Merkezi.

Diyarı, N.H. and A.K. Derneği 1956. Coğrafi Durum. *Akşehir Dergisi, March*: 12–15.

Drennan, R.D. 1988. Household Location and Compact versus Dispersed Settlement in Prehispanic Mesoamerica, in R.R. Wilk and W. Ashmore (eds) *Household and Community in the Mesoamerican Past*: 273–293. Albuquerque: University of New Mexico Press.

Düring, B. 2006. *Constructing Communities. Clustered Neighborhood Settlements of the Central Anatolian Neolithic ca. 8500-5500*. Leiden: Nederlands Instituut Voor Het Nabije Osten.

Düring, B. and A. Marciniak 2005. Households and communities in the Central Anatolian Neolithic. *Archaeological Dialogues* 12(2): 165–187.

Edgeworth, M. 2003. *Acts of Discovery: An Ethnography of Archaeological Practice* (BAR International Series 1131). Oxford: Archaeopress.

Erol, O. 1985. The Relationship between the Phases of the Development of the Konya-Karapınar Obruks and the Pleistocene Tuzgölü and Konya Pluvial Lakes. *Proceedings of the Ankara-Antalya Symposium, July Publication* 6: 207–213.

Esin, U. and S. Harmankaya 1999. Aşıklı, in M. Özdoğan and N. Başgelen (eds) *Neolithic in Turkey: The Cradle of Civilization. New Discoveries*: 115–132. Istanbul: Arkeoloji ve Sanat Publications.

Esin, U. and S. Harmankaya 2007. Aşıklı Höyük, in M. Özdoğan and N. Başgelen (eds) *Anadolu'da Uygarlığın Doğuşu ve vrupa'ya Yayılımı: Türkiye'de Neolitik Dönem, yeni kazılar, yeni bulgular*: 255–272. İstanbul: Arkeoloji ve Sanat Publications.

Feinman, G.M. and L.M. Nicholas 2012. Compact versus Dispersed Settlement in Pre-Hispanic Mesoamerica: The Role of Neighborhood Organization and Collective Action, in M.C. Arnauld, L.R. Manzanilla and M.E. Smith (eds) *The Neighborhood as a Social and Spatial Unit in Mesoamerican Cities*: 132–155. Tucson: University of Arizona Press.

Furholt, M., N. Müller-Scheeßel, M. Wunderlich, I. Cheben and J. Müller 2020. Communality and Discord in an Early Neolithic Settlement Agglomeration: The LBK Site of Vráble, Southwest Slovakia. *Cambridge Archaeological Journal* 30(3): 469–489.

Hamon, C. 2016. Debates in ethnoarchaeology today: a new crisis of identity or the expression of a vibrant research strategy? *World Archaeology* 48(5): 700–704.

Hendon, J.A. 1996. Archaeological Approaches to the Organization of Domestic Labor: Household Practice and Domestic Relations. *Annual Review of Anthropology* 25: 45–61.

Hodder, I. 1982. *The Present Past: An Introduction to Anthropology for Archaeologists*. London: Batsford.

Hodder, I. 2013. Çatalhöyük. A Summary of Recent Work Concerning Architecture, in B. Söğüt (ed.) *Stratonikeia'dan Laginaya - Ahmet Adil Tırpan Armağanı (From Stratonikeia to Lagina, Festschrift in Honour of Ahmet Adil Tırpan)*: 303–314. Istanbul: Ege Publications.

Horne, L. 1994. *Village Spaces: Settlement and Society in Northeastern Iran*. Washington, D.C.: Smithsonian Institution Press.

Hütteroth, W.D. 1974. The Influence of Social Structure on Land Division and Settlement in Inner Anatolia, in P. Benedict, E. Tümertekin and F. Mansur (eds) *Turkey: Geographic and Social Perspectives*: 19–47. Leiden: Brill.

İnalcık, H. 2009. *Devlet-i Aliye; Osmanlı İmparatorluğu Üzerine Araştırmalar-I, Seçme Eserler-II; Klasik Dönem (1302-1606): Siyasal, Kurumsal ve Ekonomik Gelişim*. Istanbul: Türkiye İş Bankası Kültür Yayınları.

Karabayır, M. 2001. *Geçmişten Günümüze Çumra*. Çumra: Çumra Belediyesi.

Keleş, B. 2002. Anadolu'da Gelişen Bazı Önemli Ticaret Merkezleri (Antalya-Kayseri-Sivas ve Sinop), in *Anadolu'da Tarihi Yollar ve Şehirler Semineri. Bildiriler*: 25–38. İstanbul: İÜ Edebiyat Fakültesi Tarih Araştırma Merkezi.

Konukçu, F. and R. Akbuğa 2006. Konya-Çura Yöresinde Yüzeysel Tuzlu Taban Suyunun Sulanan Alanlardaki Toprak-Su ve Tuz Dengesi Üzerine. *Tekirdağ Ziraat Fakültesi Dergisi* 3: 105–117.

Konyalı, İ.H. 1945. *Nasreddin Hoca'nın Şehir Akşehir. Tarihi-Turistik Klavuz*. Municipality of Akşehir: Akşehir Belediyesi.

Kramer, C. 1982. *Village Ethnoarchaeology: Rural Iran in Archaeological Perspective*. New York: Academic Press.

Kuzucuoğlu, C., R. Parish and M. Karabiyikoglu 1998. The dune systems of Konya Plain (Turkey): their relation to environmental changes in Central Anatolia during the Late Pleistocene and Holocene. *Geomorphology* 23(2–4): 257–271.

Květina, P. and M. Končelová 2013. Neolithic LBK Intrasite Settlement Patterns: A Case Study from Bylany (Czech Republic). *Journal of Archaeology* 2013: 581607, http://dx.doi.org/10.1155/2013/581607

Marciniak, A. and N. Yalman (eds) 2013. *Contesting Ethnoarchaeologies: Traditions, Theories, Prospects* (One World Archaeology 7). New York: Springer.

Matthews, W. 2012. Defining Households: Micro-Contextual Analysis of Early Neolithic Households in the Zagros, Iran, in B.J. Parker and C.P. Foster (eds) *New Perspectives on Household Archaeology*: 183–216. Winona Lake (IN): Eisenbrauns.

Naruse, T., H. Kitagawa and H. Matsubara 1997. Lake Level Changes and Development of Alluvial Fans in Lake Tuz and the Konya Basin during the Last 24,000 Years on the Anatolian Plateau, Turkey. *Japan Review* 8: 173–192.

Netting, R.R., R. Wilk and E.J. Arnould (eds) 1984. *Households: Comparative and Historical Studies of the Domestic Group*. Berkeley: University of California Press.

Ödekan, A. 1995. Mimarlik ve Sanat Tarihi, in S. Aksin (ed.) *Türkiye Tarihi 1, Osmanli Devleti'ne Kadar Türkler*: 363–496. Istanbul: Cem Yayınları.

Osborne, J.F. and P. Van Valkenburgh (eds) 2013. *Territoriality in Archaeology* (Archaeological Papers of the American Anthropological Association 22). Walden (MA): Wiley-Blackwell.

Özüdoğru, Ş. 1997. *Tarihi, Sosyal ve Kültürel Yönleriyle Hotamış*. Konya.

Pyzel, J. 2012. Preliminary results of large scale emergency excavations in Ludwinowo 7, comm. Włocławek, in R. Smolnik (ed.) *Siedlungsstruktur und Kulturwandel in der Bandkeramik*: 160–166. Dresden: Landesamt für Archäologie.

Roberts, N., P. Boyer and R. Parish 1996. Preliminary Results of Geoarchaeological Investigations at Çatalhöyük, in I. Hodder (ed.) *On the Surface: Çatalhöyük 1993-1995*: 19–40. London: British Institute at Ankara.

Sargın, S. and H. Akengin 2009. Akşehir Kırlarında Nüfus, Yerleşme ve Arazi Kullanımı. *Süleyman Demirel Üniversitesi, Fen Edebiyat Fakültesi Sosyal Bilimler Dergisi* 19: 149–168.

Şeker, C.H., H. Özaytekin, H. Negiş, İ. Gümüş, M. Dedeoğlu, E. Atmaca and Ü. Karaca 2017. Identification of regional soil quality factors and indicators: a case study on an alluvial plain (central Turkey). *Solid Earth* 8(3): 583–595.

Smith, M.E. 2010. The archaeological study of neighborhoods and districts in ancient cities. *Journal of Anthropological Archaeology* 29(2): 137–154.

Smith, M.E. and J. Novic 2012. Introduction: Neighborhoods and Districts in Ancient Mesoamerica, in M.C. Arnauld, M.E. Smith and L.R. Manzanilla (eds) *The Neighborhood as a Social and Spatial Unit in Mesoamerican Cities*: 1–26. Tucson: University of Arizona Press.

Stäuble, H. and U. Veit (eds) 2016. *Der bandkeramische Siedlungsplatz Eythra in Sachsen*. Leipzig: Professur für Ur- und Frühgeschichte der Universität.

Steadman, S.R. 2015. *Archaeology of Domestic Architecture and the Human Use of Space*. London and New York: Routledge.

Steere, B. 2017. *The Archaeology of Houses and Households in the Native Southeast*. Tuscaloosa: The University of Alabama Press.

Sümer, F. 1972. *Oğuzlar (Türkmenler) Tarihleri-Boy Teşkilatı-Destanları* (Ankara Üniversitesi Dil Tarih Coğrafya Fakültesi Yayınları 170). Ankara: Ankara Üniversitesi Basımevi.

Watson, P.J. 1979. *Archaeological Ethnography in Western Iran*. Tucson: University of Arizona Press.

Whittle, A. 1996. *Europe in the Neolithic. The creation of new worlds*. Cambridge: Cambridge University Press.

Wilk, R.R. and W.L. Rathje 1982. Household Archaeology. *American Behavioral Scientist* 25(6): 617–639.

Wylie, A. 2002. *Thinking from Things: Essays in the Philosophy of Archaeology*. Berkeley: University of California Press.

Yaeger, J. and M. Canuto 2000. Introducing an archaeology of communities, in M.A. Canuto and J. Yaeger (eds) *The Archaeology of Communities: A New World Perspective*: 1–15. London: Routledge.

Yalman, N. 2005. Çağdaş Köylerde Yapılan 'Yerleşim Mantığı' Çalışmalarının Arkeolojik Yerleşmelerin Yorumuna Katkısı. Unpublished PhD Dissertation, University of Istanbul.

Yücel, T. 1987. *Türkiye Coğrafyası* (Publications of the Institute of Research on Turkish Culture 68). Institute of Research on Turkish Culture: Ankara.

Chapter 3

From Sanctuaries to Towns:
The Role of Religion in Early Urbanization

Manuel Fernández-Götz

Abstract

This paper discusses the role of religion in early urbanization processes, arguing that in many cases cities developed at the location of pre-existing places for cultic celebrations and political assemblies. Starting with some general remarks on the role of religious gatherings as focal points for communal identity construction, a series of examples from different times and periods are listed. The chapter focuses particularly on the Late Iron Age *oppida* of temperate Europe. Recent research has uncovered evidence for public spaces and sanctuaries at numerous *oppida*, highlighting the importance of their political and religious role. On occasion, the existence of a place for cult activities preceded the concentration of a significant number of people or even the fortification of the area. These public/cultic places shaped community organization, being periodically visited by inhabitants of a large, rural environment. The results have important implications for our understanding of early centralization and urbanization processes in pre-modern societies.

Religion at the Root of Community Aggregation

From the Mesopotamian ziggurats to the urban sanctuaries of the Greek *poleis*, the public spaces within the *oppida* of temperate Europe, and the temples of pre-Hispanic Mesoamerica, religion appears to be an essential element of urbanization processes in pre-modern societies, often being at the root of the fusion of previously scattered communities. As stated by Carballo, '*As a socially transformative process, ancient urbanizations were guided by the varied cultural logic of the people undertaking these changes, both in cities and their hinterlands. Much of that logic was grounded in religion and would have likewise been in flux, meaning that urbanization was a phenomenon in which religion was both transformative and transformed by*' (2016: 19). In some cases, it has even been determined that the existence of a place for cult activities preceded the concentration of a significant number of people or even the fortification of the sites. Drawing upon different archaeological case studies and historical comparisons, this paper will explore the crucial role of sanctuaries as focal points for social aggregation and early urbanization.

The construction of collective identities through sanctuaries is a key element for the understanding of ancient societies and, in particular, of their dynamics of aggregation. Communities are largely symbolic constructs (Cohen 1985). Given the fact that public cult places often functioned as *lieux de mémoire* where foundation myths were reproduced through rituals and cult celebrations, these sites played a vital role in the symbolic construction of political and ethnic communities in Antiquity and the creation of boundaries with outside groups (Derks and Roymans 2009; Gerritsen and Roymans 2006). Major sanctuaries of civic religion, being meeting places of intergroup cult communities as well, offer some of the best possibilities for gaining access to political and ethnic constructs at different scales of social organization. Following Derks and Roymans, these sites were '*the concrete anchoring points in the landscape where the polity's core values—as exemplified in its tradition of origin—were transmitted to the wider community through recitals, dramatic performances and collective rituals*' (2009: 8). In many cases, it is possible to observe a close link between the appearance of cult centers and the emergence of politicized identities, a phenomenon already noted by Polignac (1995) in his work on the origins of the Greek *poleis*.

Identities are constructed through performing practices (Bourdieu 1977; Giddens 1984), which shape the memories of individuals and communities (Beck and Wiemer 2009; Bommas 2011). In this sense, the rituals and celebrations held at supra-local sanctuaries would have been key elements in the fostering of social cohesion, self-awareness, and shared identity. As is known from multiple ethnographic and historical examples, the performances that took place on the occasion of ceremonial public occasions would provide those attending with shared experiences that would create, reaffirm, and reinforce the symbolic ties that united communities (Earle 1997: 153). Sanctuaries would therefore be sites at which politics, religion, and the building of collective identities went hand in hand (Gerritsen and Roymans 2006).

Figure 3.1. Ruins of the ceremonial center of Göbekli Tepe
(photo by Teomancimit; CC-BY-SA-3.0; https://en.wikipedia.org/wiki/Göbekli_Tepe)

In periods of centralization, communal rituals develop to sustain the new, higher order of social organization (Kristiansen 1998: 345). In a world imbued by religion, with no distinction made between sacred and profane, ritual spaces could have served as landmarks in the territory, acting as elements that brought together different clans and lineages. One of the earliest known examples is the famous tell of Göbekli Tepe in southeastern Turkey (Dietrich *et al.* 2012; Schmidt 2006). This hill sanctuary dates back to the 10th millennium BC and provides evidence for repetitive feasts. According to the long-standing excavator Klaus Schmidt, the site with its famous T-shaped pillars would have served as a focal point of aggregation that acted as a sort of pilgrimage destination, attracting people from a large region (Figure 3.1). In a famous publication, Schmidt (2000) coined the expression '*first came the temple, then the town*,' illustrating that places of supra-local religious significance played a key role in early processes of social aggregation.

Whereas Göbekli Tepe did not develop into an urban center, we can find examples from all around the world of sanctuaries being among the oldest structures of emerging cities. This phenomenon includes many urban centers of ancient Mesopotamia, the city of Jerusalem with the Temple Mount, and the temples of Angkor Wat in Cambodia. In ancient China,

the importance of the religious component in the development of early urbanism was already stressed in Wheatley's seminal volume. According to this author, '*whenever [...] we trace back the characteristic urban form to its beginnings we arrive not at a settlement that is dominated by commerce [...] or at one that is focused on a citadel [...] but rather at a ceremonial complex*' (Wheatley 1971: 225).

Although this might not be a universal model, it was certainly a widespread phenomenon in different cultures and periods. It is to be expected that new archaeological research will expand the corpus of well-documented case studies. For instance, new archaeological investigations at the lowland Maya site of Ceibal have documented a formal ceremonial complex that was built around 950 BC, preceding the development of permanent settlement in the area (Inomata *et al.* 2015).

In Scandinavia, the site of Uppåkra in southern Sweden provides an example of a central place that was situated on a location that had ritual significance and eventually became a trading and production center (Hårdh 2000; Larsson 2007). In the Medieval period, several Scandinavian towns grew up around places where people had congregated since Antiquity to hold their assemblies, the so-called 'Things.' At these meetings of free men, disputes were settled, laws issued, and

Figure 3.2. Burial mounds at Gamla Uppsala
(photo by the author).

political decisions taken, all accompanied by public religious rites and economic activities (Sanmark *et al.* 2015–2016; Wenskus 1984). One of the most prominent cases was the 'Thing of all Swedes,' held annually at Gamla Uppsala, which combined a general assembly, a great fair, and a religious celebration (Duczko 1998). All free men who were living in the kingdom and able to wield a weapon had the right to participate at the assembly at this major judicial, royal, and sacred location (Figure 3.2). Examples of towns that originated at 'Thing' places or in their proximity include Viborg, Odense, and Ringsted in Denmark and Uppsala in Sweden.

The significance of religious pilgrimages as triggers for the development of urban centers is a phenomenon frequently observed across Medieval Europe. Pilgrimages were often linked to the cult of the tomb of a saint, for example at Santiago de Compostela in northern Spain or Esslingen in southern Germany. In any case, it is worth noting that there are also numerous cases of sites with an important ritual function that did not develop into urban settlements. Thus, contextual analyses are required to draw conclusions at the micro-, meso-, and macroscales.

Politics and Religion at the *Oppida*

In what follows, I will concentrate on examples from Late Iron Age Europe, particularly the large, fortified *oppida* that developed between the 2nd and 1st centuries BC (Figure 3.3; Fernández-Götz 2019a; Fichtl 2005, 2012a; Rieckhoff and Fichtl 2011). Traditional approaches have emphasized the role of these large, fortified sites as centers of craft production and trade (Collis 1984; Wells 1984). Without denying these economic factors, recent research shows that it is also necessary to take into account political and religious aspects (Buchsenschutz 2014; Fernández-Götz 2014c, 2018). Archaeological research is uncovering a growing

number of sanctuaries and public spaces, or 'plazas,' within the *oppida*, and even buildings that could have served for political meetings (Fichtl 2010, 2012b, 2016; Metzler *et al.* 2006; Poux 2012b). An example is the presumed meeting place of the Arvernian senate discovered at the public square of Corent close to the central sanctuary and the marketplace (Figure 3.4; Poux 2012a; Poux and Demierre 2016). The proximity between a sanctuary, a meeting place, and a market is repeatedly observed throughout history, as we can see in examples extending from the coastal sanctuaries of the ancient Mediterranean to many modern-day Buddhist temples.

The discovery of public places and sanctuaries at *oppida* sites, such as Manching, Titelberg, Martberg, Bibracte, and Corent, provides evidence for the political and religious life of Late Iron Age communities (Fernández-Götz 2014b; Fichtl 2010, 2012b, 2016; Metzler *et al.* 2006). These public spaces were fundamental arenas for interaction and collective negotiation, being comparable in their functions to the plazas known from Mesoamerica (Tsukamoto and Inomata 2014) and the Andean region (Moore 1996). Moreover, the enormous quantity of animal bones found at sites such as Titelberg (Méniel 2008) and the large number of wine amphorae documented at Bibracte and Corent (Poux 2004) provide evidence for communal festivals and banquets, probably linked to political assemblies, religious celebrations, and fairs. As is known from other examples in the ancient world (Fernández-Götz 2013; Ligt and de Neeve 1988), people would take advantage of these multitudinous encounters to deal with political, religious, social, and economic matters.

The Late Iron Age *oppida*, or at least the majority of them, served as focal points of reference that were periodically visited by inhabitants of the rural hinterland, who came for markets, political celebrations, and religious

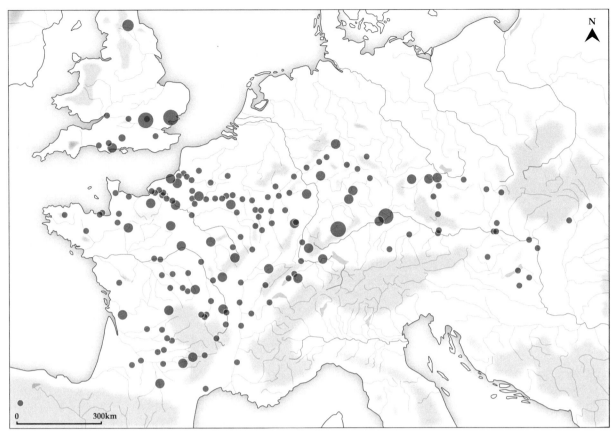

Figure 3.3. Distribution map of Late Iron Age *oppida* between
the Atlantic and East Europe (figure by the author).

Figure 3.4. Recreation of the center of the *oppidum* of Corent
with major public structures (after Poux 2014).

festivals. In addition, the large, fortified sites could have served as places of refuge during times of conflict. The public gatherings and celebrations held at the *oppida* must have been key elements in the construction of supra-local identities (Fernández-Götz and Roymans 2015; Gerritsen and Roymans 2006). Public assemblies in particular were important mechanisms of collective governance (Fernández-Götz 2013), much like those existing in societies all around the globe (cf. Blanton and Fargher 2008). Literary sources, particularly Julius Caesar, provide some information on the existence of these large collective meetings in first-century BC Gaul. The best-documented example is the Treveran assembly convened by Indutiomarus:

> '*He proclaimed an armed convention. This in the practice of the Gauls marks the beginning of a war; and by a general law all grown men are accustomed to assemble at it in arms, while the one who comes last to the assembly is put to death with every kind of torture in sight of the host. At the convention Indutiomarus declared Cingetorix an enemy and confiscated his goods. [...] This business despatched, Indutiomarus declared in the convention that he had been summoned by the Senones, the Carnutes, and several other Gallic states, and that he proposed to march to them through the borders of the Remi, laying waste their lands, and before so doing to attack the camp of Labienus*' (Caesar, *De Bello Gallico* V, 56).

We find an extremely close connection between politics and religion since calling the Treveran assembly was both a political act (preparation for war, humiliation of the principal rival for power, etc.) but also a religious one (ritual sacrifice of the last warrior to arrive).

As Wenskus (1984) noted, the inherently cultic nature of public assemblies means they would mainly be held at the great sanctuaries. Religion and politics would be two interwoven concepts, the political group also acting as a religious community (Fichtl 2005: 145–147). Bearing in mind the enormous number of people who must have congregated, it is reasonable to assume that public assemblies took place in open spaces, very often located within the *oppida*. The *oppidum* of Titelberg in Luxembourg is a particularly compelling example of this. Recovery of more than 5000 Celtic coins and evidence of Mediterranean imports attest to the prosperity of this site. The most outstanding feature, however, is the so-called public space or *area sacra* where assemblies, fairs, and religious ceremonies were held (Metzler 2006; Metzler *et al.* 2016). This large area, covering 10 ha in the eastern part of the *oppidum*, was surrounded by a mudbrick wall and a ditch containing finds that suggest ritual activities (Figure 3.5). Evidence for political decision-making within the public space is provided by the presence of voting installations from the first half of the 1st century BC. An enormous

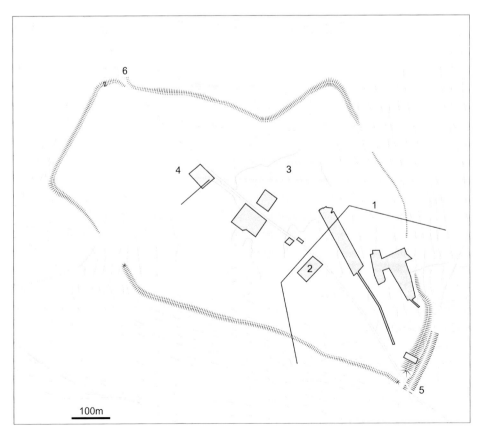

Figure 3.5. Plan of the Titelberg *oppidum*. 1: Cultic ditch that marks the boundary of the public space; 2: Excavation of the monumental center; 3: Concentration of the La Tène habitat; 4: Possible Roman military establishment; 5: East gate; 6: West gate (after Metzler *et al.* 2006, modified by the author).

quantity of animal bones suggests the existence of large-scale communal feasting. The inner chronology of Titelberg shows that the sacred space for public events was defined around the same time as the *murus gallicus* fortification, followed by the development of the settlement, artisanal production, and trade. A monumental building, developed in several stages on the highest point of the site, was finally transformed into an impressive Gallo-Roman temple in the early centuries AD.

Titelberg seems to have acted as the main center or capital of the tribal polity of the Treveri, at least in the 1st century BC. This public space is exceptionally large, and could have hosted public assemblies of the kind described by Caesar as occurring among the Treveri (see above). However, Titelberg is not the only Treveran *oppidum* with traces indicating gatherings and cult activities. Indeed, spaces for religious practices and assemblies have been identified archaeologically in six of the seven Treveran *oppida* in the Middle Rhine–Moselle region; in five cases, these are at the highest point of the respective site: Titelberg, Martberg, Wallendorf, Otzenhausen, and Kastel-Staadt (Fernández-Götz 2014a; 2014b: 143–157; Metzler *et al.* 2006). Taken as a whole, the data reflect an organization of the territory of the Treveri around the *oppida*, which, in turn, acted as focal points for social and territorial aggregations. The territory of this polity was made up of different entities, each one having an *oppidum* with a sanctuary at its core. These huge fortified centers were places for assemblies (→political role), collective rituals (→religious role), and fairs and the minting of coins (→economic role).

From Sacred Areas to Urban Settlements

As stated above, the majority of temperate European *oppida* were centers of politico-religious aggregation, which would serve as meeting places and arenas for negotiation. This is well attested by archaeology and by written sources describing the celebrations of councils, assemblies, and great communal banquets. Examples illustrating this role include the great Aeduan assembly held at the *oppidum* of *Decetia* (Caesar, *De Bello Gallico* VII, 33), the fact that Bibracte was the site of the *concilium totius Galliae*, at which Vercingetorix was proclaimed commander-in-chief of the confederation against the Romans (Caesar, *De Bello Gallico* VII, 63), or a passage that tells us that the Aeduan *vergobret* (highest magistrate) Convictolitavis and a large part of the senate met with Litaviccus at Bibracte (Caesar, *De Bello Gallico* VII, 55). Caesar's strategy of taking a key *oppidum* in order to obtain the submission of a whole polity also underlines the role of these settlements as political centers. Even at those *oppida* with significant evidence for production and trade, these economic activities often seem to have developed as by-products of the political and religious

significance of the sites (Fernández-Götz 2014c). Smith (2016) has recently proposed that most pre-modern cities were political cities in which the role that clearly predominates is the political and religious, not the economic, and the *oppida* seem to fit well within this general model.

Going a step further, many temperate European *oppida* might have had their origin in spaces for ritual and political gatherings (Fernández-Götz 2014b, 2014c; Fichtl *et al.* 2000; Metzler *et al.* 2006). In fact, there is an increasing number of examples of *oppida* where it has been proven that a place for cult activities and assemblies preceded the concentration of a significant number of people or even the fortification of the site. This phenomenon is particularly evident at Manching in Bavaria. At the center of this important *oppidum* was Temple A, the first phase of which dates back to the end of the 4th century BC (Figure 3.6; Sievers 2007; Wendling 2013). Nearby was a paved space covering an area of 50-x-80 m that may have been used as a meeting place, and several votive deposits of materials were recovered dating from between the 4th and 2nd centuries BC. This temple–plaza pairing shows similarities with the situation observed in pre-Hispanic Mesoamerica (Carballo 2016), and can also be found at other Late Iron Age *oppida*, such as Corent. In the case of Manching, the occasional Early Iron Age objects leave open the possibility that the religious significance of the temple enclosure was even older, while the presence of human bones could perhaps be related to ancestor worship. It is also interesting to note that the wall of the *oppidum*—built toward the end of the 2nd century BC—describes a circumference whose center is the previously mentioned Temple A, which existed before the settlement was founded and lay at its heart from the beginning (Figure 3.7). It is quite clear that this cannot be a matter of chance, and probably relates to cosmogonical conceptions and foundation rites, similar to the notion of the *pomerium* in ancient Rome (Rykwert 1976).

The existence of a sanctuary pre-dating the development of an *oppidum* in the same location is also clearly visible at Gournay-sur-Aronde in Picardy. The famous sanctuary's origin lay in the 4th/3rd century BC, but the *oppidum* itself did not develop until well into the 1st century BC (Brunaux *et al.* 1985). In the case of Moulay, the *oppidum* was preceded by a sanctuary from the 3rd century BC (Fichtl *et al.* 2016). Recent research at the *oppidum* of Corent, presumed to be the early first-century BC capital of the Arverni, is also significant. The excavations conducted by Poux suggest that the sanctuary was founded before the settlement developed (Poux 2012a; Poux and Demierre 2016). The establishment of links with the ancestral past can be suggested due to the location near the Late Iron Age sanctuary of a great Late Bronze Age tumulus,

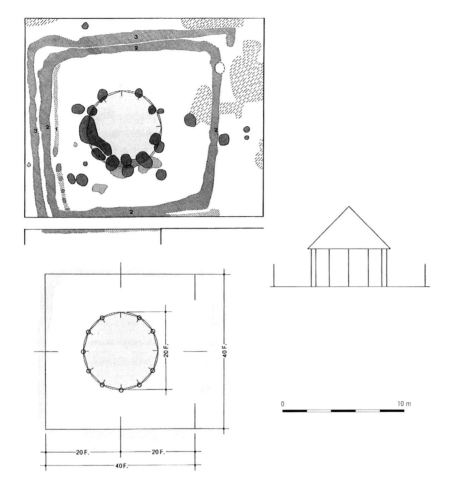

Figure 3.6. Plan of Temple A at Manching (after Sievers 2010, modified by the author).

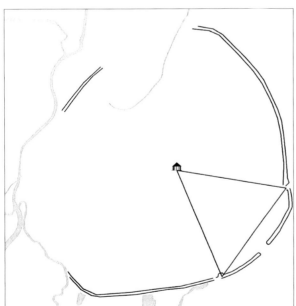

Figure 3.7. Manching. Location of the central temple and visual axes with the southern and the eastern gates, creating a perfect triangle (after Eller *et al.* 2012).

possibly identified with the tomb of a founding hero, and therefore, with the tutelary deity of the *oppidum* and perhaps even of the *civitas* (Ramona 2011; see also Fernández-Götz 2019b).

At Bibracte, the tribal capital of the Aedui, isotopic and dendrochronological dating indicates that the public space known as 'La Terrasse,' measuring 110-x-92 m and situated near a Gallo-Roman temple, could have been established in the 3rd century BC (Figure 3.8; Gruel and Richard 1998). Although this last date needs to be treated with caution, if correct, it would imply that the place was used and visited for assemblies and religious purposes well before the *oppidum* was founded at the end of the 2nd century BC (Fleischer and Rieckhoff 2002). In any case, the described phenomenon is not restricted to temperate Europe since a similar situation is also seen in Mediterranean Gaul at Iron Age sites, such as Entremont or Glanum, where the sanctuaries originated earlier than the *oppida* (Garcia 2006).

In the case of the large territorial *oppida* in Britain, Haselgrove has summarized their origins following a similar line of interpretation:

'*Several territorial oppida potentially originated as sacred locations used periodically as meeting places by widely dispersed populations, with little or no permanent occupation [...]. This role as a neutral place where otherwise separate groups came together under the auspices of the gods - for instance to elect a war leader - encouraged further development of their communal functions [...]. What had begun as a neutral meeting*

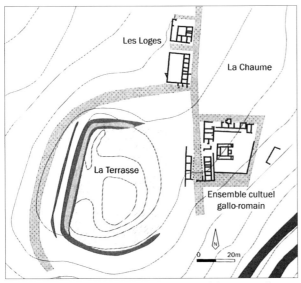

Figure 3.8. Bibracte. Late Iron Age public space of 'La Terrasse' and the nearby Gallo-Roman temple (after Fichtl 2005).

place thus gradually evolved into the recognised focus of the wider social grouping, whose identity it came to symbolise, although the local lineage heads continued to reside on their ancestral lands.' (2000: 106)

In the northwestern Iberian Peninsula, San Cibrán de Las provides an exceptional case study of sacrality in the *longue durée*, several centuries before the foundation of the *oppidum* (Álvarez-González *et al.* 2017). Radiocarbon dates imply that the site was regularly frequented from at least the 4th century BC; however, the *oppidum* did not develop until the late 2nd/early 1st century BC, when a large fortification and the urban layout were established (Prieto Martínez *et al.* 2017). The highest part, the so-called acropolis or *croa*, remained free of any living structure but was enclosed and separated from the rest of the *oppidum* by a wall (Figure 3.9). Occupation in the *oppidum* declined in the Roman period, but several inscriptions on the acropolis refer to different deities that were worshiped there, which, together with some stone sculptures with archaic features representing divinities, suggests a religious function for the enclosed area on the highest point of the site. It seems that the sacred significance of the acropolis of San Cibrán de Las can be traced back several centuries before the development of a large settlement, and continued after the *oppidum* was abandoned.

The example of San Cibrán de Las, with its acropolis on the highest point of the settlement, brings us back

Figure 3.9. Aerial view of the *oppidum* of San Cibrán de Las, with the acropolis on the top and the two concentric circles of fortifications (after Álvarez-González *et al.* 2017).

to the Treveran *oppida* of the Middle Rhine–Moselle region. As mentioned above, six of the seven *oppida* have evidence of pre-Roman sanctuaries and/or public assembly places, which in five cases are located on the highest points of their respective sites. All of them have signs of being frequented before the development of the *oppida*, mainly in the 5th and/or 4th centuries BC, and in most of them, their sanctuaries continued to be used during the Roman period, and were even monumentalized (Fernández-Götz 2014a; Metzler *et al.* 2006). Therefore, the religious significance of these sites seems to have existed before, during, and after the development of *oppida*, in a similar way as in San Cibrán de Las.

It is also interesting to note that the sacred spaces were located at the highest points of the sites in most of these cases, clearly underlining their special symbolism. As a way of segmenting space, specific places or landscapes play a crucial mnemonic role in different socioeconomic and historical contexts (for examples, see Hayden 2002; Yates 1999), something that can be observed in these European Iron Age examples as well. As a result, we should consider the possibility that many peaks were believed to have been places of exceptionally sacred nature. As noted by González-Ruibal (2006–2007: 104), any place can be associated with events, memories, and myths, but certain specific points are capable of concentrating with special intensity messages that are especially relevant for the social reproduction of groups. Amongst others, this must have been the case of these high points, which are veritable *lieux de mémoire* (Nora 1989), immersed in myths, legends, and traditions. The 'biography' of these hills would go far beyond the fleeting development of *oppida* upon them, and this long-term perspective allows a more comprehensive interpretation of their significance over time.

The above-mentioned examples demonstrate that, in many cases, the use of a place for cultic purposes and holding assemblies would have been the cause, and not the consequence, of the development of *oppida* at the sites. In a context of population increase, growing production, and flourishing of contacts with the Mediterranean world, religion must have been the principal cohesive force through which the integration of Late Iron Age communities into broader sociopolitical groupings was structured (for the role of rituals as mechanisms of sociopolitical integration, see Feinman 2016).

Conclusions: Religion as a Fostering Force in Early Urbanism

To summarize, it seems clear that ritual considerations need to be taken into account when addressing the origins of early urban centers. This conclusion coincides with a broader theoretical approach proposed by Godelier (2010), in which he questions the pre-eminence of economic relationships argued by Marxists and Liberals, placing instead religion as the basis of social order in traditional societies. Large agglomerations are usually the result of processes of population growth and increasing socioeconomic complexity, but the choice of place was often determined by earlier religious considerations and collective memories. The role of religious activities in aggregating people for ritual was foundational—once people were together, they frequently engaged in political decision-making and in exchange, which ultimately led to political and economic functions and often resulted in the development of large, permanent settlements. Although there would have been numerous exceptions to the model 'from sanctuaries to towns,' the recognition that in many cases religious and assembly spaces developed early and then other urban functions came later, has important implications for our understanding of pre-modern urbanization processes and the dynamics of collective aggregation on a global scale.

References Cited

Álvarez-González, Y., L. López González, M. Fernández-Götz and M.V. García Quintela 2017. El *oppidum* de San Cibrán de Las y el papel de la religión en los procesos de centralización en la Edad del Hierro. *Cuadernos de Prehistoria y Arqueología de la Universidad Autónoma de Madrid* 43: 217–239.

Beck, H. and H.-U. Wiemer (eds) 2009. *Feiern und Erinnern. Geschichtsbilder im Spiegel antiker Feste* (Studien zur Alten Geschichte 12). Berlin: Antike.

Blanton, R.E. and L.F. Fargher 2008. *Collective Action in the Formation of Pre-Modern States*. New York: Springer.

Bommas, M. (ed.) 2011. *Cultural Memory and Identity in Ancient Societies*. London: Continuum.

Bourdieu, P. 1977. *Outline of a Theory of Practice*. Cambridge: Cambridge University Press.

Brunaux, J.-L., P. Méniel and F. Poplin 1985. *Gournay I: les fouilles sur le sanctuaire et l'oppidum (1975-84)*. Amiens: Revue Archéologique de Picardie, nº sp.

Buchsenschutz, O. 2014. La serpe d'or et le rempart de fer, in C. Gaeng (ed.) *Archaeologia Mosellana 92. Hommage à Jeannot Metzler*: 209–214. Luxembourg: Centre National de Recherche Archéologique.

Carballo, D.M. 2016. *Urbanization and Religion in Ancient Central Mexico*. Oxford: Oxford University Press.

Cohen, A.P. 1985. *The Symbolic Construction of Community*. London and New York: Ellis Horwood.

Collis, J. 1984. *Oppida. Earliest Towns North of the Alps*. Sheffield: University of Sheffield.

Derks, T. and N. Roymans 2009. Introduction, in T. Derks und N. Roymans (eds) *Ethnic Constructs in Antiquity: The Role of Power and Tradition*: 1–10. Amsterdam: Amsterdam University Press.

Dietrich, O., M. Heun, J. Notroff, K. Schmidt and M. Zarnkow 2012. The role of cult and feasting in the emergence of Neolithic communities. New evidence from Göbekli Tepe, south-eastern Turkey. *Antiquity* 86(333): 674–695.

Duczko, W. 1998. Gamla Uppsala. *Reallexikon der Germanischen Altertumskunde* 10: 409–418.

Earle, T. 1997. *How Chiefs Come to Power: The Political Economy in Prehistory*. Stanford (CA): Stanford University Press.

Eller, M., S. Sievers, H. Wendling and K. Winger 2012. Zentralisierung und Urbanisierung – Manchings Entwicklung zur spätkeltischen Stadt, in S. Sievers and M. Schönfelder (eds) *Die Frage der Protourbanisation in der Eisenzeit*: 303–318. Dr. Rudolf Habelt, Bonn.

Feinman, G.M. 2016. Variation and change in archaic states: Ritual as a mechanism of sociopolitical integration, in J.M. Murphy (ed.) *Ritual and Archaic States*: 1–22. Gainesville: University Press of Florida.

Fernández-Götz, M. 2013. Politik, Religion und Jahrmärkte: Zur Rolle der Volksversammlungen im eisenzeitlichen und frühmittelalterlichen Europa, in R. Karl and J. Leskovar (eds) *Interpretierte Eisenzeiten 5. Fallstudien, Methoden, Theorie*: 71–82. Linz: Oberösterreichischen Landesmuseum.

Fernández-Götz, M. 2014a. Central places and the construction of collective identities in the Middle Rhine-Moselle region, in C. Popa and S. Stoddart (eds) *Fingerprinting the Iron Age: Approaches to Identity in the European Iron Age*: 175–186. Oxford: Oxbow Books.

Fernández-Götz, M. 2014b. *Identity and Power: The Transformation of Iron Age Societies in Northeast Gaul*. Amsterdam: Amsterdam University Press.

Fernández-Götz, M. 2014c. Reassessing the oppida: The role of power and religion. *Oxford Journal of Archaeology* 33(4): 379–394.

Fernández-Götz, M. 2018. Urbanization in Iron Age Europe: Trajectories, Patterns and Social Dynamics. *Journal of Archaeological Research* 26: 117–162.

Fernández-Götz, M. 2019a. A World of 200 Oppida: Pre-Roman Urbanism in Temperate Europe, in L. de Ligt and J. Bintliff (eds) *Regional Urban Systems in the Roman World, 150 BCE-250 CE*: 35–66. Leiden: Brill.

Fernández-Götz, M. 2019b. Héros fondateurs et identités collectives à l'âge du Fer, in R. Golosetti (ed.) *Mémoires de l'âge de Fer. Effacer ou réécrire le passé*: 87–100. Paris: Hermann Editeurs.

Fernández-Götz, M. and N. Roymans 2015. The Politics of Identity: Late Iron Age Sanctuaries in the Rhineland. *Journal of the North Atlantic* 8: 18–32.

Fichtl, S. 2005. *La ville celtique. Les oppida de 150 av. J.-C. à 15 ap. J.-C.* Paris: Errance.

Fichtl, S. 2010. Les places publiques dans les oppida. *L'Archéologue, archéologie nouvelle* 108: 36–40.

Fichtl, S. 2012a. *Les premières villes de Gaule. Le temps des oppida*. Lacapelle-Marival: Archéologie Nouvelle.

Fichtl, S. 2012b. Places publiques et lieux de rassemblement à la fin de l'âge du Fer dans le monde celtique, in A. Bouet (ed.) *Le forum en Gaule et dans les régions voisines*: 41–53. Bordeaux: Ausonius.

Fichtl, S. 2016. Les centres publics: sanctuaires et lieux de reunion, in S. Fichtl, E. Le Goff, A. Mathiaut-Legros and Y. Menez (eds) *Les premières villes de l'ouest. Agglomérations gauloises de Bretagne et Pays de la Loire*: 52–59. Jublains: Musée archéologique de Jublains.

Fichtl, S., E. Le Goff, A. Mathiaut-Legros and Y. Menez (eds) 2016. *Les premières villes de l'ouest. Agglomérations gauloises de Bretagne et Pays de la Loire*. Jublains: Musée archéologique de Jublains.

Fichtl, S., J. Metzler and S. Sievers 2000. Le rôle des sanctuaires dans le processus d'urbanisation, in by V. Guichard, S. Sievers and O.H. Urban (eds) *Les processus d'urbanisation à l'âge du Fer (Eisenzeitliche Urbanisationsprozesse)* (Collection Bibracte 4): 179–186. Glux-en-Glenne: Centre archéologique européen.

Fleischer, F. and S. Rieckhoff 2002. Bibracte – Eine keltische Stadt, in U. Cain and S. Rieckhoff (eds) *Fromm – Fremd – Barbarisch: Die Religion der Kelten*: 103–118. Mainz: Philipp von Zabern.

Garcia, D. 2006. Religion et société. La Gaule méridionale, in C. Goudineau (ed.) *Religion et société en Gaule*: 135–163. Paris: Errance.

Gerritsen, F. and N. Roymans 2006. Central places and the construction of tribal identities. The case of the Late Iron Age Lower Rhine region, in C. Haselgrove (ed.) *Celtes et Gaulois, l'Archéologie face à l'Histoire. 4: Les mutations de la fin de l'âge du Fer*: 251–266. Glux-en-Glenne: Centre archéologique européen.

Giddens, A. 1984. *The Constitution of Society: Outline of the Theory of Structuration*. Cambridge: Blackwell/Polity Press.

Godelier, M. 2010. *Au fondement des sociétés humaines. Ce que nous apprend l'anthropologie*. Paris: Flammarion.

González-Ruibal, A. 2006–2007. *Galaicos: poder y comunidad en el Noroeste de la Península Ibérica (1200 a.C.-50 d.C.)* (Brigantium 18–19). A Coruña: Museo Arqueolóxico e Histórico.

Gruel, K. and H. Richard 1998. Lieux publics, lieux cultuels, in K. Gruel and D. Vitali (eds) *L'oppidum de Bibracte: un bilan de onze années de recherches (1984-1995)* (Gallia 55): 31–34. Paris: CNRS.

Hårdh, B. 2000. Uppåkra – a centre in south Sweden in the 1st millennium AD. *Antiquity* 74(285): 640–648.

Haselgrove, C. 2000. The character of oppida in Iron Age Britain, in V. Guichard, S. Sievers and O.H. Urban (eds) *Les processus d'urbanisation à l'âge du Fer (Eisenzeitliche Urbanisationsprozesse)* (Collection Bibracte 4): 103–110. Glux-en-Glenne: Centre archéologique européen.

Hayden, R.M. 2002. Antagonistic tolerance. Competitive sharing of religious sites in South Asia and the Balkans. *Current Anthropology* 43(2): 205–231.

Inomata, T., J. MacLellan, D. Triadan, J. Munson, M. Burham, K. Aoyama, H. Nasu, F. Pinzón and

H. Yonenobu 2015. Development of sedentary communities in the Maya lowlands: Coexisting mobile groups and public ceremonies at Ceibal, Guatemala. *Proceedings of the National Academy of Sciences* 112(14): 4268–4273.

Kristiansen, K. 1998. *Europe before History*. Cambridge: Cambridge University Press.

Larsson, L. 2007. The Iron Age ritual building at Uppåkra, southern Sweden. *Antiquity* 81(311): 11–25.

Ligt, L. de and P.W. de Neeve 1988. Ancient periodic markets: Festivals and fairs. *Athenaeum* 66: 391–416.

Méniel, P. 2008. Les restes d'animaux de l'espace public de l'*oppidum* du Titelberg, in D. Castella and M.-F. Meylan Krause (eds) *Topographie sacrée et rituels. Le cas d'Aventicum, capitale des Helvètes*: 167–173. Basel: Archéologie suisse.

Metzler, J. 2006. Religion et politique. L'oppidum trévire du Titelberg, in C. Goudineau (ed.) *Religion et société en Gaule*: 190–202. Paris: Errance.

Metzler, J., C. Gaeng and P. Méniel 2016. *L'espace public du Titelberg* (Dossiers d'Archéologie du Centre National de Recherche Archéologique 17). Luxembourg: Centre National de Recherche Archéologique.

Metzler, J., P. Méniel and C. Gaeng 2006. Oppida et espaces publics, in C. Haselgrove (ed.) *Celtes et Gaulois, l'Archéologie face à l'Histoire. 4: Les mutations de la fin de l'âge du Fer*: 201–224. Glux-en-Glenne: Centre archéologique européen.

Moore, J.D. 1996. The Archaeology of Plazas and the Proxemics of Ritual: Three Andean Traditions. *American Anthropologist* 98(4): 789–802.

Nora, P. 1989. Between memory and history: Les lieux de mémoire. *Representations* 26: 7–24.

Polignac, F. de 1995. *Cults, Territory, and the Origins of the Greek City-State*. Chicago: University of Chicago Press.

Poux, M. 2004. *L'âge du vin. Rites de boisson, festins et libations en Gaule indépendante*. Montagnac: Éditions Monique Mergoil.

Poux, M. (ed.) 2012a. *Corent - Voyage au coeur d'une ville gauloise*. Paris: Errance.

Poux, M. 2012b. Religion, sanctuaires et pratiques cultuelles en Gaule: quarante ans d'innovations, in L. Olivier (ed.) *Le Musée d'Archéologie nationale et les gaulois du XIXe au XXIe siècle*: 151–169. Saint-Germain-en-Laye: Musée d'Archéologie nationale.

Poux, M. 2014. Enlarging oppida: Multipolar town patterns in Late Iron Age Gaul, in M. Fernández-Götz, H. Wendling and K. Winger (eds) *Paths to Complexity. Centralisation and Urbanisation in Iron Age Europe*: 156–166. Oxford: Oxbow Books.

Poux, M. and M. Demierre (eds) 2016. *Le sanctuaire de Corent (Puy-de-Dôme, Auvergne). Vestiges et rituels* (Supplément à Gallia). Paris: CNRS.

Prieto Martínez, M.P., Y. Alvarez González, M. Fernández-Götz, M.V. García Quintela, C. González García and L. López González 2017. The contribution of Bayesian analysis to the chronology of Iron Age north-western Iberia: New data from San Cibrán de Las (Galicia, Spain). *Journal of Archaeological Science: Reports* 16: 397–408.

Ramona, J. 2011. Agglomérations gauloises. Nouvelles considérations. *Les Dossiers d'archéologie H.-S.* 21: 46–51.

Rieckhoff, S. and S. Fichtl 2011. *Keltenstädte aus der Luft*. Stuttgart: Konrad Theiss.

Rykwert, J. 1976. *The Idea of a Town: The Anthropology of Urban Form in Rome, Italy and the Ancient World*. Princeton (NJ): Princeton University Press.

Sanmark, A., F. Iversen, N. Mehler and S. Semple (eds) 2015–2016. *Debating the Thing in the North II: Selected Papers from Workshops Organized by The Assembly Project*. Journal of the North Atlantic 8.

Schmidt, K. 2000. Zuerst kam der Tempel, dann die Stadt. Vorläufiger Bericht zu den Grabungen am Göbekli Tepe und am Gürcütepe 1995-1999. *Istanbuler Mitteilungen* 50: 5–41.

Schmidt, K. 2006. *Sie bauten die ersten Tempel. Das rätselhafte Heiligtum der Steinzeitjäger*. Munich: C.H. Beck.

Sievers, S. 2007. *Manching - Die Keltenstadt*. Stuttgart: Konrad Theiss.

Sievers, S. 2010. L'*oppidum* de Manching. *L'Archéologue, archéologie nouvelle* 108: 32–35.

Smith, M.E. 2016. How can archaeologists identify early cities? Definitions, types, and attributes, in M. Fernández-Götz and D. Krausse (eds) *Eurasia at the Dawn of History: Urbanization and Social Change*: 153–168. New York: Cambridge University Press.

Tsukamoto, K. and T. Inomata (eds) 2014. *Mesoamerican Plazas: Arenas of Community and Power*. Tucson: University of Arizona Press.

Wells, P.S. 1984. *Farms, Villages and Cities: Commerce and Urban Origins in Late Prehistoric Europe*. Ithaca: Cornell University Press.

Wendling, H. 2013. Manching reconsidered: New perspectives on settlement dynamics and urbanization in Iron Age Central Europe. *European Journal of Archaeology* 16(3): 459–490.

Wenskus, R. 1984. Ding. *Reallexikon der Germanischen Altertumskunde* 5: 444–455.

Wheatley, P. 1971. *The Pivot of the Four Quarters. A Preliminary Enquiry in the Origins and Character of the Ancient Chinese City*. Chicago: Aldine.

Yates, F.A. 1999. *Arts of Memory*. London and New York: Routledge.

Chapter 4

Activity Zones and Community Formation: The Role of Spatial Structure in Early Nucleated Villages

Roderick B. Salisbury

Abstract

Spatial relationships are among the most important sources of archaeological evidence, and among the most important aspects of social organization. Reconstructing spatial structure, including the locations of task areas and activity zones, is crucial for understanding craft specialization, cross-craft interactions, power structures, inclusion/exclusion, and a host of other social behaviors. In part, this is because spatial structure can be used to regulate interpersonal interactions. Along with multiscalar and diachronic approaches, comparative spatial analyses are therefore essential for understanding how spatial organization functioned to facilitate or impede the success of early settlement nucleation. Drawing on ethnographic and archaeological comparisons from Europe and North America, this contribution examines different use of space in different types of sites during the Late Neolithic on the Great Hungarian Plain. Different types of sites, even if the difference is sometimes very subtle, show different spatial patterning of houses and activity zones. Furthermore, by increasing the social significance of identity while exposing people to a greater number of communities, these differences were instrumental in facilitating the sociopolitical changes that accompanied settlement and population aggregation.

Introduction

Cycles of people moving together and moving apart are known throughout prehistory and continue today. These processes have not always, or even often, been simple, peaceful, or long-lasting. Plausible explanations about how and why people came together and stayed together or moved apart require evidence of spatial relations, the way that social units and their material correlates were arranged and interacted in relation to one another. Spatial relationships influence a host of human behaviors and interactions, including integration, inclusion/exclusion, craft specialization and cross-craft interactions, and power structures (Adler and Wilshusen 1990; Byrd 1994; Gorgues *et al.* 2017; Rebay-Salisbury *et al.* 2014; Riggs 2007). Spatial relations are also primary evidence for context, in Butzer's (1980) sense of context as the total environment in which human activity occurs. Therefore, reconstructing the spatial structure, including the locations of task areas and activity zones, is crucial for addressing most archaeological questions. While architecture is one physical reflection of social interactions and the social organization of space (Byrd 1994; Kent 1990; Pauknerová *et al.* 2013), most archaeological settings do not provide sufficient architectural remains to reconstruct all the processes involved in these social relationships. Other, complementary, methods are necessary to acquire data reflecting these processes.

The Great Hungarian Plain provides an excellent test area for exploring the many variables involved in diachronic social changes associated with these cycles of nucleation and dispersal (Gyucha *et al.* 2009, 2014; Parkinson *et al.* 2004, 2010; see also Gyucha, this volume). In particular, the record of variability in settlement organization, even within the same period and microregion, is nearly unique. During the Hungarian Late Neolithic (*c.* 5000–4500 BC), many people lived in more closely packed spaces. In this paper, I explore the spatial relationships linking spatial organization with social organization to identify the relative degree of integration within nucleated settlements and question whether there is evidence for social integration, or simply for several communities living close to one another. Here, I set out an approach integrating architectural elements—observed during excavation or reconstructed from magnetic anomalies—with artifact distributions and microremains to reconstruct the use of space within Late Neolithic settlements in eastern Hungary. I then use this spatial data to propose different levels of aggregation.

Integration, Social Organization, and Social Cohesion

Nucleation, defined here as the clustering of people and settlement features in one place (Parkinson *et al.* 2018; Wilkinson *et al.* 2004; see also 'aggregation:' Adler *et al.* 1996; Duffy *et al.* 2013; Kuijt 2000), can be encouraged by several factors, including mutual defense, hydrology (increased flooding or localization of potable water), increased interregional exchange and associated access to exotic goods, and access to resources, such as marketplaces, sacred spaces, or administrators. Nucleation does not imply that people were integrated into a community, only that population aggregated in one place. Settlement nucleation does not in itself generate a sense of community—a nucleated settlement is only a part of the process of constructing and maintaining a sense of common interest and shared values (Martín 2017; Martín and Murillo Herrera 2014). Other elements are needed—integrative mechanisms— to bring people to have a shared sense of community, to integrate people into a unified and coherent group.

Spatial relationships are among the most important elements of social organization, particularly in the early stages of nucleation. In small-scale, non-hierarchical societies, many social, political, and economic difficulties can be overcome by adjusting spatial structures. Most activities in small-scale societies take place within the domestic context, and the organization of domestic space is therefore filled with indicators relating to the range of social interactions. These include not only production and consumption, that is, economic activities long and widely recognized as belonging to the domestic sphere, but also political (Bowser and Patton 2004) and religious (Aldenderfer 2010) activities. Alternatively, some difficulties can be overcome by increasing the physical distance in the relevant spatial relationships. When sources of firewood or arable land are exhausted, people can change the relevant spatial relationships by moving. If within-group political differences erupt into violence, one part of a community can move away, a process called group fissioning (Bandy 2004). When societies become more complex, populations increase in size, political hierarchies evolve, and architecture becomes more monumental, movement can become more difficult or undesirable. This, in turn, can compel alternative forms of spatial structure.

The spatial structuring of nucleated settlements may be top-down, imposed by established or incipient rulers, or bottom-up, produced organically through people's negotiations of behavior and traditions. In either case, integrative mechanisms in some form are needed to keep people together and facilitate social cohesion. The lack of evidence for such integrative mechanisms might suggest the presence of more coercive processes. Alternatively, when combined with ample indications of population dispersal in subsequent periods, a lacuna of data for integrative facilities could indicate a bottom-up process of nucleation, without planned integrative mechanisms and with no compelling, life-or-death reason for staying put.

Spatial analysis in archaeology is very advanced and highly specialized at two scales: the household and the regional landscape. At the regional scale, landscape approaches often reflect the space–time patterning of settlements and other traces of human activity together with the physical environment. In Europe, integration of intensive surface survey, geochemical survey, large-scale geophysics, and airborne remote sensing data are revolutionizing regional analyses by facilitating broad regional comparisons of land use, exchange, and mobility (Alcock and Cherry 2004; Sarris *et al.* 2013; Sevara *et al.* 2018; cf. Galaty 2005). Household archaeology is well developed in terms of both method (Ullah 2012) and theory (Borić 2008; Chesson 2012). While the household is a useful tool for understanding production and consumption of small-scale segmentary societies, it is less helpful for seeing how communities, as groups of households, become integrated into larger communities, or contribute to tribal (Parkinson 2002) or chiefly (Anderson 1996) cycling as components of nucleated villages.

Settlements represent an intermediate scale, one that has received less attention. A settlement is not a direct archaeological correlate for a community living in a specific location. Settlements are configured by the various socioeconomic and cultural practices of the inhabitants. Nucleated settlements may be populated by the aggregation of members of several communities, and in the earliest phases of aggregation, these communities may have retained their identities and remained spatially segregated from one another, forming discrete clusters of houses within a larger settlement. The spatial layout of the built environment and related activity areas reflect this complexity and heterogeneity. Whereas household archaeology examines activities and spatial organization in and around the house, often at the microscale, settlements and settlement clusters are frequently compared to one another in terms of size and location. In part, this is because excavating entire settlements is expensive in terms of finance, time, workload, and material storage. Funding to continuously excavate the same site to answer one question over many years is rare. Publish or perish with innovative, novel, and sexy results is *de rigueur*. '*Scrupulous research on difficult problems may require years of intense work before yielding coherent, publishable results. If shallower work generating more publications is favored, then researchers interested in pursuing complex questions may find themselves without jobs*' (Smaldino and McElreath 2016).

The obvious differences between farmsteads and small villages, on the one hand, and large, nucleated centers, on the other, can conceal more subtle similarities and dissimilarities in spatial structure and limit our understanding of spatial differentiation. These subtle variations are essential for understanding how the organization of space influences the formation and maintenance of aggregated communities. Therefore, analyses and comparisons of the internal spatial structure of settlements, or discrete areas within settlements, are essential. One approach to reaching such an understanding is by placing architectural and artifactual remains within the conceptual model of activity zones and household clusters (Salisbury 2016).

Activity Zones and the Organization of Integration

Activity areas research focuses on identifying the functional use of space, providing a wealth of information about social organization, and enabling comparisons of spatial units from different periods and regions. Studies have suggested that patterns of artifact densities can aid in distinguishing between short-term and longer-term occupations, with short-term occupations represented by primary refuse and discrete activity areas within and around domestic spaces. Longer-term occupations, on the other hand, typically have secondary refuse disposal outside of the occupation areas (Hardy-Smith and Edwards 2004; Hayden and Cannon 1983; Kent 1999; Schiffer 1987). In nucleated settlements, however, space is likely to be highly constrained, secondary refuse deposits might be found in abandoned houses and pits, and activity areas are likely to be closer or overlapping. Multiple activities may take place in a single space, construction and reconstruction of buildings and features might overlap with activity areas, and waste material might be deposited in general-purpose dumps. Ambiguous results from geochemical analyses of a house cluster at the Late Neolithic nucleated settlement of Szeghalom-Kovácshalom in the Körös region, for example, was interpreted as being caused by overlapping activities (Salisbury 2016: 195–196).

Activity Zones—Definition and Description

Despite these caveats, activity areas research has proved useful for understanding spatial organization and its relationship to social organization as well as daily social and economic activities, public versus private spaces, and waste management (Hayden 1997; Milek and Roberts 2013). An activity zone is a larger spatial analytical unit than an activity area and is defined as the areas in and around a house or settlement where members of the household or community conduct different kinds of activities (Oetelaar 1993; Salisbury 2013, 2016). Identification of activity zones via microremains is one way to overcome the difficulties presented by archaeological formation processes that obscure activity areas. These can include identifying the boundaries between family or communal front and back zones (for households, e.g., Oetelaar 1993; Salisbury 2012) or extended household units, or crafts and work areas (Salisbury 2017). From these boundaries, we can scale up to clusters of houses.

The model presented here is an expansion of a model first developed for activity zones within household clusters (Salisbury 2012), expanded to accommodate multiple households, thus enabling investigation of small villages, house clusters, neighborhoods, and other small, local communities. A household cluster refers to the domestic features that are associated with a household and are archaeologically visible (Bogucki and Grygiel 1981; Flannery 1976; Jongsma and Greenfield 2003; Winter 1976). The household cluster is distinct from a cluster of houses. The twin strengths of the activity zones model lie first in including the interactions and behaviors that leave measurable, in situ material remains, and second in demonstrating that different zones are the loci of different behaviors. Preparation of food and discard of waste, activities that necessarily occur each day, have specific areas assigned to them; therefore, the residues of these activities should occur in particular locations, forming zones. At the scale of house clusters, these differences are based on whether areas are used primarily for a single household or for a larger group.

At the scale of single households, there is a household front zone—a multifunctional space used for entertaining family guests, as well as for household workspace, which is generally kept clean. Next is the household back zone—an area of intensive activity and storage of personal or household possessions as well as primary waste (Oetelaar 1993: 666; Salisbury 2012: Figure 6). When discussing waste streams, for example, the primary discard location is often within the household cluster, and secondary discard occurs in a communal midden, as seen for example in Iroquoian villages, such as the Eaton site (Salisbury 2001) and the Calvert site (Timmins 1997).

For a house cluster or hamlet, the spatial areas are defined as the communal front and back zones. The communal front zone comprises an open space accessible to all members of the resident households and serving as an arena for feasts, ceremonies, meetings, and economic activities by intra- or intervillage visitors. The communal back zone is the space where members of the community store shared possessions, keep livestock, maintain latrines and middens, and conduct other 'messy and space-consuming activities that are essential to the continuity of the community as a coherent unit' (Oetelaar 1993: 667).

Methods for Identifying Activity Zones

Ethnoarchaeological and archaeological evidence for geochemical, geophysical, and microrefuse signatures of specific workspaces, marketplaces, plazas, middens, and other areas can be combined with the identification of features and architectural patterns in excavations to model the spatial organization of house clusters. These can then be compared and contrasted to find evidence for more or less segregated or integrated groups. A methodological approach to finding these patterns focuses on microremains, including microartifacts, such as lithic microdebitage, bone and charcoal fragments, and metal globules, as well as macrobotanicals and soil chemistry. These are added, depleted, or altered in presumed occupation surfaces (e.g., Coronel et al. 2015; Milek and Roberts 2013; Nolan and Redmond 2015; Parker and Sharratt 2017; Salisbury 2016, 2017; Terry et al. 2015; Vyncke et al. 2011).

Although larger pieces of debris are often removed from in situ contexts (LaMotta and Schiffer 1999; Parker and Sharratt 2017), microremains, and in particular soil chemical residues, are likely to remain in situ and reveal patterning of activity zones and task areas (Salisbury 2013, 2016, 2017; Ullah 2012). This approach is used extensively in Mesoamerican archaeology for finding activity locations within houses and house compounds (Barba and Ortiz 1992; Sampietro and Vattuone 2005). These studies were particularly helpful for identifying areas associated with the preparation, storage, and consumption of foodstuffs. Similar methods employed in Europe include, for example, multielement chemistry to distinguish stabling and domestic areas at an Iron Age house in Denmark (Hjulström and Isaksson 2009) and to identify activity areas within Late Neolithic and Early Copper Age settlements in Hungary (Salisbury 2012, 2013, 2016). Taking into account the probability that areas used for only one activity are unlikely within small farmsteads or agricultural hamlets, Salisbury (2012, 2013, based on Bogucki and Grygiel 1981; Winter 1976) focused on zones of activities and produced an idealized model of household and communal activity zones to augment earlier household cluster models. Placing these remains in a larger context provided by geophysical prospection and/or large-scale excavation provides the most robust interpretations.

Activity zones and related spatial structuring are useful for interpreting domestic production and relationships between households. Comparisons of sets of household activity zones between sites or different parts of one site provide information to extrapolate relative levels of integration and the presence of potential integrative spaces. In the following regional case study from the Great Hungarian Plain, geophysical and architectural data are presented and interpreted in terms of activity zones and the household cluster model, augmented where possible with evidence from microrefuse and macroartifact distributions. I posit that the process there was bottom-up and organic, and did not result in a fully integrated community.

Late Neolithic Aggregation on the Great Hungarian Plain

The case study region examined here is the Great Hungarian Plain, a fertile, low-lying alluvial plain in the geographic center of Europe, covering an area of about 100,000 km², with an average elevation of about 100 m above sea level (Figure 4.1). Relatively homogeneous soils form an extremely flat landscape, with depth to groundwater in modern times averaging 3–4 m.

In this paper, my temporal focus is the Late Neolithic (c. 5000–4500 BC). The transition from the Middle Neolithic to Late Neolithic (c. 5200–5000 BC) on the Great Hungarian Plain corresponds with a robust trend toward settlement nucleation, while the succeeding Late Neolithic to Early Copper Age transition (c. 4600–4500 BC) coincides with a similarly strong trend to settlement dispersal (see Gyucha, this volume). The analysis of Late Neolithic settlement patterns is almost certainly an analysis of settlement nucleation, wherein demographic aggregation, rather than demographic increase, contributed to the growth of population size.

The eastern Carpathian Basin and northern Balkans are traditionally held as having three basic Neolithic settlement types: single-layer or flat sites, tells (settlement mounds of earth and building materials that represent centuries of occupation), and tell-like mounds (Chapman 1981; Kalicz and Raczky 1987a: 15–16). In some cases, tells were seen to act as central places, tethering several smaller flat sites within microregional settlement clusters (Kalicz and Raczky 1987a; Parkinson and Gyucha 2012b; Raczky 1995). Results of regional research in the first two decades of the 21st century demand a reconsideration of this settlement typology (Gyucha et al. 2013, 2015; Raczky et al. 2015; Salisbury et al. 2013). There are small farmsteads of a single house or a few houses that may or may not have been occupied at the same time, there are house clusters, sometimes enclosed by ditches and sometimes linearly aligned, and large super-sites comprising tells or large, flat settlements. These latter sites have received the most research attention. More recent explorations indicate that these super-sites typically contain a tell within an extended horizontal settlement (Gyucha et al. 2015; Raczky and Anders 2014, 2016; Raczky et al. 2015). Furthermore, horizontal sites might not be tethered to a large central site. For example, in the Körös region of the Great Hungarian Plain, there is no tell or super-site in the approximately 40-km-long section around Csárdaszállás, between the Szarvas-Kovácshalom and Békés-Povád clusters (Salisbury 2016), and intensive surface and geophysical surveys have not turned up evidence for houses surrounding the tell at Vésztő-Mágor (Sarris et al. 2013). The lack of radiocarbon dates for smaller settlements, or for clusters of houses in larger, extended settlements, hinders interpretation of the relationships between the different site types.

Evidence for nucleation, from dispersed settlements to loose clusters of settlements and eventually to nucleated sites, including both a tell or tell-like

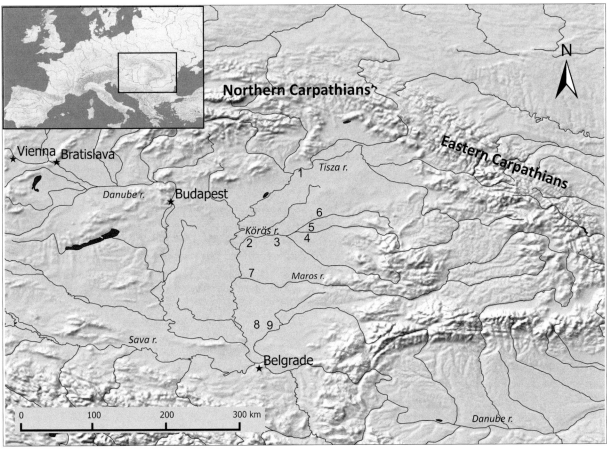

Figure 4.1. Case study area in the eastern Carpathian Basin within Hungary, with locations of major settlements mentioned in the text. 1: Polgár-Csőszhalom; 2: Öcsöd-Kováshalom; 3: Csárdaszállás-Félhalomdűlő; 4: Vésztő-Mágor; 5: Szeghalom-Kovácshalom; 6: Berettyóújfalu-Herpály; 7: Hódmezővásárhely-Gorzsa; 8: Uivar; 9: Parţa (figure by the author).

mound surrounded by houses, is seen in the Tiszazug and Körös regions (Gyucha *et al.* 2015; Parkinson and Gyucha 2012b; Raczky and Füzesi 2016), the Polgár Island region of the northeastern Great Hungarian Plain (Mesterházy *et al.* 2019; Raczky and Anders 2016; Raczky *et al.* 2015), and the Serbian Vojvodina (Hofmann *et al.* 2019). Furthermore, these nucleated settlement clusters appear to have been placed at more or less even intervals along major waterways; for example, in the Tiszazug region (Raczky and Füzesi 2016) and the Körös region (Gyucha 2015).

Researchers have observed that the organization of space on flat settlements was different from that seen in tell excavations (Draşovean 2007; Raczky 2009; Raczky and Füzesi 2016; Salisbury 2016). However, the focus on opening large sections of tells to observe vertical stratigraphy and collect datable material has resulted in a concomitant lack of information about the horizontal distribution of features and spatial patterning at off-tell spaces and flat settlements. Therefore, we do not know much about the differences in the use of space, subsistence economy, or status of the people in these different site types. The authors cited above are

amongst the very few who are systematically tackling this desideratum. What we do know is that the tells and tell-like mounds were typically surrounded by one or more ditches and palisades (Gyucha *et al.* 2015; Raczky and Anders 2014; Salisbury *et al.* 2013), that spatial subdivisions of houses and activity areas on tells were apparently planned (Kalicz 1995; Raczky 2009), and the distribution and orientation of houses were different on-tell and off-tell (Hofmann *et al.* 2019; Raczky and Anders 2010). House size and spatial divisions within houses were likely also quite different, but we currently lack sufficient data to state this unequivocally for on-tell occupations. That is, houses in some on-tell habitation layers might be the same size and shape, with the same internal and external activity areas, as off-tell houses, but this has not been investigated sufficiently.

The variety of different proxies and types of available data compounds this problem of research bias. There is a distressing lack of intensive and comprehensive comparative spatial data that can be generated by using integrated methods, such as soil chemistry, microrefuse, macrobotanicals, geophysics, airborne laser scanning, excavation, and macroartifacts distributions. Instead, most projects have employed at most two or three of these methods, usually magnetometry and excavation. Therefore, to assess the current state of knowledge about spatial patterning in aggregated settlements, we must combine these disparate datasets as much as possible.

Late Neolithic domestic structures were rectangular, timber-framed, wattle-and-daub buildings. Houses on tells were frequently multiroomed and occasionally two-storied, possibly as a result of spatial limitations imposed by ditches and palisades. The presence of a cult-corner or room, internal storage facilities, and a hearth or oven in each of the other rooms at Hódmezővásárhely-Gorzsa suggests that each room served as the domestic quarters for a nuclear, or fireside, family (Horváth 2005: 55; Parkinson 2002: 403–405, 2006: 125–128; but for a dissenting opinion, see Siklósi 2013).

Several kinds of activities could serve to integrate people into a single community. These activities could be intentional acts of coming together, such as feasts and rituals, or could act unintentionally by generating a feeling of togetherness, such as the disposal of waste in common areas. Religion is one social function that could have served an integrative purpose, and for which evidence appears to be restricted to tells on the Great Hungarian Plain. For example, houses in one habitation layer at Berettyóújfalu-Herpály enclosed a central area where a sacrificial pit was found (Kalicz and Raczky 1984). Assemblages of presumably ritual materials have been unearthed at Berettyóújfalu-Herpály (Kalicz and Raczky 1987b), Hódmezővásárhely-Gorzsa (Horváth 1987), Vésztő-Mágor (Hegedűs and Makkay 1987), and Polgár-Csőszhalom (Anders and Raczky 2013; Raczky and Sebők 2014). The recovery of 'cultic corners' with clay altars and figurine fragments in some houses on tells suggests that at least some religious practices were conducted at the household level; that is, at the same level as production (e.g., Raczky et al. 2018).

The search for centralized shrines or sacred precincts has had some apparent success. Hegedűs and Makkay (1987), for example, argued that an assemblage from a structure at Vésztő-Mágor contains too many finds of 'cultic character' to be for domestic religious practice. The finds are larger, more elaborate, and more numerous than usual, and the room floor had been re-plastered several times. They infer from this assemblage the presence of a community shrine. Similarly, central buildings used for special communal functions, as indicated by atypical artifact assemblages, have been uncovered at Parța in the Romanian Banat and interpreted as sanctuaries (Drașovean 2007). However, these interpretations have been questioned, most strongly by Lichter (2014), who points out that cultic buildings are rarely, if ever, structurally distinct

from domestic structures, and ritual paraphernalia in these special structures are found in association with grinding stones, storage vessels, loom weights, and other secular objects. Unequivocal evidence has not been found for temples or specialized ritual structures (Lichter 2014; Naumov 2013). The opposite appears true—excavation data indicate that at least some rituals were practiced in domestic structures (e.g., Horváth 1987; Kalicz and Raczky 1987b; Raczky et al. 2018), and sacred or symbolic materials were part of the Late Neolithic domestic assemblages in southeastern Europe (Bánffy 1990–1991; Crnobrnja et al. 2009). Therefore, cultic findings could be evidence for part-time religious specialization, wealthier families occupying some houses, or simply more stable occupational duration enabling the accumulation of material over time. In any case, what is lacking is evidence that these places served to integrate on- and off-tell groups through ritual interactions, or that people from off-tell visited these locations. At Polgár-Csőszhalom, evidence has been found for ritual behaviors performed off-tell and the potential for discrete ritual communities. In addition to figurines found at the flat settlement, deposits in wells and reconstructions of the ritual behaviors that generated these deposits suggest that these ritual activities involved groups larger than single households, but did not comprise the entire community at Polgár-Csőszhalom (Anders and Raczky 2013).

A second difference between tells and flat settlements is seen in the placement of ovens and cooking facilities. Houses on tells typically contained ovens or plastered hearths, in many cases one in every room; ovens or cooking areas are rarely found outside of the houses. Off-tell houses typically lacked this feature. Formation processes, including plowing and erosion, might have removed evidence for these features, as suggested for Polgár-Csőszhalom (Raczky and Anders 2010), but existing evidence suggests that more of these activities took place outdoors in off-tell settings. For example, sedimentary chemistry results at the Late Neolithic horizontal site Csárdaszállás-Félhalomdűlő suggests a food preparation and cooking area, with significant inputs of fish or shellfish between a longhouse and the nearby paleochannel (Salisbury 2013). A similar area has been proposed for a cluster of longhouses approximately 300 m south–southeast of the tell at Szeghalom-Kovácshalom, with evidence for a hearth or oven (Salisbury 2016).

Communal storage of surplus, with implications for communal sharing, can also serve to bring people together, while hoarding by families or lineages can lead to strife. Differences in food storage practices at Mississippian sites have been interpreted as evidence that incipient elites tried to leverage surplus in power relations, while also noting the differences between domestic storage and actual surplus (Barrier 2011). On the Great Hungarian Plain, internal storage containers, in the forms of very large, thick clay pots or clay storage bins built into the architecture, are known from tell excavations (Hegedűs and Makkay 1987; Horváth 1987; Kalicz and Raczky 1984). These features have typically not been found in the few existing off-tell excavations. In the rare cases where they have been recovered, such as in Trench XV at the horizontal settlement adjacent to the Uivar tell in the Banat, the houses have been interpreted as unique and having a 'special function' (Draşovean and Schier 2010: 179). In the most extensive off-tell excavations in Hungary, excavators could not positively identify food storage pits or containers in the flat settlement at Polgár-Csőszhalom (Anders and Raczky 2013). Increased efforts to identify storage facilities, whether they are pits, built-in bins, or entire buildings, would contribute to our understanding of social interactions and integration. For example, research from Çatalhöyük indicates that food was stored in individual houses, while animal skulls were publicly displayed as reminders of feasts and sharing, thereby offsetting potential conflicts related to hoarding (Bogaard et al. 2009).

Similarly, waste disposal appears to have been different between tells and horizontal settlements. Again referencing Polgár-Csőszhalom, each excavated building in the flat settlement had a refuse pit associated with it. No such pits were identified on the tell (Raczky and Anders 2008: 43). Geochemical surveys at the Late

Neolithic flat settlement of Csárdaszállás-Félhalomdűlő suggested that at least some refuse was deposited in middens associated with longhouses, while patterns at the tell-like mound of Csárdaszállás-Temetőhalom-dűlő suggest that organic waste was deposited at the edges of the settlement, near the surrounding ditch (Salisbury 2013, 2016; Salisbury et al. 2013).

Spatial patterning on many of these large sites indicates planned arrangement of architectural elements and open spaces (e.g., Parţa: Draşovean 2007; Draşovean and Schier 2010; Hódmezővásárhely-Gorzsa: Horváth 1987, 2005; Öcsöd-Kováshalom: Raczky 1987, 2009; Raczky and Füzesi 2016). Houses tended to be placed close together in an ordered arrangement, often separated by narrow passages that might have served to restrict access to central areas (Bailey 1999; Chapman 1989; Draşovean and Schier 2010; Hegedűs and Makkay 1987). Houses were built side-by-side and so close together that some houses must have shared a common wall, as observed at Berettyóújfalu-Herpály and Polgár-Csőszhalom (Kalicz and Raczky 1984; Raczky and Anders 2008) as well as at Parţa (Draşovean 2007). At Polgár-Csőszhalom, houses on the tell were arranged in a 'radial pattern with their long axes oriented toward the center of the site' (Raczky and Anders 2008: 41). On flat settlements, in contrast, houses were arranged less regularly and more often linearly, such as at Csárdaszállás-Félhalomdűlő (Figure 4.2) and in the extended horizontal settlement around the tell of

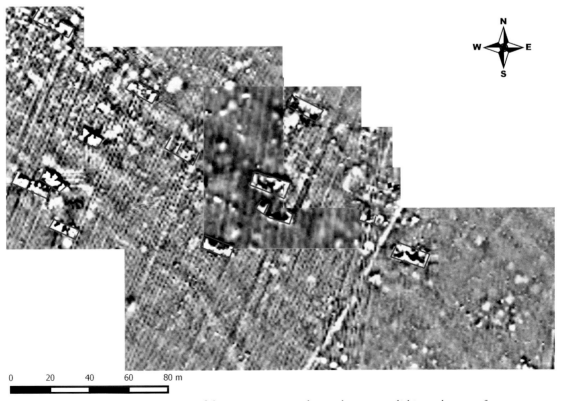

Figure 4.2. Interpretation of the magnetic anomalies at the Late Neolithic settlement of Csárdaszállás-Félhalomdűlő in the Körös region, eastern Hungary (figure by the author).

Szeghalom-Kovácshalom (Gyucha *et al.* 2015; Niekamp and Sarris 2014; see also Gyucha, this volume).

Most of the tell sites contained residential/production areas, central/communal areas, and either internal or external cemeteries. The consistency of patterning allows the extension of the activity zones model, from a single household unit model to a model of house clusters, and is applied to the spatial organization of these settlements, albeit in a preliminary form based only on features identified through survey and excavation. In some cases, several houses, pits, wells, and outbuildings combine to form discrete house clusters within larger Late Neolithic settlements. For example, within the total site area of 21 ha at Öcsöd-Kováshalom were eight discrete settlement units, separated from one another by 'empty' spaces. This has been interpreted as evidence that the communities occupying individual farmsteads or hamlets moved closer to one another, but maintained their political autonomy, as evidenced by their spatial integrity (Raczky and Füzesi 2016).

At Öcsöd-Kováshalom, houses were surrounded by open activity zones containing hearths, evidence for lithic and bone working, and large refuse pits that had presumably been opened for clay extraction and reused for waste disposal (Raczky 2009: 105). This zone appears to equate to the communal back zone for the house cluster. This distinct zone surrounded the buildings in the central zone, suggesting that associated activities were performed by members of an integrated community (Raczky and Anders 2008; Raczky and Füzesi 2016). Geochemical patterns at Csárdaszállás-Félhalomdűlő and Szeghalom-Kovácshalom indicate open areas of low chemical enrichment around the houses, with a surrounding zone of pits, middens, and food preparation areas. Based on the pattern of domestic structures and other features at these sites, low chemical enrichment suggests cleaned and/or high-traffic areas that were part of the front zones. Examples could include pathways and entrances, forming the communal front zones for house clusters. The surrounding activity zone has been interpreted as the back zone. On the other sides of the houses were areas enriched in phosphates and potassium; most likely these areas were used as middens or animal pens, with the discard of manure and ash. On the other side of the houses were pits, as identified in coring and magnetograms, and chemical signatures for food preparation. In general, these zones fall within the general distribution of surface artifacts (Salisbury 2016).

Activity Zones in Comparison and Discussion

From the data presented in the preceding section, we can delineate several sets of activities that were integrative at a small scale of several households,

without necessarily integrating everyone living in a nucleated settlement. In many cases, these sets of activities took place within a bounded area of a house cluster, with each cluster containing ritual facilities, cooking areas, storage facilities, trash pits, and wells. Multiple clusters were not found at every Late Neolithic settlement across the eastern Carpathian Basin, and the relative proximity of houses, presence of tell mounds, and processes of aggregation and separation varied. Nevertheless, the general pattern that emerges is settlements comprising multiple house clusters separated by ditches, paleomeanders, fences, or open spaces. A comparison of activity zones and the distribution of facilities in the Hungarian dataset with findings from nucleated settlements in other regions supports the interpretation of nucleated settlements being composed of smaller, well-integrated groups, whilst suggesting research directions that might yield data for higher-level integration.

During later prehistory in the eastern woodlands of North America, agriculturalists in central and western New York State and southern Ontario after *c.* AD 1300 experienced two phases of gradual village fusion or aggregation. This process, dubbed community coalescence (Birch 2010, 2012; Kowalewski 2006), also shows evidence for increasing settlement size over time. The standard explanation for Iroquoian integration has been that aggregation was a response to increased conflict between villages or tribes over access to hunting grounds and favorable trade with Europeans. Birch, however, has argued that archaeological evidence for increasing conflict amongst Iroquoian groups is a reflection of '*internal, as opposed to external, village politics*' during a '*period of major social and political realignment*' (2010: 30–31) with individuals and groups striving to sustain their influence and identity, or even survival. Furthermore, coalescence comprises cultural transformations that accompany population aggregation. Transformations include not only subsistence intensification, largely by default, but also mechanisms for social integration.

Iroquoian villages in New York and southern Ontario, especially the early villages, had longhouses with interior and exterior pits, and refuse areas outside the doors and at the edges of the village (Engelbrecht 2003, 2014). A significant difference between the Hungarian and Iroquoian examples is that the Iroquoian settlements were entirely enclosed by their palisades or hillslopes. Over time, populations aggregated in fewer settlements, and both settlements and their defensive enclosures grew in size and complexity. There are some early exceptions; the Eaton site—an Iroquoian village dating to *c.* AD 1550 and probably occupied by members of the Erie nation (Engelbrecht 2014; Salisbury and Engelbrecht 2018)—had only a partial palisade and the distribution of longhouses was irregular. The Draper site in Ontario (*c.* AD 1450–1500) provides a good example that may be more typical. Over time, this Huron nation settlement increased in size through the addition of new clusters of longhouses. Each longhouse cluster was spatially discrete, and this pattern was retained as the site expanded. New houses were not aligned with existing houses, even though this would have reduced the effort of expanding the surrounding palisade (Birch 2012). At the Mantle site, occupied a few decades after Draper, probably by members of the same community, an open common area and activity areas shared by members of several longhouses were identified (Archaeological Services Inc. 2012: 109, 114).

Birch (2010, 2012) argues that the defensive functions often assigned to palisades (e.g., Engelbrecht 2009; Keener 1999) should be accompanied by the recognition of their social and symbolic importance. Similar to arguments made by Bailey (2000: 273–276) for the Balkan Neolithic, enclosures serve as social boundaries that include and exclude. Palisades can symbolize the establishment of place and the shared efforts of time, energy, and raw materials for newly forming communities as well as restricting access and visibility to villages, or parts of villages (Bailey 2000: 274; Keeley 1996: 55; Parkinson and Duffy 2007: 101). By dividing people into groups, enclosures can simplify the integration of those within, as appears to be the case in the Iroquoian example. When used to divide some part of a settlement from other parts, features, such as ditches or fences, can make it more difficult to integrate the larger community. Following the arguments by Birch for enclosures as integrative mechanisms and by Bailey for enclosures as mechanisms of exclusion, one can suggest that people on enclosed tells were integrating themselves but excluding inhabitants of the flat settlement. Of course, it is possible that the tell was indeed a fortified village, where dispersed people gathered during times of war, but evidence for large-scale interpersonal violence in the Late Neolithic is lacking on the Great Hungarian Plain and across Southeast Europe.

Contrast these processes with evidence from Mississippian settlement patterns in the North American Southeast *c.* AD 950–1350, which also reflects a process of demographic nucleation, planned towns and ceremonial centers were part of a complex and stratified society. The largest center was Cahokia, a polity situated on the Mississippian river floodplain, home to *c.* 15,000 people, and known for having more than 120 mounds, a walled inner district, and multiple ceremonial wood henges (Alt 2012; Woods 2004). The subsistence part of the Mississippian economy relied heavily on intensive maize agriculture and the large-scale re-settlement of farmers (Anderson 2017; Pauketat 2003; Woods 2004). More socially complex, evincing top-down integration, the Mississippian polity shows

clear evidence for overt use of the built environment to structure interactions and movement. Although the range of variability in the sizes and shapes of structures probably reflects demographic diversity, residential compounds and sacred spaces were clearly marked, building styles indicated function, and walls were used to block sight lines (Alt 2012). The evidence further indicates that construction works at Cahokia were periodic and completed very quickly, implying large-scale coordination of communal effort (Alt 2012; Alt *et al.* 2010). Much like the case of Iroquoian coalescence, participating in communal construction activities presumably contributed to community integration at Cahokia, even if the impetus for integrative activities was imposed from the top down.

The spatial organization and size of domestic spaces provide a second line of evidence for interpreting Late Neolithic society on the Great Hungarian Plain. In the North American Southwest, house size was dependent on both the number of inhabitants and how closely set other houses were as well as on environmental and economic factors; houses in closely-packed nucleated villages tended to be larger than those in more dispersed settlements (Dohm 1990). In eastern Hungary, although we lack conclusive data, house size and complexity appears to have depended on proximity to other houses, and limited data available suggests differences in form, floor space, and house placement between on- and off-tell houses (e.g., Hofmann *et al.* 2019; Raczky and Anders 2010).

Zuni pueblo communities had living (domestic) rooms, storage rooms, and ceremonial rooms (shrines), the latter distinct from the widely known *kivas*. Shrines were typically living rooms that were specially prepared for ceremonies, thus serving a double function (Creamer 1993; Steele 2007). The closest analogy for Late Neolithic settlements on the Great Hungarian Plain is the storage/cultic rooms identified in houses on several tells. These rooms could have shared secular and sacred functions at various times, although some rituals could have been associated with the successful harvest of the stored grains. Functionally, these rooms appear to have provided a space for some members of the community to conduct rituals that would have served as integrative mechanisms, but we lack evidence for whether these were members of one particular household, an extended household, lineage, or other groups, possibly clans or similar fraternal organizations that crossed between house clusters. If we were to assume that people from the flat settlements needed to go to clan, fraternity, or other ritual associations on the tells, then we are forced to assume that when they dispersed, they no longer needed to participate in these rituals with the associated ritual paraphernalia. Early Copper Age researchers previously argued for the significance of newly established cemeteries as central spiritual and communal spaces that were used by multiple communities (Bailey 1997: 52; Chapman 1997: 149; Raczky and Anders 2009: 16). This is difficult to support, however, in light of the small size of these cemeteries and evidence for other potential sacred places, such as enclosures containing pits at Füzesabony-Pusztaszikszó and Szarvas-Cigány-ér-part (Kállay 1988; Makkay 1980–1981) and wells at Gyula-Remete-Iskola and Körösladány-Bikeri (Gyucha 2015: 181). If we assume that spiritual or ritual needs were already being met off-tell, then systems of part-time ritual practitioners using part-time sacred spaces within the household cluster could have carried over after dispersal. The caveat, of course, is that we lack evidence for these spaces and practices.

As noted, a household cluster includes the houses, pits, and discrete activity zones used by a household (Salisbury 2012, 2016; Winter 1976). In some cases, such as at Csárdaszállás-Félhalomdűlő, one or more houses appear to have shared spaces for food preparation and refuse disposal. Comparison with results from the Iroquoian Draper and Mantle sites suggests that this pattern of refuse disposal may be evidence for a less integrated community. Of 22 middens identified at Draper, all were used by two or more longhouses (Birch 2012; Finlayson 1985: 398), and the longhouses were distributed in an irregular pattern suggesting no central planning. In contrast, a single, large midden was used during the early years of Mantle site occupation, and two middens were utilized following a village expansion that created a large barrow trench. Birch (2012: 664) interprets these results as indicative of highly structured refuse disposal patterns at Mantle, matching the more structured layout of longhouses.

Houses at Öcsöd-Kováshalom were surrounded by open activity zones, containing hearths, debris from working lithics and bone, and large refuse pits (Raczky 2009: 105). Intensive research, including geophysical and phosphate surveys as well as excavations, conducted by the Körös Regional Archaeological Project at Vésztő-Bikeri, an Early Copper Age site on the Great Hungarian Plain, also indicates zonation of activities. Although we did not do microrefuse analysis, samples collected for flotation yielded macrobotanical remains. Within a settlement enclosed by a ditch and palisade system, three spatially discrete activity zones were identified (Gyucha 2015: 127; Parkinson et al. 2010). Houses clustered in the center of the settlement formed the inner zone. No cooking hearths, ovens, or kilns were found inside the structures. These houses were occupied partially successively, so new constructions may have removed some of the communal front zone. Phosphate levels were lowest in this central zone. A ring of pits, food preparation areas, and a well formed the second zone. The macrobotanical remains indicate that food preparation took place in both the inner and

middle zones (Gyucha 2015: Figure 5.33; Yerkes et al. 2021). The third zone consists of the space along the enclosure, with sheet middens, butchering waste, and elevated phosphate and magnetic susceptibility values (Hardy et al. 2021; Nicodemus and Kovács 2021; Yerkes et al. 2007). These activity patterns from immediately after the dispersal from Late Neolithic large sites (4459–4253 cal BC; Yerkes et al. 2009) suggest that the spatial organization of house clusters remained consistent over time.

An activity zones model can be applied to the spatial organization of settlements (Figure 4.3), and the archaeological correlates of the specific behaviors tested during future research. For example, the 'clean' inner zone of domestic architecture, low artifact density, and depletion of most chemical elements reflect the household and communal front zones, maintained for cleanliness and probably trampled by constant foot traffic. The middle zone of food preparation, ovens, pits, and wells, representing the family back zones, should contain macrobotanicals, bone fragments, phytolith concentrations, pits, and chemical signatures of fires, butchering, food preparation, and assorted other production activities, such as grinding pigments, flint knapping, or working bone. The outer zone is the communal back zone, with community middens, areas for keeping livestock, and other shared 'dirty' activities.

Integration and Partition

Bottom-up approaches, such as those in Iroquoia or on the Great Hungarian Plain, are more likely to fit egalitarian social structures. Top-down approaches, such as those of Mississippian chiefdoms where maximizing control over the economy and local population was a primary objective of the Mississippian elite, generate spatial patterns that are homogeneous and very persistent. This is evident at both the regional scale in the placement of administrative centers and the local scale in the organization of architecture. In contrast, evidence from the eastern Carpathian Basin suggests that control was not a primary driver of nucleation and centralization. In Hungary, this early aggregation ultimately collapsed and the population dispersed, but we do not find evidence for excessive violence. That is, and unlike evidence from the Linearbandkeramik (Golitko and Keeley 2007; Meyer et al. 2015; Orschiedt and Haidle 2006), we do not find mass graves or multiple bodies with clear markers of interpersonal violence. Burning of houses appears to have been deliberate but restricted to single houses at the end of their use-life, rather than settlement-wide destruction. Mississippian examples suggest that kinship identity became less important and that new identities formed based on something other than kinship—perhaps vocation or craft specialization. The Hungarian examples indicate that in the Late Neolithic,

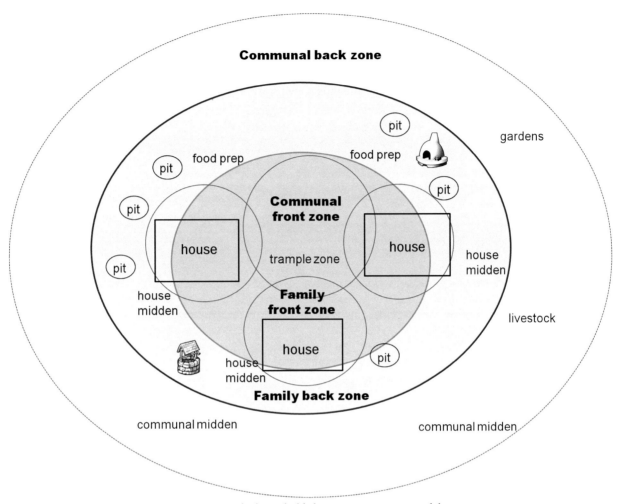

Figure 4.3. The household cluster activity zones model
(figure by the author).

kinship or household membership may have been the primary identity, and this then facilitated group fissioning at the end of the period.

Results from the Neolithic Great Hungarian Plain also imply efforts to self-segregate, to maintain privacy and identity, not on an individual level but rather at the level of families or lineages within the larger tribal group. This is most pronounced in the largest and most densely populated villages. This is similar to the Iroquoian examples, where we know that matrilineage was an important identity. However, the highly organized pattern of houses on some Neolithic tells suggests a centralized decision-making process. In conjunction with a few examples of possible part-time craft specialization at Kundruci and Okolište in Central Bosnia (Furholt 2012; Müller *et al.* 2013), this implies nascent efforts at sociopolitical control. Therefore, one interpretation of nucleated Late Neolithic villages is that they represent people coming together to be closer to centers of resource accumulation, specialized craft production, and possibly to religious or ritual specialists. Results from the southern Great Hungarian Plain, at least, also suggest that changes in

groundwater levels made these places more attractive (Gulyás and Sümegi 2011). During periods of major social and political realignment, individuals, lineages, and community segments had to work to reposition themselves in relation to one another (Birch 2010: 30–31). Something similar may have happened at the end of the Hungarian Neolithic on the Great Hungarian Plain when a combination of factors led to settlement nucleation and associated demographic packing. This, in turn, might have resulted in reduced mobility and reduced access to resources. Lacking an external threat, the population responded to these limitations by dispersing.

Possible integrative areas have been identified in central areas at Parţa, Uivar, Polgár-Csőszhalom, and Berettyóújfalu-Herpály (Draşovean 2007; Kalicz and Raczky 1984; Raczky and Sebők 2014). This central area is the communal front zone. Each of the multiroom houses contains a storage room and ovens or hearths. The house itself, then, contains much of the family front and back zones. This is not unlike Çatalhöyük, where rooms were divided into 'clean' areas of a central space and northern platforms and a 'dirty' southern part, containing domestic installations (e.g., ovens, cooking tools) with food storage, including clay grain bins, typically in small rooms in the walls of the main living space (Steele 2007, citing Mellaart 1967). Therefore, evidence for integration of people inhabiting the tells appears to be sound. Even the spatial restrictions imposed by houses placed close together and surrounded by ditches and palisades could encourage nucleation (Engelbrecht 2009). However, this cannot so easily be extended to entire aggregated settlements. Ritual or religious activities appear to have been practiced at several organizational scales. A deposit of ritual paraphernalia, including a large face pot, was recovered in a communal space between three houses at Öcsöd-Kováshalom as well as evidence is available for rituals performed inside the houses (Raczky et al. 2018: 129). These findings were interpreted as indicating that subsistence and ritual activities intertwined in Late Neolithic daily life for the members of these houses, perhaps an extended household (Raczky et al. 2018: 135).

Sharing of food through formal feasts as an integrative mechanism has been invoked to explain people living together in Iroquoian societies (Salisbury and Engelbrecht 2018), and also at Çatalhöyük, where people were able to have private food storage while remaining closely integrated (Bogaard et al. 2009). Excavations at Szeghalom-Kovácshalom in the early and mid-20th century uncovered hearths and ash deposits containing large quantities of animal bones (Gyucha et al. 2019). The great amounts of wild animal bones from the Polgár-Csőszhalom tell have been interpreted as evidence for large, communal feasts (Anders and Raczky 2013). Whether this involved the entire community, tell and off-tell, is not clear, but the hypothesized feasting as an integrative mechanism on the Great Hungarian Plain warrants further investigation.

The centrality of the cooking hearth to the integration of the household is widely recognized (Chang 1958; Lowell 1999; Riggs 2017). The identification of external cooking and food preparation areas at Late Neolithic flat settlements, and the possibility that these were shared by several houses (Raczky and Anders 2008; Salisbury 2013, 2016), suggests that integration was focused on the extended household or lineage. There is a possibility that indoor and outdoor hearths signify seasonal occupations, as seen for example in the American Southwest (Kent 1992; Lowell 1995, 1999), but existing data, which does not address seasonality, does not support this. Rather, the present state of knowledge lends itself to the interpretation of semi-autonomous lineages living near to one another, but not 'together.'

The argument, summarized by Raczky and Anders (2008: 41–43) and Siklósi (2013: 240) based on data and interpretations of several Late Neolithic settlements from across eastern Hungary, is that task areas and workspaces on some tells were used by all members of the community living on the tell, while similar activity zones could be identified with specific houses or house clusters in the flat settlements. This supports an interpretation of tell communities being distinct from the various discrete communities in the flat settlements. This also suggests that the regional settlement pattern of core and satellite settlements could be correct in terms of group identity.

Conclusions

Assessment of settlement-scale data indicates that the Late Neolithic of the Great Hungarian Plain involved a high degree of population aggregation, but small communities constructed their own 'subvillages,' visible as house clusters, within larger settlements or settlement clusters. Within each of these house clusters, small-scale integration is evident in patterns of activity zones, refuse disposal, and possibly ritual behaviors. These house clusters worked well as integrative units because they allowed small groups to retain their identity and simplified decision-making processes. However, they also may have facilitated group fissioning. On the Great Hungarian Plain, the transition from the Late Neolithic to the Early Copper Age is more remarkable for settlement and population dispersal, de-nucleation, than for copper. That is, although house clusters helped to integrate people in aggregated settlements, they did nothing for mitigating intragroup discord.

At the regional scale, we might have a system of integration within individual communities or settlement clusters, with no upper-level interactions between these clusters; that is, each settlement cluster (tell-based cluster) could have been autonomous. The presence of ceramic house models, baby burials in association with houses, and ritual or cultic assemblages found within houses imply a house-based or household identity that might have contributed to household cohesion whilst reinforcing distinctiveness from other households (Bailey 2000: 268–269). Exchange of goods and people may have taken place, but with no requirements for aid in time of trouble. This would describe the entire settlement system on the Great Hungarian Plain, and likewise offers one hypothesis for sections within the settlement system that lack a tell or super-site, e.g., around Csárdaszállás.

Debate continues about whether or not processes of nucleation during the Neolithic in Southeast Europe included the development of sociopolitical hierarchies (Müller et al. 2013; Parkinson and Gyucha 2012a; Parkinson et al. 2018; Porčić 2019), but centralization of power is not required for nucleation (Kowalewski 2006). Corporate decision-making strategies can account for the structure and construction of nucleated settlements, including massive and elaborate ditch and palisade constructions, in eastern Hungary and elsewhere.

As Haggis (2013) points out, the material assemblages and spatial data from nucleated settlements are frequently insufficient for ascertaining the actual form or process of aggregation. This is certainly the case for the Neolithic on the Great Hungarian Plain, where we have detailed excavation data from small portions of settlement mounds, but relatively little data about the material components and spatial organization of off-tell settlements. We also lack detailed analyses of the differences in site formation processes for the tell and flat settlement components, although the preserved diversity of built areas at several sites, such as Szeghalom-Kovácshalom (Gyucha et al. 2019), provides opportunities to dig into this issue in the future.

This paper generates more questions than answers, and I recognize that I am producing a typical conclusion that 'we need more research.' This is justifiable because most discussions of what the available evidence tells us about how people used various spaces, and how community members were socially, economically, and politically organized, are more hypotheses than interpretations. Data for these processes are many times insufficient. Identifying zones of activities, and defining zones associated with households and those associated with supra-household groups and whole communities, will help us to reconstruct the spatial order that is essential for understanding early nucleated settlements. To do this, we need to collect data at the appropriate analytical scales. If the same activities were enacted at each house cluster and the clusters were all contemporaneous, then the behaviors should leave the same signatures in the archaeological record. This does require controlling for apparent variability introduced by site formation processes. Samples for thin-section microscopy, soil chemistry, soil biomarkers, microrefuse, and macrobotanical analyses will enable us to identify the locations of activities while augmenting larger-scale data from surface collections, geophysics, and excavations. Research focus on activity zones will enable us to identify where people chose to conduct activities, how these activities related to other neighborhoods, and how segregated individual clusters were.

References Cited

Adler, M.A., T. Van Pool and R.D. Leonard 1996. Ancestral Pueblo Population Aggregation and Abandonment in the North American Southwest. *Journal of World Prehistory* 10(3): 375–438.

Adler, M.A. and R.H. Wilshusen 1990. Large-Scale Integrative Facilities in Tribal Societies: Cross-Cultural and Southwestern US Examples. *World Archaeology* 22(2): 133–146.

Alcock, S.E. and J.F. Cherry (eds) 2004. *Side-by-Side Survey: Comparative Regional Studies in the Mediterranean World*. Oxford: Oxbow Books.

Aldenderfer, M. 2010. Gimme That Old Time Religion: Rethinking the Role of Religion in the Emergence of Social Inequality, in T.D. Price and G.M. Feinman (eds) *Pathways to Power: New Perspectives on the Emergence of Social Inequality*: 77–94. New York: Springer.

Alt, S.M. 2012. Making Mississippian at Cahokia, in T.R. Pauketat (ed.) *The Oxford Handbook of North American Archaeology*: 497–508. Oxford: Oxford University Press.

Alt, S.M., J.D. Kruchten and T.R. Pauketat 2010. The Construction and Use of Cahokia's Grand Plaza. *Journal of Field Archaeology* 35(2): 131–146.

Anders, A. and P. Raczky 2013. Háztartások és települési egység viszonya Polgár-Csőszhalom késő neolitikus lelőhelyén (The relation between households and settlement units at the Late Neolithic settlement of Polgár-Csőszhalom). *Ősrégészeti Levelek/Prehistoric Newsletters* 13: 78–101.

Anderson, D.G. 1996. Chiefdoms: Cycling in the Late Prehistoric Southeast, in J.F. Scarry (ed.) *Political Structure and Change in the Prehistoric Southeastern United States*: 231–252. Gainesville: University Press of Florida.

Anderson, D.G. 2017. Mississippian Beginnings: Multiple Perspectives on Migration, Monumentality, and Religion in the Prehistoric Eastern United States, in G.D. Wilson (ed.) *Mississippian Beginnings*: 298–321. Gainesville: University of Florida Press.

Archaeological Services Inc. 2012. The Archaeology of the Mantle Site (AlGt–334): Report on the Stage 3–4 Mitigative Excavation of Part of Lot 22, Concession 9, Town of Whitchurch-Stouffville, Regional Municipality of York, Ontario. Report on File. Toronto: Ontario Ministry of Culture, Tourism and Sport.

Bailey, D.W. 1997. Impermanence and flux in the landscape of early agricultural southeastern Europe, in J. Chapman and P. Dolukhanov (eds) *Landscapes in Flux: Central and Eastern Europe in Antiquity* (Colloquia Pontifica 3): 41–58. Oxford: Oxbow Books.

Bailey, D.W. 1999. What is a tell? Settlement in fifth millennium Bulgaria, in J. Brück and M. Goodman (eds) *Making Places in the Prehistoric World: Themes in Settlement Archaeology*: 94–111. London: UCL Press.

Bailey, D.W. 2000. *Balkan Prehistory: Exclusion, Incorporation and Identity*. London and New York: Routledge.

Bandy, M.S. 2004. Fissioning, Scalar Stress, and Social Evolution in Early Village Societies. *American Anthropologist* 106(2): 322–333.

Bánffy, E. 1990–1991. Cult and Archaeological Context in Central- and South-Eastern Europe in the Neolithic and the Chalcolithic. *Antaeus* 19–20: 183–251.

Barba, L. and A. Ortiz 1992. Análisis químico de pisos de ocupación: Un caso etnográfico en Tlaxcala, Mexico. *Latin American Antiquity* 3(1): 63–82.

Barrier, C.R. 2011. Storage and relative surplus at the Mississippian site of Moundville. *Journal of Anthropological Archaeology* 30(2): 206–219.

Birch, J. 2010. Coalescence and conflict in Iroquoian Ontario. *Archaeological Review from Cambridge* 25(1): 27–46.

Birch, J. 2012. Coalescent Communities: Settlement Aggregation and Social Integration in Iroquoian Ontario. *American Antiquity* 77(4): 646–670.

Bogaard, A., M. Charles, K.C. Twiss, A. Fairbairn, N. Yalman, D. Filipović, G.A. Demirergi, F. Ertug, N. Russell and J. Henecke 2009. Private pantries and celebrated surplus: storing and sharing food at Neolithic Çatalhöyük, Central Anatolia. *Antiquity* 83(321): 649–668.

Bogucki, P.I. and R. Grygiel 1981. The household cluster at Brześć Kujawski 3: small-site methodology in the Polish Lowlands. *World Archaeology* 13(1): 59–72.

Borić, D. 2008. First Households and 'House Societies' in European Prehistory, in A. Jones (ed.) *Prehistoric Europe:* 109–142. Malden (MA): Blackwell.

Bowser, B.J. and J.Q. Patton 2004. Domestic Spaces as Public Places: An Ethnoarchaeological Case Study of Houses, Gender, and Politics in the Ecuadorian Amazon. *Journal of Archaeological Method and Theory* 11(2): 157–181.

Butzer, K.W. 1980. Context in Archaeology: An Alternative Perspective. *Journal of Field Archaeology* 7(4): 417–422.

Byrd, B.F. 1994. Public and Private, Domestic and Corporate: The Emergence of the Southwest Asian Village. *American Antiquity* 59(4): 639–666.

Chang, K.C. 1958. Study of the Neolithic Social Grouping: Examples from the New World. *American Anthropologist* 60(2): 298–334.

Chapman, J. 1981. *The Vinča Culture of South-East Europe* (BAR International Series 117). Oxford: British Archaeological Reports.

Chapman, J. 1989. The early Balkan village, in S. Bökönyi (ed.) *Neolithic of Southeastern Europe and its Near Eastern Connections* (Varia Archaeologica Hungarica 2): 33–53. Budapest: Archaeological Institute of the Hungarian Academy of Sciences.

Chapman, J. 1997. Places as timemarks – the social construction of landscapes in Eastern Hungary, in J. Chapman and P. Dolukhanov (eds) *Landscapes in Flux: Central and Eastern Europe in Antiquity* (Colloquia Pontifica 3): 137–162. Oxford: Oxbow Books.

Chesson, M.S. 2012. Homemaking in the Early Bronze Age, in B.J. Parker and C.P. Foster (eds) *New Perspectives on Household Archaeology:* 45–79. Winona Lake (IN): Eisenbrauns.

Coronel, E.G., S. Hutson, A. Magnoni, C. Balzotti, A. Ulmer and R.E. Terry 2015. Geochemical analysis of Late Classic and Post Classic Maya marketplace activities at the Plazas of Cobá, Mexico. *Journal of Field Archaeology* 40(1): 89–109.

Creamer, W. 1993. *The Architecture of Arroyo Hondo* (Arroyo Hondo Archeological Series 7). Santa Fe (NM): School of American Research Press.

Crnobrnja, A., Z. Simijć and M. Janković 2009. Late Vinča culture settlement at Crkvine in Stubline (Household organization and urbanization in the Late Vinča culture period). *Starinar* 59: 9–25.

Dohm, K. 1990. Effect of Population Nucleation on House Size for Pueblos in the American Southwest. *Journal of Anthropological Archaeology* 9(3): 201–239.

Draşovean, F. 2007. The neolithic tells from Parţa and Uivar (South-west Romania). Similarities and differences of the organization of social space. *Analele Banatului* 15: 19–32.

Draşovean, F. and W. Schier 2010. The Neolithic tell sites of Parţa and Uivar (Romanian Banat). A comparison of their architectural sequence and organization of social space, in S. Hansen (ed.) *Leben auf dem Tell als soziale Praxis* (Kolloquien zur Vor- und Frühgeschichte 14): 165–187. Bonn: Dr. Rudolf Habelt.

Duffy, P.R., W.A. Parkinson, A. Gyucha and R.W. Yerkes 2013. Coming Together, Falling Apart: A Multiscalar Approach to Prehistoric Aggregation and Interaction on the Great Hungarian Plain, in J. Birch (ed.) *From Prehistoric Villages to Cities: Settlement Aggregation and Community Transformation:* 44–62. New York: Routledge.

Engelbrecht, W.E. 2003. *Iroquoia: The Development of a Native World.* Syracuse (NY): Syracuse University Press.

Engelbrecht, W.E. 2009. Defense in an Iroquois Village, in L.E. Miroff and T.D. Knapp (eds) *Iroquois Archaeology and Analytic Scale:* 179–187. Knoxville: University of Tennessee Press.

Engelbrecht, W.E. 2014. Unnotched Triangular Points on Village Sites. *American Antiquity* 79(2): 353–367.

Finlayson, W.D. 1985. *The 1975 and 1978 Rescue Excavations at the Draper Site: Introduction and Settlement Patterns* (Mercury Series, Archaeological Survey of Canada Paper 130). Ottawa: National Museum of Man.

Flannery, K.V. 1976. The Early Formative Household Cluster on the Guatemalan Pacific Coast, in K.V. Flannery (ed.) *The Early Mesoamerican Village:* 31–34. New York: Academic Press.

Furholt, M. 2012. Kundruci: Development of Social Space in a Late Neolithic Tell-Settlement in Central Bosnia, in R. Hofmann, F.-K. Moetz and J. Müller (eds) *Tells: Social and Environmental Space* (Universitätsforschungen zur prähistorischen Archäologie 207): 203–219. Bonn: Dr. Rudolf Habelt.

Galaty, M.L. 2005. European Regional Studies: A Coming of Age? *Journal of Archaeological Research* 13(4): 291–336.

Golitko, M. and L.H. Keeley 2007. Beating ploughshares back into swords: warfare in the Linearbandkeramik. *Antiquity* 81(312): 332–342.

Gorgues, A., K. Rebay-Salisbury and R.B. Salisbury (eds) 2017. *Material Chains in Late Prehistoric Europe and the Mediterranean: Time, Space, and Technologies of Production*. Bordeaux: Ausonius Éditions.

Gulyás, S. and P. Sümegi 2011. Riparian environment in shaping social and economic behavior during the first phase of the evolution of Late Neolithic tell complexes in SE Hungary (6th/5th millennia BC). *Journal of Archaeological Science* 38(10): 2683–2695.

Gyucha, A. 2015. *Prehistoric Village Social Dynamics: The Early Copper Age in the Körös Region* (Prehistoric Research in the Körös Region 2). Budapest: Archaeolingua.

Gyucha, A., P.R. Duffy and W.A. Parkinson 2013. Prehistoric human-environmental interactions on the Great Hungarian Plain. *Anthropologie* 51(2): 157–168.

Gyucha, A., W.A. Parkinson and R.W. Yerkes 2009. A multi-scalar approach to settlement pattern analysis: the transition from the Late Neolithic to the Early Copper Age on the Great Hungarian Plain, in T.L. Thurston and R.B. Salisbury (eds) *Reimagining Regional Analyses: The Archaeology of Spatial and Social Dynamics*: 100–129. Newcastle: Cambridge Scholars Publishing.

Gyucha, A., W.A. Parkinson and R.W. Yerkes 2014. The Transition from the Late Neolithic to the Early Copper Age: Multi-Disciplinary Investigations in the Körös Region of the Great Hungarian Plain, in W. Schier and F. Draşovean (eds) *The Neolithic and Eneolithic in Southeast Europe: New Approaches to Dating and Cultural Dynamics in the 6th to 4th millennium BC* (Prähistorische Archäologie in Südosteuropa 28): 273–296. Rahden/Westfalen: Marie Leidorf.

Gyucha, A., W.A. Parkinson and R.W. Yerkes 2019. The Evolution of a Neolithic Tell on the Great Hungarian Plain: Site Formation and Use at Szeghalom-Kovácshalom. *Journal of Field Archaeology* 44(7): 458–479.

Gyucha, A., R.W. Yerkes, W.A. Parkinson, N. Papadopoulos, A. Sarris, P.R. Duffy and R.B. Salisbury 2015. Settlement Nucleation in the Neolithic: A Preliminary Report of the Körös Regional Archaeological Project's Investigations at Szeghalom-Kovácshalom and Vésztő-Mágor, in S. Hansen, P. Raczky, A. Anders and A. Reingruber (eds) *Neolithic and Copper Age between the Carpathians and the Aegean Sea. Chronologies and Technologies from the 6th to the 4th Millennium BCE* (Archäologie in Eurasien 31): 129–142. Bonn: Dr. Rudolf Habelt.

Haggis, D.C. 2013. Social Organization and Aggregated Settlement Structure in an Archaic Greek City on Crete (ca. 600 BC), in J. Birch (ed.) *From Prehistoric Villages to Cities: Settlement Aggregation and Community Transformation*: 63–86. New York: Routledge.

Hardy, M., M.L. Galaty, R.B. Salisbury and D.M. Billingsley 2021. Soil Chemistry, in W.A. Parkinson, A. Gyucha and R.W. Yerkes (eds) *Bikeri: Two Copper Age Villages on the Great Hungarian Plain*: 65–74. Los Angeles: Cotsen Institute of Archaeology at UCLA.

Hardy-Smith, T. and P.C. Edwards 2004. The garbage crisis in prehistory: artefact discard patterns at the Early Natufian site of Wadi Hammeh 27 and the origins of household refuse disposal strategies. *Journal of Anthropological Archaeology* 23(3): 253–289.

Hayden, B. 1997. Observations on the Prehistoric Social and Economic Structure of the North American Plateau. *World Archaeology* 29(2): 242–261.

Hayden, B. and A. Cannon 1983. Where the Garbage Goes: Refuse Disposal in the Maya Highlands. *Journal of Anthropological Archaeology* 2(2): 117–163.

Hegedűs, K. and J. Makkay 1987. Vésztő-Mágor: A settlement of the Tisza culture, in L. Tálas and P. Raczky (eds) *The Late Neolithic of the Tisza Region*: 85–104. Budapest and Szolnok: Kossuth Kiadó and Szolnok County Museum.

Hjulström, B. and S. Isaksson 2009. Identification of activity area signatures in a reconstructed Iron Age house by combining element and lipid analyses of sediments. *Journal of Archaeological Science* 36(1): 174–183.

Hofmann, R., A. Medović, M. Furholt, I. Medović, T.S. Pešterac, S. Dreibrodt, S. Martini and A. Hofmann 2019. Late Neolithic multicomponent sites of the Tisza region and the emergence of centripetal settlement layouts. *Praehistorische Zeitschrift* 94(2): 351–378.

Horváth, F. 1987. Hódmezővásárhely-Gorzsa: A settlement of the Tisza culture, in L. Tálas and P. Raczky (eds) *The Late Neolithic of the Tisza Region*: 31–46. Budapest and Szolnok: Kossuth Kiadó and Szolnok County Museum.

Horváth, F. 2005. Gorzsa. Előzetes eredmények az újkőkori tell 1978 és 1996 közötti feltárásából (Gorzsa. Preliminary results of the excavation of the Neolithic tell between 1978–1996), in L. Bende and G. Lőrinczy (eds) *Hétköznapok Vénuszai*: 51–83. Hódmezővásárhely: Móra Ferenc Múzeum.

Jongsma, T. and H.J. Greenfield 2003. The Household Cluster Concept in Archaeology, in L. Nikolova (ed.) *Early Symbolic Systems for Communication in Southeast Europe* (BAR International Series 1139): 21–24. Oxford: British Archaeological Reports.

Kalicz, N. 1995. Siedlungsstruktur der neolithischen Herpály-Kultur in Ostungarn, in A. Aspes (ed.) *Settlement Patterns between the Alps and the Black Sea 5th to 2nd Millenium B.C.* (Memorie del Museo Civico di Storia Naturale di Verona, Sezione Scienze dell'Uomo 4): 67–75. Verona-Lazise: Museo Civico di Storia Naturale.

Kalicz, N. and P. Raczky 1984. Preliminary Report on the 1977–82 Excavations at the Neolithic and Bronze Age Tell Settlement of Berettyóújfalu-Herpály. Part I. Neolithic. *Acta Archaeologica Academiae Scientiarum Hungaricae* 36: 85–136.

Kalicz, N. and P. Raczky 1987a. The Late Neolithic of the Tisza region: A survey of recent archaeological research, in L. Tálas and P. Raczky (eds) *The Late Neolithic of the Tisza Region:* 11–29. Budapest and Szolnok: Kossuth Kiadó and Szolnok County Museum.

Kalicz, N. and P. Raczky 1987b. Berettyóújfalu-Herpály: A settlement of the Herpály culture, in L. Tálas and P. Raczky (eds) *The Late Neolithic of the Tisza Region:* 105–125. Budapest and Szolnok: Kossuth Kiadó and Szolnok County Museum.

Kállay, Á.S. 1988. Rézkori áldozati leletegyüttes Füzesabony határában (Kupferzeitlicher Opferfundkomplex in der Gemarkung von Füzesabony). *Agria* 24: 21–50.

Keeley, L. 1996. *War Before Civilization.* New York: Oxford University Press.

Keener, C. 1999. An Ethnohistorical Analysis of Iroquois Assault Tactics Used against Fortified Settlements of the Northeast in the Seventeenth Century. *Ethnohistory* 46(4): 777–807.

Kent, S. (ed.) 1990. *Domestic Architecture and the Use of Space: An Interdisciplinary Cross-Cultural Study.* Cambridge: Cambridge University Press.

Kent, S. 1992. Studying Variability in the Archaeological Record: An Ethnoarchaeological Model for Distinguishing Mobility Patterns. *American Antiquity* 57(4): 635–660.

Kent, S. 1999. The Archaeological Visibility of Storage: Delineating Storage from Trash Areas. *American Antiquity* 64(1): 79–94.

Kowalewski, S.A. 2006. Coalescent Societies, in T.J. Pluckhahn and R. Ethridge (eds) *Light on the Path: The Anthropology and History of the Southeastern Indians:* 94–122. Tuscaloosa: University of Alabama Press.

Kuijt, I. 2000. People and Space in Early Agricultural Villages: Exploring Daily Lives, Community Size, and Architecture in the Late Pre-Pottery Neolithic. *Journal of Anthropological Archaeology* 19(1): 75–102.

LaMotta, V.M. and M.B. Schiffer 1999. Formation processes of house floor assemblages, in P.N. Allison (ed.) *The Archaeology of Household Activities:* 19–29. London: Routledge.

Lichter, C. 2014. 'Temples' in the Neolithic and Copper Age in Southeast Europe? *Documenta Praehistorica* 41: 119–136.

Lowell, J.C. 1995. Illuminating Fire-Feature Variability in the Grasshopper Region of Arizona. *Kiva* 60(3): 351–369.

Lowell, J.C. 1999. The Fires of Grasshopper: Enlightening Transformations in Subsistence Practices through Fire-Feature Analysis. *Journal of Anthropological Archaeology* 18(4): 441–470.

Makkay, J. 1980–1981. Eine Kultstätte der Bodrogkeresztúr-Kultur in Szarvas und Fragen der sakralen Hügel. *Mitteilungen des Archäologischen Instituts der Ungarischen Akademie der Wissenschaften* 10–11: 45–57.

Martín, A.J. 2017. Population Nucleation and Functional Interdependence in Prehistoric Coastal Ecuador. *Social Evolution and History* 16(2): 20–51.

Martín, A.J. and M. Murillo Herrera 2014. Networks of interaction and functional interdependence in societies across the Intermediate Area. *Journal of Anthropological Archaeology* 36: 60–71.

Mellaart, J. 1967. *Çatal Hüyük. A Neolithic Town in Anatolia.* New York: McGraw-Hill.

Mesterházy, G., G. Serlegi, B. Vágvölgyi, A. Füzesi and P. Raczky 2019. A szociális folyamatok színterei Polgár-Csőszhalom késő neolitikus településének összefüggéseiben (Arenas of Social Dynamics on the Late Neolithic Settlement of Polgár-Csőszhalom). *Archaeologiai Értesítő* 144(1): 1–32.

Meyer, C., C. Lohr, D. Gronenborn and K.W. Alt 2015. The massacre mass grave of Schöneck-Kilianstädten reveals new insights into collective violence in Early Neolithic Central Europe. *Proceedings of the National Academy of Sciences* 112(36): 11217–11222.

Milek, K.B. and H.M. Roberts 2013. Integrated geoarchaeological methods for the determination of site activity areas: a study of a Viking Age house in Reykjavik, Iceland. *Journal of Archaeological Science* 40(4): 1845–1865.

Müller, J., R. Hofmann, N. Müller-Scheeßel and K. Rassmann 2013. Neolithische Arbeitsteilung: Spezialisierung in einem Tell um 4900 v. Chr, in A. Anders and G. Kulcsár (eds) *Moments in Time: Papers Presented to Pál Raczky on His 60th Birthday* (Ősrégészeti Tanulmányok/Prehistoric Studies 1): 407–420. Budapest: L'Harmattan.

Naumov, G. 2013. Embodied Houses: the Social and Symbolic Agency of Neolithic Architecture in the Republic of Macedonia, in D. Hofmann and J. Smyth (eds) *Tracking the Neolithic House in Europe: Sedentism, Architecture and Practice:* 65–94. New York and Heidelberg: Springer.

Nicodemus, A., Zs.E. Kovács and R.W. Yerkes 2021. The Faunal Assemblages, in W.A. Parkinson, A. Gyucha and R.W. Yerkes (eds) *Bikeri: Two Early Copper Age Villages on the Great Hungarian Plain:* 317–346. Los Angeles: Cotsen Institute of Archaeology at UCLA.

Niekamp, A. and A. Sarris 2014. Utilizing Magnetic Prospection and GIS to Examine Settlement Organization in Neolithic Southeastern Europe, in F. Giligny, F. Djindjian, L. Costa, P. Moscati and S. Robert (eds) *CAA2014 21st Century Archaeology: Concepts, Methods and Tools:* 53–64. Oxford: Archaeopress.

Nolan, K.C. and B.G. Redmond 2015. Geochemical and geophysical prospecting at three multicomponent sites in the Southwestern Lake Erie Basin: A pilot study. *Journal of Archaeological Science: Reports* 2: 94–105.

Oetelaar, G.A. 1993. Identifying Site Structure in the Archaeological Record: An Illinois Mississippian Example. *American Antiquity* 58(4): 662–687.

Orschiedt, J. and M.N. Haidle 2006. The LBK Enclosure at Herxheim: Theatre of War or Ritual Centre? References from Osteoarchaeological Investigations. *Journal of Conflict Archaeology* 2(1): 153–167.

Parker, B.J. and N. Sharratt 2017. Fragments of the Past: Microartifact Analysis of Use Surfaces at Tumilaca la Chimba, Moquegua, Peru. *Advances in Archaeological Practice* 5(1): 71–92.

Parkinson, W.A. 2002. Integration, Interaction, and Tribal 'Cycling:' The Transition to the Copper Age on the Great Hungarian Plain, in W.A. Parkinson (ed.) *The Archaeology of Tribal Societies* (Archaeological Series 15): 391–438. Ann Arbor (MI): International Monographs in Prehistory.

Parkinson, W.A. 2006. *The Social Organization of Early Copper Age Tribes on the Great Hungarian Plain* (BAR International Series 1573). Oxford: Archaeopress.

Parkinson, W.A. and P.R. Duffy 2007. Fortifications and Enclosures in European Prehistory: A Cross-Cultural Perspective. *Journal of Archaeological Research* 15(2): 97–141.

Parkinson, W.A. and A. Gyucha 2012a. Long-Term Social Dynamics and the Emergence of Hereditary Inequality: A Prehistoric Example from the Carpathian Basin, in T.K. Kienlin and A. Zimmermann (eds) *Beyond Elites: Alternatives to Hierarchical Systems in Modelling Social Formations* (Universitätsforschungen zur prähistorischen Archäologie 215): 243–249. Bonn: Dr. Rudolf Habelt.

Parkinson, W.A. and A. Gyucha 2012b. Tells in Perspective: Long-Term Patterns of Settlement Nucleation and Dispersal in Central and Southeast Europe, in R. Hofmann, F.-K. Moetz and J. Müller (eds) *Tells: Social and Environmental Space* (Universitätsforschungen zur prähistorischen Archäologie 207): 105–116. Bonn: Dr. Rudolf Habelt.

Parkinson, W.A., A. Gyucha, R.W. Yerkes, M.R. Morris, A. Sarris and R.B. Salisbury 2010. Early Copper Age Settlements in the Körös Region of the Great Hungarian Plain. *Journal of Field Archaeology* 35(2): 164–183.

Parkinson, W.A., W.P. Ridge and A. Gyucha 2018. Village nucleation and centralisation in the Later Neolithic of South-Eastern Europe: A long-term, comparative approach, in S. Dietz, F. Mavridis, Ž. Tankosić and T. Takaoğlu (eds) *Communities in Transition: The Circum-Aegean Area during the 5th and 4th Millennia BC:* 17–26. Oxford: Oxbow Books.

Parkinson, W.A., R.W. Yerkes and A. Gyucha 2004. The Transition to the Copper Age on the Great Hungarian Plain: The Körös Regional Archaeological Project Excavations at Vésztő-Bikeri and Körösladány-Bikeri, Hungary, 2000–2002. *Journal of Field Archaeology* 29(1): 101–121.

Pauketat, T.R. 2003. Resettled Farmers and the Making of a Mississippian Polity. *American Antiquity* 68(1): 39–66.

Pauknerová, K., R.B. Salisbury and M. Baumanová 2013. Human-landscape interaction in prehistoric Central Europe: analysis of natural and built environments. *Anthropologie* 51(2): 131–142.

Porčić, M. 2019. Evaluating Social Complexity and Inequality in the Balkans between 6500 and 4200 BC. *Journal of Archaeological Research* 27(3): 335–390.

Raczky, P. 1987. Öcsöd-Kováshalom: A settlement of the Tisza culture, in L. Tálas and P. Raczky (eds) *The Late Neolithic of the Tisza Region:* 61–83. Budapest and Szolnok: Kossuth Kiadó and Szolnok County Museum.

Raczky, P. 1995. Neolithic settlement patterns in the Tisza region of Hungary, in A. Aspes (ed.) *Settlement Patterns between the Alps and the Black Sea 5th to 2nd Millenium B.C.* (Memorie del Museo Civico di Storia Naturale di Verona, Sezione Scienze dell'Uomo 4): 77–86. Verona-Lazise: Museo Civico di Storia Naturale.

Raczky, P. 2009. Archaeological Data on Space Use at a Tell-Like Settlement of the Tisza Culture (New results from Öcsöd-Kováshalom, Hungary), in F. Draşovean, D.L. Ciobotaru and M. Maddison (eds) *Ten Years After: The Neolithic of the Balkans as Uncovered by the Last Decade of Research* (Bibliotheca Historica et Archaeologica Banatica 49): 101–124. Timişoara: Editura Marineasa.

Raczky, P. and A. Anders 2008. Late Neolithic spatial differentiation at Polgár-Csőszhalom, eastern Hungary, in D.W. Bailey, A. Whittle and D. Hofmann (eds) *Living Well Together? Settlement and Materiality in the Neolithic of South-East and Central Europe:* 35–53. Oxford: Oxbow Books.

Raczky, P. and A. Anders 2009. Régészeti kutatások egy késő neolitikus településen – Polgár-Bosnyákdomb (Előzetes jelentés) (Archaeological research at a late neolithic settlement – Polgár-Bosnyákdomb (Preliminary report). *Archaeologiai Értesítő* 134(1): 5–21.

Raczky, P. and A. Anders 2010. Activity loci and data for spatial division at a Late Neolithic site-complex (Polgár-Csőszhalom: a case study), in S. Hansen (ed.) *Leben auf dem Tell als soziale Praxis* (Kolloquien zur Vor- und Frühgeschichte 14): 143–163. Bonn: Dr. Rudolf Habelt.

Raczky, P. and A. Anders 2014. Szentpéterszeg-Kovadomb. Egy késő neolitikus lelőhely tér-képei (Szentpéterszeg-Kovadomb. Image-scapes of a Late Neolithic settlement), in A. Anders, Cs. Balogh and A. Türk (eds) *Avarok Pusztái: Régészeti tanulmányok Lőrinczy Gábor 60. születésnapjára:* 23–42. Budapest: Martin Opitz Kiadó.

Raczky, P. and A. Anders 2016. Polgár-Bosnyákdomb, a Late Neolithic tell-like settlement on Polgár Island (NE Hungary). Preliminary results of the investigations. *Folia Quaternaria* 84: 99–122.

Raczky, P., A. Anders, K. Sebők, P. Csippán and Zs. Tóth 2015. The Times of Polgár-Csőszhalom. Chronologies of Human Activities in a Late Neolithic Settlement in Northeastern Hungary, in S. Hansen, P. Raczky, A. Anders and A. Reingruber (eds) *Neolithic and Copper Age between the Carpathians and the Aegean Sea. Chronologies and Technologies from the 6th to the 4th Millennium BCE* (Archäologie in Eurasien 31): 21–48. Bonn: Dr. Rudolf Habelt.

Raczky, P. and A. Füzesi 2016. Öcsöd-Kováshalom: A retrospective look at the interpretations of a Late Neolithic site. *Dissertationes Archaeologicae* 3(4): 9–42.

Raczky, P., A. Füzesi and A. Anders 2018. Domestic and Symbolic Activities on a Tell-Like Settlement at Öcsöd-Kováshalom in the Tisza Region, in S.A. Luca (ed.) *The Image of Divinity in the Neolithic and Eneolithic. Ways of Communication*: 117–140. Suceava: Editura Karl A. Romstorfer.

Raczky, P. and K. Sebők 2014. The outset of Polgár-Csőszhalom tell and the archaeological context of a special central building, in S. Forţiu and A. Cintar (eds) *ArheoVest II: In Honorem Gheorghe Lazarovici. Interdisciplinaritate în Arheologie*: 51–100. Szeged: JATEPress Kiadó.

Rebay-Salisbury, K., A. Brysbaert and L. Foxhall (eds) 2014. *Knowledge Networks and Craft Traditions in the Ancient World: Material Crossovers*. London: Routledge.

Riggs, C.R. 2007. Architecture and Identity at Grasshopper Pueblo, Arizona. *Journal of Anthropological Research* 63(4): 489–513.

Riggs, C.R. 2017. Hearths, 'Kivas,' and Households at the Pigg Site: An Architectural Strong Analytical Case from Southwest Colorado, in M.B. Schiffer, C.R. Riggs and J.J. Reid (eds) *The Strong Case Approach in Behavioral Archaeology*: 87–103. Salt Lake City: University of Utah Press.

Salisbury, R.B. 2001. Lithic and Ceramic Cross-Mends at the Eaton Site. *The Bulletin: Journal of the New York State Archaeological Association* 117: 49–56.

Salisbury, R.B. 2012. Soilscapes and settlements: remote mapping of activity areas in unexcavated small farmsteads. *Antiquity* 86(331): 178–190.

Salisbury, R.B. 2013. Interpolating geochemical patterning of activity zones at Late Neolithic and Early Copper Age settlements in eastern Hungary. *Journal of Archaeological Science* 40(2): 926–934.

Salisbury, R.B. 2016. *Soilscapes in Archaeology: Settlement and Social Organization in the Neolithic of the Great Hungarian Plain* (Prehistoric Research in the Körös Region 3). Budapest: Archaeolingua.

Salisbury, R.B. 2017. Links in the chain: evidence for crafting and activity areas in late prehistoric cultural soilscapes, in A. Gorgues, K. Rebay-Salisbury and R.B. Salisbury (eds) *Material chains in late prehistoric Europe and the Mediterranean: time, space, and technologies of production* (Mémoires 48): 47–65. Bordeaux: Ausonius Éditions.

Salisbury, R.B., G. Bertók and G. Bácsmegi 2013. Integrated Prospection Methods to Define Small-Site Settlement Structure: a Case Study from Neolithic Hungary. *Archaeological Prospection* 20(1): 1–10.

Salisbury, R.B. and W. Engelbrecht 2018. Broken points and social cohesion in Iroquoian villages: A point refit study. *Journal of Anthropological Archaeology* 51: 104–112.

Sampietro, M.M. and M.A. Vattuone 2005. Reconstruction of activity areas at a formative household in northwest Argentina. *Geoarchaeology* 20(4): 337–354.

Sarris, A., N. Papadopoulos, A. Agapiou, M.C. Salvi, D.G. Hadjimitsis, W.A. Parkinson, R.W. Yerkes, A. Gyucha and P.R. Duffy 2013. Integration of geophysical surveys, ground hyperspectral measurements, aerial and satellite imagery for archaeological prospection of prehistoric sites: the case study of Vésztő-Mágor Tell, Hungary. *Journal of Archaeological Science* 40(3): 1454–1470.

Schiffer, M.B. 1987. *Formation Processes of the Archaeological Record*. Albuquerque: University of New Mexico Press.

Sevara, C., G. Verhoeven, M. Doneus and E. Draganits 2018. Surfaces from the Visual Past: Recovering High-Resolution Terrain Data from Historic Aerial Imagery for Multitemporal Landscape Analysis. *Journal of Archaeological Method and Theory* 25(2): 611–642.

Siklósi, Zs. 2013. *Traces of Social Inequality during the Late Neolithic in the Eastern Carpathian Basin* (Dissertationes Pannonicae Ser. IV. Vol. 3). Budapest: Eötvös Loránd University, Institute of Archaeological Sciences.

Smaldino, P.E. and R. McElreath 2016. The natural selection of bad science. *Royal Society Open Science* 3:160384, https://doi.org/10.1098/rsos.160384

Steele, L.D. 2007. The Neolithic settlement at Çatalhöyük and Pueblo ethnoarchaeology. *British School at Athens Studies* 15: 37–46.

Terry, R.E., D.A. Bair and E.G. Coronel 2015. Soil Chemistry in the Search for Ancient Maya Marketplaces, in E.M. King (ed.) *The Ancient Maya Marketplace: The Archaeology of Transient Space*: 138–167. Tucson: University of Arizona Press.

Timmins, P.A. 1997. *The Calvert Site: An Interpretive Framework for the Early Iroquoian Village* (Archaeological Survey of Canada Paper 156). Hull: Canadian Museum of Civilization.

Ullah, I.I.T. 2012. Particles of the past: microarchaeological spatial analysis of ancient house floors, in B.J. Parker and C.P. Foster (eds) *New Perspectives on Household Archaeology*: 123–138. Winona Lake (IN): Eisenbrauns.

Vyncke, K., P. Degryse, E. Vassilieva and M. Waelkens 2011. Identifying domestic functional areas. Chemical analysis of floor sediments at the Classical-Hellenistic settlement at Düzen Tepe (SW Turkey). *Journal of Archaeological Science* 38(9): 2274–2292.

Wilkinson, T.J., J. Ur and J. Casana 2004. From Nucleation to Dispersal: Trends in Settlement Pattern in the

Northern Fertile Crescent, in J.F. Cherry and S.E. Alcock (eds) *Side-by-Side Survey: Comparative Regional Studies in the Mediterranean World*: 195–205. Oxford: Oxbow Books.

Winter, M. 1976. The Archaeological Household Cluster in the Valley of Oaxaca, in K.V. Flannery (ed.) *The Early Mesoamerican Village*: 25–31. New York: Academic Press.

Woods, W.I. 2004. Population nucleation, intensive agriculture, and environmental degradation: The Cahokia example. *Agriculture and Human Values* 21(2): 255–261.

Yerkes, R.W., A Gyucha and K. Kasper 2021. The Floral Assemblages, in W.A. Parkinson, A. Gyucha and R.W. Yerkes (eds) *Bikeri: Two Early Copper Age Villages on the Great Hungarian Plain*: 347–364. Los Angeles: Cotsen Institute of Archaeology at UCLA.

Yerkes, R.W., A. Gyucha and W.A. Parkinson 2009. A Multiscalar Approach to Modeling the End of the Neolithic on the Great Hungarian Plain Using Calibrated Radiocarbon Dates. *Radiocarbon* 51(3): 1071–1109.

Yerkes, R.W., A. Sarris, T. Frolking, W.A. Parkinson, A. Gyucha, M. Hardy and L. Catanoso 2007. Geophysical and geochemical investigations at two early copper age settlements in the Körös River Valley, Southeastern Hungary. *Geoarchaeology* 22(8): 845–871.

Chapter 5

Population Aggregation and Social Transformations in Middle-Range Societies: A Comparative Study of Neolithic Nucleated Settlements on the Great Hungarian Plain

Attila Gyucha

Abstract

This study explores the evolution of prehistoric nucleated settlements and their impacts on long-term sociocultural developments in 'middle-range' village societies. The geographic focus is the Great Hungarian Plain where an overall tendency toward population aggregation occurred for the first time during the later Neolithic. I employ a multiscalar, diachronic, comparative approach to interpret information related to the built environment of the Late Neolithic (*c.* 5000–4500 BC) as it relates to the origins, development, and aftermath of nucleated sites. The analysis indicates highly similar settlement patterns in three different microregions but implies a great deal of variation in layout and organization at the site level. The models I propose to explain these patterns both highlight the significance of social behavioral principles in the gravitation of Neolithic populations toward centers and emphasize the underlying importance of preexisting sociocultural differences and the role of unique, site-level sociopolitical dynamics in community cohesion. I argue that divergent developments at large Late Neolithic settlements largely contributed to shifts in long-lasting cultural traditions across the Great Hungarian Plain during the transition between the Neolithic and Copper Age.

Introduction

Numerous studies of historical and modern settings demonstrate that population aggregation into urban sites was frequently generated by broad-scale societal changes. These studies also shed light on the unequaled capacities of cities to trigger leaps in sociocultural developments (Clark 2016; Fox 1977; Glaeser 2011; Mumford 1961; Pirenne 1952; Southall 1998), and similar interpretations have been invoked concerning urban centers in ancient civilizations (Algaze 2008; Creekmore and Fisher 2014; Marcus and Sabloff 2008; Smith 2003; Storey 2020; Yoffee 2017). The emergence and long-term impact of large, nucleated settlements within prehistoric, stateless societies, however, has been the focus of less, and much less systematic, research. In most contexts worldwide, it remains unclear whether the demographic processes that led to population aggregations within so-called 'middle-range' or village societies followed processes analogous to those in pre-modern and modern cities. Similarly, little research has been aimed directly at understanding whether the sociocultural trajectories of nucleated village sites produced social outputs similar to those in urban configurations within state-level societies.

Recent advances in archaeological field and analytical methods facilitate in addressing these questions.

These advances, in particular GIS, remote sensing, and absolute dating, enable us to study the spatial organization of archaeological sites at multiple social and geographic scales, from local to regional, within a diachronic framework. This paper takes advantage of these methodological developments while relying on the theoretical premises that the layout and architecture of settlements preserve the histories and traditions of the occupants, offering insights into social and political configurations and providing valuable information about cultural and ideological preferences (see, for example, Hillier and Hanson 1984; Kostof 1991; Lefebvre 1991; Parker Pearson and Richards 1994; Rapoport 1982, 1994).

In this paper, a multiscalar approach is applied to investigate the evolution of nucleated settlements on the Great Hungarian Plain during the Late Neolithic (*c.* 5000–4500 BC). Using information about the built environment at various scales, from house structures to regional settlement patterns, I assess: 1) how demographic processes paved the way for the evolution of nucleated settlements; 2) how sociopolitical processes generated specific architectural spatial configurations, and; 3) how cultural processes related to site structure and site histories. A comparative perspective is employed to make inferences about the degree of variation in the built space at Late Neolithic nucleated sites and to elucidate the origins of settlement

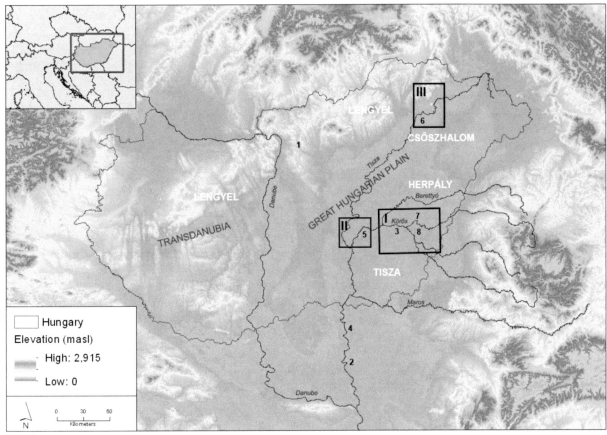

Figure 5.1. Sites, archaeological groups, and regions mentioned in the text.
I: Central Körös Valley; II: Tiszazug; III: Upper Tisza Valley; 1: Aszód-Papi földek; 2: Borđoš;
3: Csárdaszállás-Félhalomdűlő; 4: Čoka-Kremenjak; 5: Öcsöd-Kováshalom; 6: Polgár-Csőszhalom;
7: Szeghalom-Kovácshalom; 8: Vésztő-Mágor (figure by the author).

trajectories and the demographic, sociopolitical, and cultural processes behind these trajectories.

Specifically, I focus on three regions on the Great Hungarian Plain where archaeological datasets to study the critical aspects of Late Neolithic settlement developments at various scales are available: the Central Körös Valley, the Tiszazug, and the Upper Tisza Valley (Figure 5.1). In these areas, systematic surface surveys have yielded diachronic information about Neolithic settlement patterns. In addition, long-term, multidisciplinary archaeological research at the large, nucleated Late Neolithic sites of Szeghalom-Kovácshalom, Öcsöd-Kováshalom, and Polgár-Csőszhalom allows for productive analyses of settlement layout and organization in each of these regions.

The results indicate that although the initial impetus for aggregation may have been highly diverse, similar basic social behavioral motivations accounted for the later growth of large sites during the Late Neolithic, generating analogous, and roughly contemporaneous, settlement processes across the Great Hungarian Plain. At the local scale, however, a great degree of variability characterized the spatial development and organization of these sites. I suggest that differences in traditions

and social practices in local communities, a lack of shared cosmology and planning principles as well as disparities in political institutions and mechanisms to ensure social cohesion contributed to this variability. Finally, I argue that developments at these large settlements played a critical role in the overall cultural changes that unfolded throughout the region at the end of the Neolithic.

Nucleation on the Great Hungarian Plain in the Neolithic: The Archaeological Record

Spatial Organization at the Regional and Microregional Scales: Settlement Patterns

A trend toward nucleation of sedentary villagers occurred for the first time in Europe during the 7th millennium BC. This process is thought to have primarily been demonstrated by stratified tell sites, the earliest of which developed in Thessaly, Greece. With the spread of additional migratory groups, the Early Neolithic period brought about new farming settlements throughout southeastern Europe, including the formation of tells across the southern Balkans in the first half of the 6th millennium BC (Bailey 2000; Perlés 2001; Rosenstock 2006).

In other areas of southeastern Europe, for hundreds of years, early farming communities employed more mobile settlement strategies, with relatively frequent relocation of hamlets and small villages. Over the final centuries of the 6th millennium BC, however, large horizontal settlements and tell sites developed in these regions as well. During this time, the northernmost distribution of tells extended into the Great Hungarian Plain. As in other regions, tell formation on the Plain has been attributed to the permanent aggregation and lasting co-residence of previously dispersed groups (Makkay 1982; Parkinson and Gyucha 2012; Raczky 2015).

By the beginning of the 5th millennium BC, agglomeration processes peaked and farming villages unprecedented in size and population dominated the physical and social landscape of the Great Hungarian Plain for generations. These tells and large, horizontal sites, which we refer to as 'nucleated settlements,' developed in each of the three archaeologically defined Late Neolithic groups on the Great Hungarian Plain—the Tisza, Herpály, and Csőszhalom (see Figure 5.1; Kalicz 1995; Kalicz and Raczky 1987; Raczky 1992).

In the past few decades, a few regions of the Great Hungarian Plain have been subject to systematic, full-coverage archaeological surface surveys. These investigations have produced valuable datasets to study diachronic changes in settlement patterns, and permit us to explore the nucleated Late Neolithic settlements in their broader geographic contexts. Below, I review the available information concerning the development of Late Neolithic settlement patterns at the regional scale, as well as in specific microregions, within the Central Körös Valley, the Tiszazug, and the Upper Tisza Valley (see Figure 5.1).

The Central Körös Valley and the Szeghalom Microregion. Over the course of the Archaeological Topography of Hungary project (*Magyarország Régészeti Topográfiája,* hereafter MRT; Ecsedy *et al.* 1982; Jankovich *et al.* 1989, 1998; Szatmári in prep), the location and extent of archaeological sites were mapped for nearly 4000 km² in Békés County, including *c.* 2900 km² of the Central Körös Valley (see Figure 5.1). During the Late Neolithic, Tisza-type ceramic assemblages featured the majority of this region, while Herpály assemblages prevailed in the northeastern section.

The MRT dataset indicates a significant decrease in the number and increase in the size of settlements from the Middle Neolithic (*c.* 5500–5000 BC) to the Late Neolithic (*c.* 5000–4500 BC), and this has often been associated with nucleation processes across the Central Körös Valley (Gyucha *et al.* 2009; Parkinson 2006; Sherratt 1983). Recent regional analysis revealed spatially distinct settlement clusters in this area, with

12 contemporaneous nucleated sites, including tells and large, horizontal settlements, typically surrounded by small satellite sites and separated by 6 to 20 km from one another (Gyucha 2015). All nucleated Late Neolithic settlements were abandoned by no later than *c.* 4600/4500 BC, and small, highly dispersed villages prevailed in the Central Körös Valley during the subsequent Early Copper Age (*c.* 4500–4000 BC) (Gyucha *et al.* 2014; Parkinson *et al.* 2021).

I explored the settlement cluster in the Szeghalom microregion, located in the north-central section of the Central Körös Valley (Figure 5.2), to assess the scale of population aggregation from the Middle to the Late Neolithic. In this microregion, within a 5-km radius around the central Szeghalom-Kovácshalom tell site, 16 Middle Neolithic and one Late Neolithic, small, 0.5- to 2-ha settlements are known. When a 10-km radius is considered, the number of identified Middle Neolithic sites is 49, and the Late Neolithic sites include three hamlets and another tell site, Vésztő-Mágor (see Hegedűs and Makkay 1987).

Tiszazug and the Öcsöd Microregion. In the Tiszazug region, west of the Central Körös Valley, in the floodplain between the Körös River and the Tisza River, extensive surface surveys covered 564 km² (see Figure 5.1). Although the complete dataset has yet to be published, the surveys identified 178 Middle Neolithic and 11 Late Neolithic settlement sites, exhibiting remarkably similar densities of Middle and Late Neolithic sites in this region as those of the neighboring Central Körös Valley (Raczky and Füzesi 2016). Furthermore, the unoccupied zones between the large settlements of the three identified Late Neolithic spatial clusters in the Tiszazug also are similar in extent. Data regarding the Early Copper Age settlement pattern is currently unavailable for this area.

The microregion incorporated in the present study is centered on the large Öcsöd-Kováshalom settlement (Figure 5.3). One additional Late Neolithic site was identified within a 5-km radius of Öcsöd-Kováshalom. Concerning the preceding period, the surface surveys registered some 28 Middle Neolithic settlements in this area. When a 10-km radius is applied, there are 76 Middle Neolithic and three Late Neolithic sites.

The Upper Tisza Valley and the Polgár Island. The international Upper Tisza Project in the 1990s collected settlement data for an area of *c.* 3000 km² in northeastern Hungary (Chapman 1994; Chapman and Laszlovszky 2010). Surface surveys occurred in three spatially unconnected blocks. A specific microregion of about 67 km² within the Polgár Block, the alluvial plain of the Polgár Island near the Tisza River, has been subject to systematic archaeological research during the past decades (Füzesi *et al.* 2016); however, owing

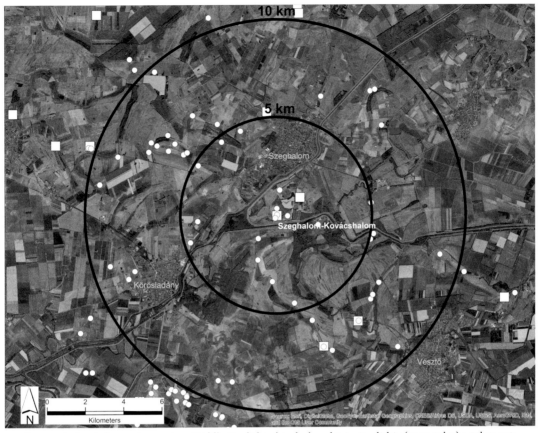

Figure 5.2. Szeghalom microregion: Middle Neolithic (circles) and Late Neolithic (rectangles) settlements in 5- and 10-km radius around Szeghalom-Kovácshalom (figure by the author).

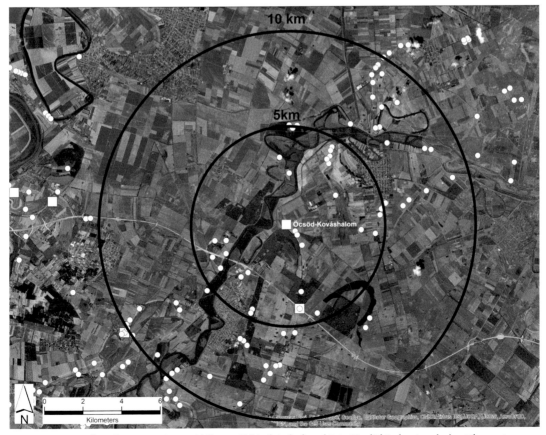

Figure 5.3. Öcsöd microregion: Middle Neolithic (circles) and Late Neolithic (rectangles) settlements in 5- and 10-km radius around Öcsöd-Kováshalom (figure by the author).

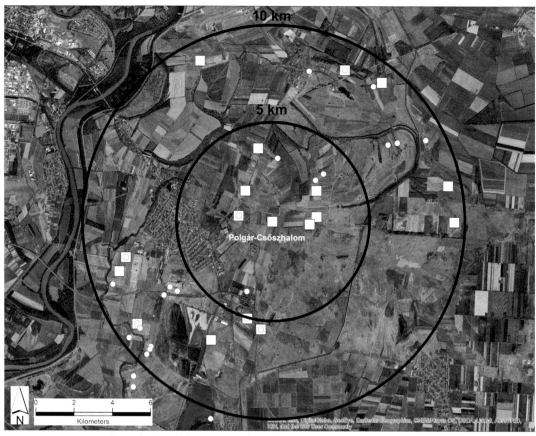

Figure 5.4. Polgár Island: Middle Neolithic (circles) and Late Neolithic (rectangles) settlements
in 5- and 10-km radius around Polgár-Csőszhalom (figure by the author).

to extensive grasslands, about 50% of the microregion was not surveyed (A. Füzesi, personal communication). The investigations on the Polgár Island have produced chronologically more refined results than in the Szeghalom and Öcsöd microregions (Raczky 2019). The earlier Middle Neolithic (ALP II–III) occupation of the Polgár Island is represented by some 20 sites, measuring 1 to 5 ha in extent. Nucleation of some of these villages seems to have occurred at the end of the Middle Neolithic (ALP IV), with a decrease in settlement number to eight and an increase in settlement size ranging from 5 to 10 ha (Raczky and Anders 2009). Population estimates suggest that 100 to 200 individuals lived at these sites (Raczky and Anders 2012). In the Late Neolithic, 18 sites, assigned to the Csőszhalom group, were inhabited on the Polgár Island; of these, the Polgár-Csőszhalom settlement complex is the largest (Figure 5.4). As in the Central Körös Valley, population dispersal from Polgár-Csőszhalom terminated by *c.* 4600/4500 BC, leading to a network of small, dispersed settlements in the landscape by the Early Copper Age (Raczky *et al.* 2014b).

Spatial Layout at the Local Scale: Settlement Organization

For nearly 100 years, research into the Late Neolithic focused on tell sites to a great extent throughout southeastern Europe. These studies provided initial insights into site layout, indicating typically densely occupied settlements. Population estimates for tells, commonly based on the horizontal extent and the extrapolation of the floor areas of exposed structures, range between about a hundred to a few thousand inhabitants (Hofmann 2015; Souvatzi 2008; Todorova and Vajsov 1993).

In the course of the past two decades, the scope of archaeological research has expanded beyond the spatial limits of tells across southeastern Europe (e.g., Hansen *et al.* 2010; Medović *et al.* 2014; Naumov 2016). These investigations—fueled by methodological advances, remote sensing in particular—have revealed that a majority of tells were not stand-alone sites but were integral parts of settlement complexes with a contemporaneous village in their immediate surroundings. In terms of size, these external sites bear a resemblance to the large horizontal settlements of the Late Neolithic without tells in their territories (e.g., Crnobrnja *et al.* 2009; Pappa and Besios 1999). In several cases, these horizontal sites have multiple tell-like mounds within their confines (e.g., Sherratt 1984).

Information from the increasing number and expanding scale of state-of-the-art investigations on the Great Hungarian Plain provides us with an opportunity to begin to reconstruct the spatial organization of Late Neolithic nucleated settlements and to make inferences about the social processes that contributed to their evolution. Below, I summarize the available information about settlement layout and organization from the nucleated Late Neolithic sites of Szeghalom-Kovácshalom, Öcsöd-Kováshalom, and Polgár-Csőszhalom. These sites are located in microregions with data on settlement patterns described above and have been subject to extensive geophysical prospection, systematic surface survey, and excavation that permit us to discuss site size, layout, and chronological development. Although several other Late Neolithic nucleated sites have recently been explored on the Great Hungarian Plain (Draşovean and Schier 2010; Hofmann et al. 2019a; Marić et al. 2016; Neumann et al. 2014; Raczky and Anders 2014; Schier and Draşovean 2020; Stanković Pešterac et al. 2014), their current state of research and/or the published results do not allow for addressing settlement development from a multiscalar perspective.

Szeghalom-Kovácshalom. The Szeghalom-Kovácshalom tell, located in the Central Körös Valley (see Figure 5.1), has been studied from the beginning of the 20th century (Bakay 1971; Darnay 1905; Szeghalmi 1913a, 1913b). Throughout the past decade, systematic gridded surface collections, geophysical and geochemical surveys as well as targeted excavations have been conducted on and around the tell (Gyucha et al. 2015, 2019; Papadopoulos et al. 2014; Parkinson et al. 2018; Salisbury 2016).

The tell is located along a paleochannel of the Sebes-Körös River and covers 1.25 ha (Figure 5.5). The current stratigraphic sequence measures a maximum of 3.5 m in thickness. Recent studies, based on the integration of data from old excavations and new research, indicate that the tell was a residential site during its early use (c. 5200/5100 to 4950/4900 BC) (Gyucha et al. 2019; Parkinson et al. 2018). Later, a moat was built to encircle the tell, and subsequent campaigns of extensive sediment depositions resulted in the elevation of the tell. In this stage (c. 4950/4900 to 4850/4800 BC), primarily non-profane, communal activities were performed at the site. In the final phase of its Neolithic development, a graveyard was established on the tell.

Gridded surface surveys and geophysical prospection demonstrated that an external settlement developed around the tell, extending across a total of c. 90 ha (Gyucha et al. 2015). In addition to anomalies interpreted

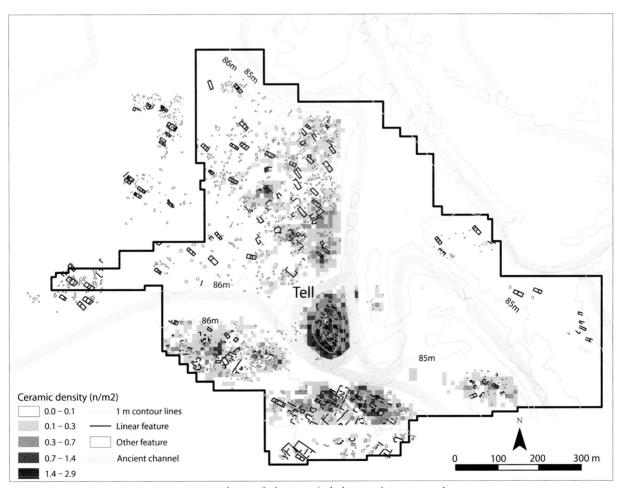

Figure 5.5. The Szeghalom-Kovácshalom settlement complex
(adapted from Gyucha et al. 2019).

as pits, kilns, hearths, and wells, the magnetic survey identified nearly 170 rectilinear, typically northwest–southeast oriented anomalies interpreted as structures (see Figure 5.5). These anomalies represent exclusively burned buildings and unburnt structures have not been identified, therefore, the total number of structures might have been greater at the site. The ceramic assemblages from the gridded surface collections and excavations, as well as radiocarbon dates from a number of exposed structures, have established that the overwhelming majority of these buildings were constructed in the Late Neolithic. The size of the structures across the external settlement ranges between 12 and 859 m², with an average of 97 m²; most of the clearly identifiable architectural magnetic anomalies measure 60 to 200 m². Spatial and statistical analyses indicate clusters of buildings, arranged around an empty space in several cases (Niekamp and Sarris 2015).

Absolute chronological studies revealed that the initial occupation at the external settlement occurred at the turn of the 6th and 5th millennia BC (Gyucha *et al.* 2019). The early structures were constructed close to the tell and at higher elevations along the Sebes-Körös River. Occupation at lower elevations farther from the tell and the river developed gradually over time. Along with Tisza materials, the surface collections and excavations confirmed the presence of non-local, Herpály style, sherds at the site.

Settlement expansion peaked after 4950/4900 BC at the external site, coinciding with the deliberate elevation of the tell and its transformation into a communal venue. The uppermost tell layers have been lost, likely due to erosion and plowing, and therefore, the termination date of the Neolithic tell development remains unknown. Radiocarbon dates from the external site indicate that the Szeghalom-Kovácshalom settlement complex was abandoned sometime after 4650/4600 BC.

Öcsöd-Kováshalom. Information about the internal organization of Öcsöd-Kováshalom, the largest Late Neolithic site in the Tiszazug region (see Figure 5.1), derives from surface collections, stratigraphic coring, geophysical prospection, and excavations (e.g., Füzesi and Raczky 2018; Füzesi *et al.* 2020a, 2020b; Raczky 1987, 2009; Raczky and Füzesi 2016; Raczky *et al.* 1985, 2018). The site, located along a Hármas-Körös River paleochannel, has eight, spatially distinct settlement nuclei of *c.* 0.3 to 0.9 ha, totaling 4–5 ha within an area of about 21 ha (Figure 5.6; Füzesi *et al.* 2020b). Coring suggests there were unoccupied areas between these settlement nuclei. A recent magnetic survey has revealed an arc of three concentric ditches at the site, with the outer ditch measuring 500 m and the inner ditch measuring 250 m in diameter. The ditches seem to have been made up of discontinuous segments and had several attached, round structures of 30–40 m in diameter along the outermost ditch (Raczky *et al.* 2018).

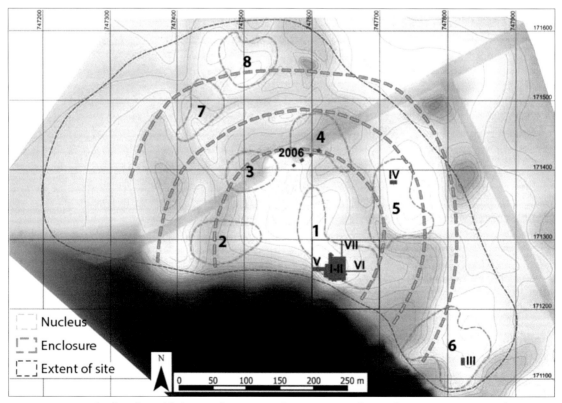

Figure 5.6. The Öcsöd-Kováshalom settlement complex. Roman numbers indicate excavation trenches, Arabic numbers mark settlement nuclei (modified from Füzesi and Raczky 2018 by the author).

It has been argued that the ditch segments were dug subsequently and were backfilled shortly after their construction over the course of communal campaigns to create a collective monument (Füzesi *et al.* 2020a, 2020b).

The central section of a nucleus in the southeastern part of Öcsöd-Kováshalom was extensively excavated. The anthropogenic layers included a variety of settlement features and constitute a tell-like stratigraphy of 1.3–1.6 m in depth. Two major construction phases (A and B) were defined, with northwest–southeast oriented, closely aligned buildings of *c.* 35 to 140 m² in size. A rectangular ditch with a fence that encircled these structures in Phase A was out of use during Phase B. Building density increased in this later phase. Both Phases A and B have been estimated to represent *c.* 100 years of occupation at this tell-like nucleus (Raczky and Füzesi 2016). Radiocarbon dates place the life span of the Öcsöd-Kováshalom settlement between 5200 and 4980 BC.

Polgár-Csőszhalom. The Polgár-Csőszhalom settlement complex is situated south of a Tisza River paleochannel in the Upper Tisza Valley (see Figure 5.1). The tell and the surrounding external settlement have been excavated since the 1950s and recent surface collections and geophysical surveys mapped the spatial extent and layout of the settlement complex (e.g., Bánffy and Bognár-Kutzián 2007; Füzesi *et al.* 2016; Mesterházy *et al.* 2019; Raczky 2018; Raczky and Anders 2008; Raczky *et al.* 1994, 2014a).

On the tell, the maximum thickness of vertical stratigraphy measures 3.6 to 4 m (Raczky 2018). The excavations uncovered a central, two-story structure with ritual objects that date to the initial stage of tell development (Raczky and Sebők 2014). Thereafter, 34 to 38 superimposing, small buildings were erected in a radial pattern on the tell. Similar to the first-phase central structure, these buildings may have been burned down. In the later phase, no structures were constructed on the tell and, as seen at Szeghalom-Kovácshalom, the mound is thought to have been deliberately built up (Raczky 2018; Raczky *et al.* 2011). Magnetic prospection revealed a palisaded multiditch system with four entrances around the tell (Figure 5.7). The enclosure, and hence the horizontal dimension of the tell, is believed to have been expanded over time. The number of ditches changed from one to three and the enclosed area increased from 20–25 to 180–190 m in diameter. The construction and use of the tell–enclosure unit date between *c.* 4900/4800 and 4500/4450 BC (Raczky *et al.* 2015).

Based on information collected during surface surveys and magnetic prospection, the external settlement covered *c.* 67 ha around the tell (Figure 5.7; Füzesi *et al.* 2016; Raczky 2018). In the eastern section of the site, highway salvage work exposed an area of *c.* 3.3 ha, uncovering 80 Late Neolithic unburnt houses and other features associated with the buildings (Raczky and Anders 2008, 2010; Raczky *et al.* 2011). The excavations and recent geophysical studies indicate rows and clusters of northwest–southeast oriented structures, ranging between *c.* 5–7-x–10–15 m in size (Füzesi *et al.* 2016; Raczky and Anders 2010). Based on extrapolation, *c.* 400 houses are assumed to have been constructed across the external site in the Late Neolithic (Raczky 2019). A circular, double-ditch enclosure of 40-x-60 m in diameter also was identified by the geophysical survey

Figure 5.7. The Polgár-Csőszhalom settlement complex. 1: Enclosed tell; 2: Ditch and palisade
enclosure in the horizontal site (modified from Mesterházy *et al.* 2019 by the author).

in the western section of the settlement (Füzesi *et al.* 2016).

Radiocarbon samples from the eastern part of the horizontal settlement yielded dates between *c.* 4900 and 4700 BC, indicating a north–south expansion of the site over time, with the earliest features located along the river (Raczky *et al.* 2015). However, samples from the double-ditch enclosure west of the tell date to *c.* 4700–4600 BC (Raczky *et al.* 2014a), implying chronological differences between the use of the eastern and western settlement zones as well.

Marked differences have been proposed for the use of the tell and the external settlement. It is argued that residential activities occurred at the external site, while the tell was a locale for ceremonies and rituals (Raczky 2019; Raczky and Anders 2006, 2008; Raczky *et al.* 2011). In addition, ceramic studies revealed an abundance of objects with stylistic elements from an array of neighboring and more remote regions. The architectural design of the enclosure system around the tell also is interpreted as evidence for interactions between the local Csőszhalom and Lengyel communities who lived west of the Upper Tisza Valley and in Transdanubia (Raczky 2002; Raczky *et al.* 2007, 2015).

Nucleation on the Great Hungarian Plain during the Neolithic: Interpretation

The Evolution of Late Neolithic Settlement Patterns

The results of systematic surface surveys in the Central Körös Valley, the Tiszazug, and the Polgár Island indicate the permanent aggregation of numerous, previously dispersed, small-scale Neolithic communities into a few, large settlements. A general trend toward nucleation began already in the later phase of the Middle Neolithic, around 5200/5100 BC, on the Great Hungarian Plain and this process climaxed at the beginning of the 5th millennium BC. The radical decrease in site number from the Middle to the Late Neolithic in each studied area suggests that the primary source of influx into these nucleated centers likely were the settlements located in the immediate microregions, *c.* 5–10 km in radius.

Scholars regularly argue for the focal roles of nucleated sites in their respective microregions regarding political organization, communal and ritual performances, and interregional interaction across southeastern Europe (Chapman 1994; Link 2006: 72–73; Meier-Arendt 1991; Müller 2017; Runnels *et al.* 2009; Starnini *et al.* 2015; Whittle 1996, 2018). The Late Neolithic settlement patterns on the Great Hungarian Plain permit us to assume that these sites—including tells and large, commonly tell-centered, settlement complexes—

functioned as centers of autonomous political units. Small, contemporaneous sites frequently occurred in their proximity (e.g., Gyucha 2015; Kalicz and Raczky 1987; Makkay 1982), but the lack of systematic research into the relationship between the nucleated centers and these 'satellite' sites makes it difficult to comment on how they interacted. Based on data from the Central Körös Valley and the Tiszazug, Late Neolithic political units on the Great Hungarian Plain may have extended over a couple of hundred square kilometers and their centers may have been inhabited by 70–100% of these units' total population.

These political units appear to have been spatially separated (Gyucha 2015; Gyucha *et al.* 2014; Parkinson 2006), but they were not isolated. The shared material culture and practices within each of the three major contemporaneous archaeological groups on the Plain (i.e., Tisza, Herpály, Csőszhalom) imply intensive interactions among them. In addition, recent stylistic, compositional, and technological analyses of various materials provided evidence for regular interactions across the boundaries of the Tisza and Herpály groups (Riebe 2021).

In the course of these interactions, the permanent movement of people through sociopolitical and cultural boundaries also commonly occurred. When relocation took place between communities producing highly similar material culture, its scale and regularity are notoriously difficult to ascertain in the archaeological record. Nevertheless, it tends to reveal itself when movements occurred between communities featuring marked differences in technology and decorative style. In this regard, recent studies of pottery from Aszód-Papi földek have provided important data. This large Late Neolithic site is located in the contact zone of the Tisza and Lengyel archaeological groups (see Figure 5.1), and attributes of both decorative styles are commonly present in its ceramic assemblage (Kalicz 1985, 2008). Petrographic studies of numerous samples demonstrated that each studied vessel was produced locally (Kreiter *et al.* 2017), suggesting the co-residence and admixture of Tisza and Lengyel groups at Aszód-Papi földek. Similar, stylistically mixed assemblages are known from other Late Neolithic sites in the contact zones between major archaeological groups, including Szeghalom-Kovácshalom and Polgár-Csőszhalom (see above) as well as several other nucleated sites in northern Serbia, such as Borđoš and Čoka-Kremenjak (Banner 1960; Hofmann *et al.* 2019a; Medović *et al.* 2014; see also Mirković-Marić and Marić 2017). Thus, the archaeological record from sites situated in the boundary zones of groups with markedly distinctive material culture testifies to a significant degree and high frequency of residential mobility during the Late Neolithic not only within these zones but likely across the entire Great Hungarian Plain. These data also indicate that population movement frequently drifted toward large centers from both neighboring microregions and more remote areas.

Late Neolithic nucleated settlements were abandoned around the middle of the 5th millennium BC throughout the Plain. As survey data from the Central Körös Valley and Polgár Island illustrate, by the Early Copper Age, dispersed settlement patterns developed, with much smaller and more ephemeral sites (Kovács 2016; Parkinson et al. 2010, 2021; Szilágyi 2010). Regional-scale, diachronic settlement studies from the Central Körös region show that many of the spatially distinct clusters of Early Copper Age villages occurred in the same territories that were occupied during the Late Neolithic (Gyucha 2015; Gyucha et al. 2014). These clusters might exemplify the perpetuation of Late Neolithic higher-order political units into the Copper Age.

The Evolution of Late Neolithic Nucleated Settlements

Settlement data from Szeghalom-Kovácshalom, Öcsöd-Kováshalom, and Polgár-Csőszhalom indicates a high degree of variation at different scales—from household and neighborhood organization to overall settlement layout—at the large, nucleated Late Neolithic settlements on the Great Hungarian Plain.

Both within and between these sites, marked variability characterized the organization of households. Buildings at each studied site exhibit a broad range of sizes, with some structures several times larger than the smallest ones. Although functional differences also may in part be responsible for this pattern, excavations indicate that the majority of structures were residential (i.e., houses). When average floor areas are compared between sites, buildings at the external Szeghalom-Kovácshalom site appear to have been much larger than those in other regions of the Great Hungarian Plain. Although data from systematic statistical studies currently are available solely from Szeghalom-Kovácshalom, the average floor area at Öcsöd-Kováshalom and Polgár-Csőszhalom may have been 10–30% smaller than that of Szeghalom-Kovácshalom, and when the majority of structures are considered, this value might be 65–70%. Buildings at other Late Neolithic settlements on the Plain typically also are significantly smaller than those at Szeghalom-Kovácshalom (e.g., Kalicz and Raczky 1984; Medović et al. 2014; Niekamp and Sarris 2015), however, some larger structures were constructed at several sites (for an overview, see Kalicz and Kovács 2010). Furthermore, as Tisza settlements across the Central Körös Valley demonstrate, including Szeghalom-Kovácshalom, Öcsöd-Kováshalom, as well as Csárdaszállás-Félhalomdűlő with several structures of c. 160 square meters (Salisbury et al. 2013b; see also Salisbury, this volume), houses were organized and used

differently even within a single archaeological group where otherwise people shared very similar material culture and social practices.

Within settlements, neighborhoods composed of multiple households have been recorded at large Late Neolithic sites, however, their layout and organization differed. At Öcsöd-Kováshalom, the eight neighborhoods were separated spatially from one another by tens of meters, and this arrangement seems to have persisted over the course of the entire life span of the settlement. By contrast, at Szeghalom-Kovácshalom, unoccupied zones between the neighborhoods appear to have been much smaller, and, as their less pronounced presence in the central zones of the external settlement indicates, neighborhood organization changed over time. At these two sites, the internal spatial arrangement of neighborhoods also differed substantially. At Szeghalom-Kovácshalom, several of the neighborhoods were laid out surrounding small plazas, whereas at Öcsöd-Kováshalom, central, empty spaces were absent, and fenced household units were constructed. Concerning the external settlement at Polgár-Csőszhalom, although the organization of individual households—with residential structures and additional features, such as wells, pits, and burials—is well established, sufficient data to elucidate neighborhood layout and organization is currently unavailable. Regarding integrative architecture, although structures interpreted as shrines were unearthed on some Late Neolithic tells (Hegedűs and Makkay 1987; Lazarovici and Lazarovici 2004), similar features associated with specific neighborhoods have not been identified at contemporaneous settlements on the Great Hungarian Plain.

Similar to households and neighborhoods, settlement-scale layout and organization also exhibit a high degree of variation at the three studied sites. The formation of thick strata in the central zones and how these formation processes related to community development likely differed at each site. At Öcsöd-Kováshalom, the tell-like nucleus is interpreted as a residential area that was occupied permanently for several centuries, where recurrent construction and destruction episodes accounted for the formation of the anthropogenic sequence. By contrast, at Szeghalom-Kovácshalom, though similar processes led to tell development in the initial phase, this was followed by deliberate mounding and a functional shift toward the use of the tell as a communal space. Like this latter phase at Szeghalom-Kovácshalom, the evolution of the Polgár-Csőszhalom tell is understood as the creation of a central place for ceremonial activities through the construction of a mound and an enclosure system (e.g., Raczky et al. 2011). Shared aspects among these sites include the development of large villages tethered to the central loci a few generations after the initial settlement phases as well as the northwest–southeast orientation of structures in these external settlements.

Finally, large-scale construction works that required a great expenditure of labor occurred at each studied Late Neolithic site. The deliberate elevation of tells and the construction of ditches, and possibly ramparts, would have demanded the lasting participation of a large proportion or the entirety of the local communities. However, as with features at the household and neighborhood levels, the structural attributes of enclosures at Late Neolithic sites reflect a high degree of variation. The moat around the Szeghalom-Kovácshalom tell, the Polgár-Csőszhalom multiple enclosure system with clearly defined entrances encircling the tell, and the extremely large triple-ditch structure at Öcsöd-Kováshalom with gaps and attached round structures all reflect the concept of spatial demarcation, but they also represent substantially different design principles.

Modeling Variability in Settlement Patterns: Drivers of Nucleation in the Late Neolithic

The archaeological record does not support explanations that rely on push factors for the aggregation processes and the emergence of large sites on the Great Hungarian Plain at the beginning of the Late Neolithic. Neither settlement nor mortuary data indicate an increase in the degree of intergroup conflicts or encroachment from outside populations. Climate perturbations resulting in some hydrological changes may have occurred (see Gulyás and Sümegi 2011; Salisbury *et al.* 2013a), but there is no convincing evidence for a widespread shift in regional climatic and environmental conditions that would have required the agglomeration of dispersed communities into select, environmentally favorable locations.

Instead, the trend toward population nucleation at the turn of the 6th and 5th millennia BC may be explained by internal social processes that made a few villages more attractive than others. Similar to other parts of the world where large, permanent communities emerged through immigration, the social value of specific sites, related to their religious importance or their founding communities, could have been acted as a captivating 'magnet' (for similar mechanisms in other parts of the world, see Adler 1989; Düring 2013; Kelly 2019; see also Fernández-Götz, this volume). As in other cultural contexts (see Adler *et al.* 1996; Kusimba 2008; Sindbaek 2007; see also Fulminante, this volume), a high degree of connectedness of some settlement communities, resulting in better access to raw materials and other commodities through interregional exchange networks, also could have triggered aggregation.

Testing any hypotheses concerning the *original impetus for nucleation* to the Late Neolithic magnet sites is a problematic endeavor. It is particularly because its archaeological correlates commonly are encapsulated into the lowermost sequence of multilayered sites, and these layers representing initial settlement phases have not been extensively excavated on the Great Hungarian Plain. Yet, based on diachronic studies on local-scale settlement organization and microregional settlement patterns, the *general process of nucleation* unfolded on the Plain through the influx and permanent settlement of small-scale, previously dispersed, more mobile and autonomous communities to a few select sites, predominantly from adjacent microregions. Below, I elaborate on this description and propose an explanation for this general process. A social behavioral approach that focuses on individual and group motivations as they relate to nucleation is used in order to elucidate the *impetus for population growth* at large Late Neolithic settlements after their initial stage of development.

The archaeological record indicates the lack of centralized political structures on the Great Hungarian Plain prior to the evolution of large Neolithic sites. The small, scattered village communities lived in egalitarian sociopolitical settings where intra- and intercommunity cooperation and solidarity were key adaptive mechanisms. In the absence of centralized political control, decisions about settlement relocation might have been made by the villagers or supra-village councils. Data from Szeghalom-Kovácshalom and Polgár-Csőszhalom suggest that the nucleated Late Neolithic settlements commonly grew large through subsequent inward flows of people from many of these villages, sometimes in the course of multiple generations. Over time, the original impetus for nucleation—religious, economic, or others in nature—may have been complemented, then overrode, by benefits that the new social configurations of large settlements offered.

Within these new contexts, the previous local- and microregional-scale networks composed of hamlets and villages, and bonded by kinship and other corporate affiliations, would have been fundamentally reorganized. That is to say, the former intercommunity social and economic networks that enabled the access of small and scattered communities to various resources and commodities, assured security and safety in bad times, provided marriage partners, and promoted communal activities were spatially rearranged and became consolidated at a single location in the landscape—the context of a nucleated settlement. Thus, these previous networks many times did not disintegrate—in particular during the initial stages of nucleation—but their nodes and lines were reconfigured and centered within the emerging large sites. The synergistic impact developed through the co-residence of individuals and groups that had participated in these networks rendered the nucleated Late Neolithic sites powerful entities where a wide range of socioeconomic institutions, mechanisms, and functions operated to ensure order and cohesion.

For groups who chose to continue living in isolated settings, the social and economic benefits of nucleated settlements, established and advanced through the actions and interactions of the initial-stage aggregated groups, were missed. Over time, they may have been treated differently by those who lived at and took part in the everyday life of large villages. The evolution of nucleated communities paved way for the formation and solidification of new identities and failing to actively participate in daily practices and face-to-face interactions might have resulted in these isolated groups becoming strangers. Therefore, they could not equally reap the benefits provided by these large sites, such as circulation of information and goods, participation in ritual activities, obtaining alliance in case of violent conflicts, or pooling resources after bad harvests. Under these circumstances, instead of the low cost of a great deal of spatially condensed interactions, interpreted as a major driver of urbanization worldwide and through the ages (e.g., Gaspar and Glaeser 1998; Ortman *et al.* 2014; Smith 2019), the high cost of exclusion would have incited permanent population aggregation to the large Late Neolithic settlements. Eventually, the displacement and reconfiguration of previous networks channeled the isolated groups into a social vacuum, which put them at stake in the long run. Thus, the *original impetus for nucleation* featured by a *want-to-join*, pull attitude might have switched to a *must-join*, push attitude as the paramount *impetus for population growth* at nucleated settlements.

Modeling Variability in Settlement Organization: The Outcomes of Nucleation in the Late Neolithic

While microregional settlement patterns evolved similarly likely due to analogous social processes, the high degree of organizational variability discerned on multiple scales at Late Neolithic large settlements on the Great Hungarian Plain—from household to neighborhood to settlement-scale organization—suggests profoundly divergent paths in local-scale social developments. The different trajectories may have emerged primarily due to two major factors: 1) differences in social and cultural practices and norms among subgroups at large sites that developed already prior to their aggregation, and 2) differences in mechanisms and institutions introduced during the course of the development of nucleated sites to secure community integrity and cohesion, in response to internal social dynamics.

Regarding preexisting differences, the archaeological record indicates marked variation with respect to the spatial organization of households and settlements on the Great Hungarian Plain before the Late Neolithic. The size and internal arrangements of households at Early Neolithic Körös and Middle Neolithic Alföld Linear Pottery sites exhibit overall similarities within each respective period across the region (Anders and Siklósi 2012; Domboróczki *et al.* 2017; Horváth 1989; Raczky 2006). By contrast, the later Middle Neolithic Szakálhát phase appears to have been characterized by a higher degree of variability (Hegedűs 1983; Horváth 1989; Szénászky 1979, 1988). This shift in the organization of households signals the discontinuation of former, widely practiced Neolithic traditions to more heterogeneous family unit configurations prior to the development of aggregated settlements at the end of the Middle Neolithic period.

Variation in neighborhood organization at the three sites considered in this paper suggests that aggregation and integration into the social fabric of large villages may have developed in different ways across the Great Hungarian Plain. Specifically, these processes may have occurred through the establishment of neighborhoods either by previously autonomous communities that lived in the same village or through the co-residence of multiple extended families stemming from different hamlets or villages. The occupants of these latter neighborhood units may have been linked by clan affiliations, and their aggregation many times could have been a gradual, sequential process. The archaeological record suggests that groups from outside particular microregions, with sometimes substantially different cultural traditions, also may have participated in the evolution of large Late Neolithic settlements.

Thus, the significant degree of variability documented in household and neighborhood organization at Szeghalom-Kovácshalom, Öcsöd-Kováshalom, and Polgár-Csőszhalom is reflective of the external demographic growth of these settlements. Moreover, this variability might be indicative of the co-residence of groups that in their earlier developments, frequently already during the later stage of the Middle Neolithic, had different ideas and preferences in respect to the social composition and related spatial organization of their households and settlements. In this way, the Late Neolithic nucleated sites may be understood as spatially realigned new confederacies (for similar processes, see Birch 2019), where novel, including in particular cohesive place-based, identities formed.

Concerning means of securing community integrity and cohesion, the high degree of variation in the overall layout and integrative architectures at nucleated Late Neolithic settlements on the Great

Hungarian Plain indicates a variety of responses and resolutions to mitigate and overcome challenges related to the co-residence of many hundreds, or sometimes thousands, of inhabitants (cf. Bandy 2004; Dunbar 2011; Feinman 2011; Johnson 1982). In contrast to these sites, the large settlements of many ancient middle-range and state-level societies exhibit a remarkable degree of organizational similarities, suggesting shared planning ideas and principles in place (e.g., Kenoyer 1991; Müller *et al.* 2018; Renfrew and Cherry 1986; Smith 2017; Snodgrass 2012: 234–257). The similar layout as well as the presence and regular spatial associations of specific architectural features and public spaces in these settlements usually are explained by centralized political control, peer-polity interaction, and shared cosmologies. While some architectural features and their associations (e.g., spatial separation of tells by enclosures) commonly occurred during the Late Neolithic, there were no shared ideas and resultant overarching design principles that would have regulated the initial layout and spatial growth of large sites across the Great Hungarian Plain. In fact, as the Tisza sites of Öcsöd-Kováshalom and Szeghalom-Kovácshalom illustrate, regular planning ideas were absent even within the sphere of specific regional cultural traditions. Instead, as the high degree of variation in settlement layouts and integrative features demonstrates, the occupants of these sites seem to have employed community-specific measures adapted to the local challenges that occurred as a result of increasing population size and density as well as sociocultural heterogeneity. Many of these measures can be considered as social innovations to develop and sustain group identity and integrity (see Gyucha 2019). Although some of these innovations may have been borrowed by multiple communities, the fundamentally different local trajectories prevented overall regularities from occurring in the organization of large Late Neolithic settlements.

Some integrative mechanisms to achieve social cohesion were similar at these sites. Conformity may have served as one of these mechanisms. The pursuit of conformity may be manifested in the common, northwest–southeast, alignment of buildings at many large Late Neolithic settlements throughout the Great Hungarian Plain (for an alternative interpretive scenario, see Vondrovský 2018). Although profound differences can be observed in their structure and use, the presence of integrative architecture is also a commonality at these sites. These features include enclosures, were created through the collective actions of the villagers, and are typically located in or near the oldest zones of nucleated sites, especially tells. Their construction frequently resulted in permanent communal spaces to provide social anchors for the occupants and ensure integrity. In addition

to individual households, these venues evidently were the loci of rituals, and other, more inclusive, ceremonies.

As opposed to many other prehistoric contexts worldwide (e.g., Adler 2002; Hofmann *et al.* 2019b; Manzanilla 2009), little archaeological evidence is available for neighborhood-level communal spaces where differing subgroup traditions would have been practiced. Thus, rituals seem to have been regulated, and possibly in some cases consolidated, at the settlement level. The only contemporaneous Late Neolithic large settlement with presumably multiple communal places is Polgár-Csőszhalom where ceremonies could have been performed by and/or for a different audience in the enclosure within the horizontal site than on the tell.

Concluding Remarks: Late Neolithic Nucleated Settlements as Arenas of Social and Cultural Change

The fusion of numerous, previously dispersed, communities into a few select places might have been fueled by similar social processes on the Great Hungarian Plain during the Late Neolithic. However, as the built environment of these sites indicate, radically unique settlement biographies grew out of these processes. The differences might have stemmed predominantly from the markedly divergent pathways in local-scale social and political developments. These pathways likely occurred due to the interplay between previous social and cultural differences among constituent groups as well as the development of social mechanisms and institutions over the course of individual settlement trajectories.

Nevertheless, the nucleated Late Neolithic settlements were not only dynamic 'laboratories' to advance new sociopolitical organizations to cope with challenges associated with population size, density, and heterogeneity. They also may have been catalysts for profound cultural shifts on the Great Hungarian Plain. Regionalization in material culture began as early as the Middle Neolithic and continued into the Late Neolithic, shedding light on increasing disparities in cultural values, belief systems, and associated symbols among societies in the macroregion (Kalicz and Makkay 1977; Kalicz and Raczky 1987; Parkinson 2006). The development of large Late Neolithic sites amplified these transformations—toward microscale cultural variations. This process evolved through the regular and lasting interactions of groups with diverse practices and traditions in the context of nucleated settlements. Over time, these interactions culminated in new ideas, narratives, and syntheses about the sociocultural evolution and history of the specific large communities. The built environment of Late Neolithic sites indicates that particular spots in the settlements, including many tells, were transformed into community-scale integrative monuments to link past, 'global' heritage with emerging, 'local' cultural values.

Microscale cultural variations occurring simultaneously at numerous centers on the Plain, and resulting in the formation of an array of profoundly different microtraditions, may have been the final, ultimate stimulant for the dissolution of the Neolithic worldview that had characterized the previous one and a half millennia. Thus, similar to ancient, pre-industrial, and modern cities (Boyar and Fleet 2010; de Souza Briggs 2004; Glaeser 2011; Hall 1998; Redfield and Singer 1954; Smith 2019; Wirth 1938), the Late Neolithic nucleated settlements of the Great Hungarian Plain with their large and diverse communities were configurations that triggered substantive sociocultural changes at the macroregional scale.

The disintegration of Neolithic worldview coincided with the abandonment of nucleated sites in the middle of the 5th millennium BC across the Plain. In regard to the built environment, small, dispersed villages were founded by neighborhood units that relocated from the large settlements (Gyucha et al. 2014; Parkinson et al. 2021). Although some elements of the Neolithic traditions persisted in these Early Copper Age villages (Gyucha 2015; Raczky and Anders 2012; Raczky et al. 2014b; Salisbury 2016), this process concurred with fundamental shifts in symbology, practices, and material culture (Bognár-Kutzián 1972). Over a few generations, microscale cultural variations were replaced by a markedly homogeneous, macroregional cultural tradition throughout the Great Hungarian Plain at the onset of the Copper Age.

Acknowledgments

I thank Pál Raczky and András Füzesi to provide access to regional settlement data for the Polgár Island and Tiszazug regions.

References Cited

Adler, M.A. 1989. Ritual Facilities and Social Integration in Nonranked Societies, in W.D. Lipe and M. Hegmon (eds) *The Architecture of Social Integration in Prehistoric Pueblos*: 35–52. Cortez (CO): Crow Canyon Archaeological Center.

Adler, M.A. 2002. Building Consensus: Tribes, Architecture, and Typology in the American Southwest, in W.A. Parkinson (ed.) *The Archaeology of Tribal Societies* (International Monographs in Prehistory, Archaeological Series 15): 155–172. Ann Arbor: University of Michigan.

Adler, M.A., T. van Pool and R.D. Leonard 1996. Ancestral Pueblo Population Aggregation and Abandonment in the North American Southwest. *Journal of World Prehistory* 10(3): 375–438.

Algaze, G. 2008. *Ancient Mesopotamia at the Dawn of Civilization: The Evolution of an Urban Landscape*. Chicago: University of Chicago Press.

Anders, A. and Zs. Siklósi (eds) 2012. *The First Neolithic Sites in Central/South-East European Transect. Vol. III. The Körös Culture in Eastern Hungary* (BAR International Series 2334). Oxford: Archaeopress.

Bailey, D.W. 2000. *Balkan Prehistory: Exclusion, Incorporation and Identity*. London: Routledge.

Bakay, K. 1971. A régészeti topográfia munkálatai Békés megyében 1969-ben. *Békés Megyei Múzeumok Közleményei* 1: 135–153.

Bandy, M.S. 2004. Fissioning, Scalar Stress, and Social Evolution in Early Village Societies. *American Anthropologist* 106(2): 322–333.

Bánffy, E. and I. Bognár-Kutzián 2007. *The Late Neolithic Tell Settlement at Polgár-Csőszhalom, Hungary. The 1957 Excavation* (BAR International Series S1730 and Central European Series 4). Oxford and Budapest: Archaeopress and Archaeolingua.

Banner, J. 1960. The Neolithic Settlement on the Kremenyák Hill at Csóka. *Acta Archaeologica Academiae Scientiarum Hungaricae* 12: 1–56.

Birch, J. 2019. Settlement Aggregation and Geopolitical Realignment in the Northeastern Woodlands, in A. Gyucha (ed.) *Coming Together: Comparative Approaches to Population Aggregation and Early Urbanization*: 349–367. Albany (NY): SUNY Press.

Bognár-Kutzián, I. 1972. *The Early Copper Age Tiszapolgár Culture in the Carpathian Basin* (Archaeologia Hungarica 42). Budapest: Akadémiai Kiadó.

Boyar, E. and K. Fleet 2010. *A Social History of Ottoman Istanbul*. Cambridge: Cambridge University Press.

Chapman, J. 1994. Social power in the early farming communities of Eastern Hungary: Perspectives from the Upper Tisza region. *A Jósa András Múzeum Évkönyve* 36: 79–91.

Chapman, J. and J. Laszlovszky 2010. Introduction to the Upper Tisza Project, in J. Chapman, M. Gillings, E. Magyari, R. Shiel, B. Gaydarska and C. Bond (eds) *The Upper Tisza Project: Studies in Hungarian Landscape Archaeology. Book 2: Settlement Patterns in the Bodrogköz Block* (BAR International Series 2087): 1–27. Oxford: Archaeopress.

Clark, G. 2016. *Global Cities: A Short History*. Washington, D.C.: Brookings Institution Press.

Creekmore III, A.T. and K.D. Fisher (eds) 2014. *Making Ancient Cities: Space and Place in Early Urban Societies*. Cambridge and New York: Cambridge University Press.

Crnobrnja, A., Z. Simić and M. Janković 2009. Late Vinča culture settlement at Crkvine in Stubline: Household organization and urbanization in the Late Vinča culture period. *Starinar* 59: 9–25.

Darnay, K. 1905. Szeghalmi ásatásról. *Archaeologiai Értesítő* 1905: 66–70.

de Souza Briggs, X. 2004. Civilization in Color: The Multicultural City in Three Millennia. *City and Community* 3(4): 311–342.

Domboróczki, L., A. Kalli, M. Makoldi and E. Tutkovics 2017. The Füzesabony-Gubakút Settlement Development Model of the Alföld Linear Pottery Culture in the Light of the Recent Archaeological Discoveries at Hejőpapi-Szeméttelep (2008–2011) and Bükkábrány-Bánya VII-Vasúti Dűlő (2009–2011). *Journal of Historical Archaeology & Anthropological Sciences* 2(2): 00046, DOI:10.15406/jhaas.2017.02.00046

Draşovean, F. and W. Schier 2010. The Neolithic tell sites of Parţa and Uivar (Romanian Banat). A comparison of their architectural sequence and organization of social space, in S. Hansen (ed.) *Leben auf dem Tell als soziale Praxis* (Kolloquien zur Vor- und Frühgeschichte 14): 165–187. Bonn: Dr. Rudolf Habelt.

Dunbar, R.I.M. 2011. Constraints on the Evolution of Social Institutions and Their Implications for Information Flow. *Journal of Institutional Economics* 7(3): 345–371.

Düring, B.S. 2013. The anatomy of a prehistoric community: Reconsidering Çatalhöyük, in J. Birch (ed.) *From Prehistoric Villages to Cities: Settlement Aggregation and Community Transformation:* 23–43. New York and London: Routledge.

Ecsedy, I., L. Kovács, B. Maráz and I. Torma (eds) 1982. *Magyarország Régészeti Topográfiája 6. Békés Megye Régészeti Topográfiája: A szeghalmi járás (IV/1).* Budapest: Akadémiai Kiadó.

Feinman, G.M. 2011. Size, Complexity, and Organizational Variation: A Comparative Approach. *Cross-Cultural Research* 45(1): 37–58.

Fox, R.G. 1977. *Urban Anthropology: Cities in Their Cultural Settings.* Englewood Cliffs (NJ): Prentice-Hall.

Füzesi, A., G. Mesterházy, G. Serlegi, G. Márkus and P. Raczky 2016. Polgár-Csőszhalom: Results of the new multidisciplinary investigations of a Late Neolithic settlement in the Tisza region. *Hungarian Archaeology* Autumn 2016:1–13. Electronic document: http://files.archaeolingua.hu/2016O/Fuzesi_et_al_E16OSZ.pdf, accessed on August 2, 2021

Füzesi, A. and P. Raczky 2018. Öcsöd-Kováshalom. Potscape of a Late Neolithic site in the Tisza region. *Dissertationes Archaeologicae ex Instituto Archaeologico Universitatis de Rolando Eötvös nominatae* Ser. 3. No. 6: 43–146.

Füzesi, A., K. Rassmann, E. Bánffy, H. Hoehler-Brockmann, G. Kalla, N. Szabó, M. Szilágyi and P. Raczky 2020a. Test excavation of the 'pseudo-ditch' system of the Late Neolithic settlement complex at Öcsöd-Kováshalom on the Great Hungarian Plain. *Dissertationes Archaeologicae ex Instituto Archaeologico Universitatis de Rolando Eötvös nominatae* Ser. 3. No. 8: 141–164.

Füzesi, A., K. Rassmann, E. Bánffy and P. Raczky 2020b. Human Activities on a Late Neolithic Tell-like Settlement Complex of the Hungarian Plain (Öcsöd-Kováshalom), in A. Blanco-González and T.L. Kienlin (eds) *Current Approaches to Tells in the Prehistoric Old World:* 139–162. Oxford: Oxbow Books.

Gaspar, J. and E.L. Glaeser 1998. Information Technology and the Future of Cities. *Journal of Urban Economics* 43(1): 136–156.

Glaeser, E. 2011. *Triumph of the City: How Our Greatest Invention Makes Us Richer, Smarter, Greener, Healthier and Happier.* London: Penguin Press.

Gulyás, S. and P. Sümegi 2011. Riparian environment in shaping social and economic behavior during the first phase of the evolution of Late Neolithic tell complexes in SE Hungary (6th/5th millennia BC). *Journal of Archaeological Science* 38(10): 2683–2695.

Gyucha, A. 2015. *Prehistoric Village Social Dynamics: The Early Copper Age in the Körös Region* (Prehistoric Research in the Körös Region 2). Budapest: Archaeolingua.

Gyucha, A. 2019. Population Aggregation and Early Urbanization from a Comparative Perspective: An Introduction, in A. Gyucha (ed.) *Coming Together: Comparative Approaches to Population Aggregation and Early Urbanization:* 1–35. Albany (NY): SUNY Press.

Gyucha, A., W.A. Parkinson and R.W. Yerkes 2009. A Multi-Scalar Approach to Settlement Pattern Analysis: The Transition from the Late Neolithic to the Early Copper Age on the Great Hungarian Plain, in T. Thurston and R.B. Salisbury (eds) *Reimagining Regional Analyses: The Archaeology of Spatial and Social Dynamics:* 100–129. Cambridge: Cambridge Scholars Publishing.

Gyucha, A., W.A. Parkinson and R.W. Yerkes 2014. The Transition from the Late Neolithic to the Early Copper Age: Multidisciplinary Investigations in the Körös Region of the Great Hungarian Plain, in W. Schier and F. Draşovean (eds) *The Neolithic and Eneolithic in Southeast Europe: New Approaches to Dating and Cultural Dynamics in the 6th to 4th Millennium BC:* 273–296. Marie Leidorf, Rahden/Westfalen.

Gyucha, A., W.A. Parkinson, and R.W. Yerkes 2019. The Development of a Neolithic Tell on the Great Hungarian Plain: Site Formation and Use at Szeghalom-Kovácshalom. *Journal of Field Archaeology* 44(7): 458–479.

Gyucha, A., R.W. Yerkes, W.A. Parkinson, N. Papadopoulos, A. Sarris, P.R. Duffy and R.B. Salisbury 2015. Settlement Nucleation in the Neolithic: A Preliminary Report of the Körös Regional Archaeological Project's Investigations at Szeghalom-Kovácshalom and Vésztő-Mágor, in S. Hansen, P. Raczky, A. Anders and A. Reingruber (eds) *Neolithic and Copper Age between the Carpathians and the Aegean Sea. Chronologies and Technologies from the 6th to the 4th Millennium BCE* (Archäologie in Eurasien 31): 129–142. Bonn: Dr. Rudolf Habelt.

Hall, P. 1998. *Cities in Civilization: Culture, Innovation, and Urban Order.* London: Weidenfeld & Nicolson.

Hansen, S., M. Toderaş, A. Reingruber, I. Gatsov, M. Kay, P. Nedelcheva, D. Nowacki, A. Röpke, J. Wahl and J. Wunderlich 2010. Pietrele 'Măgura Gorgana'. Bericht über die Ausgrabungen und geomorphologischen Untersuchungen im Sommer 2009. *Eurasia Antiqua* 16: 43–96.

Hegedűs, K. 1983. The Settlement of the Neolithic Szakálhát Group at Csanytelek-Újhalastó. *Móra Ferenc Múzeum Évkönyve* 1982–1983(1): 7–54.

Hegedűs, K. and J. Makkay 1987. Vésztő-Mágor: A Settlement of the Tisza Culture, in L. Tálas and P. Raczky (eds) *The Late Neolithic of the Tisza Region: A Survey of Recent Excavations and Their Findings:* 85–104. Budapest and Szolnok: Kossuth Press and Szolnok County Museums.

Hillier, B. and J. Hanson 1984. *The Social Logic of Space.* Cambridge: Cambridge University Press.

Hofmann, R. 2015. The Bosnian Evidence: The New Late Neolithic and Early Copper-Age Chronology and Changing Settlement Patterns, in S. Hansen, P. Raczky, A. Anders and A. Reingruber (eds) *Neolithic and Copper Age between the Carpathians and the Aegean Sea. Chronologies and Technologies from the 6th to the 4th Millennium BCE* (Archäologie in Eurasien 31): 219–241. Bonn: Dr. Rudolf Habelt.

Hofmann, R., A. Medović, M. Furholt, I. Medović, T. Stanković Pešterac, S. Dreibrodt, S. Martini and A. Hofmann 2019a. Late Neolithic multicomponent sites of the Tisza region and the emergence of centripetal settlement layouts. *Praehistorische Zeitschrift* 94(2): 351–378.

Hofmann, R., J. Müller, L. Shatilo, M. Videiko, R. Ohlrau, V. Rud, N. Burdo, M. Dal Corso, S. Dreibrodt and W. Kirleis 2019b. Governing Tripolye: Integrative architecture in Tripolye settlements. *PLoS ONE* 14(9): e0222243, https://doi.org/10.1371/journal.pone.0222243

Horváth, F. 1989. A Survey on the Development of Neolithic Settlement Pattern and House Types in the Tisza Region, in S. Bökönyi (ed.) *Neolithic of Southeastern Europe and its Near Eastern Connections* (Varia Archaeologica Hungarica 2): 85–101. Budapest: Institute of Archaeology of the Hungarian Academy of Sciences.

Jankovich, D., J. Makkay and B.M. Szőke (eds) 1989. *Magyarország Régészeti Topográfiája 8. Békés Megye Régészeti Topográfiája: A szarvasi járás (IV/2).* Budapest: Akadémiai Kiadó.

Jankovich, D., P. Medgyesi, E. Nikolin, I. Szatmári and I. Torma (eds) 1998. *Magyarország Régészeti Topográfiája 10. Békés Megye Régészeti Topográfiája: Békés és Békéscsaba környéke (IV/3).* Budapest: Akadémiai Kiadó.

Johnson, G.A. 1982. Organizational Structure and Scalar Stress, in C. Renfrew, M. Rowlands and B.A. Segraves-Whallon (eds) *Theory and Explanation in Archaeology:* 389–421. New York: Academic Press.

Kalicz, N. 1985. *Kőkori falu Aszódon* (Múzeumi Füzetek 32). Aszód: Petőfi Múzeum.

Kalicz, N. 1995. Siedlungsstruktur der neolithischen Herpály-Kultur in Ostungarn, in A. Aspes (ed.) *Settlement Patterns between the Alps and the Black Sea 5th to 2nd Millennium B. C.* (Memorie del Museo Civico di Storia Naturale di Verona, Sezione Scienze dell'Uomo 4): 67–75. Verona: Museo Civico di Storia Naturale.

Kalicz, N. 2008. Aszód: ein gemischter Fundort der Lengyel- und Theiss-Kultur. *Communicationes Archaeologicae Hungariae* 2008: 5–54.

Kalicz, N. and K. Kovács 2010. Háztípusok az aszódi késő neolitikus lelőhelyen (House types at the Late Neolithic settlement of Aszód). *Ősrégészeti Levelek* 12: 31–47.

Kalicz, N. and J. Makkay 1977. *Die Linienbandkeramik in der Grossen Ungarischen Tiefebene* (Studia Archaeologica VII). Budapest: Akadémiai Kiadó.

Kalicz, N. and P. Raczky 1984. Preliminary report on the 1977–1982 excavations at the Neolithic and Bronze Age tell-settlement of Berettyóújfalu–Herpály. Part I. Neolithic. *Acta Archaeologica Academiae Scientiarum Hungaricae* 36: 85–136.

Kalicz, N. and P. Raczky 1987. The Late Neolithic of the Tisza Region: A Survey of Recent Archaeological Research, in L. Tálas and P. Raczky (eds) *The Late Neolithic of the Tisza Region:* 11–29. Budapest and Szolnok: Kossuth Press and Szolnok County Museums.

Kelly, J. 2019. Contextualizing Aggregation and Nucleation as Demographic Processes Leading to Cahokia's Emergence as an Incipient Urban Center, in A. Gyucha (ed.) *Coming Together: Comparative Approaches to Population Aggregation and Early Urbanization:* 105–133. Albany (NY): SUNY Press.

Kenoyer, J.M. 1991. The Indus Valley Tradition of Pakistan and Western India. *Journal of World Prehistory* 5(4): 331–385.

Kostof, S. 1991. *The City Shaped: Urban Patterns and Meanings through History.* Boston: Little Brown.

Kovács, K. 2016. Településszerkezeti sajátosságok Kenderes–Kulis kora rézkori lelőhelyén: az elmúlt évtizedek kutatási eredményei (The Characteristics of Settlement Structure at the Early Copper Age Site Kenderes–Kulis. The Results of Research Conducted in the Past Decades). *Tisicum* 25: 55–63.

Kreiter, A., N. Kalicz, K. Kovács, Zs. Siklósi and O. Viktorik 2017. Entangled traditions: Lengyel and Tisza ceramic technology in a Late Neolithic settlement in northern Hungary. *Journal of Archaeological Science: Reports* 16: 589–603.

Kusimba, C. 2008. Early African Cities: Their Role in the Shaping of Urban and Rural Interaction Spheres, in J. Marcus and J.A. Sabloff (eds) *The Ancient City. New*

Perspectives on Urbanism in the Old and New World: 229–246. Santa Fe (NM): School for Advanced Research.

Lazarovici, C.-M. and G. Lazarovici 2004. *Neoliticul. Vol. 1. Architectura neoliticului şi epocii Cuprului din Romania* (Bibliotheca Archaeologica Moldaviae 4). Iaşi: Trinitas.

Lefebvre, H. 1991. *The Production of Space.* Translated by D. Nicholson-Smith. Maiden (MA): Wiley-Blackwell.

Link, T. 2006. *Das Ende der neolithischen Tellsiedlungen. Ein kulturgeschichtliches Phänomen des 5. Jahrtausends v. Chr. im Karpatenbecken* (Universitätsforschungen zur prähistorischen Archäologie 134). Bonn: Dr. Rudolf Habelt.

Makkay, J. 1982. *A magyarországi neolitikum kutatásának új eredményei: Az időrend és a népi azonosítás kérdései.* Budapest: Akadémiai Kiadó.

Manzanilla, L.R. 2009. Corporate life in apartment and barrio compounds at Teotihuacan, Central Mexico: craft specialization, hierarchy and ethnicity, in L.R. Manzanilla and C. Chapdelaine (eds) *Domestic Life in Prehispanic Capitals. A Study of Specialization, Hierarchy and Ethnicity* (Memoirs 46): 21–42. Ann Arbor: University of Michigan, Museum of Anthropology.

Marcus, J. and J.A. Sabloff (eds) 2008. *The Ancient City: New Perspectives on Urbanism in the Old and New World.* Santa Fe (NM): School for Advanced Research.

Marić, M., N. Mirković-Marić, B. Molloy, D. Jovanović, P. Mertl, L. Milašinović and J. Pendić 2016. New Results of the Archaeological Excavations on the Site Gradište near Iđoš: Season 2014. *Glasnik* 32: 125–153.

Medović, A., R. Hofmann, T. Stanković Pešterac, S. Dreibrodt, I. Medović and R. Pešterac 2014. The Late Neolithic settlement mound Borđoš near Novi Bečej, Serbian Banat, in a multiregional context – Preliminary results of geophysical, geoarchaeological and archaeological research. *Rad Muzeja Vojvodine* 56: 53–77.

Meier-Arendt, W. 1991. Zu Tells und Tellartigen Siedlungen im Spätneolithikum Ost-Ungarns, Siebenbürgens und des Banat: Überlegungen zu Entstehung und Funktion. *Banatica* 11: 77–85.

Mesterházy, G., G. Serlegi, B. Vágvölgyi, A. Füzesi and P. Raczky 2019. A szociális folyamatok színterei Polgár-Csőszhalom késő neolitikus településének összefüggéseiben (Arenas of social dynamics on the Late Neolithic settlement of Polgár-Csőszhalom). *Archaeologiai Értesítő* 144: 1–32.

Mirković-Marić, N. and M. Marić 2017. Late Neolithic Tisza sites in the Serbian part of Banat. *Archaeologiai Értesítő* 142: 1–34.

Müller, J. 2017. From the Neolithic to the Iron Age – Demography and Social Agglomeration: The Development of Centralized Control?, in M. Fernández-Götz and D. Krausse (eds) *Eurasia at the Dawn of History: Urbanization and Social Change:* 106–124. Cambridge: Cambridge University Press.

Müller, J., R. Hofmann, R. Ohlrau and L. Shatilo 2018. The social constitution and political organisation of Tripolye mega-sites: hierarchy and balance, in H. Meller, D. Gronenborn and R. Risch (eds) *Überschuss ohne Staat-Politische Formen in der Vorgeschichte/ Surplus without the State-Political Forms in Prehistory* (Tagungen des Landesmuseums für Vorgeschichte Halle 18): 247–260. Halle/Saale: Landesamt für Denkmalpflege und Archäologie Sachsen-Anhalt, Landesmuseum für Vorgeschichte.

Mumford, L. 1961. *The City in History.* New York: Harcourt, Brace, and World.

Naumov, G. 2016. Tell communities and wetlands in Neolithic Pelagonia, Republic of Macedonia. *Documenta Praehistorica* 43: 327–342.

Neumann, D., Zs. Siklósi, R. Scholz and M. Szilágyi 2014. Preliminary report on the first season of fieldwork in Berettyóújfalu-Szilhalom. *Dissertationes Archaeologicae ex Instituto Archaeologico Universitatis de Rolando Eötvös nominatae* Ser. 3 No. 2: 377–403.

Niekamp, A. and A. Sarris 2015. Utilizing Magnetic Prospection and GIS to Examine Settlement Organization in Neolithic Southeastern Europe, in F. Giligny, F. Djindjian, L. Costa, P. Moscati and S. Robert (eds) *CAA 2014 – 21st Century Archaeology. Proceedings of the 42nd Annual Conference on Computer Applications and Quantitative Methods in Archaeology:* 53–64. Oxford: Archaeopress.

Ortman, S.G., A.H.F. Cabaniss, J.O. Sturm and L.M.A. Bettencourt 2014. The Pre-History of Urban Scaling. *PLOS ONE* 9(2): e87902, https://doi.org/10.1371/journal.pone.0087902

Papadopoulos, N.G., A. Sarris, W.A. Parkinson, A. Gyucha, R.W. Yerkes, P.R. Duffy and P. Tsourlos 2014. Electrical resistivity tomography for the modelling of cultural deposits and geomorphological landscapes at Neolithic sites: a case study from southeastern Hungary. *Archaeological Prospection* 21: 169–183.

Pappa, M. and M. Besios 1999. The Neolithic Settlement at Makriyalos, Northern Greece: Preliminary Report on the 1993–1995 Excavations. *Journal of Field Archaeology* 26(2): 177–195.

Parker Pearson, M. and C. Richards 1994. Architecture and Order: Spatial Representation and Archaeology, in M. Parker Pearson and C. Richards (eds) *Architecture and Order: Approaches to Social Space:* 34–66. London: Routledge.

Parkinson, W.A. 2006. *The Social Organization of Early Copper Age Tribes on the Great Hungarian Plain* (BAR International Series 1573). Oxford: Archaeopress.

Parkinson, W.A. and A. Gyucha 2012. Tells in Perspective: Long-Term Patterns of Settlement Nucleation and Dispersal in Central and Southeast Europe, in R. Hofmann, F.-K. Moetz and J. Müller (eds) *Tells: Social and Environmental Space:* 105–116. Bonn: Dr. Rudolf Habelt.

Parkinson, W.A., A. Gyucha, P. Karkanas, N. Papadopoulos, G. Tsartsidou, A. Sarris, P.R. Duffy and R.W. Yerkes 2018. A Landscape of Tells: Geophysics and Microstratigraphy at Two Neolithic Tell Sites on the Great Hungarian Plain. *Journal of Archaeological Science: Reports* 19: 903–924.

Parkinson, W.A., A. Gyucha and R.W. Yerkes (eds) 2021. *Bikeri: Two Copper Age Villages on the Great Hungarian Plain*. Los Angeles: Cotsen Institute of Archaeology at University of California.

Parkinson, W.A., R.W. Yerkes, A. Gyucha, A. Sarris, M. Morris and R.B. Salisbury 2010. Early Copper Age Settlements in the Körös Region of the Great Hungarian Plain. *Journal of Field Archaeology* 35(2): 164–183.

Perlès, C. 2001. *The early Neolithic in Greece. The first farming communities in Europe*. Cambridge: Cambridge University Press.

Pirenne, H. 1952. *Medieval Cities: Their Origins and the Revival of Trade*. Princeton (NJ): Princeton University Press.

Raczky, P. 1987. Öcsöd-Kováshalom: A Settlement of the Tisza Culture, in L. Tálas and P. Raczky (eds) *The Late Neolithic of the Tisza Region*: 61–83. Budapest and Szolnok: Kossuth Press and Szolnok County Museums.

Raczky, P. 1992. The Tisza Culture of the Great Hungarian Plain. *Studia Praehistorica* 11–12: 162–176.

Raczky, P. 2002. Evidence of contacts between the Lengyel and the Tisza–Herpály Cultures at the Late Neolithic site of Polgár-Csőszhalom (Relationship between Central European and Balkan ritual practice and sacral thought in the Upper Tisza Region). *Budapest Régiségei* 36: 79–92.

Raczky, P. 2006. House-Structures under Change on the Great Hungarian Plain in Earlier Phases of the Neolithic, in N. Tasić and C. Grozdanov (eds) *Homage to Milutin Garašanin*: 379–398. Belgrade: Serbian Academy of Sciences and Arts.

Raczky, P. 2009. Archaeological data on space use at a tell-like settlement of the Tisza Culture (New results from Öcsöd-Kováshalom, Hungary), in F. Draşovean, D.L. Ciobotaru and M. Maddison (eds) *Ten Years After: The Neolithic of the Balkans, as Uncovered by the Last Decade of Research*: 101–124. Timişoara: Editura Marineasa.

Raczky, P. 2015. Settlement in South-east Europe, in C. Fowler, J. Harding and D. Hofmann (eds) *The Oxford Handbook of Neolithic Europe*: 235–254. Oxford: Oxford University Press.

Raczky, P. 2018. A Complex Monument in the Making at the Late Neolithic Site of Polgár-Csőszhalom (Hungary), in A.T. Bács, Á. Bollók and T. Vida (eds) *Across the Mediterranean - Along the Nile: Studies in Egyptology, Nubiology and Late Antiquity Dedicated to László Török on the Occasion of His 75th Birthday*: 15–60. Budapest: Archaeolingua.

Raczky, P. 2019. Cross-Scale Settlement Morphologies and Social Formations in the Neolithic of the Great Hungarian Plain, in A. Gyucha (ed.) *Coming Together: Comparative Approaches to Population Aggregation and Early Urbanization*: 259–294. Albany (NY): SUNY Press.

Raczky, P. and A. Anders 2006. Social dimensions of the Late Neolithic settlement of Polgár-Csőszhalom (Eastern Hungary). *Acta Archaeologica Academiae Scientiarum Hungaricae* 57: 17–33.

Raczky, P. and A. Anders 2008. Late Neolithic spatial differentiation at Polgár-Csőszhalom, eastern Hungary, in D. Bailey, A. Whittle and D. Hofmann (eds) *Living Well Together? Settlement and Materiality in the Neolithic of South-East and Central Europe*: 35–53. Oxford: Oxbow Books.

Raczky, P. and A. Anders 2009. Settlement history of the Middle Neolithic in the Polgár micro-region (The development of the Alföld Linearband Pottery in the Upper Tisza Region, Hungary), in J.K. Kozłowski (ed.) *Interactions Between Different Models of Neolithisation North of the Central European Agro-Ecological Barrier* (Prace Komisji Prehistorii Karpat PAU 5): 31–50. Kraków: Polish Academy of Arts and Sciences.

Raczky, P. and A. Anders 2010. The times they are a-changin': revisiting the chronological framework of the Late Neolithic settlement complex at Polgár-Csőszhalom, in P. Kalábková, B. Kovár, P. Pavúk and J. Šuteková (eds) *PANTA RHEI. Studies in Chronology and Cultural Development of the South-Eastern and Central Europe in Earlier Prehistory Presented to Juraj Pavúk on the Occasion of his 75th Birthday* (Studia Archaeologica et Mediaevalia 11): 357–378. Bratislava: Comenius University.

Raczky, P. and A. Anders 2012. Neolithic enclosures in Eastern Hungary and their survival into the Copper Age, in F. Bertemes, P.F. Biehl and H. Meller (eds) *Neolithische Kreisgrabenanlagen in Europa/ Neolithic Circular Enclosures in Europe* (Tagungen des Landesmuseums für Vorgeschichte Halle 8): 271–309. Halle/Saale: Landesamt für Denkmalpflege und Archäologie Sachsen-Anhalt, Landesmuseum für Vorgeschichte.

Raczky, P. and A. Anders 2014. Szentpéterszeg-Kovadomb. Egy késő neolitikus lelőhely tér-képei, in A. Anders, Cs. Balogh and A. Türk (eds) *Avarok pusztái – Régészeti tanulmányok Lőrinczy Gábor 60. születésnapjára/Avarum solitudines. Archaeological studies presented to Gábor Lőrinczy on his sixtieth birthday* (MTA BTK MŐT Kiadványok 2, Opitz Archaeologica 6): 23–42. Budapest: Martin Opitz Kiadó.

Raczky, P., A. Anders and L. Bartosiewicz 2011. The Enclosure System of Csőszhalom and its Interpretation, in S. Hansen and J. Müller (eds) *Sozialarchäologische Perspektiven: gesellschaftlicher Wandel 5000–1500 v. Chr. zwischen Atlantik und Kaukasus* (Archäologie in Eurasien 24): 57–79. Darmstadt: Philipp von Zabern.

Raczky, P., A. Anders, N. Faragó and G. Márkus 2014a. Short report on the 2014 excavations at Polgár-Csőszhalom. *Dissertationes Archaeologicae ex Instituto*

Archaeologico Universitatis de Rolando Eötvös nominatae Ser. 3 No. 2: 363–376.

Raczky, P., A. Anders, K. Sebők, P. Csippán and Zs. Tóth 2015. The Times of Polgár-Csőszhalom: Chronologies of Human Activities in a Late Neolithic Settlement in Northeastern Hungary, in S. Hansen, P. Raczky, A. Anders and A. Reingruber (eds) *Neolithic and Copper Age between the Carpathians and the Aegean Sea. Chronologies and Technologies from the 6th to the 4th Millennium BCE* (Archäologie in Eurasien 31): 21–48. Bonn: Dr. Rudolf Habelt.

Raczky, P., A. Anders and Zs. Siklósi 2014b. Trajectories of Continuity and Change between the Late Neolithic and the Copper Age in Eastern Hungary, in W. Schier and F. Draşovean (eds) *The Neolithic and Eneolithic in Southeast Europe: New approaches to dating and cultural dynamics in the 6th to 4th Millennium BC* (Prähistorische Archäologie in Südosteuropa 28): 319–346. Berlin: Marie Leidorf.

Raczky, P., L. Domboróczki and Zs. Hajdú 2007. The site of Polgár-Csőszhalom and its cultural and chronological connections with the Lengyel culture, in J.K. Kozłowski and P. Raczky (eds) *The Lengyel, Polgár and related cultures in the Middle/Late Neolithic in Central Europe*: 49–70. Kraków: Polish Academy of Arts and Sciences.

Raczky, P. and A. Füzesi 2016. Öcsöd-Kováshalom. A retrospective look at the interpretations of Late Neolithic site. *Dissertationes Archaeologicae ex Instituto Archaeologico Universitatis de Rolando Eötvös nominatae* Ser. 3. No. 4: 9–42.

Raczky, P., A. Füzesi and A. Anders 2018. Domestic and Symbolic Activities on a Tell-Like Settlement at Öcsöd-Kováshalom in the Tisza Region, in *The Image of Divinity in the Neolithic and Eneolithic: Ways of Communication*: 117–140. Suceava: Editura Karl A. Romstorfer.

Raczky, P., W. Meier-Arendt, K. Kurucz, Zs. Hajdú and Á. Szikora 1994. Polgár-Csőszhalom. A Late Neolithic settlement in the Upper Tisza region and its cultural connections. Preliminary report. *A Jósa András Múzeum Évkönyve* 36: 231–240.

Raczky, P. and K. Sebők 2014. The outset of Polgár-Csőszhalom tell and the archaeological context of a special central building, in S. Forţiu and A. Cîntar (eds) *Arheovest II: In honorem Gheorge Lazarovici*: 51–100. Szeged: JATEPress.

Raczky, P., P. Seleanu, G. Rózsa, Cs. Siklódi, G. Kalla, B. Csornay, H. Oravecz, M. Vicze, E. Bánffy, S. Bökönyi and P. Somogyi 1985. Öcsöd-Kováshalom: The Intensive Topographical and Archaeological Investigation of a Late Neolithic Site. Preliminary Report. *Mitteilungen des Archäologischen Instituts der ungarischen Akademie der Wissenschaften* 14: 251–278.

Rapoport, A. 1982. *The Meaning of the Built Environment: A Nonverbal Communication Approach*. Beverly Hills (CA): Sage.

Rapoport, A. 1994. Spatial Organization and the Built Environment, in T. Ingold (ed.) *Companion Encyclopedia of Anthropology: Humanity, Culture, and Social Life*: 460–502. London: Routledge.

Redfield, R. and M.B. Singer 1954. The Cultural Role of Cities. *Economic Development and Cultural Change* 3(1): 53–73.

Renfrew, C. and J.F. Cherry (eds) 1986. *Peer Polity Interaction and Socio-Political Change*. Cambridge: Cambridge University Press.

Riebe, D. 2021. *Redefining Archaeological Cultures: Boundaries and Interactions during the Late Neolithic on the Great Hungarian Plain* (Prehistoric Research in the Körös Region 5). Budapest: Archaeolingua.

Rosenstock, E. 2006. Early Neolithic tell settlements of South-East Europe in their natural setting: A study in distribution and architecture, in I. Gatsov and H. Schwarzberg (eds) *Aegean - Marmara - Black Sea: The Present State of Research on the Early Neolithic*: 115–125. Langenweissbach: Beier&Beran.

Runnels, C.N., C. Payne, N.V. Rifkind, C. White, N.P. Wolff and S.A. LeBlanc 2009. Warfare in Neolithic Thessaly. A Case Study. *Hesperia* 78: 165–194.

Salisbury, R.B. 2016. *Soilscapes in Archaeology: Settlement and Social Organization in the Neolithic of the Great Hungarian Plain* (Prehistoric Research in the Körös Region 3). Budapest: Archaeolingua.

Salisbury, R., G. Bácsmegi and P. Sümegi 2013a. Preliminary environmental historical results to reconstruct prehistoric human-environmental interactions in Eastern Hungary. *Central European Journal of Geosciences* 5(3): 331–343.

Salisbury, R.B., G. Bertók and G. Bácsmegi 2013b. Integrated Prospection Methods to Define Small-site Settlement Structure: a Case Study from Neolithic Hungary. *Archaeological Prospection* 20(1): 1–10.

Schier, W. and F. Draşovean (eds) 2020. *Uivar 'Gomilă' – A Prehistoric Tell Settlement in the Romanian Banat. Vol. I. Site, Architecture, Stratigraphy and Dating* (Prähistorische Archäologie in Südosteuropa 32). Rahden/Westfalen: Marie Leidorf.

Sherratt, A. 1983. The Development of Neolithic and Copper Age Settlement in the Great Hungarian Plain, Part I: The Regional Setting. *Oxford Journal of Archaeology* 1(3): 287–316.

Sherratt, A. 1984. The Development of Neolithic and Copper Age Settlement in the Great Hungarian Plain, Part II: Site Survey and Settlement Dynamics. *Oxford Journal of Archaeology* 2(1): 13–41.

Sindbaek, S.M. 2007. Networks and nodal points: The emergence of towns in early Viking Scandinavia. *Antiquity* 81(311): 119–132.

Smith, M.E. 2017. The Teotihuacan Anomaly: The Historical Trajectory of Urban Design in Ancient Central Mexico. *Open Archaeology* 3: 175–193.

Smith, M.E. 2019. Energized Crowding and the Generative Role of Settlement Aggregation and

Urbanization, in A. Gyucha (ed.) *Coming Together: Comparative Approaches to Population Aggregation and Early Urbanization*: 37–58. Albany (NY): SUNY Press.

Smith, M.L. (ed.) 2003. *The Social Construction of Ancient Cities*. Washington, D.C.: Smithsonian Institution Press.

Snodgrass, A. 2012. *Archaeology and the Emergence of Greece*. Edinburgh: Edinburgh University Press.

Southall, A. 1998. *The City in Time and Space*. Cambridge: Cambridge University Press.

Souvatzi, S.G. 2008. *A Social Archaeology of Households in Neolithic Greece: An Anthropological Approach*. Cambridge: Cambridge University Press.

Stanković Pešterac, T., R. Hofmann, A. Medović, S. Dreibrodt and I. Medović 2014. Multidisciplinary Archaeological Research at the Late Neolithic site Bordjoš (Borjas) near Novi Bečej (Northern Serbia) – Geoelectrical prospection of a house, in S. Forţiu and A. Cîntar (eds) *Arheovest II: In honorem Gheorge Lazarovici*: 545–562. Szeged: JATEPress.

Starnini, E., Gy. Szakmány, S. Józsa, Zs. Kasztovszky, V. Szilágyi, B. Maróti, B. Voytek and F. Horváth 2015. Lithics from the Tell Site Hódmezővásárhely-Gorzsa (Southeast Hungary): Typology, Technology, Use and Raw Material Strategies during the Late Neolithic (Tisza Culture), in S. Hansen, P. Raczky, A. Anders and A. Reingruber (eds) *Neolithic and Copper Age between the Carpathians and the Aegean Sea. Chronologies and Technologies from the 6th to the 4th Millennium BCE* (Archäologie in Eurasien 31): 105–128. Bonn: Dr. Rudolf Habelt.

Storey, G.R. 2020. *The Archaeology of Ancient Cities*. New York: Eliot Werner.

Szatmári, I. (ed.) in prep *Magyarország Régészeti Topográfiája. A gyulai és sarkadi járás*.

Szeghalmi, Gy. 1913a. Ásatás a szeghalmi Kovácsha-lomban (Első közlemény). *Archaeologiai Értesítő* 1913: 37–52.

Szeghalmi, Gy. 1913b. Ásatás a szeghalmi Kovácsha-lomban (Második közlemény). *Archaeologiai Értesítő* 1913: 123–141.

Szénászky, G.J. 1979. A korai Szakálháti csoport települése Battonyán (The settlement of the early Szakálhát group at Battonya). *Archaeologiai Értesítő* 106: 67–77.

Szénászky, G.J. 1988. A korai szakálháti kultúra Battonyán (Funde aus der frühen Szakálhát-Kultur von Battonya). *Békés Megyei Múzeumok Közleményei* 11: 5–29.

Szilágyi, M. 2010. Kora rézkori település és árokrendszer Szolnok-Zagyvaparton (Frühkupferzeitliche Sied-lung und Grabensystem von Szolnok-Zagyvapart). *Archaeologiai Értesítő* 135: 183–199.

Todorova, H. and I. Vajsov 1993. *Novokamennata epoha v Balgarija*. Sofia: Nauka i Iskustvo.

Vondrovský, V. 2018. Let the Sunshine In The Issue of Neolithic Longhouse Orientation. *European Journal of Archaeology* 21(4): 528–549.

Whittle, A. 1996. *Europe in the Neolithic: The creation of new worlds*. Cambridge: Cambridge University Press.

Whittle, A. 2018. *The Times of Their Lives. Hunting History in the Archaeology of Neolithic Europe*. Oxford: Oxbow Books.

Wirth, L. 1938. Urbanism as a Way of Life. *American Journal of Sociology* 44(1): 1–24.

Yoffee, N. (ed.) 2017. *Early Cities in Comparative Perspective, 4000 BCE–1200 CE*. Cambridge: Cambridge University Press.

Chapter 6

Large Settlements of the Funnel Beaker Culture
in Lesser Poland:
Instruments of Social Cohesion and Cultural Conversion

Marek Nowak, Klaus Cappenberg, Marta Korczyńska,
and Magdalena Moskal-del Hoyo

Abstract

At the beginning of the 4th millennium BC, a new archaeological unit, the southeastern variant of the Funnel Beaker culture developed in southeastern Poland. From *c.* 3600 BC, the growth of the area occupied by some settlements of this culture can be observed in the archaeological record. In the second half of the 4th millennium BC, the biggest settlements reached the size of approximately 35 ha. These became microregional centers around which the wider settlement networks were organized. Due to the disappearance of most of the smaller sites in the last quarter of the 4th and in early 3rd millennia BC, one can assume that a significant part of the local population moved to these large settlements. The communities of these large, nucleated settlements were characterized by a trans-egalitarian social structure, probably with nominal leaders. The decision-making competencies of these leaders extended not only to large settlements but also to the sphere of regional interactions. Large settlements under consideration were, in great measure, established through the integration of local, late Lengyel–Polgár populations into the Funnel Beaker cultural system. The settlements became symbolic reference points that permitted the development and maintenance of a new 'Funnel Beaker identity.' This paper examines the processes by which this integration occurred and the role of a distinctive identity in maintaining population aggregation.

Introduction

At the turn of the 5th and 4th millennia BC, as a result of complicated interactions between central European, post-Linear Pottery Neolithic, and still 'non-neolithized' Late Mesolithic societies inhabiting North-Central and North Europe, a new type of Neolithic culture was formed (e.g., Kabaciński *et al.* 2015; Klassen 2004; Sørensen 2014). In archaeological terms, it has been defined as the Funnel Beaker culture (*Trichterbecherkultur* in German, hereafter TRB; e.g., Midgley 1992) or the Funnel Beaker complex (Furholt *et al.* 2014). During the first half of the 4th millennium BC, this unit spread over all of North and East-Central Europe as well as the neighboring southern Scandinavian zone. Around 3800/3700 BC, some groups of TRB also appeared in Lesser Poland (*Małopolska*) (Figure 6.1; Nowak 2017b).

By the end of the first half of the 4th millennium BC, TRB replaced late, post-Linear Pottery culture groups (i.e., Lengyel–Polgár ones: Kadrow 2017; Kadrow and Zakościelna 2000) and covered almost all of Lesser Poland. Thus, the Lesser Poland branch of TRB became an important component of this archaeological phenomenon. It is frequently described as its southeastern group (hereafter SE TRB; e.g., Midgley 1992; Nowak 2017b). TRB definitively disappeared in

this region during the period *c.* 3100–2800 BC, being infiltrated, transformed, and replaced by the Baden culture, the Globular Amphorae cultural expansion, and finally by the spread of the Corded Ware culture.

Within SE TRB, an unusually large number of sites have been recorded (Figure 6.2). We can only estimate this number at *c.* 10,000 sites in the region, based mainly on results of surveys conducted during the Archaeological Record of Poland program (*Archeologiczne Zdjęcie Polski*; e.g., Nowak 2001; Pelisiak 2018).

In terms of size and function, there are very different sites in the SE TRB. Among these is a small group of settlements that stand out due to their large size. They are present in western (Bronocice, Mozgawa), middle (Ćmielów, Grzegorzewice-Zagaje, Kamień Łukawski, Stryczowice, Zawichost-Pieczyska), and eastern Lesser Poland as well as the adjacent part of western Ukraine (Gródek Nadbużny, Zimno; see Figure 6.1).

These sites, owing to their spectacular dimensions, had become a topic of interest to the researchers of 'Polish' Neolithic before World War II (Jażdżewski 1936). Intensive excavations were carried out on most of them in the 1950s and 1960s (Ćmielów: Podkowińska 1950, 1951, 1955, 1957, 1961; Gródek Nadbużny: Jażdżewski 1958; Poklewski 1958; Kamień Łukawski: Kempisty 1965,

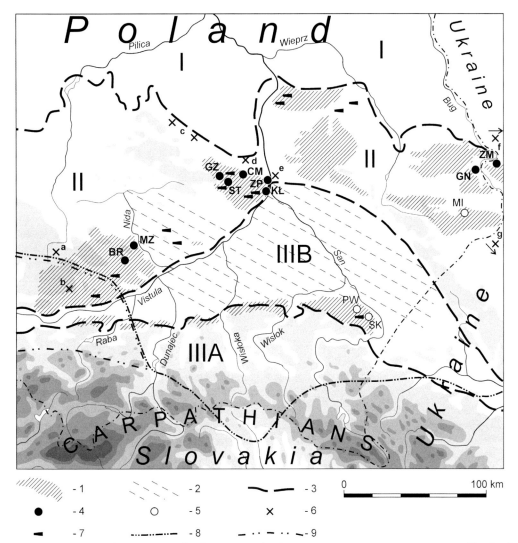

Figure 6.1. Location of SE TRB. I: Lowland zone; II: Upland zone; IIIA: Mountain zone; IIIB: Zone of foreland plateaus, plains, and basins; 1: Loess landscape; 2: Para-lowland landscape; 3: Approximate boundaries between major ecological units; 4: Large SE TRB settlements: BR = Bronocice, MZ = Mozgawa, GZ = Grzegorzewice-Zagaje, ST = Stryczowice, CM = Ćmielów, ZP = Zawichost-Pieczyska, KŁ = Kamień Łukawski, GN = Gródek Nadbużny, ZM = Zimno; 5: potential SE TRB large settlements: MI = Mikulin, PW = Pawłosiów, SK = Skołoszów; 6: Outcrops of major flint raw materials used by SE TRB: a: G-type Jurassic flint, b: Cracow-type Jurassic flint, c: 'Chocolate' flint, d: 'Stripped' flint, e: Świeciechów flint, f: Volhynian flint, g: Dniester flint; 7: Monumental tombs (most important megalithic and wooden long barrows); 8: Southern border of SE TRB settlement area; 9: Dispersed SE TRB settlements (figure by M. Nowak).

1966; Zawichost-Pieczyska: Balcer 1966, 1967; Zimno: Bronicki *et al.* 1998). Unfortunately, for various reasons, the results of these investigations still have not fully been published. In the 1970s, an interdisciplinary project focusing on the site of Bronocice was implemented (Kruk and Milisauskas 1981, 1983), resulting in a large number of publications regarding various aspects of this research (Kruk and Milisauskas 1990, 2018; Kruk *et al.* 1996, 2016, 2018; Milisauskas and Kruk 1984, 1989, 1990, 1991; Milisauskas *et al.* 2012, 2016). However, a complete, monographic synthesis of the investigations at this site has not been produced so far. Nevertheless, Bronocice is undoubtedly the best-recognized site of the SE TRB. At present, another research project is underway to comprehensively examine a large settlement at

Mozgawa (Korczyńska *et al.* 2019; Moskal-del Hoyo *et al.* 2018), and the search for other large settlements in eastern and southeastern Lesser Poland is ongoing (T. Chmielewski and M. Rybicka, personal communication; see potential large settlements on Figure 6.1).

To recapitulate, the level of recognition of these sites is diverse. Based on available data, however, we believe that it is possible to propose reliable interpretations and conclusions. Attention should be paid particularly to the favorable fact that fairly large areas of these sites have either been excavated (for example, several hectares at Bronocice, Ćmielów, and Gródek Nadbużny) or surveyed by using non-invasive methods (for example, dozens of hectares at Mozgawa).

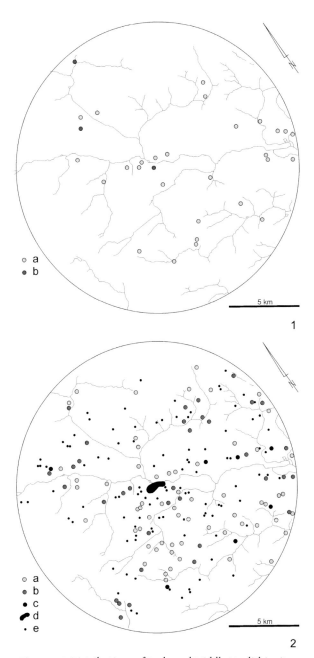

Figure 6.2. Distributions of Early and Middle Neolithic sites in the Bronocice microregion. 1: Lengyel–Polgár complex (33 sites): a: 0.5–3.0 ha, b: 4.5–5.5 ha; 2: SE TRB (106 sites, excluding Beaker/Baden horizon): a: < 2 ha, b: 2.1–4.9 ha, c: 5.0–10.0 ha, d: Large site at Bronocice (up to 21 ha), e: Stray finds (modified from Kruk *et al.* 1996 by M. Korczyńska).

We believe that these large SE TRB sites may be the remnants of settlements of exceptional importance both in economic and social terms. Among other roles, they might have been centers where decisions were made that regulated social functioning on micro- and mesoregional scales. Moreover, they were cultural reference points that contributed to and greatly facilitated the 'Funnel Beaker' acculturation of local Neolithic populations of late post-Linear Pottery (late Lengyel–Polgár) origin. In this paper, we argue that there are premises that render these assumptions reasonable.

Characteristics of the Large Sites of SE TRB

Spatial Extent

Into the group of large settlements of the southeastern branch of TRB, sites ranging from a dozen to approximately 35 ha are included. Areas of such size are perhaps not particularly impressive when compared to large sites in some other Neolithic/Eneolithic cultures, such as the Trypillia mega-sites covering several hundred hectares (e.g., Gaydarska 2020; Müller *et al.* 2016b; see also Diachenko and Zubrow, this volume). However, it is important to compare these dimensions to the averaged spatial extent of sites of the archaeological unit under consideration. The majority of SE TRB sites cover 1–2 ha, and the rare instances of settlements described as middle size usually do not exceed 2–5 ha and measure only exceptionally 6–10 ha (see Figure 6.2.2; e.g., Jastrzębski 1988; Kruk and Milisauskas 1999; Milisauskas and Kruk 1984; Nowak 1993; Pelisiak 2005; Rybicka *et al.* 2019; Zych 2008).

Environmental Context

The large SE TRB settlements are located in a hilly and loessy landscape, and similar sites have not been identified in other ecological zones (see Figure 6.1). Currently, the loess uplands constitute the most fertile areas, and there is no reason to doubt that it was similar in the Neolithic. These sites are situated at high, topographically prominent points on the loess hills and headlands, elevated above flood plains. During the Neolithic period, these locations were even more clearly marked in the landscape since the surrounding valleys now are filled with thick alluvia dating to the younger Holocene (e.g., Poręba *et al.* 2012; Szwarczewski 2009, 2013). Although we could say that these locations offered defensive qualities, the SE TRB settlements were not routinely enclosed by ditches and/or palisades. The general lack of fortifications cannot be explained by the small spatial extent of the excavations; certainly, this is not the case at Bronocice, Ćmielów, or Gródek Nadbużny. Bronocice is the only site where a ditch was discovered, protecting the settlement from one side (Milisauskas and Kruk 1990). This ditch dates to the late phase of the period under discussion (c. 3100/3000–2900/2800 BC).

Internal Layout and Structure

The spatial organization of large SE TRB sites is not clear. Their excavated parts are characterized by a tangle of different kinds and large quantities of anthropogenic features. For instance, a combination of aerial photography and geomagnetic survey revealed the presence of at least 1700 pits densely covering the entire area of the site at Mozgawa (Figure 6.3; Korczyńska *et al.* 2019).

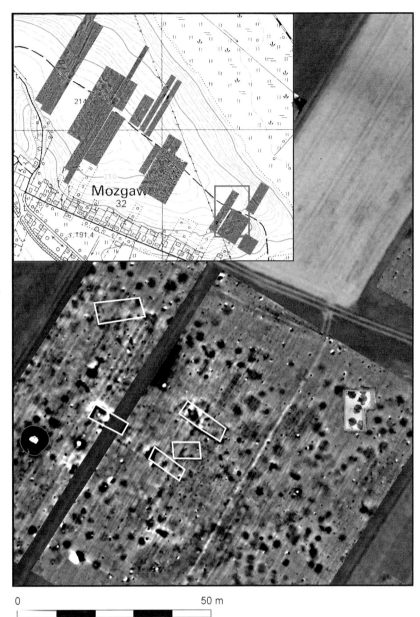

Figure 6.3. Results of geomagnetic prospection in the southeastern part of Mozgawa. White quadrangles indicate potential houses (figure by K. Cappenberg, M. Korczyńska, and J. Ociepka).

0   50 m

There are few obvious remains of buildings at these settlements. This also holds for other sorts of SE TRB sites as well as for sites of other groups of the TRB. The evident cases are restricted to remains of a house type commonly called *ploschchadka* (after a Ukrainian term; for examples, see Müller *et al.* 2016a, 2016b). Such houses were built of clay on wooden frames. Archaeologically, they typically are recorded as roughly quadrangular concentrations of a large number of daub fragments, often with construction imprints. A significant amount of such fragments is flat since they originate from plaster applied to floors or walls. Houses of this type are very characteristic of the Cucuteni–Trypillia culture in present-day Ukraine. Thus, it is no wonder that in the SE TRB area we find them primarily at its eastern margins, such as at Gródek Nadbużny and Zimno (Gumiński 1989; Rybicka 2017). However, it is possible that such structures also were erected in the western

parts of Lesser Poland, as suggested by some findings at Bronocice (Kruk and Milisauskas 1981; Milisauskas *et al.* 2016) and Mozgawa (Płoszaj 2016). The observed daub concentrations at SE TRB sites imply a maximum house size of approximately 15-x-5 m.

Because remains of the *ploschchadka* type are infrequently found, some researchers, based on indirect evidence, such as systems of pits surrounding empty spaces, conjecture the existence of other house structures (Balcer 1989; Kulczycka-Leciejewiczowa 2002; Milisauskas *et al.* 2016; see also Figure 6.3). If this holds, it seems reasonable to assume that the majority of TRB buildings must have been constructed in a different way than the earlier Neolithic structures; that is, in a way that did not leave archaeologically visible traces. This does not necessarily mean that they were flimsy and short-lived; log houses, for example,

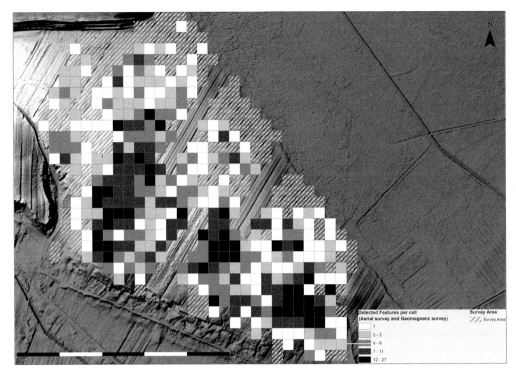

Figure 6.4. Reconstructed density of anthropogenic features at Mozgawa (figure by K. Cappenberg and M. Korczyńska).

are quite solid, but usually do not leave any traces (Kulczycka-Leciejewiczowa 2002).

As a consequence of the scarcity of house remains, we also have very little data about the organization of households. The site of Gródek Nadbużny provides some information in this regard. By analyzing the distribution of settlement remains, Gumiński (1989) concluded that there could have been at least nine settlement nuclei, consisting of up to a few households, which each encompassed one *ploschchadka* and other related features. However, there also were nuclei with only one household (Gumiński 1989: 16–20, 29). A reconstruction generated for Mozgawa, based on data from non-invasive surveys, seems to suggest a similar situation (Figure 6.4), with three settlement nuclei probably composed of several households.

The spatial arrangement of features at SE TRB sites suggests that the buildings commonly surrounded open places. A good example is the rectangular empty place, measuring *c.* 25–30-x-8–10 m, found within the maze of features at Ćmielów. In the center of this place, a single pit was discovered, which contained an exceptionally large number of well-preserved amphora and pitcher fragments, richly decorated with zoomorphic motifs (Podkowińska 1961). The empty area would correspond with the so-called public space in some concepts of spatial behaviors (e.g., Fleischer 2014; Palyvou 2004). For some researchers, however, such an arrangement would instead be indicative of the existence of a house; in this case, a quite large one with a possible cellar. Admittedly, a proper decision between these alternatives does not seem possible.

Traces of intensive production activities have been recorded in large SE TRB settlements. This includes especially flint tool production made on good quality raw materials (see Figure 6.1). It is notable that these sites were not located close to a given outcrop but at a distance of 30 to 80 km. The site of Ćmielów, based on the presence of 'striped' and Świeciechów flints, provides an outstanding example of lithic manufacturing. In his detailed study, Balcer (2002) managed, among other things, to discern the northern sector of the site where this activity was mainly performed. At least three other sites have provided evidence for similar situations, including Gródek Nadbużny (based on Volhynian flints; Gumiński 1989), Zawichost-Pieczyska (Świeciechów flint; Balcer 1967), and Bronocice (Jurassic G flint; Kruk and Milisauskas 1981, 1983). However, it must be emphasized that these villages were inhabited by farmers and not by full-time specialist flintknappers.

Close relationships with flint outcrops and flint production are not characteristic of all large SE TRB settlements. Some of them, from the perspective of chipped stone *chaîne opératoire*, can be described as 'user settlements.' Inhabitants of these sites almost exclusively used imported ready-made tools, mostly made on long, regular blades. Interestingly, significant numbers of these imported tools were made of distant raw materials. Perhaps even more interesting are findings of unprocessed blade blanks of the same raw materials. For example, in Mozgawa, finished tools and blade blanks made of Świeciechów flint distinctly predominate. This flint is not the closest one geographically, the outcrops of Jurassic flints are located closer (see Figure 6.1), but, apart from

Volhynian flint, the Świeciechów flint certainly is the best quality.

Burials in settlement pits are distinctive features at almost all large SE TRB settlements (e.g., Balcer 1966; Kempisty 1965). These burials exhibit all the typical features of the general TRB ritual, such as the placement of the body in an extended position and a very modest amount of grave goods, with many of the burials completely lacking them. An exceptional find is the collective Grave XIII from Bronocice. Altogether, 17 individuals were identified, including 10 children ranging from 6 months to 10 years of age, two women about 18 years old, two men aged 18 and 25 years, and a 15-year-old of indeterminate sex (Milisauskas et al. 2016: 92–101). The layout of the bodies did not follow TRB traditions. This feature is associated with the late settlement phase at Bronocice, characterized by strong Baden culture influences. For this reason and judging from some anatomical traits, a recent hypothesis is that the feature represents a burial of people of foreign origin (Milisauskas et al. 2016: 98–101).

Chronology

The available chronological information, a large proportion of which are AMS dates (cf. Nowak 2017a),

shows that large settlements in SE TRB developed no earlier than approximately 3600 BC, as demonstrated by radiocarbon dates from Bronocice (Kruk and Milisauskas 1990, 2018; Kruk et al. 2018; Milisauskas et al. 2016), Mozgawa (Korczyńska et al. 2019), Ćmielów (Bakker et al. 1969; Breuning 1987: 159–160), Gródek Nadbużny (Bronicki et al. 2003; Jastrzębski 1991), and Zimno (Bronicki et al. 2003). As for the time of their abandonment, it is possible that they persisted until the end of SE TRB, c. 2900/2800 BC. The only exception seems to be Ćmielów, which can be placed between c. 3600 and 3300 BC, but even at that site one date indicates abandonment c. 3100–2900 BC.

Bronocice and Mozgawa: Two Case Studies

Data from Bronocice are of great help in the matter of chronology and spatial development of the SE TRB settlements due to research conducted by Kruk and Milisauskas (Figure 6.5; Kruk and Milisauskas 1990, 2018; Kruk et al. 1996, 2016, 2018; Milisauskas and Kruk 1984, 1989; Milisauskas et al. 2016). In the BR I phase (c. 3750/3700 BC; chronology according to Nowak 2017a), only a small settlement of c. 2 ha existed in Zone C. After the late Lublin-Volhynian culture, TRB people appeared on the site again c. 3600 BC. The village was probably occupied by a TRB community until c. 2800

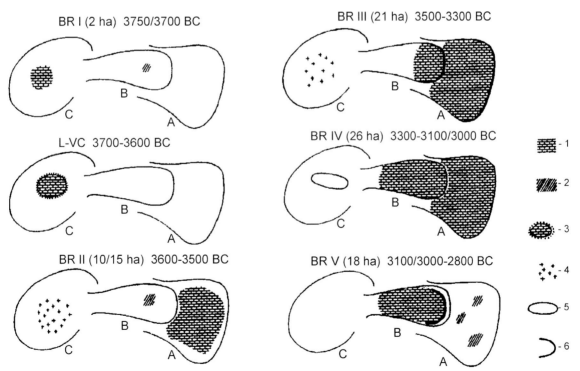

Figure 6.5. Development of the Bronocice site. A, B, C: Basic zones of the site; BR I to III: Settlement phases of the Funnel Beaker culture; BR IV and V: Settlement phases of the Funnel Beaker culture, with influences from the Baden culture (i.e., Beaker/ Baden assemblages); L–VC: Lublin–Volhynian culture (late Lengyel–Polgár) settlement; 1: Occupied area; 2: Distribution of areas in use beyond the extent of the site in a given phase; 3: Lublin–Volhynian fortification; 4: Cemetery in BR II and III (and later?) phases; 5: Enclosure dating to the BR IV phase; 6: Fortification of the BR V phase (adapted from Kruk et al. 1996). Note that the chronology of phases has been slightly modified (see Nowak 2017a), therefore, differences occur when compared to earlier publications (i.e., Kruk and Milisauskas 1990; Kruk et al. 1996, 2016; Milisauskas et al. 2016) (figure by M. Nowak).

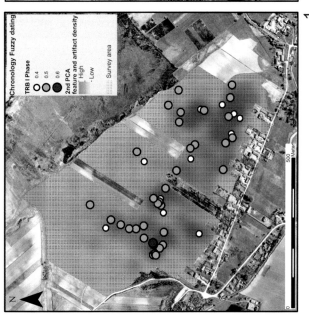

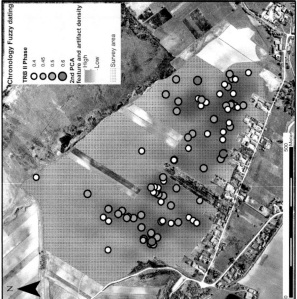

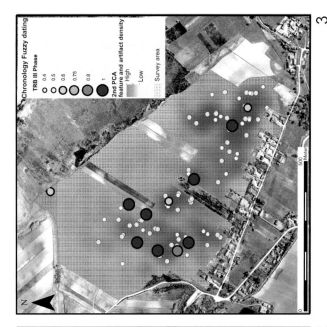

Figure 6.6. 'Fuzzy' chronology of Funnel Beaker culture surface findings at Mozgawa (1–3). Typological dating (which does not quite fit to the absolute dating, see text): TRB I: c. 3600–3500 BC; TRB II: c. 3500–3300 BC; TRB III: c. 3300–3100/2900 BC (figure by K. Cappenberg and M. Korczyńska).

BC, during phases BR II to BR V. Over the course of this period, the spatial extent of the settlement changed. In the BR II phase (c. 3600–3500 BC), the site may have measured 10–15 ha, and occupation took place mainly in Zone A. The size of the settled area grew over time up to 26 ha in the BR IV phase (c. 3300–3100/3000 BC), then decreased again to 18 ha in the BR V phase (c. 3100/3000–2800 BC). In the period of c. 3500–3100/3000 BC, all zones of the site seem to have been utilized, and after 3100/3000 BC, predominantly Zone B was in use. Thus, not all the zones were utilized continuously, simultaneously, and for the same purpose over time. For instance, in Zone C, there was a cemetery in the BR II and BR III phases, and possibly also a bit longer, followed by a variously interpreted (e.g., kraal) small enclosure in the BR IV phase. Obtaining radiocarbon dates from all phases of each part of the site utilized by TRB people, except Zones A and C in the BR V phase, is an issue of intrinsic importance for the reconstruction of site development. The case of Bronocice can be acknowledged as reflecting long-term adherence to a particular place.

The recently investigated site of Mozgawa is also significant for assessing chronology and dynamics of intrasite development at large SE TRB settlements (Korczyńska et al. 2019; Moskal-del Hoyo et al. 2018). Radiocarbon dates indicate inhabitation between 3600 and 3100 BC at this site. As regards the spatial distribution of these dates, it is important to note that all sections of the site, a total of 30–35 ha, were occupied in the period of c. 3600–3400/3350 BC. Dates from the central and southeastern sections of Mozgawa suggest that these zones were still inhabited between 3400/3350 and 3250 BC. Finally, it is possible that after c. 3250 BC, only the southeastern section was utilized, in an area of slightly over 10 ha.

Only four small areas have been excavated at Mozgawa so far, and therefore, the spatial representativeness of radiocarbon and ceramic typological data is much lower than at Bronocice. Results from surface collections can also facilitate in answering questions regarding site development. Typology-based dating of surface findings (mainly pottery), based on a fuzzy logic approach (e.g., Farinetti et al. 2010), implies that the entire area of the site was settled during all phases of the TRB development (Figure 6.6). Further investigations are needed to settle this contradiction between data from excavations and surface surveys.

Discussion

Early Development of SE TRB

For about 200 years, SE TRB people lived in small and medium-sized settlements. When located in loess zones, the former did not exceed 1–2 ha (Kruk 1980; Milisauskas and Kruk 1984), and settlements outside of loess zones were often smaller (Nowak 1993, 2001). The few medium-size sites occur only in loess zones, and their extent usually did not exceed 4–5 ha (Kruk *et al.* 1996; Milisauskas and Kruk 1984).

The early SE TRB consisted of microregional groups that maintained fairly clear social borders (Nowak 1993). We could hypothesize that such groups were composed of no more than 150 individuals, based on spatial data (Nowak 1993), ethnographic observations (Lehmann *et al.* 2014), and psychological/neurobiological interpretations of human behavior (Dunbar 2016). Such a scale reflects limits of recognized kinship (Dunbar 2016: 91), among other aspects.

Units of this kind often erected sepulchral monuments (unchambered barrows or so-called megadendrons; see Libera and Tunia 2006; Tunia 2006), indicating the presence of leaders who were buried in the central graves of such monuments. It cannot be ruled out that among these leaders were persons who brought the first TRB groups from the lowland zone. Over time, they became mythical ancestors whose worship was celebrated in chapels routinely built within these monuments (e.g., Florek 2008; Przybyła and Tunia 2013). Significantly enough, although grave goods buried with the deceased in these monuments are scarce, in several cases, it contains single copper artifacts (daggers and axes; Przybyła and Tunia 2013; K. Tunia, personal communication). Objects made of copper are rather uncommon in SE TRB, and not only in its early phase. Therefore, individuals who were endowed with such items to carry them into the netherworld had to occupy an extremely prominent role in their communities. Thus, local groups would have leaders that stood out due to their personal status rather than their wealth. In the early SE TRB, this position may have been associated with being a member of the founding lineage. It was manifested, and visible to others, by a public cult of the founding ancestor, interred in the locally oldest sepulchral monument. Thus, sepulchral monuments symbolically reflected the founding history and mythology of all members of these groups, and created and maintained historical and mythological identity ('people of monuments,' 'people who were brought here by those who were buried in monuments'). It is not a coincidence that usually flat cemeteries were established next to such monuments (Florek 2008; Garbacz 2006) as if symbolically adding the rank-and-file members of a given community to this history and mythology.

'Classic' Period of SE TRB

After *c.* 3600 BC, the number of SE TRB sites increased significantly, coinciding with the disappearance of the last groups of the Lengyel–Polgár complex (L–PC) in Lesser Poland. These changes took place due to cultural transformations within L–PC, which consisted of abandoning the 'old' cultural model in favor of the 'new' one, that is, the SE TRB (Nowak 2009, 2013, 2014a). This made SE TRB a unit of significant demographic dimensions.

These processes were not only connected with transformations in the material culture. Among other changes, the most spectacular was the almost complete coverage of the landscape by SE TRB sites, both within the fertile loess 'islands,' used previously by Early Neolithic groups (see Figure 6.2), and in areas between such 'islands,' which had not been utilized by these earlier groups. Although SE TRB settlements were not uniformly distributed over the entire landscape, and sites in loess areas were still more numerous, unlike the earlier Neolithic, the presence of TRB groups is evident even in less fertile zones.

Compared to the preceding period, there are many more SE TRB sites in this 'classic' phase; taking into account the number of sites with radiocarbon dates (Nowak 2009), few dozen times more sites can be assigned to the classic phase. Given the quantitative relations of ceramics with early and classic features, this difference does not seem exaggerated. A clear numerical predominance also occurs in relation to L–PC, although it does not seem to be so radical. For example, calculations for the southeastern part of the discussed area gave about 180 sites for L–PC and almost 900 for SE TRB (Pelisiak 2018).

Most of small and medium-size SE TRB settlements were occupied for shorter durations than those of comparable size L–PC sites (for comparisons, see Burchard 1973, 1977; Nowak 2014b; Rook and Nowak 1993; Valde-Nowak *et al.* 2015; Włodarczak 2013 and Godłowska *et al.* 1987; Grabowska and Zastawny 2011; Nowak 2010, 2014b). This suggests that the much greater number of classic phase TRB sites, relative to both L–PC and the early SE TRB, does not testify exclusively to population growth but also was a result of a greater degree of mobility (see Bogucki 2008; Kruk and Milisauskas 1999: 142–143).

Because Funnel Beaker sites cover the landscape more or less evenly, we are not able to discern microregional clusters. This problem probably results from insufficient quantity and quality of chronological data. Therefore, it is plausible that the available evidence represents a palimpsest of sequential movements between microregions. However, the areas and boundaries of consecutively settled microregions might have changed over time, so that shifts in social boundaries may have been more frequent than during the Lengyel–Polgár period, which had been more stable in this regard. That is, boundaries that had been actively maintained by L–PC communities became more fluid, contributing to the more dispersed SE TRB settlement pattern. In the late L–PC groupings, the disintegration of social units of various scales took place when they joined the system of the SE TRB information flow.

Nucleation Processes in the 'Classic' SE TRB

Settlement nucleation occurred around 3600 BC, in the context of the transformations described above. Villages evolved that were significantly larger than those remaining from previous periods. However, the number of these large sites was fairly low; assuming that not all settlements have been identified, this number across the entire SE TRB should not be greater than approximately 50. These sites were inhabited for a long time, probably over 500 years, during which the zones occupied by the inhabitants might have shifted sequentially but always exceeded c. 10 ha.

There were, and there are, dynamic relations between repetitive social practices and their environmental contexts, as well as artifacts and ecofacts, including the construction of place, as environmental and material realities shaped and were shaped and influenced by social practices (Salisbury 2016: 19–22). Understanding these relations leads to more or less reliable reconstructions of the former based on the latter. Obviously, there also have been positive correlations between the size of the settled area and the number of people inhabiting it. Exceeding the next population thresholds required the occurrence of new decision-making levels that aimed at coping with social and other stressors (Dunbar 2016).

From 3600 BC, there was a significant demographic increase in some settlements of SE TRB. For example, for the settlement of Bronocice in the BR III phase, population has been estimated at approximately 500 individuals (Kruk et al. 1996; Milisauskas and Kruk 1984). These villages prevailed over other settlements within their respective regions in terms of extent and population and developed through demographic and settlement nucleation (Milisauskas and Kruk 1984: Table 8).

A challenging question is why large TRB settlements were founded only in zones of fertile, loess uplands. The placement of settlements may have been affected by very different factors, including, but not restricted to, ecological and environmental advantages and access to specific raw materials. Decision-making processes leading to the establishment of settlements may also have considered social factors, or even psychological, political, and ideological ones.

We should emphasize that although the large TRB settlements were located in the same zones as the L–PC settlements, they were founded from scratch (Gródek Nadbużny might be the only exception; see Gumiński 1989; Jastrzębski 1991), sometimes with a preceding phase of a smaller settlement. In contrast to many smaller sites of SE TRB, settlement continuation from the Early Neolithic has not been recorded at these large villages. This phenomenon can be considered as an expression of a partial, conscious break with previous settlement and cultural traditions.

At about 3600/3500 BC, evidence indicates a shift toward slash-and-burn agriculture that corresponded to the use of extensive areas in the vicinity of large sites. This is reflected primarily by geomorphological data, such as diluvial layers dated to the Middle Neolithic, which indicate intensive erosion processes caused by human activity (Kruk et al. 1996; Moskal-del Hoyo et al. 2018; Poręba et al. 2012; Śnieszko 1985; Szwarczewski 2009). This also correlated with some opening of the landscape, suggested by palynological and malacological data (Jersak and Śnieszko 1987; Moskal-del Hoyo et al. 2018).

These processes led to the appearance of more open, forest-steppe or steppe-like, landscapes. The inhabitants of large sites, for the first time in the Neolithic, actively and fundamentally transformed significant parts of their natural environments. Such behavior, which can be described as 'taming of the landscape,' became an essential part of their identity. When people transform their environment, in the long run, these changes also influence themselves, affecting their conceptualization of place, time, and identity (Salisbury 2016: 251). Living in a transformed environment may have affirmed identity at large settlements in the TRB period (i.e., 'people of fire'), as opposed to groups that had not changed their environments, especially if this transformation by burning was initiated by the inhabitants of these villages or their ancestors. Thus, a semi-open, park-like landscape surrounding the large settlements became a source of collective identity for people living in them, enabling them to offset some variability and providing a mental constituent that separated them from others. A sense of connection with a very specific landscape generated emotional ties 'that Neustupný (1991, 1998b) argued are essential in the construction of community areas, and that others refer to as the "moral community"' (Salisbury 2016: 255; see also Whittle 2003).

As mentioned above, currently, there are few known building remains from large SE TRB settlements. These remains, as well as analogies from smaller settlements and the other TRB groups, indicate that in this culture, including the large villages discussed here, there were no strict patterns in this respect (Kulczycka-Leciejewiczowa 2002; Milisauskas et al. 2016; Nowak 2009: 351–370, with further literature; Pelisiak 2003).

The built environment that the inhabitants interacted with daily in large SE TRB settlements may have consisted of a dozen or so concentrations of houses. Compared with Early Neolithic examples, in which well-preserved outlines of houses demonstrate advanced standardization, these houses were not homogeneous in terms of construction technique and size. The layout of the SE TRB houses within the spatial concentrations did not follow strictly defined spatial rules. This, again, is in marked contrast to Early Neolithic patterns. Furthermore, although local TRB communities technically were capable of erecting large architectural structures, exemplified by the above-mentioned monumental megalithic tombs and tombs built of earth and wood (Nowak 2017b), there are no indications of the construction of exceptionally big structures at the settlements.

Regularities in architecture, as occurred in the Early Neolithic of Lesser Poland, suggest a widely held set of cultural conventions (Salisbury 2016: 251), and its absence in the SE TRB indicates that such conventions did not exist over the course of that period. The lack of a particular pattern of house construction may imply that there was no uniform mental image in regard to how settlements should look, and that architectural conventions did not have significant cultural importance. Thus, it did not communicate any specific social and/or ideological meaning (including a lack of adherence to some of the earlier building traditions; see Nowak 2009: 366). One can conclude that this phenomenon was the result of a social structure, in which small, relatively autonomous family units (households), in the form of nuclear families, prevailed in the social sphere (see Kukawka 1997; Kulczycka-Leciejewiczowa 2002: 45). This sort of social organization also contributed to the creation and maintenance of their identity (i.e., 'free household people,' as opposed to L–PC identity). These observations indicate that settlement layouts developed through the everyday cooperation of and negotiation between family units (Salisbury 2016: 251).

Burials in large settlements were scantily equipped; as regards flat burials found outside of these settlements, both in isolation and in cemeteries, there are no differences in this respect. It seems likely that some part of the population of large settlements was buried on the spot and others outside since cemeteries have been recorded close to settlements (see Bronocice; Milisauskas et al. 2016). Differences in wealth and status do not seem to have occurred between these two groups, however, some other kinds of social differences may have existed between them. We can only speculate some corporate form of social differentiation within the populations of SE TRB large settlements.

Craft production activities concentrated on the large villages. Flint working is a factor that impacted internal layout, which is the most evident at the site of Ćmielów. Such a system was a part of the built environment of the settlement, reflecting the diversity of residents. However, it is difficult to answer the question of whether there was any hierarchy related to this diversity. Undoubtedly, the production of chipped stone tools in these villages far exceeded the needs of their residents (Balcer 2002). Therefore, these settlements were centers of the distribution of finished tools made from the best raw materials. More importantly, the large SE TRB sites were not only production centers but also nodes in the distribution system of blade blanks. It is reasonable to assume that there existed some distinguished specialist groups, such as producers and middlemen. People who were involved in these activities were not necessarily richer or more influential, although we know that this often happens especially in the case of middlemen, rather they may have constituted a complementary component of the socioeconomic system. The distribution of high-quality flint raw materials could have created a kind of interaction sphere, or spheres, that extended beyond SE TRB.

To better understand the importance of SE TRB large settlements, their surroundings also should be taken into account. In contrast to the Early Neolithic period, large SE TRB settlements are distinguished by their size relative to that of other sites in their respective regions. This might imply a system in which such settlements were the centers of economic and sociopolitical organizations at the micro- and/or mesoregional scale. The population of a given large settlement, or at least part of it, was endowed with decision-making competencies in respect to the village itself as well as to a territory beyond its borders.

Kruk and Milisauskas (1999; Milisauskas and Kruk 1984, 1989) postulated that integrated agricultural agglomerations appeared in the loess uplands of Lesser Poland during the SE TRB, organized according to different rules than in the Early Neolithic period (see also Balcer 2002; Jastrzębski 1988; Pelisiak 2018). They argued that a hierarchical system, consisting of paramount large villages, medium-size settlements, and small sites, was formed after the mid-4th millennium BC, and local communities were structured by decision-making competencies of more than one level (Kruk and Milisauskas 1999: 141).

According to Kruk and Milisauskas (1999: 126), proportions between large, medium, and small settlements come to 1:10:25 in well-studied loess areas, not including sites identified as camps and by stray finds. All of these categories of sites would have been components of organizational units, usually covering several hundred square kilometers, which can be associated with the concept of a 'communal world' (Neustupný 1998a: 19, 39–41).

Alas, we must admit that a precise determination of the boundaries of such organizational units is speculative. As already highlighted, the relatively uniform and dense spatial distribution of the Funnel Beaker sites in the landscape and the unavailability of a high-resolution chronological framework contribute to this problem. One way or another, if this image of the classic SE TRB settlement is a kind of chronological palimpsest, postulated communal worlds would comprise a stable, long-term center (i.e., a large settlement) and several groups (consisting of hamlets and single households) that moved relatively frequently, perhaps after one generation, between consecutively used areas in specific microregions.

Based on data on the built environment, there is no evidence to indicate advanced social hierarchy in large SE TRB settlements. There were no central and prominent buildings, richly equipped burials, and 'wealthier' neighborhoods within these sites. The architectural, or in another word, visual, 'egalitarianism' lasted for a long time. Inevitably, it also influenced the organization of the society, inhibiting the development of more advanced social diversity, including hereditary hierarchical structures.

It is therefore possible to wonder whether the analogy with nucleation processes in the Trypillia culture is applicable here. Namely, it has recently been suggested that for this culture, particularly for its mega-sites, social structures were characterized by the lack of clear social hierarchy (Müller et al. 2016a, 2016b; see also Gaydarska and Chapman 2020a, 2020b). These sites would be central decision-making centers, persisting not so much as a result of social hierarchy, but because of a kind of social contract. The establishment of such centers is considered as a result of conscious political decisions (Müller 2016a: 15). Furthermore, these communities constituted a 'social experiment of living together' (Müller 2016b: 302), although this interpretation is perhaps a bit risky.

Certainly, there must have been some forms of leadership and social control at large SE TRB settlements. Many terms used in social evolution theory could be proposed, which refer to social structures and ways of exercising authority in contexts when inequality of wealth and perhaps status does

not equal formal hierarchy and power (Renfrew and Bahn 2016). However, in our opinion, the concept of 'trans-egalitarian societies' is particularly useful for understanding SE TRB settlements, strongly promoted by Bogucki (1999: 208–258, with further references). This term is to

> '... describe societies which are neither egalitarian nor politically stratified. [...] these societies were moving beyond the constraints of the egalitarian households of late foragers and early farmers into a social environment of competition and differentiation. Yet the relationships among households over time were still fluid and had not become ossified into rigid hierarchical structures. "Leadership" had not yet become completely transformed into "power"' (Bogucki 1999: 209)

The reason for the formation of trans-egalitarian societies was the presence of aggrandizing individuals who became nominal leaders without institutionalized, genealogy-based status. Judging by the existence of separate nuclei of houses within the discussed, large SE TRB settlements, there could have been even several of such nominal leaders at a given settlement. Probably one of them, perhaps representing the largest household concentration, was more influential or aspired to be more important. Their authority and prestige 'grew from their ability as heads of households [and factions] to pursue successful accumulation strategies and to hold other households in economic and social debt' (Bogucki 1999: 257–258). Such leaders could have emerged and disappeared. Defense, trade, and other relations functioned within the context of 'trusted networks' 'rather as formal functions of a leadership elite' (Bogucki 1999: 217–218). Another typical feature of trans-egalitarian societies would be an increase in activities related to trade and mortuary ceremonialism (Bogucki 1999: 256). It seems quite possible that the nominal leaders were interred in unchambered long barrows or megadendrons, which were also erected in the classic phase of SE TRB (Libera and Tunia 2006).

Progress of Nucleation in the Late SE TRB

In the last quarter of the 4th and the early 3rd millennia BC, many of the smaller SE TRB sites were abandoned. Judging from this, one could assume that a significant, and perhaps the greater, part of local populations concentrated in large settlements. For instance, Milisauskas and Kruk (1989: 83) evaluated that level at c. 56%.

What can be considered as the cause of such a process? The most influential hypothesis proposed by Kruk (1980) assumes that progressive deforestation eventually caused a crisis when there was no longer anything to burn. This forced the inhabitants of the

SE TRB clusters to move into the central settlements and start intensive farming, utilizing simple ards or plows with oxen as draft animals. Iconographic data suggesting the use of draft animals at this time and in this region (Milisauskas and Kruk 1991; Milisauskas *et al.* 2012: 137–138; Uzarowicz-Chmielewska 1978) and an impression of a yoke on a horn core from the BR V phase at Bronocice (Milisauskas and Kruk 1991) may corroborate such an argument, however, it must be noted that images directly representing plowing are unavailable in the archaeological record. It is also worth mentioning that the use of draft animals is considered to have been a factor facilitating the establishment and maintenance of large Trypillia settlements (Müller 2016b; Müller and Rassman 2016).

Interestingly enough, large SE TRB sites are often characterized by culturally mixed archaeological materials. The so-called Beaker–Baden assemblages in western Lesser Poland are the best examples of such correlation (Zastawny 2008). Baden influences can also be suggested for Ćmielów and Gródek Nadbużny (Burchard *et al.* 1991; Przybył 2017; Zastawny 2015). Furthermore, a ditch discovered in Bronocice (Kruk and Milisauskas 1981), as well as other fortifications recently found through aerial photography and verified by surface findings, but not necessarily associated with SE TRB large settlements (Przybyła *et al.* 2015), belong to the phase featured by Baden influences. These enclosures may be considered as a result of these influences since similar structures have been recorded fairly frequently in Baden culture contexts (e.g., Nowak and Zastawny 2015). However, political threats leading to the intensification of nucleation during the late phase of SE TRB can also be postulated.

One way or another, even populous communities that inhabited large settlements should be reckoned with during the period in question. Exceeding the next demographic levels should result in increased social control and stratification. Nevertheless, based on available archaeological premises, it is difficult to say unequivocally whether this was the case, and this lack of clarity is somewhat daunting. In any case, there are visible influences from outside of the TRB world and maybe even indications of foreign settlers at some large SE TRB villages. It is quite plausible that these settlements transformed into multicultural emporia controlling economic exchange.

Disappearance of SE TRB

The large SE TRB settlements disappeared around 2900/2800 BC, as did the entire SE TRB. Subsequently, mainly local branches of the Corded Ware culture (CWC) evolved throughout Lesser Poland, most probably representing communities of semi-nomadic shepherds (Włodarczak 2006). Undoubtedly, it is possible that processes toward social and cultural disintegration occurred already during the late, nucleated SE TRB. The roots of these processes might have included insufficient resources available for the growing populations at the nucleated settlements and social tensions within these egalitarian communities, possibly associated with their scale and the lack of institutionalized social hierarchies (Gyucha 2015: 286). An interesting proposal regarding insufficient natural resources for nucleated communities is the lack of available wood, postulated by some researchers (Kruk 1980; Kruk and Milisauskas 1999), and not only in the case of Lesser Poland (e.g., Gyucha 2015: 85–87). Possibly, it is not accidental that the size of some large SE TRB villages decreased in their final stages; this might have been the case for Bronocice and Mozgawa as well. Such disintegration surely facilitated the transformation of SE TRB toward local CWC.

Conclusions

Our research aimed at modeling the social and economic processes behind the development of large settlements of SE TRB, in order to gain a better understanding of how decisions to nucleate affected the sociocultural trajectories of the Middle Neolithic groups in Lesser Poland (see also Gyucha *et al.* 2015: 129).

During the classic SE TRB, in some areas of Lesser Poland, settlement systems tethered to centers of *c.* 10–35 ha appeared. These systems were characterized by trans-egalitarian social structures, with nominal, aggrandizing leaders who controlled the flow of certain goods and supervised neighboring territories (i.e., the communal world). That is, their decision-making powers extended not only to groups inhabiting large settlements but also to the sphere of microregional populations. Their status did not result from inheritance but rather from personal merits. Not all these social features were present in the early SE TRB or the preceding L-PC.

Finally, it should be emphasized that a significant part of the SE TRB population constituted descendants of the L-PC. For those people, in deviating from traditional cultural patterns and 'Funnel Beaker acculturation,' a need emerged to generate a new identity. Sepulchral monuments were not significant symbols of this new identity. Therefore, in the conditions of the profound change of the previous spatial functioning, combined with anthropogenic transformations of the environment, it was necessary to construct new, visible reference points, understandable for all the 'carriers' of the new cultural system. In other words, residents of the SE TRB large settlements were people of 'Funnel Beaker origin' and Early Neolithic origin, culturally transformed into the SE TRB. The decline of the large

SE TRB settlements *c.* 2900/2800 BC was preceded and intensified by processes of internal disintegration caused by ecological stressors.

Acknowledgments

This paper, particularly concerning investigations at Mozgawa, was financially supported by projects conducted by the National Science Center in Poland, including Archaeological, Archaeobotanical and Palaeoenvironmental Research in the Western Part of the Nida Basin (2013/11/B/HS3/03822; PI: M. Moskal-del Hoyo) and Agriculture and Palaeodietary Development in Neolithic and Bronze Ages on the Basis of Stable Carbon and Nitrogen Isotope Values in Biological Remains (2013/10/M/HS3/00537; PI: A. Mueller-Bieniek). Geomagnetic prospection has been conducted in the framework of a cooperation with Professur für Metallzeiten, Institut für Ur- und Frühgeschichte Universität zu Köln. We greatly appreciate the support provided by Tobias L. Kienlin and Jakob Ociepka in that matter. The authors are also grateful to A. Wacnik, A. Mueller-Bieniek, P. Szwarczewski, K. Kotynia, and M. Płoszaj for their kind permissions to utilize unpublished data. We are also thankful to J.M. del Hoyo-Melendez for proofreading the final manuscript.

References Cited

Bakker, J.A., J.C. Vogel and T. Wiślański 1969. TRB and other C14 dates from Poland (c. 4350–1350 BC and 800–900 AD). *Helinium* 9: 3–27, 209–238.

Balcer, B. 1966. Odkrycie szkieletu ludzkiego w jamie 16 w obrębie osady kultury pucharów lejkowatych w Zawichoście, pow. Sandomierz. *Rocznik Muzeum Świętokrzyskiego* 4: 29–33.

Balcer, B. 1967. Stanowisko Pieczyska (Zbrza Wielka) w Zawichoście-Podgórzu, pow. Sandomierz, w świetle pierwszych wykopalisk. *Wiadomości Archeologiczne* 32: 290–375.

Balcer, B. 1989. Z badań nad budownictwem w kulturze pucharów lejkowatych. Podziemia osady na wzgórzu Gawroniec w Ćmielowie, woj. tarnobrzeskie. *Archeologia Polski* 34: 267–367.

Balcer, B. 2002. *Ćmielów, Krzemionki, Świeciechów. Związki osady neolitycznej z kopalniami krzemienia.* Warszawa: Instytut Archeologii i Etnologii Polskiej Akademii Nauk.

Bogucki, P. 1999. *The Origins of Human Society.* Malden and Oxford: Blackwell.

Bogucki, P. 2008. *Forest Farmers and Stockherders: Early Agriculture and Its Consequences in North-Central Europe.* 2nd edition. Cambridge: Cambridge University Press.

Breuning, P. 1987. *14C-Chronologie des Vorderasiatischen, Südost- und Mittel-europäischen Neolithikums.* Köln and Wien: Böhlau.

Bronicki, A., S. Kadrow and A. Zakościelna 2003. Radiocarbon dating of the Neolithic settlement in Zimne, Volhynia, in light of the chronology of the Lublin-Volhynia culture and the south-eastern group of the Funnel Beaker culture. *Baltic-Pontic Studies* 12: 22–67.

Bronicki, A., H. Ochrimenko and A. Zakościelna 1998. Badania weryfikacyjno-sondażowe wyżynnej osady neolitycznej na stanowisku 'Grodzisko' w Zimnem, rej. Włodzimierz Wołyński (Ukraina). *Archeologia Polski Środkowowschodniej* 3: 12–30.

Burchard, B. 1973. Ze studiów nad chronologią kultury pucharów lejkowatych w zachodniej części Małopolski, in J. Machnik (ed.) *Z badań nad neolitem i wczesną epoką brązu w Małopolsce:* 107–120. Wrocław: Ossolineum.

Burchard, B. 1977. Wyniki badań wykopaliskowych na stan. 1 w Niedźwiedziu, gm. Słomniki, woj. Kraków, w latach 1965–1973. *Sprawozdania Archeologiczne* 29: 59–81.

Burchard, B., S. Jastrzębski and J. Kruk 1991. Some Questions at Funnel Beaker Culture South-Eastern Group – An Outline, in D. Jankowska (ed.) *Die Trichterbecherkultur. Neue Forschungen und Hypothesen, Teil II:* 95–102. Poznań: Instytut Prahistorii Uniwersytetu im. A. Mickiewicza and Zakład Archeologii Wielkopolski Instytutu Historii Kultury Materialnej Polskiej Akademii Nauk.

Dunbar, R. 2016. *Human Evolution: Our Brains and Behavior.* London: Penguin Books.

Farinetti, E., S. Hermon and F. Nicolucci 2010. Fuzzy logic application to artifact surface survey data, in F. Nicolucci and S. Hermon (eds) *Beyond the Artifacts: Digital Interpretation of the Past:* 125–129. Budapest: Archaeolingua.

Fleischer, J. 2014. The complexity of public space at the Swahili town of Songo Mnara, Tanzania. *Journal of Anthropological Archaeology* 35(1): 1–22.

Florek, M. 2008. Cmentarzyska kultury pucharów lejkowatych na Wyżynie Sandomierskiej. Historia i stan badań. *Wiadomości Archeologiczne* 60: 97–123.

Furholt, M., M. Hinz, D. Mischka, G. Noble and D. Olausson (eds) 2014. *Landscapes, Histories and Societies in the Northern European Neolithic* (Frühe Monumentalität und soziale Differenzierung 4). Kiel and Bonn: Institut für Ur- und Frühgeschichte der CAU and Dr. Rudolf Habelt.

Garbacz, K. 2006. Dwa grobowce z Grzybowa, pow. Staszów na tle zjawiska rozpowszechniania się idei megalitycznej w grupie południowo-wschodniej kultury pucharów lejkowatych, in J. Libera and K. Tunia (eds) *Idea megalityczna w obrządku pogrzebowym kultury pucharów lejkowatych:* 307–333. Lublin and Kraków: Instytut Archeologii i Etnologii Polskiej Akademii Nauk and Instytut Archeologii Uniwersytetu Marie Curie-Skłodowskiej.

Gaydarska, B. (ed.) 2020. *Early Urbanism in Europe: The Trypillia Megasites of the Ukrainian Forest-Steppe*. Warsaw and Berlin: De Gruyter.

Gaydarska, B. and J. Chapman 2020a. Conclusions, in B. Gaydarska (ed.) *Early Urbanism in Europe: The Trypillia Megasites of the Ukrainian Forest-Steppe*: 508–528. Warsaw and Berlin: De Gruyter.

Gaydarska, B. and J. Chapman 2020b. Discussion, in B. Gaydarska (ed.) *Early Urbanism in Europe: The Trypillia Megasites of the Ukrainian Forest-Steppe*: 415–507. Warsaw and Berlin: De Gruyter.

Godłowska, M., J.K. Kozłowski, L. Starkel and K. Wasylikowa 1987. Neolithic settlement at Pleszów and changes in the natural environment in the Vistula valley. *Przegląd Archeologiczny* 34: 133–159.

Grabowska, B. and A. Zastawny 2011. Materiały kręgu lendzielsko-polgarskiego ze st. 5 w Modlnicy, pow. Krakowski, in J. Kruk and A. Zastawny (eds) *Modlnica, st. 5: Od neolitu środkowego do wczesnej epoki brązu*: 95–172. Kraków: Krakowski Zespół do Badań Autostrad.

Gumiński, W. 1989. *Gródek Nadbużny. Osada kultury pucharów lejkowatych*. Wrocław: Ossolineum.

Gyucha, A. 2015. *Prehistoric Village Social Dynamics: The Early Copper Age in the Körös Region* (Prehistoric Research in the Körös Region 2). Budapest: Archaeolingua.

Gyucha, A., R.W. Yerkes, W.A. Parkinson, A. Sarris, N. Papadopoulos, P.R. Duffy, and R.B. Salisbury 2015. Settlement Nucleation in the Neolithic: A Preliminary Report of the Körös Regional Archaeological Project's Investigations at Szeghalom-Kovácshalom and Vésztő-Mágor, in S. Hansen, P. Raczky, A. Anders and A. Reingruber (eds) *Neolithic and Copper Age between the Carpathians and the Aegean Sea: Chronologies and Technologies from the 6th to the 4th Millennium BCE* (Archäologie in Eurasien 31): 129–142. Bonn: Dr. Rudolf Habelt.

Jastrzębski, S. 1988. Kultura pucharów lejkowatych w międzyrzeczu Huczwy i Bugu – analiza osadnicza. *Prace i Materiały Zamojskie* 3: 5–25.

Jastrzębski, S. 1991. The settlement of the Funnel Beaker Culture at Gródek Nadbużny, the Zamość District, site 1C – brief characteristics, in D. Jankowska (ed.) *Die Trichterbecherkultur. Neue Forschungen und Hypothesen, Teil II*: 189–196. Poznań: Instytut Prahistorii Uniwersytetu Adama Mickiewicza, Zakład Archeologii Wielkopolski Instytutu Historii Kultury Materialnej Polskiej Akademii Nauk.

Jażdżewski, K. 1936. *Kultura pucharów lejkowatych w Polsce zachodniej i środkowej*. Poznań: Polskie Towarzystwo Prehistoryczne.

Jażdżewski, K. 1958. Uwagi ogólne o osadzie neolitycznej w Gródku Nadbużnym w pow. hrubieszowskim, st. 1C. *Archeologia Polski* 2: 279–284.

Jersak, J. and Z. Śnieszko 1987. Zmiany środowiska geograficznego w późnym vistulianie i holocenie na obszarach lessowych Wyżyny Miechowskiej i Opatowsko-Sandomierskiej, in J. Jersak (ed.) *Wybrane zagadnienia paleogeografii czwartorzędu - holocen*: 7–24. Katowice: Uniwersytet Śląski.

Kabaciński, J., S. Hartz, D.C.M. Raemaekers and T. Terberger (eds) 2015. *The Dąbki Site in Pomerania and the Neolithisation of the North European Lowlands (c. 5000-3000 calBC)* (Archäologie und Geschichte im Ostseeraum/Archaeology and History of the Baltic 8). Rahden/Westfalen: Marie Leidorf.

Kadrow, S. 2017. The Danubian world and the dawn of the metal ages, in P. Włodarczak (ed.) *The Past Societies. The Polish Lands from the First Evidence of Human Presence to the Early Middle Ages, Vol. 2: 5500-2000 BC*: 63–106. Warszawa: Institute of Archaeology and Ethnology of the Polish Academy of Sciences.

Kadrow, S. and A. Zakościelna 2000. An outline of the evolution of Danubian cultures in Małopolska and western Ukraine. *Baltic-Pontic Studies* 9: 187–255.

Kempisty, E. 1965. Grób kultury pucharów lejkowatych w Kamieniu Łukawskim, pow. Sandomierz. *Wiadomości Archeologiczne* 31: 159–162.

Kempisty, E. 1966. Materiały do osadnictwa kultury pucharów lejkowatych na terenie Gór Pieprzowych, w pow. Sandomierz. *Wiadomości Archeologiczne* 32: 137–148.

Klassen, L. 2004. *Jade und Kupfer: Untersuchungen zum Neolithisierungsprozess im westlichen Ostseeraum unter besonderer Berücksichtigung der Kulturentwicklung Europa 5500-3500 BC*. Moesgård: Jutland Archaeological Society.

Korczyńska, M., K. Cappenberg, M. Nowak, P. Szwarczewski and M. Moskal-del Hoyo 2019. Multi-methodological approaches to investigate large archaeological sites: The case study of the Eneolithic settlement in Mozgawa, western Lesser Poland. *Journal of Archaeological Science: Reports* 27: 101941.

Kruk, J. 1980. *Gospodarka w Polsce południowo-wschodniej w V-III tysiącleciu p.n.e.* Wrocław: Ossolineum.

Kruk, J., S.W. Alexandrowicz, S. Milisauskas and Z. Śnieszko 1996. *Osadnictwo i zmiany środowiska naturalnego wyżyn lessowych. Studium archeologiczne i paleogeograficzne nad neolitem w dorzeczu Nidzicy*. Kraków: Instytut Archeologii i Etnologii Polskiej Akademii Nauk.

Kruk, J., M. Lityńska-Zając and S. Milisauskas 2016. *Gospodarka roślinna w neolicie. Studium przypadku (Neolithic plant cultivation at Bronocice)*. Kraków: Institute of Archaeology and Ethnology of the Polish Academy of Sciences.

Kruk, J. and S. Milisauskas 1981. Wyżynne osiedle neolityczne w Bronocicach. *Archeologia Polski* 26: 65–113.

Kruk, J. and S. Milisauskas 1983. Chronologia absolutna osadnictwa neolitycznego z Bronocic, woj. kieleckie. *Archeologia Polski* 28: 257–320.

Kruk, J. and S. Milisauskas 1990. Radiocarbon dating of Neolithic assemblages from Bronocice. *Przegląd Archeologiczny* 37: 195–234.

Kruk, J. and S. Milisauskas 1999. *Rozkwit i upadek społeczeństw rolniczych neolitu*. Kraków: Instytut Archeologii i Etnologii Polskiej Akademii Nauk.

Kruk, J. and S. Milisauskas 2018. *Bronocice: The Chronology and Development of a Neolithic Settlement of the Fourth Millennium BC*. Kraków: Institute of Archaeology and Ethnology, Polish Academy of Sciences.

Kruk, J., S. Milisauskas and P. Włodarczak 2018. *Real Time: Radiocarbon Dates and Bayesian Analysis of the Neolithic Settlement at Bronocice, Fourth Millennium BC*. Kraków: Institute of Archaeology and Ethnology, Polish Academy of Sciences.

Kukawka, S. 1997. *Na rubieży środkowoeuropejskiego świata rolniczego. Społeczności Ziemi Chełmińskiej w IV tysiącleciu p.n.e.* Toruń: Uniwersytet Mikołaja Kopernika.

Kulczycka-Leciejewiczowa, A. 2002. Kilka uwag o budownictwie ludności kultury pucharów lejkowatych, in A. Abramowicz and J. Maik (eds) *Budownictwo i budowniczowie w przeszłości*: 39–48. Łódź: Instytut Archeologii i Etnologii Polskiej Akademii Nauk.

Lehmann, J., P.C. Lee and R.I.M. Dunbar 2014. Unravelling the evolutionary functions of communities, in R.I.M. Dunbar, C. Gamble and J.A.J. Gowlett (eds) *Lucy to Language: The Benchmark Papers*: 245–276. Oxford: Oxford University Press.

Libera, J. and K. Tunia (eds) 2006. *Idea megalityczna w obrządku pogrzebowym kultury pucharów lejkowatych*. Kraków and Lublin: Instytut Archeologii i Etnologii Polskiej Akademii Nauk and Instytut Archeologii Uniwersytetu Marii Curie Skłodowskiej w Lublinie.

Midgley, M. 1992. *TRB Culture. The First Farmers of the North European Plain*. Edinburgh: Edinburgh University Press.

Milisauskas, S. and J. Kruk 1984. Settlement organization and the appearance of low level hierarchical societies during the Neolithic in the Bronocice microregion, southeastern Poland. *Germania* 62: 1–30.

Milisauskas, S. and J. Kruk 1989. Economy, migration, settlement organization, and warfare during the Late Neolithic in Southeastern Poland. *Germania* 67: 77–96.

Milisauskas, S. and J. Kruk 1990. Neolitische Befestigungen und die Einfriedung von Bronocice. *Jahresschrift für mitteldeutsche Vorgeschichte* 73: 231–236.

Milisauskas, S. and J. Kruk 1991. Utilization of cattle for traction during the later Neolithic in Southeastern Poland. *Antiquity* 65(248): 561–566.

Milisauskas, S., J. Kruk, M.-L. Pipes and E. Haduch 2016. *Neolithic Human Burial Practices. The Interpretation of Funerary Behaviors at Bronocice*. Kraków: Institute of Archaeology and Ethnology of the Polish Academy of Sciences.

Milisauskas, S., J. Kruk, M.-L. Pipes and D. Makowicz-Poliszot 2012. *Butchering and Meat Consumption in the Neolithic: The Exploitation of Animals at Bronocice*. Kraków: Instytut Archeologii i Etnologii Polskiej Akademii Nauk.

Moskal-del Hoyo, M., A. Wacnik, W.P. Alexandrowicz, R. Stachowicz-Rybka, J. Wilczyński, S. Wędzicha, P. Szwarczewski, M. Korczyńska, K. Cappenberg and M. Nowak 2018. Open country species persisted in loess regions during the Atlantic phase: New multidisciplinary data from southern Poland. *Review of Palaeobotany and Palynology* 253: 49–69.

Müller, J. 2016a. Demography and Social Agglomeration: Trypillia in a European Perspective, in J. Müller, K. Rassmann and M. Videiko (eds) *Trypillia Mega-Sites and European Prehistory 4100-3400 BCE* (Themes in Contemporary Archaeology 2): 7–16. London and New York: Routledge.

Müller, J. 2016b. Human Structure Social Space: What We Can Learn from Trypillia?, in J. Müller, K. Rassmann and M. Videiko (eds) *Trypillia Mega-Sites and European Prehistory 4100-3400 BCE* (Themes in Contemporary Archaeology 2): 301–304. London and New York: Routledge.

Müller, J. and K. Rassman 2016. Introduction, in J. Müller, K. Rassmann and M. Videiko (eds) *Trypillia Mega-Sites and European Prehistory 4100-3400 BCE* (Themes in Contemporary Archaeology 2): 1–7. London and New York: Routledge.

Müller, J., R. Hofmann and R. Ohlrau 2016a. From domestic households to mega-structures: proto-urbanism?, in J. Müller, K. Rassmann and M. Videiko (eds) *Trypillia Mega-Sites and European Prehistory 4100-3400 BCE* (Themes in Contemporary Archaeology 2): 253–268. London and New York: Routledge.

Müller, J., K. Rassmann and M. Videiko (eds) 2016b. *Trypillia Mega-Sites and European Prehistory 4100-3400 BCE* (Themes in Contemporary Archaeology 2). London and New York: Routledge.

Neustupný, E. 1991. Community areas of prehistoric farmers in Bohemia. *Antiquity* 65(247): 326–331.

Neustupný, E. 1998a. Structures and events: The theoretical basis of spatial archaeology, in E. Neustupný (ed.) *Space in Prehistoric Bohemia*: 9–44. Praha: Institute of Archaeology, Academy of Sciences of the Czech Republic.

Neustupný, E. 1998b. The transformation of community areas into settlement areas, in E. Neustupný (ed.) *Space in Prehistoric Bohemia*: 45–61. Praha: Institute of Archaeology, Academy of Sciences of the Czech Republic.

Nowak, M. 1993. *Osadnictwo kultury pucharów lejkowatych we wschodniej części Niecki Nidziańskiej*. Kraków: Instytut Archeologii Uniwersytetu Jagiellońskiego.

Nowak, M. 2001. Osadnicze i socjo-polityczne modele południowo-wschodniej grupy kultury pucharów lejkowatych, in J.K. Kozłowski and E. Neustupný (eds) *Archeologia przestrzeni. Metody i wyniki badań* struktur osadniczych w dorzeczach górnej Łaby i Wisły: 127–152. Kraków: Polska Akademia Umiejętności and Akademie Věd České Republiky.

Nowak, M. 2009. Drugi etap neolityzacji ziem polskich. Kraków: Instytut Archeologii Uniwersytetu Jagiellońskiego.

Nowak, M. 2010. Późna faza cyklu lendzielsko-polgarskiego w zachodniej Małopolsce w świetle wyników badań wykopaliskowych w Podłężu, stanowisko 17 (powiat wielicki). Śląskie Sprawozdania Archeologiczne 52: 49–90.

Nowak, M. 2013. Settlement and economy of the TRB in Lesser Poland: transformation or continuity?, in S. Kadrow and P. Włodarczak (eds) Environment and Subsistence – Forty Years After Janusz Kruk's 'Settlement studies…' (Studien zur Archäologie in Ostmitteleuropa 11): 245–260. Rzeszów and Bonn: Institute of Archaeology Rzeszów University and Dr. Rudolf Habelt.

Nowak, M. 2014a. Identity of FBC societies in the upper Vistula river basin, in M. Furholt, M. Hinz, D. Mischka, G. Noble and D. Olausson (eds) Landscapes, Histories and Societies in the Northern European Neolithic (Frühe Monumentalität und soziale Differenzierung 4): 85–196. Bonn: Institut für Ur- und Frühgeschichte der CAU Kiel and Dr. Rudolf Habelt.

Nowak, M. 2014b. Późny etap rozwoju cyklu lendzielsko-polgarskiego w zachodniej Małopolsce, in K. Czarniak, J. Kolenda and M. Markiewicz (eds) Szkice neolityczne. Księga poświęcona pamięci prof. dr hab. Anny Kulczyckiej-Leciejewiczowej: 239–284. Wrocław: Instytut Archeologii i Etnologii Polskiej Akademii Nauk.

Nowak, M. 2017a. Do ¹⁴C dates always turn into an absolute chronology? The case of the Middle Neolithic in western Lesser Poland. Documenta Praehistorica 44: 240–271.

Nowak, M. 2017b. Ubiquitous settlers, consequent farmers, and monument builders, in P. Włodarczak (ed.) The Past Societies: The Polish Lands from the First Evidence of Human Presence to the Early Middle Ages, Vol. 2: 5500-2000 BC: 125–170. Warszawa: Institute of Archaeology and Ethnology of the Polish Academy of Sciences.

Nowak, M. and A. Zastawny (eds) 2015. The Baden Culture around the Western Carpathians. Kraków: Krakowski Zespół do Badań Autostrad.

Palyvou, C. 2004. Outdoor space in Minoan architecture: 'community and privacy'. British School at Athens Studies 12: 207–217.

Pelisiak, A. 2003. Osadnictwo. Gospodarka. Społeczeństwo. Studia nad kulturą pucharów lejkowatych na Niżu Polskim. Rzeszów: Wydawnictwo Uniwersytetu Rzeszowskiego.

Pelisiak, A. 2005. Osadnictwo i gospodarka w neolicie we wschodniej części Karpat polskich. Konfrontacja informacji archeologicznych i palinologicznych, in K. Wasylikowa, M. Lityńska-Zając and A. Bieniek

(eds) Roślinne ślady człowieka: 29–52. Kraków: Instytut Botaniki im. W. Szafera Polskiej Akademii Nauk.

Pelisiak, A. 2018. Centrum i peryferia osadnictwa w neolicie i wczesnej epoce brązu na wschodnim Podkarpaciu i we wschodniej części polskich Karpat (Core and Peripheries of the Neolithic and Early Bronze Age Settlements on the Eastern Carpathian Forelands and the Eastern Part of Polish Carpathians). Rzeszów: Instytut Archeologii Uniwersytetu Rzeszowskiego, Fundacja Rzeszowskiego Ośrodka Archeologicznego.

Płoszaj, M. 2016. Polepa konstrukcyjna z osady kultury pucharów lejkowatych w Mozgawie, pow. pińczowski (stanowisko 1-3). Unpublished Masters thesis, Jagiellonian University.

Podkowińska, Z. 1950. Osada neolityczna na górze Gawroniec w Ćmielowie, pow. Opatów. Wiadomości Archeologiczne 17: 95–146.

Podkowińska, Z. 1951. Prace wykopaliskowe na stanowisku 'Gawroniec-Pałyga' w Ćmielowie, w pow. opatowskim 1950 R. Wiadomości Archeologiczne 18: 201–242.

Podkowińska, Z. 1955. Sprawozdanie z prac wykopaliskowych na górze Gawroniec (Pałyga) w Ćmielowie, pow. opatowski w 1954 r. Sprawozdania Archeologiczne 1: 11–27.

Podkowińska, Z. 1957. Sprawozdanie z prac wykopaliskowych prowadzonych w 1955 r. w Ćmielowie na stanowisku Gawroniec-Pałyga. Sprawozdania Archeologiczne 3: 24–47.

Podkowińska, Z. 1961. Spichrze ziemne na osadzie kultury pucharów lejkowatych na Gawrońcu-Pałydze w Ćmielowie, pow. Opatów. Archeologia Polski 6: 21–63.

Poklewski, T. 1958. Osada kultury pucharów lejkowatych w Gródku Nadbużnym, pow. Hrubieszów (stanowisko 1C). Archeologia Polski 2: 287–328.

Poręba, G., Z. Śnieszko and P. Moska 2012. New perspectives of dating prehistoric soil erosion in loess areas. Sprawozdania Archeologiczne 64: 113–148.

Przybył, A. 2017. From south to north. Baden culture people and their neighbors, in P. Włodarczak (ed.) The Past Societies: The Polish Lands from the First Evidence of Human Presence to the Early Middle Ages, Vol. 2: 5500-2000 BC: 171–210. Warszawa: Institute of Archaeology and Ethnology of the Polish Academy of Sciences.

Przybyła, M.M., P. Szczepanik and M. Podsiadło 2015. Eneolithic enclosure in Gniazdowice, Proszowice district, Lesser Poland, in the light of non-destructive research methods, in M. Nowak and A. Zastawny (eds) The Baden Culture around the Western Carpathians: 337–352. Kraków: Krakowski Zespół do Badań Autostrad.

Przybyła, M.M. and K. Tunia 2013. Investigations in 2012 of the southern part of the Funnel Beaker culture temenos at Słonowice near the Małoszówka river. Fourth report, in S. Kadrow and P. Włodarczak (eds)

Environment and Subsistence – forty years after Janusz Kruk's 'Settlement studies...' (Studien zur Archäologie in Ostmitteleuropa 11): 139–162. Rzeszów and Bonn: Institute of Archaeology Rzeszów University and Dr. Rudolf Habelt.

Renfrew, C. and P. Bahn 2016. *Archaeology. Theories, Methods, and Practice*. 7th edition. London: Thames & Hudson.

Rook, E. and M. Nowak 1993. Sprawozdanie z badań wielokulturowego stanowiska w Krakowie – Prądniku Czerwonym, w latach 1990 i 1991. *Sprawozdania Archeologiczne* 45: 35–72.

Rybicka, M. 2017. *Kultura trypolska – kultura pucharów lejkowatych. Natężenie kontaktów i ich chronologia*. Rzeszów: Instytut Archeologii Uniwersytetu Rzeszowskiego and Fundacja Rzeszowskiego Ośrodka Archeologicznego.

Rybicka, M., A. Hawinskyj and W. Pasterkiewicz 2019. *Leżnica, stanowisko Czub – osiedle kultury pucharów lejkowatych na zachodnim Wołyniu*. Rzeszów: Wydawnictwo Uniwersytetu Rzeszowskiego.

Salisbury, R.B. 2016. *Soilscapes in Archaeology. Settlement and Social Organization in the Neolithic of the Great Hungarian Plain* (Prehistoric Research in the Körös Region 3). Budapest: Archaeolingua.

Śnieszko, Z. 1985. *Paleogeografia holocenu w dolinie Sancygniówki*. Wrocław: Ossolineum.

Sørensen, L. 2014. *From Hunter to Farmer in Northern Europe. Migration and Adaptation during the Neolithic and Bronze Age*. Oxford: Wiley.

Szwarczewski, P. 2009. The Formation of Deluvial and Alluvial Cones as a Consequence of Human Settlement on a Loess Plateau: An Example from the Chroberz Area (Poland). *Radiocarbon* 51(2): 445–455.

Szwarczewski, P. 2013. Szkic położenia geologiczno-geomorfologicznego stanowisk w Stryczowicach, woj. Świętokrzyskie, in A. Uzarowicz-Chmielewska and B. Sałacińska (eds) *Osady neolityczne w Stryczowicach, woj. świętokrzyskie* (Materiały Starożytne i Wczesnośredniowieczne 10): 251–256. Warszawa: Państwowe Muzeum Archeologiczne.

Tunia, K. 2006. 'Temenos' kultury pucharów lejkowatych w Słonowicach, pow. Kazimierza Wielka. Badania 1979-2002. Trzecie sprawozdanie, in J. Libera and K. Tunia (eds) *Idea megalityczna w obrządku pogrzebowym kultury pucharów lejkowatych*: 335–340. Lublin and Kraków: Instytut Archeologii i Etnologii Polskiej Akademii Nauk and Instytut Archeologii Uniwersytetu Marie Curie-Skłodowskiej.

Uzarowicz-Chmielewska, A. 1978. Wielokulturowa osada w Ostrowcu Świętokrzyskim, woj. Kielce. *Materiały Archeologiczne* 18: 5–51.

Valde-Nowak, P., A. Gil-Drozd, A. Kraszewska and M. Paternoga 2015. The Proto-Boleraz grave in the Western Beskids, in M. Nowak and A. Zastawny (eds) *The Baden Culture around the Western Carpathians*: 191–219. Kraków: Krakowski Zespół do Badań Autostrad.

Whittle, A. 2003. *The Archaeology of People. Dimensions of Neolithic Life*. London and New York: Routledge.

Włodarczak, P. 2006. *Kultura ceramiki sznurowej na Wyżynie Małopolskiej*. Kraków: Instytut Archeologii i Etnologii Polskiej Akademii Nauk.

Włodarczak, P. 2013. Projekt badań chronologii absolutnej eneolitu i początków epoki brązu w Małopolsce, in I. Cheben and M. Soják (eds) *Otázky neolitu a eneolitu našich krajín – 2010. Zborník referátov z 29. Pracovného stretnutia bádateľov pre výskum neolitu a eneolitu Čiech, Moravy a Slovenska, Vršatské Podhradie, 27.-30.9.2010*: 373–387. Nitra: Archeologický ústav Slovenskéj Akademie Vied.

Zastawny, A. 2008. The Baden and the Funnel Beaker-Baden Settlement in Lesser Poland, in M. Furholt, M. Szmyt and A. Zastawny (eds) *The Baden Complex and the Outside World* (Studien zur Archäologie in Ostmitteleuropa 4): 177–188. Bonn: Dr. Rudolf Habelt.

Zastawny, A. 2015. The Baden complex in Lesser Poland – horizons of cultural influences, in M. Nowak and A. Zastawny (eds) *The Baden Culture around the Western Carpathians*: 119–150. Kraków: Krakowski Zespół do Badań Autostrad.

Zych, R. 2008. *Kultura pucharów lejkowatych w Polsce południowo-wschodniej*. Rzeszów: Instytut Archeologii Uniwersytetu Rzeszowskiego and Fundacja Rzeszowskiego Ośrodka Archeologicznego.

Chapter 7

Spatio-Demographic Structure and Social Organization: A Linear Trajectory or Overlapping Trends?

Aleksandr Diachenko and Ezra B.W. Zubrow

Abstract

An oversimplified understanding of general systems theory in archaeology co-relates the concepts of population growth, social complexity, and economy. To analyze how the spatial layout of large settlements are the outcomes of the interactions of highly diverse social, political, economic, and religious orders, we argue and focus on more universal and less diverse characteristics, such as population, spatial location, and economic subsistence. Recent studies have demonstrated discontinuities between demographic trends and socioeconomic transformations worldwide. By developing a multiscalar analysis and estimations based on the application of Central Place Theory to Cucuteni–Tripolye settlements and their systems, this paper presents deep non-linear patterns of demographic growth that in many cases can be wrongly taken for specific types of sociopolitical organization. Furthermore, we show that this growth takes place even though simulations demonstrate that large settlements would only last four generations. 'Satellite' settlements that were branched off from the settlements of medium and large size in our case study represent demographic self-regulation caused by density dependence.

Introduction

Neolithic and Bronze Age nucleated settlements have long been a subject of archaeological attention because they provide the physical evidence that is used in a variety of theoretically and substantively important archaeological domains. For example, there are case studies and generalizations based upon these sites covering a wide range of topics, including the development of a) typo-chronologies; b) urbanization processes; c) population characterizations; d) new social relationships; and e) new administrative structures. The last topic is caused largely by relatively high estimates for population size and density. Since Childe (1950), these variables are used to trace significant transformations of nucleated settlements and interpret their importance compared to small sites in their surroundings.

Population size and density as well as their related variables—settlement size, number of dwellings, thickness of cultural layer, density of dwellings—are taken as proxies for the order of sites in settlement hierarchies (for an overview, see Duffy 2015). This approach has met a certain amount of reasonable critique in recent decades. At the same time, much more complicated 'hidden' trajectories of demographic development at different spatial scales were identified with this approach (Crema 2014; Crema *et al.* 2016; DeLong and Burger 2015; Diachenko and Zubrow 2015; Duffy 2015; Feinman 2011, 2013; Flannery 1998; Fletcher 1995, 2006; Gaydarska 2016; Haas *et al.* 2015; Hamilton *et al.* 2007, 2009, 2016; Hofmann *et al.* 2016; Lobo *et al.*

2020; Ortman *et al.* 2015). Population density using built spaces within sites as a proxy is reconsidered as a variable that reflects different developmental trajectories of sites representing differential population control or individual and societal benefits (e.g., Cesaretti *et al.* 2016; Furholt 2016; Müller 2017). This study proposes an explanation for the formation of spatial hierarchy, linking spatio-demographic patterns at the scale of particular sites to the spatial hierarchy at the regional scale. We will start with consideration of the 'market' distribution of population in non-market socioeconomic systems, and then present the case study of Tripolye settlements and settlement systems in modern Ukraine. Case study results are discussed from the perspective of demographic self-regulation causing the spatial structure of prehistoric settlements and settlement systems.

Underlying all community organizations are certain realities. This is true for all societies. It makes no difference whether they are in Africa, North America, Europe, the Middle East, or Asia. It makes no difference whether they are Neolithic, Bronze Age, Iron Age, Roman, or even the Medieval or later historic periods. Over time and space, separately or conjoined, communities go through organization and disorganization, integration and disintegration, growth and decline, stability and instability. The determinants and consequences of these processes underlie both this case study and the book. One must avoid the insularity of a particular geography, the parochialism of a particular time period, the provincialism of a particular culture, and the professionalism of a particular discipline.

This book's editors have suggested, '*The spatial layout of large settlements results from the interactions of social, political, economic, and religious orders.*' We believe we should first focus on universal characteristics, such as population, spatial location, and economic subsistence, before focusing on the more specialized and diversified characteristics.

In this case study, we use Christaller's (1966) Central Place Theory (originally published in 1933), demographic and spatial variables, in addition to proxies. We argue that the fundamentals of Central Place Theory are the fundamentals of community organization, representing one ideal form of a self-regulated community organization from prehistory until today. Furthermore, in our real case, the optimization takes place regardless of whether a market is present. Hence, the underlying principle of Central Place Theory concerns self-regulated spatial distributions of populations.

'Market' Distribution of Population in Non-Market Socioeconomic Systems: The Issue

Direct links between the spatio-demographic structure of prehistoric populations and their socioeconomic development were to a great extent caused by the application to archaeological data of models developed in analytical geography (for the most recent overview, see Nakoinz and Knitter 2016). These models link the order of places in a spatial hierarchy, fixed population values, the number and size of the complementary regions, and the range of goods and services. Central Place Theory remains one the most influential in this set of models. Widely applied to modern and archaeological data in the 1960s and 1970s, Central Place Theory was an easy fit because Christaller's principles were suitable for the general systems theory and considered as one of the cornerstones of processual archaeology (for Central Place Theory in archaeology, see Clarke 1977; Crumley 1976; Hodder and Orton 1976; Nakoinz 2019; Pollard 1980; Smith 1974; for system analysis, see Bertalanffy 1968; Clarke 1968; Flannery 1968). On one hand, the reduction in the use of this set of spatial models over the following decades was caused by post-processual critiques. On the other hand, this reduction resulted from the failure of the models caused by extending their application to problems for which they were not designed. This resulted in some notorious discrepancies between the model and the empirical data. The latter issue is currently being resolved by modifications in the models; for example, by the incorporation of Central Place Theory into network analysis (e.g., Nakoinz 2012). Considering the utility of this model in multiscalar analysis and the fruitful outcomes of its application in archaeology, we argue that Central Place Theory is a powerful tool for studying demographic self-organization.

The basic assumptions of Christaller's original model and terminology must be re-examined for a model to be appropriate for archaeological research. A 'central place' is defined as a '*center, which provides other settlements of the region with the main (central) goods and services*' (Christaller 1966: 16). Since central places are not equal in their functions, centers of the high spatial order possess a wider range of goods and services which they supply to the centers of the low order. Territories serviced by central places are the complementary regions.

Following Christaller (1966), the model is based on five initial assumptions. These are:

1. An unbounded space with a homogeneous distribution of purchasing power.
2. Central goods to be obtained from the nearest central place.
3. All parts of a space to be served by a central place; the complementary regions must completely fill the plain.
4. Consumer movement to be minimized.
5. No excess surplus to be earned by any one central place.

In terms of these conditions, given an optimum location of settlements in space, the group of identical central places will have complementary regions in the shape of regular hexagons, while central places themselves will constitute a grid in the shape of regular triangles (Haggett 1979). Christaller (1966) defined three main types of optimization of socioeconomic systems reflected in their spatial structure. Optimization is described by K-values determined by the number of serviced places related to one central place. K-values equal to 3, 4, and 7 are the basic K-values, introduced by Christaller, that reflect the location of sites in order to optimize, respectively, the market system, transportation, and administration in a region. It should be, however, noted that later work of geographers on empirical data resulted in the conclusion that settlement systems characterized by K-value of $K = 7$ are extremely rare in the real world (M.J. Woldenberg, personal communication) or even do not exist at all (Parr 1995). Other types of optimization are known as well. For instance, Johnston (1972) found settlement systems with a K-value of $K = 2$ in the ancient Near East. This type of optimization also was found by Berry (1967) in the distribution of central and served places in Iowa and Northern Dakota in the 1960s.

Two methods developed in analytical geography are useful for estimating the K-values of archaeological settlement systems. The first concerns the location of settlements and their order in the spatial hierarchy, while the second deals with the distribution of population at different orders of spatial hierarchy.

The model proposed by Beckman and McPherson (1970) allows the estimation of the K-values concerning to highest spatial orders (Formula 1) or third spatial order and lower orders (Formula 2) as follows:

$$N_2 = N_1(K-1), (1)$$

$$N_n = N_{n-1}K \ (n \geq 3), (2)$$

where N_1 and N_2 are the number of settlements of, respectively, the first and the second rank in the spatial hierarchy, N_n is the number of settlements of the third spatial rank and lower ranks, n is the rank in the spatial hierarchy, and K is Christaller's K-value.

Beckman's (1958) model describes the distribution of population at different orders of spatial hierarchy as follows:

$$p_m = \frac{ks^{m-1}r}{(1-k)^m}, (3)$$

where p_m is the population of the city of order m, r is the rural population in the market area of the town at order 1, and k is the ratio of city size to rural and town population served. The variable s is the parameter of system optimization.

The relationship between the variable s from Formula 3 and Christaller's K-values was discussed in analytical geography for several years (e.g., Dacey 1966; Parr 1969). Accepting earlier critiques, Beckman and McPherson (1970) concluded that s equals $K-1$ for the two highest orders of spatial hierarchy, while s equals K for the third and lower orders.

As represented in its basic assumptions, both the theoretical part of Christaller's work and empirical evidence used by him are completely based upon the concept of the market as an organizational principle. A market is any medium through which parties engage in economic transactions for exchanging ownership or use. It does not need to be based upon either money or spatial contiguity, as recently shown by the bitcoin phenomenon. For Christaller, even distance between settlements in space is considered from a costs perspective. He introduced the terms 'economic distance' determined by the '*cost of freight, insurance, and storage; time of travel; and loss of weight or space in transit. Similarly, as regards passenger travel, the economic distance was calculated by the cost of transportation; the time required; and the discomfort of travel.*' The 'range of a good' is considered as '*the farthest distance the dispersed population is willing to go in order to buy a good offered at a place – a central place*' (Christaller 1966: 22).

Critiques in the decades since the model was first applied in archaeology have raised an important question considering the application of this model to archaeological data (e.g., Crumley 1976; Evans 1980). If Central Place Theory is based on organizational principles of the market economy, then could it justifiably be applied to settlement systems of prehistoric, non-market populations (e.g., Crumley 1976; Evans 1980; Hirth 1998; Minc 2006)? Polanyi (1944) argued that non-market societies do not fit the rational decision assumptions or the rules of supply and demand of market economies (i.e., substantivist viewpoint). Thus, his followers were forced to reject Christaller's view when it came to non-market societies.

We may re-assess and re-express this question. If Central Place Theory initially was based on the organizational principles of market economy and could not be applied to prehistoric settlement systems, then why do numerous archaeological and cultural anthropological studies find 'market distributions' of prehistoric and ethnographic settlements (e.g., Johnson 1972; Pollard 1980; Smith 1974; Zubrow 1975)? Furthermore, why would these distributions fall into appropriate spatial hierarchies, with appropriate ratios of settlement size?

'Market' Distributions of Populations in Non-Market Socioeconomic Systems: A Case Study

Considering the issue of well-developed settlement hierarchies in prehistory, we decided to discuss the application of Central Place Theory to Cucuteni–Tripolye (also Cucuteni–Trypillia) settlements and their systems in modern Ukraine. Over the course of two millennia, the territory of this unit expanded from a small region around the Prut, Siret, and Dniester river valleys to become the largest cultural unit in eastern Europe. At its maximum, it occupied the area from the Carpathians to the eastern bank of the Dnieper, and from the forest zone of modern Ukraine to the northwestern coast of the Black Sea, in the territories of modern Moldova, Romania, and Ukraine. The taxonomic structure of the cultural unit is complex (for example, see Dergachev 1980; Ryzhov 2012; Tsvek 2006). Sites with similar assemblages of material culture, mainly ceramic complexes, are grouped into types. Several types of sites form local groups which, considering transformations in the material culture over time, are combined into 'lines of development;' the latter term was introduced by Dergachev (1980) to mark the evolutionary chains in material culture. Lines of development form five cultures of the cultural complex: Precucuteni, Ariuşd, Cucuteni, Eastern Tripolye, and Western Tripolye (Ryzhov 2012; Tsvek 2006). Recently, and somewhat confusingly, the term 'Tripolye' has been used simultaneously for the Eastern Tripolye and Western Tripolye cultures. The time span and area increase along this taxonomic hierarchy, while differences in material culture grow.

Particularly, we worked with the settlement systems of Vladimirovsko-Tomashovskaya line of the Western Tripolye culture between the Southern Bug and Dnieper rivers in the territory of modern Ukraine (Ryzhov 2012). Sites of these local groups include mega-sites that recently became a topic of wide international discussions in that they are the largest Neolithic settlements of southeastern Europe (Chapman *et al.* 2014; Gaydarska 2015, 2016, 2020; Menotti and Korvin-Piotrovskiy 2012; Müller *et al.* 2016b; Ohlrau 2020). All mega-sites located in the Southern Bug and Dnieper Interfluve exceed 100 ha in size, while some of them measure 210 ha to 340 ha.

The latest relative chronology of Cucuteni–Tripolye is based on the correlation between ceramic seriation and probabilities of population movement derived from a gravity model. Ryzhov's (2012) original relative chronology is based on pottery seriation. Recent results of correspondence analysis carried out for pottery generally confirm this chronological scheme (Müller *et al.* 2016a). In Ryzhov's (2012) scheme, sites

are combined into three local groups (Vladimirovskaya, Nebelevskaya, and Tomashovskaya) that form a single line of development. Its chronology is subdivided into phases and stages (Diachenko and Menotti 2012; Ryzhov 2012). Since the latest stage of the Vladimirovskaya group chronologically overlaps with the earliest phase of the Nebelevskaya group, and the latest phase of the Nebelevskaya group chronologically overlaps with the earliest phase of the Tomashovskaya group, the relative chronology of the Vladimirovsko-Tomashovskaya line was combined into 10 analytical periods that include only synchronous settlements (Diachenko and Zubrow 2015; Diachenko *et al.* 2020). The average duration of the analytical period covers a time range of about 50 years (Kruts 1989), but the duration of mega-sites exceeded the duration of the analytical period, measuring approximately 100 years (cf. Chapman and Gaydarska 2016; Diachenko 2012; Gaydarska 2020; Harper 2019; Müller *et al.* 2016a; Ohlrau 2020; Ohlrau *et al.* 2016). As we shall see later, the chronology of the mega-sites supports our conclusion that most of them would not exceed the life span of four generations.

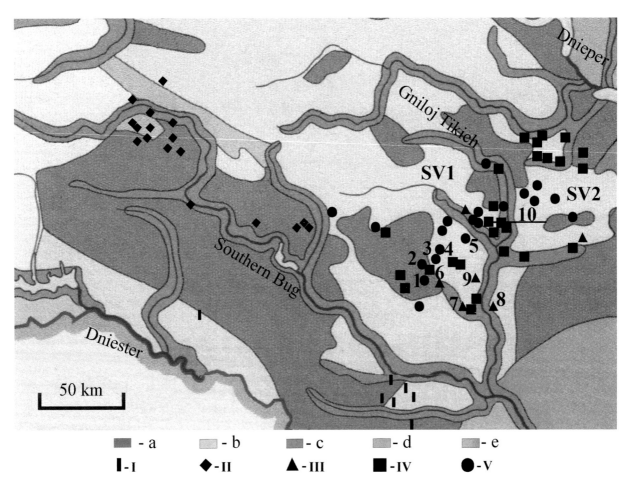

Figure 7.1. Tripolye sites in the Southern Bug and Dnieper Interfluve and neighboring regions. Landscapes: a: Forest-steppe upland dissected landscapes; b: Loess upland terrace landscapes; c: Floodplain landscapes; d: Pine forest terraces; e: Northern steppe upland and slope landscapes. Settlements: I: Chechelnitskaya local group; II: Srednebugskaya local group; III: Vladimirovskaya local group; IV: Nebelevskaya local group; V: Tomashovskaya local group. Sites: 1: Tomashovka; 2: Sushkovka; 3: Dobrovody; 4: Talianki; 5: Maidanetske; 6: Nebelevka; 7: Vladimirovka; 8: Fedorovka; 9: Peregonovka; 10: Glubochek (figure by A. Diachenko).

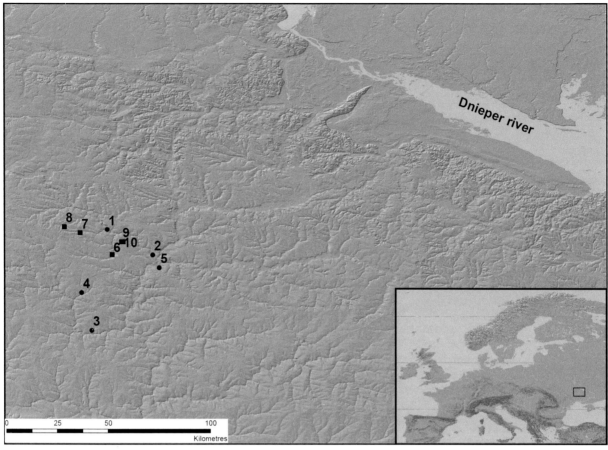

Figure 7.2. Settlement clusters, with the centers at Nebelevka and Maidanetske. 1: Gordashivka 1; 2: Kryvi Kolena; 3: Leshchivka; 4: Nebelevka; 5: Pischane; 6: Maidanetske; 7: Moshuriv 1; 8: Romanivka; 9: Talne 2; 10: Talne 3. Circles indicate settlements of the first phase of the Nebelevskaya group and the final stage of the Vladimirovskaya group. Squares indicate settlements of the second stage of the third phase of the Tomashovskaya group (figure by A. Diachenko).

At the regional scale, all the Tripolye settlements are highly clustered (Figure 7.1). These clusters are located in two specific areas and are labeled as Spatial Variation 1 and 2 (hereinafter, SV1 and SV2). Each of them consisted of smaller-scale spatial groups. The Gniloj Tikich River constitutes the border between SV1 and SV2 (Diachenko 2012). The models of Beckman (1958) and Beckman and McPherson (1970) were already applied to clusters of synchronous sites (Diachenko 2012, 2013). However, the recently obtained, high-precision geomagnetic plans of settlements require new interpretations (Chapman *et al.* 2014, 2016; Rassmann *et al.* 2016). Settlement systems of synchronous sites with centers at Nebelevka and Maidanetske, belonging to the 4th and the 9th analytical periods, respectively, are considered (Figure 7.2). For population estimates according to Beckmann's model, we used the number of dwellings, in order to avoid issues of estimations presented by the average number of people per house. New, high-precision geomagnetic settlement plans include more dwellings than the old plans. Therefore, we can calculate the correlation coefficient used to project the total number of buildings for sites where geomagnetic surveys have not been conducted (Diachenko 2016). Based on simulation of

family growth, 78.4% of the dwellings are assumed to have been synchronous at each site (Diachenko 2016; Diachenko and Menotti 2012).

Let us consider the settlement group that includes the mega-site Nebelevka, dating to *c.* 3950–3900 BC. The order of 'rural' population from Central Place Theory is represented by the small settlements of Leshchevka and Peschane, while 'central places' are exemplified by the medium-size settlement of Krivye Kolena and the large settlement of Nebelevka. Taking into account the critiques from Chapman and Gaydarska (2016) about the structure of the settlement system with a center at Nebelevka and the number of sites within it, we should consider the settlement cluster with a center at Nebelevka that had a three-tiered hierarchy, or two settlement clusters occurred with centers at Krivye Kolena and Nebelevka that each had a two-tiered hierarchy (Table 7.1). According to Formulas 1 and 2, the *K*-value of *K* = 2 characterizes each case.

The settlement cluster that includes the mega-site of Maidanetske, dating to 3700–3650 BC, has a three-tiered hierarchy. The order of 'rural' population from

Site	Size (hectares)	Number of synchronous dwellings	Reference
Nebelevka	238	1064	Chapman and Gaydarska 2016
Krivye Kolena	38.2	399	Diachenko and Menotti 2012
Leshchevka	11.8	149	Diachenko and Menotti 2012
Peschane	16.3	206	Diachenko and Menotti 2012

Table 7.1. Settlement cluster with a 'center' at Nebelevka.

Site	Size (hectares)	Number of synchronous dwellings	Reference
Maidanetske	210	2327	Rassmann *et al.* 2014
Romanovka	57.7	603	Diachenko and Menotti 2012
Moshurov 1	7.1	31	Diachenko and Menotti 2012
Talnoe 2	4.9	61	Diachenko and Menotti 2012
Talnoe 3	3.1	39	Diachenko and Menotti 2012

Table 7.2. Settlement cluster with a 'center' at Maidanetske.

Assumed 'center'	Assumed number of orders in spatial hierarchy	Assumed number of orders for the 'central places' in spatial hierarchy	K-value
Nebelevka	3	2	*c.* 0.87
Nebelevka	2	1	1
Krivye Kolena	2	1	1
Maidanetske	3	2	*c.* 1.22

Table 7.3. *K*-values dependent upon spatial hierarchy.

Central Place Theory is represented by the small settlements of Moshurov 1, and Talnoe 2 and 3, while 'central places' are exemplified, respectively, by the medium-size settlement of Romanovka and the large settlement of Maidanetske (Table 7.2). The 'satellite' sites near Maidanetske are located across the stream. Christaller's (1966) Central Place Theory does not predict this unusual location. Especially given that $K = 2$ is the closest integer K-value that describes the whole settlement system.

Now let us consider the distribution of population at different spatial orders. Formula 3 includes four knowns and one unknown. Hence, we may estimate this variable by rewriting this equation as follows:

$$s = \sqrt[m-1]{\frac{p_m(1-k)^m}{kr}}, (4)$$

where p_m is the population of the city of order m, r is the rural population in the market area of the town at order 1, and k is the ratio of city size to rural and town population served. The variable s is the parameter of system optimization (Beckmann 1958).

Table 7.3, based on Equation 4, provides the names of 'assumed centers,' assumed number of orders

in the spatial hierarchy, number of orders for the assumed central places, and actual K-values. Since the K-value is approximately 1, Nebelevka and Krivye Kolena are self-servicing settlements. The K-values of the three-tiered hierarchical systems centered at Nebelevka and Maidanetske increase from $K = 0.87$ to $K = 1.22$. Although both values are close to 1, the increase represents increased optimization of the distribution of population.

A particular set of assumptions is necessary for both scenarios to be possible. These are that the population is not seasonally shifting or migrating, that the villages persist in their spatial locations, and that the spatial orders remain the same. The obtained results would be significantly changed considering the possibility of seasonal movement of these populations from centers to 'satellites.'

If the K-values are calculated based on spatial location (Beckmann and McPherson 1970), or based on spatial location weighted by population (Beckmann 1958), one would get significantly different results. This difference might be explained by the seasonal migratory scenario. Over the long term, societies have tried various ways to optimize the location of settlements and the distribution of populations. The impact of these various strategies also may have influenced the patterns we see.

Finally, the *K*-value of *K* = 1, obtained for the distribution of population, may also be explained from the perspective of models developed in theoretical ecology. However, before discussing these explanatory models, we need to present the results obtained by analyzing the stabilization points in carrying capacity.

Spatio-Demographic Structure of Prehistoric Settlements and Their Systems and Demographic Self-Regulation

Our recent study of stabilization points, natural population growth, and migrations is based upon the same set of data (Diachenko and Zubrow 2015). Estimates confirmed that the Tripolye population growth fits the model defined by May (1976) and Feigenbaum (1978, 1979). It is based upon multiple iterations of the logistic equation:

$$P_{x+1} = gP_x(1 - P_x), (5)$$

where *C* is the carrying capacity and *g* is the rate of population growth. P_x is the initial population, and P_{x+1} is the population after time *x*+1. P_x and P_{x+1} are expressed as percentages of 1 which corresponds to the maximum carrying capacity (*C* = 1).

The iterations lead to the transition from simple periodic behavior to a regime with complex aperiodic growth. Most of the bifurcation points are followed by period doubling. This means that for one previous period there are now two periods within the same time span. Stabilization points are dependent on the growth rate, *g*. If *g* exceeds 1 but it is less than 2, the population stabilizes near the following value:

$$P_s = \frac{g-1}{g}, (6)$$

If *g* is within the range between 2 and 3, the population oscillates around the same value (Formula 6), and then stabilizes near it. If *g* is greater than 3 and less than 3.45, the population oscillates between two values determined by the growth rate. If *g* exceeds 3.45 but it is less than 3.54, the population oscillates between four values, etc. Once *g* exceeds the Feigenbaum constant (*g* ≈ 4.669201609), the system completely falls into chaotic behavior (Feigenbaum 1978, 1979; May 1976).

When empirical data significantly exceeded the predicted model values, then there is immigration of new population into the Southern Bug and Dnieper Interfluve, while in the cases, when model data significantly exceed the empirical values, there is emigration of population from the region (Diachenko and Zubrow 2015). The first process corresponds to

significant changes in the material culture (Ryzhov 2012). The second process is confirmed by the formation of new settlements east of the analyzed region as well as an increase in population outside the analyzed region (see Figure 7.1).

We hypothesize that stabilization points resulting from deep non-linear trends in demographic development do not directly correspond to socioeconomic organization. This is confirmed by a general correspondence between the model and the empirical data. Furthermore, explanations for the deviations correlate with the formation of new settlements and rapid changes in ceramic complexes (Diachenko and Zubrow 2015).

As shown by Formula 5, carrying capacity is not the single factor that influences stabilization points in population growth. They also are dependent on population density and growth rate. The specific relationship between the latter two variables is known as the 'Allee-effect' or 'density-dependence' (Lockwood *et al.* 2007). The density of dwellings within the largest sites of the settlement clusters, an imperfect proxy of population density, will be used in this paper for analyzing the demographic development of Tripolye populations. These estimates are presented in Table 7.4.

Stabilization in population density is estimated to be proportional to *c.* 10–10.5 dwellings per 1 ha. In the case of three migration waves into the region, the related values range from 10.9 to 11.1 dwellings per 1 ha. In two other cases, including one that represents another migration wave (the case of Nebelevka), the density of dwellings stabilized at *c.* 4.1–4.8 dwellings per 1 ha.

The weak and the strong Allee-effects are illustrated in Figure 7.3. Given all possible combinations of population densities and growth rates, the bifurcation point is represented by the greatest density on the x-axis that will produce the highest possible growth rate on the y-axis. Moreover, examination of the weak Allee-effect suggests that growth rates and density both increase as one moves from a to b. However, as one moves past the bifurcation point and moves from c to d, density increases but growth diminishes.

In addition, there are two differences between the weak and the strong Allee-effects. The first is that as one moves upwards toward e and f in the strong Allee-effect, there can be decreasing negative growth and increasing density that is transformed later into increasing growth and increasing density prior to the bifurcation point. This is not possible in the weak Allee-effect where all the initial growth is positive. Second, the shape of the a–d curve and the e–h curve is different. The slope of the growth density curve is greater for the strong Allee-effect relative to the weak Allee-effect. The system is dynamic. Once the population density exceeds the

Settlement/analytical period	Absolute dates (cal BC)	Settlement size (hectares)	Number of synchronous dwellings	Density of dwellings (dwellings per 1 hectare)
Tomashovka / 10	3650–3600	117.4	1169	10
Maidanetske / 9	3700–3650	210	2327	11.1
Talianki / 8	3750–3700	340	1631	4.8
Dobrovody / 7	3800–3750	130	1411	10.9
Sushkovka / 6	3850–3800	76.9	803	10.4
Glubochek / 5	3900–3850	100	906	9.1
Nebelevka / 4	3950–3900	260	1064	4.1
Peregonovka / 3	4000–3950	50	523	10.5
Vladimirovka / 2	4050–4000	50.2	523	10.5
Fedorovka / 1	4100–4050	122.7	1335	10.9

Table 7.4. Density of dwellings at the largest Tripolye settlements of the SV1 in the Southern Bug and Dnieper Interfluve (modified from Hofmann *et al.* 2016).

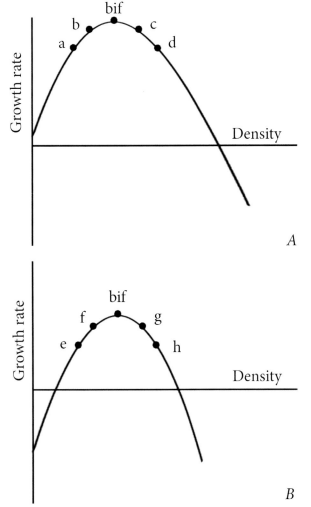

Figure 7.3. Graphs showing the weak (*A*) and strong (*B*) Allee-effect (adapted from Lockwood *et al.* 2007).

branched-off from the settlements of medium and large size in our case study, and represent demographic self-regulation caused by density-dependence. This assumption is verified via comparison of the bifurcation points in the density of dwellings and the number of satellites corresponding to the large settlements. Additional corroboration comes from the general trends in changes in the density of dwellings and waves of immigration (Tables 7.4 and 7.5). Chronologically, the smooth decrease in density of dwellings took place after the waves of immigration, i.e., in periods 2, 3, and 10. Furthermore, it is important to distinguish that there was at least one rapid decline in the density of dwellings during a period of immigration. There was also a second rapid decline, for which we do not yet have an explanation (see Table 7.4).

The formation of 'satellites' during analytical periods 4 and 9 was associated with immigration into the region. Similarly, they are associated during the analytical periods 5 and 10 after the immigration waves (Table 7.5). The correlation between the density of dwellings and the formation of 'satellites' confirms the influence of deep demographic self-organizing trends on the spatio-demographic development of settlements and settlement systems. This confirmation is reinforced by the results of the application of Beckmann's (1958) model.

Demographic Structure: The Dynamic Perspective

There cannot be community organization or spatial organization, settlement nucleation, markets, and/or non-market dynamics without adequate population to maintain the settlements in their specific locations over time. The above demographic self-regulation as reflected in Central Place Theory relies upon occupied settlements. Therefore, it is appropriate to understand the demographic parameters that place boundaries

bifurcation point, the decrease in population size causes decreases in population density, bringing the population back toward the bifurcation point. This allows us to infer that the 'satellite' settlements were

Table 7.5. Small villages that were branched-off from the largest settlements.

Analytical period	Absolute dates (cal BC)	Largest settlement	Small settlements that were branched-off from the mega-sites
10	3650–3600	Tomashovka	Gorodnitsa
9	3700–3650	Maidanetske	Talnoe 2, Talnoe 3
8	3750–3700	Talianki	-
7	3800–3750	Dobrovody	-
6	3850–3800	Sushkovka	-
5	3900–3850	Glubochek	Kolodistoe 1, Kolodistoe 2
4	3950–3900	Nebelevka	Leshchevka
3	4000–3950	Peregonovka	-
2	4050–4000	Vladimirovka	-
1	4100–4050	Fedorovka	-

on the sustainability of the 'satellite' villages and central places. If too many villages go extinct, the spatial organization is destroyed. If central places grow too much, the potential of mortality factors, such as disease, increases. Therefore, we analyze the demographic parameters that would be necessary to maintain such a structure. In order to discover the demographic parameters that would sustain the geographic structure, we simulated various types of mortality events that would potentially destroy the spatio-demographic structure.

We use both moderate and high rates of mortality and morbidity, which unlike the modern situation, were frequent rather than rare.[1] We will find in our simulations that life expectancy was short. Even with everyone entering the productive labor force at a very young age, economic dependence, the cohort-specific dependency ratios, would be a major problem affecting the spatio-demographic structure of Tripolye settlements (Velikanova 1963). One must remember that for most people more than half of their lives were spent growing up. The life expectancy for most Copper Age settlements is generally accepted to be between 25 and 35 (Galor and Moav 2007). One should not lose sight of this, as one of our reviewers pointed out. This short life-span has many effects, not the least of which is the relative lack of experience of the principal decision-makers in these communities, given that they were probably in their 20s, or even early 20s.

Recently, the issues of the correlation between mortality and fertility rates in Neolithic Europe after the introduction of agriculture are being actively debated (Bocquet-Appel *et al.* 2009; Shennan 2008, 2013). Following Shennan's (2008) assumptions, we are more concerned about the possible influence of

mortality rates on the spatio-demographic structure of Cucuteni–Tripolye populations in our simulations.

Lacking cemeteries in the analyzed region, we do not know how much mortality there was in our case. This does not mean that there is nothing left to be discovered about the survival of these large villages. Peasant and pastoral societies frequently are conservative, and thus we model them as being initially stationary or stable. Briefly, these population distributions have rather particular characteristics (Alho 2008; Bratadan 2016; Coale and Demeny 1966; Keyfitz and Caswell 2005). A stationary population has had constant birth and death rates in balance for a long period of time. The result is both the number and the percentage of people in every age cohort remain constant. In other words, neither the size nor the structure of the population pyramid changes over time. A stable population does not change in structure but may either grow or decrease in number. Only the percentage of the population in each cohort remains the same.[2] Although we do not believe that the Tripolye villages were perfectly stationary or stable populations, we feel justified in initially modeling them as stationary or stable populations for this paper.

Therefore, for a moment, we will assume that the approximately 5000 people who lived in these large villages are distributed in either a stationary or a stable distribution. The value of 5000 people is based on the estimated population of Nebelevka as well as some other mega-sites (cf. Chapman *et al.* 2016; Diachenko 2016; Gaydarska 2020; Ohlrau 2020; Ohlrau *et al.* 2016).

Next, we assume from the perspective of the villager that mortality changes unpredictably. There are random epidemics, raids, and periods of bad harvests of plants or animals. One can simulate what happens to the village with random changes in mortality. To do so, we used

---

[1] Today, such rates are factors only for the aged. In prehistory, they influenced all the cohorts with special prominence for the young. Mortality came on the thrumming wings of disease, the clashing screams of raiding and warfare, and the hollow echoes of famine.

[2] That is to say, the population pyramid may become bigger or smaller, but the shape remains the same.

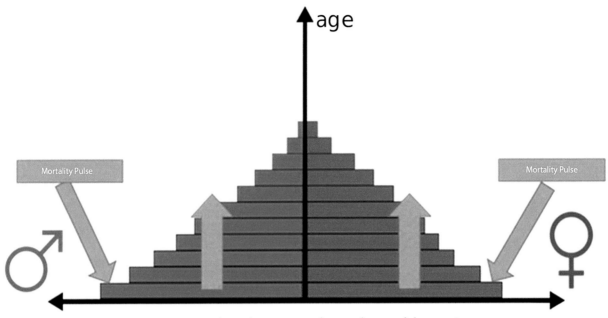

Figure 7.4. Mortality pulses impacting lower cohorts and then moving upward through the pyramid (figure by E.B.W. Zubrow).

random generators to change mortality and applied it to the village demographic structure. The changes in mortality followed random normal distributions, random f distributions, random t distributions, random uniform distributions, random binomial distributions, random geometric distributions, and random hypergeometric distributions.

Several simplifying conventions should be specified to improve transparency. First, we treat the random mortality changes as being similar to 'pulses.' Temporally, the change is a rapid, one-time change that takes place instantaneously when perceived from our level of temporal resolution. Once changed, it does not change back in the same period. Moreover, temporally there always is the possibility of a second pulse that may or may not be of the same magnitude, and we do not assume that the pulses have a standard frequency. Second, once a change has been made, the impact of the changing mortality caused by the pulse drifts over time into older cohorts. Third, the mortality pulses influence both male and female mortality equally. We recognize that female mortality is related to fertility, and we see the reproductive effect of younger female cohorts becoming older. However, we do not take into account that the random mortality pulses *de novo* may be different for males and females in this study. Fourth, for this paper, the pulses influenced mortality in the lowest cohorts initially, and then drifted into the older cohorts. As above, we recognize that there could be mortality pulses that affect only older cohorts (i.e., age-specific warfare) or all cohorts simultaneously, but we do not simulate them in our simplified model (Figure 7.4). Fifth, the in-migration and outmigration rate remains constant before and after the pulse. Of these

assumptions, the third and the fifth are probably the least likely.

For the simulations, the original stationary or stable population was classed into five-year cohorts. Numerous simulations were run with the same type of random distribution of the mortality pulses and with the same parameters. From each, there were different results because the mortality pulse is created randomly. However, they were frequently similar. Then, more simulations were run for the same random distribution but altering the parameters (e.g., the median changes from 5 to 0.05, etc.). Finally, the type of random distribution was changed (e.g., from normal to f, etc.), and the same entire process was repeated. Figure 7.5 is a typical result, showing the number of survivors at the end of the cohort. The cohort is labeled by the year it begins.

The results are summarized. The overall average cohort life expectancy is 16.5 years for all the simulations. This value is the average of all the cohorts' life expectancies for all the simulations. This tells us that most of the time, the life expectancy is sufficient for a percentage of the population to grow from one to the next cohort. However, the range is from 61.2 years in one t distribution to as short as 3.21 years in one uniform distribution. The latter is too short for the survival of the population. Not surprisingly, the average cohort life expectancy varies by the type of distribution. They are normal 25.18, f 21.94, t 49.13, uniform 7.03, binomial 7.35, geometric 13.7, and hypergeometric 10.23. In other words, on average, the impact of random mortality pulses varies widely, but usually does not extinguish the population.

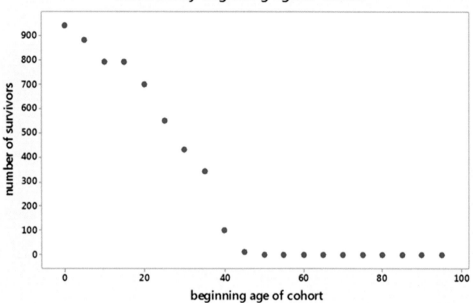

Figure 7.5. The number of survivors at the end of each cohort whose beginning age is listed on the x axis—a geometric c simulation (figure by E.B.W. Zubrow).

The average height of the population pyramid or the average of the oldest members of the oldest cohorts for our simulations is the following: normal distributions 50, f 55, t 70, uniform 35, binomial 21, geometric 47, and hypergeometric 44.

However, there are specific parameter settings for f, u, binomial, geometric, and hypergeometric distributions that rapidly extinguish the population (Table 7.6). In fact, 28% of all the simulations result in the extinction of the population in one generation. This means that one could expect one in every four villages to go extinct in one generation or that one village could last four generations, with all the others going extinct. The latter is substantiated by both the radiocarbon dating and the sequential population movement (cf. Chapman and Gaydarska 2016; Diachenko 2012; Harper 2016; Kruts 1989; Müller et al. 2016a; Videiko 2013). The archaeologically validated sequential population movement is once in approximately four generations. To summarize our results simply, we suggest that most of the villages for which we see archaeological evidence are among the lucky 25% that would survive for four generations.

Discussion

To analyze how the spatial layout of large settlements are the outcomes of the interactions of highly diverse social, political, economic, and religious orders, we focus on the more universal and less diverse characteristics, such as population, spatial location, and economic subsistence. Two observations arise from this study. First, prehistoric demographic self-regulation is the underlying principle creating spatial hierarchy, as inferred from the analysis of Tripolye settlement hierarchy using Central Place Theory. Second, small random increases in mortality to what would be stationary or stable populations frequently result in demographic collapse or population-village extinction in approximately four generations. This conclusion arose through simulations that projected changes to age structure over time. Traditionally, certain values of population size, density, or related variables were associated with specific types of social organization and administration of the inhabitants of nucleated settlements. In the battleground of the modern literature, these views are retreating and losing ground (Crema 2014; Crema et al. 2016; Delong and Burger 2015; Duffy 2015).

Our new results agree with Feinman's (2013) note emphasizing the increased variability of social organizations corresponding to increasing population size. This case study not only shows that four generations seems to be an approximate limit for the Tripolye mega-sites, but that there seem to have been two simultaneous responses when villages became extinct, as we see they did in the simulations. To maintain the spatio-demographic pattern reflected by Central Place Theory, the population would have had to shift locations to maintain the geographic pattern, and they would have had to change the network structure. The formation of Tripolye settlement systems that included both the mega-sites and 'satellite'-sites represent demographic self-regulation caused by density-dependence. 'Satellite' settlements were branched-off from the settlements of medium and large size in our case study. This assumption is confirmed by comparison of the bifurcation points in density of

	Average cohort life expectancy	Maximum age	Parameter 1	Parameter 2
Normal distribution			Mean	Standard deviation
normal a	6.86	35	5	0.25
normal b	39.87	35	0.5	0.01
normal c	16.24	> 60	1	1
normal d	26.14	> 60	1	0.5
normal e	36.55	> 60	0.5	0.5
f distribution			Numerator degrees of freedom	Denominator degrees of freedom
f a	24.8	> 60	1	100
f b	28.54	> 60	1	50
f c	22.6	15–25	1	1
f d	11.83	0–20	10	1
t distribution			Degrees of freedom	
t a	62.1	> 60	1	
t b	40.38	> 60	5	
t c	45.46	> 60	10	
Uniform distribution			Lower endpoint	Upper endpoint
u a	3.21	0–5	0	100
u b	3.98	0–5	0	50
u c	10.21	45	0	10
u d	6.29	20	5	
u e	11.47	> 60	0	10
Binomial distribution			Number of trials	Event probability
binomial a	4.9	15	100	0.1
binomial b	3.7	0	100	0.5
binomial c	2.83	0	100	0.9
binomial d	4.47	0–5	100	0.2
binomial e	23.98	> 60	100	0.01
binomial f	7.2	45	100	0.05
Geometric distribution			Event probability	
geometric a	4.35	0	20	0.01
geometric b	4.36	5–10	20	0.05
geometric c	12.81	15–40	20	0.2
geometric d	21.61	> 60	20	0.8
geometric e	25.68	> 60	20	0.9
Hypergeometric distribution			Event count	Sample size
hypergeometric a	6.18	20	100	100
hypergeometric b	3.7	5	500	100
hypergeometric c	4.3	5	250	100
hypergeometric d	7.4	30	100	100
hypergeometric e	8.7	60–75	25	100
hypergeometric f	31.09	> 60	10	100

Table 7.6. Summary results from simulations of the demographic structure of prehistoric villages when mortality is randomly impacted by different types of random distributions.

dwellings and the number of satellites corresponding to the large settlements.

We systematically increased the degree of freedom in our simulations, and as we did so, the degree of volatility of the impact moved closer and closer to 'complete randomness.' This helps us to understand how occasional small factors may influence demographic self-regulation. What the results show is that relatively small random factors impacting mortality that sometimes are repeated create such massive demographic collapse that the villages are abandoned. More specifically, increased mortality may affect younger cohorts, and thus reduce anyone in the fertility periods as the mortality drifts upwards through the cohorts. Alternatively, it may impact one gender over another, for there are many ways to create a massive demographic collapse. Once volatility enters the system, increasing changes may occur. This is a typical demographic snowball effect. It becomes more and more difficult to rectify.

Conclusions

Finally, historically in archaeology the analyzed Tripolye mega-sites were taken as a proxy of the formation of chiefdoms and the reconstruction of social complexity in prehistoric Europe (e.g., Videiko 2013). This may or may not be the case. Our study shows that the real situation and the underlying mechanisms are far more complex for the interaction between the developments of hierarchy as seen in Central Place Theory, and demographic self-regulation is the result of many different interactions, including random mortality. In short, what we have shown is that the traditional explanations of hierarchical settlement patterns for hierarchical socioeconomic structure camouflage a very complex set of interactions creating a mirage. This should not be a surprise when understanding that the reality of such large and sophisticated settlements has many interactions that mask causation. Our approach provides a novel understanding of not only such large and complex settlements but also helps unmask the principles of spatial organization in prehistory.

References Cited

Alho, J. 2008. Migration, fertility, and aging in stable population. *Demography* 43(3): 641–650.

Beckmann, M.J. 1958. City hierarchies and the distribution of city size. *Economic Development and Culture Change* 6: 243–248.

Beckmann, M.J. and J.C. McPherson 1970. City size distribution in a central place hierarchy: an alternative approach. *Journal of Regional Science* 10(1): 25–33.

Berry, B.J.L. 1967. *Geography of Market Centers and Retail Distribution*. Englewood Cliffs (NJ): Prentice-Hall.

Bertalanffy, L. 1968. *General System Theory: Foundations, Development, Applications*. New York: George Braziller.

Bocquet-Appel J.-P., S. Naji, M. van der Linden and J.K. Kozłowski 2009. Detection of diffusion and contact zones of early farming in Europe from the space-time distribution of 14C dates. *Journal of Archaeological Science* 36(3): 807–820.

Bratadan, C. 2016. Emigration and the stable population model: Migration effects on the demographic structure of the sending country, in R. Schoen (ed.) *Dynamic Demographic Analysis*: 217–225. Dordrecht: Springer.

Cesaretti, R., J. Lobo, L.M.A. Bettencourt, S.G. Ortman and M.E. Smith 2016. Population-Area Relationship for Medieval European Cities. *PLoS ONE* 11(10): e0162678, https://doi.org/10.1371/journal.pone.0162678

Chapman, J. and B. Gaydarska 2016. Low-Density Agrarian-Based Cities: A Principle of the Past and Present, in J. Müller, K. Rassmann and M. Videiko (eds) *Trypillia Mega-Sites and European Prehistory 4100-3400 BCE* (Themes in Contemporary Archaeology 2): 181–193. London and New York: Routledge.

Chapman, J., B. Gaydarska and D. Hale 2016. Nebelivka: Assembly Houses, Ditches, and Social Structure, in J. Müller, K. Rassmann and M. Videiko (eds) *Trypillia Mega-Sites and European Prehistory 4100-3400 BCE* (Themes in Contemporary Archaeology 2): 117–132. London and New York: Routledge.

Chapman, J., M. Videiko, D. Hale, B. Gaydarska, N. Burdo, K. Rassmann, C. Mischka, J. Müller, A. Korvin-Piotrovskiy and V. Kruts 2014. The Second Phase of the Trypillia Mega-Site Methodological Revolution: A New Research Agenda. *European Journal of Archaeology* 17(3): 369–406.

Childe, V.G. 1950. The urban revolution. *The Town Planning Review* 21: 3–17.

Christaller, W. 1966. *Central Places in Southern Germany*. Englewood Cliffs (NJ): Prentice-Hall.

Clarke, D.L.L. 1968. *Analytical Archaeology*. London: Routledge.

Clarke, D.L.L. (ed.) 1977. *Spatial Archaeology*. London: Routledge.

Coale, A.J. and P. Demeny 1966. *Regional Model Life Tables and Stable Populations*. Princeton (NJ): Princeton University Press.

Crema, E.R. 2014. A Simulation Model of Fission–Fusion Dynamics and Long-Term Settlement Change. *Journal of Archaeological Method and Theory* 21: 385–404.

Crema, E.R., A. Kandler and S. Shennan 2016. Revealing patterns of cultural transmission from frequency data: equilibrium and non-equilibrium assumptions. *Scientific Reports* 6: 39122, https://doi.org/10.1038/srep39122

Crumley, C.A. 1976. Toward a Locational Definition of State Systems of Settlement. *American Anthropologist* 78(1): 59–73.

Dacey, M.F. 1966. Population of places in a central place hierarchy. *Journal of Regional Studies* 6(2): 27–33.

DeLong, J.P. and O. Burger 2015. Socio-Economic Instability and the Scaling of Energy Use with Population Size. *PLoS ONE* 10(6): e0130547, https://doi.org/10.1371/journal.pone.0130547

Dergachev, V.A. 1980. *Sites of the Late Tripolye*. Kishinev: Shtiintsa.

Diachenko, A. 2012. Settlement system of West Tripolye culture in the Southern Bug and Dnieper interfluve: formation problems, in F. Menotti and A.G. Korvin-Piotrovskiy (eds) *The Tripolye Culture Giant-Settlements in Ukraine: Formation, Development and Decline*: 116–138. Oxford: Oxbow Books.

Diachenko, A. 2013. Hierarchic settlement systems and the issue of archaeological sampling, in A. Pozikhovski, J. Rogozinski and M. Rybicka (eds) *Na Pograniczu Kultury Pucharow Lejkowatych i Kultury Tripolskiej*: 9–14. Rzeszow: Mitel.

Diachenko, A. 2016. Demography Reloaded, in J. Müller, K. Rassmann and M. Videiko (eds) *Trypillia Mega-Sites and European Prehistory 4100-3400 BCE* (Themes in Contemporary Archaeology 2): 181–194. London and New York: Routledge.

Diachenko, A. and F. Menotti 2012. The gravity model: monitoring the formation and development of the Tripolye culture giant-settlements in Ukraine. *Journal of Archaeological Science* 39(4): 2810–2817.

Diachenko, A., I. Sobkowiak-Tabaka and S. Ryzhov 2020. Approaching the unification and diversity of pottery assemblages: The case of Western Tripolye culture ceramics in the Southern Bug and Dnieper interfluve, 4100–3600 cal BC. *Documenta Praehistorica* 47: 522–535.

Diachenko, A. and E.B.W. Zubrow 2015. Stabilization Points in Carrying Capacity: Population Growth and Migrations. *Journal of Neolithic Archaeology* 17: 1–15.

Duffy, P.R. 2015. Site size hierarchy in middle range societies. *Journal of Anthropological Archaeology* 37: 85–99.

Evans, S.T. 1980. Spatial Analysis of Basin of Mexico Settlement: Problems with the Use of the Central Place Model. *American Antiquity* 45(4): 866–875.

Feigenbaum, M.J. 1978. Quantitative universality for a class of nonlinear transformations. *Journal of Statistical Physics* 19: 25–52.

Feigenbaum, M.J. 1979. The universal metric properties of nonlinear transformations. *Journal of Statistical Physics* 21: 669–706.

Feinman, G.M. 2011. Size, Complexity, and Organizational Variation: A Comparative Approach. *Cross-Cultural Research* 45(1): 37–58.

Feinman, G.M. 2013. The emergence of social complexity, in D.M. Carballo (ed.) *Cooperation and Collective Action: Archaeological Perspectives*: 35–56. Boulder: University of Colorado Press.

Flannery, K.V. 1968. Archeological systems theory and Early Mesoamerica, in B.J. Meggers (ed.) *Anthropological Archeology in the Americas*: 67–87. Washington, D.C.: Anthropological Society of Washington.

Flannery, K.V. 1998. The Ground Plans of Archaic States, in G.M. Feinman and J. Marcus (eds) *Archaic States*: 15–58. Santa Fe (NM): School for Advanced Research Press.

Fletcher, R. 1995. *The Limits to Settlement Growth*. Cambridge: Cambridge University Press.

Fletcher, R. 2006. Materiality, space, time, and outcome, in J. Bintliff (ed.) *A Companion to Archaeology*: 110–114. Oxford: Blackwell.

Furholt, M. 2016. Settlement layout and social organisation in the earliest European Neolithic. *Antiquity* 90(353): 1196–1212.

Galor, O. and O. Moav 2007. *The Neolithic revolution and contemporary variations in life expectancy* (Working Paper, No. 2007-14). Providence (RI): Brown University, Department of Economics.

Gaydarska, B. 2015. Giant-settlements or proto-cities: The false opposition, in A. Diachenko, F. Menotti, S. Ryzhov, K. Bunyatyan and S. Kadrow (eds) *The Cucuteni-Tripolye Cultural Complex and Its Neighbours: Essays in Memory of Volodymyr Kruts*: 35–56. Lviv: Astrolabe.

Gaydarska, B. 2016. The city is dead! Long live the city! *Norwegian Archaeological Review* 49: 40–57.

Gaydarska, B. (ed.) 2020. *Early Urbanism in Europe: The Trypillia Megasites of the Ukrainian Forest-Steppe*. Warsaw and Berlin: De Gruyter.

Haas, W.R., C.J. Klink, G.J. Maggard and M.S. Aldenderfer 2015. Settlement-Size Scaling among Prehistoric Hunter-Gatherer Settlement Systems in the New World. *PLoS ONE* 10(11): e0140127, https://doi.org/10.1371/journal.pone.0140127

Haggett, P. 1979. *Geography. A Modern Synthesis*. New York: Harper and Row.

Hamilton, M.J., O. Burger, J.P. DeLong, R.S. Walker, M.E. Moses and J.H. Brown 2009. Population stability, cooperation, and the invisibility of the human species. *Proceedings of the National Academy of Sciences of the USA* 106(30): 12255–12260.

Hamilton, M.J., J. Lobo, E. Rupley, H. Youn and G.B. West 2016. The ecological and evolutionary energetics of hunter-gatherer residential mobility. *Evolutionary Anthropology* 25(3): 124–132.

Hamilton, M.J., B.T. Milne, R.S. Walker, O. Burger and J.H. Brown 2007. The complex structure of hunter-gatherer social network. *Proceedings of the Royal Society B* 274(2): 2195–2202.

Harper, T.K. 2016. Climate, migrations, and false cities on the Old European periphery: A spatio-demographic approach to understanding the Tripolye giant-settlements. Unpublished PhD dissertation, State University of New York at Buffalo.

Harper, T.K. 2019. Demography and climate in Late Eneolithic Ukraine, Moldova, and Romania: Multiproxy evidence and pollen-based regional corroboration. *Journal of Archaeological Science: Reports* 23: 973–982.

Hirth, K.G. 1998. The Distributional Approach: A New Way to Identify Marketplace Exchange in the Archaeological Record. *Current Anthropology* 39(4): 451–476.

Hodder, I. and C. Orton 1976. *Spatial Analysis in Archaeology*. Cambridge: Cambridge University Press.

Hofmann, R., A. Diachenko and J. Müller 2016. Demographic trends and socio-economic dynamics: Some issues of correlation, in S. Țerna and B. Govedarica (eds) *Interactions, Changes and Meanings: Essays in Honor of Igor Manzura on the Occasion of his 60th Birthday:* 193–198. Kishinev: Stratum Plus.

Johnson, G.A. 1972. A test of the utility of the Central Place Theory in archaeology, in by P.J. Ucko, R. Tringham and G.W. Dimbleby (eds) *Man, Settlement and Urbanism:* 769–787. London: Duckworth.

Keyfitz, N. and H. Caswell 2005. *Applied Mathematical Demography*. New York: Springer.

Kruts, V.A. 1989. Regarding the history of Tripolye culture population in the Southern Bug and Dnieper interfluve, in S.S. Berezanskaya (ed.) *Prehistoric Archaeology: Materials and Studies:* 117–132. Kiev: Naukova Dumka.

Lobo, J., L. Bettencourt, M.E. Smith and S. Ortman 2020. Settlement scaling theory: Bridging the study of ancient and contemporary urban systems. *Urban Studies* 57(4): 731-747.

Lockwood, J., M.F. Hoopes and M.P. Marchetti 2007. *Invasion Ecology*. Oxford: Blackwell.

May, R.L. 1976. Simple mathematical models with very complicated dynamics. *Nature* 261: 459–467.

Menotti, F. and A. Korvin-Piotrovskiy (eds) 2012. *The Giant-Settlements of the Tripolye Culture: Formation, Development and Decline*. Oxford: Oxbow Books.

Minc, L.D. 2006. Monitoring regional market systems in prehistory: Models, methods, and metrics. *Journal of Anthropological Archaeology* 25(1): 82–116.

Müller, J. 2017. Inheritance, population development and social identities Southeast Europe 5200–4300 BCE, in M. Gori and M. Ivanova (eds) *Balkan Dialogues: Negotiating Identity between Prehistory and the Present:* 156–168. London: Routledge.

Müller, J., R. Hofmann, L. Brandtstätter, R. Ohlrau and M. Videiko 2016a. Chronology and Demography: How Many People Lived in a Mega-Site?, in J. Müller, K. Rassmann and M. Videiko (eds) *Trypillia Mega-Sites and European Prehistory 4100-3400 BCE* (Themes in Contemporary Archaeology 2)*:* 137–170. London and New York: Routledge.

Müller, J., K. Rassmann and M. Videiko (eds) 2016b. *Trypillia Mega-Sites and European Prehistory 4100-3400 BCE* (Themes in Contemporary Archaeology 2). London and New York: Routledge.

Nakoinz, O. 2012. Models of Centrality. *Journal of Ancient Studies* 3: 217–233.

Nakoinz, O. 2019. *Zentralität. Theorie, Methoden und Fallbeispiele zur Analyse zentraler Orte* (Berlin Studies of the Ancient World 56). Berlin: Pro Business.

Nakoinz, O. and D. Knitter 2016. *Modelling Human Behavior in Landscapes: Basic Concepts and Modelling Elements*. Dordrecht: Springer.

Ohlrau, R. 2020. *Maidanets'ke: Development and Decline of a Trypillia Mega-Site in Central Ukraine* (Scales of Transformations in Prehistoric and Archaic Societies 7). Leiden: Sidestone Press.

Ohlrau, R., M. Dal Corso, W. Kirleis and J. Müller 2016. Living on the edge? Carrying capacities of Trypillian settlements in the Buh-Dnipro interfluve, in J. Müller, K. Rassmann and M. Videiko (eds) *Trypillia Mega-Sites and European Prehistory 4100-3400 BCE* (Themes in Contemporary Archaeology 2)*:* 207–220. London and New York: Routledge.

Ortman, S.G., A.H.F. Cabaniss, J.O. Sturm and L.M.A. Bettencourt 2015. Settlement scaling and increasing returns in an ancient society. *Science Advances* 1(1): 1e1400066, https://advances.sciencemag.org/content/1/1/e1400066

Parr, J. 1969. City hierarchies and the distribution of city size: a reconsideration of Beckmann's contribution. *Journal of Regional Science* 9(2): 239–253.

Parr, J.B. 1995. Alternative approaches to market-area structure in the urban system. *Urban Studies* 32(8): 1317–1329.

Polanyi, K. 1944. *The Great Transformation. The Political and Economic Origins of Our Time*. Boston: Beacon.

Pollard, H.P. 1980. Central Places and Cities: A Consideration of the Protohistoric Tarascan State. *American Antiquity* 45(4): 677–696.

Rassmann, K., A. Korvin-Piotrovskiy, M. Videiko and J. Müller 2016. The new challenge for site plans and geophysics: Revealing the settlement structure of giant settlements by means of geomagnetic survey, in J. Müller, K. Rassmann and M. Videiko (eds) *Trypillia Mega-Sites and European Prehistory 4100-3400 BCE* (Themes in Contemporary Archaeology 2)*:* 29–54. London and New York: Routledge.

Ryzhov, S. 2012. Relative chronology of the giant-settlement period BII – CI, in F. Menotti and A.G. Korvin-Piotrovskiy (eds) *The Tripolye Culture Giant-Settlements in Ukraine: Formation, Development and Decline:* 79–115. Oxford: Oxbow Books.

Shennan, S. 2008. Population processes and their consequences in Early Neolithic Central Europe, in J.-P. Bocquet-Appel and O. Bar-Yosef (eds) *The Neolithic Demographic Transition and Its Consequences:* 315–329. New York: Springer.

Shennan, S. 2013. Demographic continuities and discontinuities in Neolithic Europe: Evidence, methods and implications. *Journal of Archaeological Method and Theory* 20(2): 300–311.

Smith, C.A. 1974. Economics of marketing systems: models from economic geography. *Annual Review of Anthropology* 3: 167–201.

Tsvek, O.V. 2006. *Settlements of Eastern Tripolye Culture (A Brief Overview)*. Kiev: IA NASU.

Velikanova, M.S. 1975. *Paleoanthropology of Prut and Dniester Interfluve*. Moscow: Nauka.

Videiko, M. 2013. *Comprehensive Study of the Large Settlements of Trypillia Culture, V – IV mil. BC*. Saarbrücken: Lambert.

Zubrow, E.B.W. 1975. *Prehistoric Carrying Capacity. A Model*. Menlo Park (CA): Cummings.

Chapter 8

Sanctuaries and Settlements:
Spatial Organization in the Nuragic Landscapes of Sardinia

Ruth Beusing

Abstract

Monumental architecture is commonly regarded as a means for consolidating political dominance and supporting social cohesion within and between communities. Sardinia's monumental Nuragic culture of the Middle Bronze Age to Early Iron Age introduced different types of monumental buildings for profane and religious purposes, including settlement monuments (*nuraghi*) as well as tombs and sanctuaries. The dense distribution of these monuments in the landscape suggests their importance as landmarks but also as beacons for structural networks. There are many ways to study the social impact of these monuments. This paper analyzes the intervisibility between the monuments and addresses changing relations between profane and religious architecture to decipher the reciprocal impact of places within cultural landscapes and their social meaning over the roughly 1100 years of the Nuragic culture in Sardinia. From a survey of the entire island, this study focuses on a smaller sample region, a mesoregion in southern-central Sardinia. The results are discussed in terms of the inclusivity and exclusivity of the representative architecture in its cultural and environmental context.

Introduction

Why and *how* people settle landscapes have been focal research questions in archaeology since the outset of the discipline. The erection of sanctuaries, in particular, encompasses more than just people coming to emotional terms with the supernatural. Sanctuaries are a connector for the expression of kinship, politics, identity, and other aspects of the socially constructed world. Monuments can serve as symbols of social cohesion and membership in a larger community, thereby serving an integrative function as was discussed in detail for megaliths in Northwest Europe (Chapman 1981; Renfrew 1976).

Rituals are also a conduit between the cosmological and the everyday routine, a visible venue for the assertion of group identities. The reuse of sacred places over time has been suggested as a primary contributor to large-scale aggregation and complex societies (e.g., Fernandez-Götz, this volume). In the Nuragic culture of Sardinia, places exclusively used as sacred venues, other than burial places, appear to be a late invention, culminating in the Early Iron Age (hereafter EIA) (see Table 8.1).

The occurrence of new sanctuaries, in particular water-temples, is evidence of a changing ritual pattern in the Nuragic culture. Water-temples are cult buildings centered on wells/*pozzi*, stone-lined shafts or chambers dug to various depths to capture subterranean water, and on fonts/*fonti*, superficial stone basins or chambers for collecting spring-water (Webster 2014). The architecture of water-temples exemplifies exquisite masonry. Several of the wells consist of a shaft or chamber construction with a corbelled dome that required elaborate skills in statics (e.g., Santa Christina, Paulilatino, Santa Vittoria, Serri). The fonts indicate similar masonry skills as can be seen in the house-like construction of Su Tempiesu, together with anteroom and waterworks (for more details and further literature on the examples, see Ialongo 2011; Webster 2014). The typology of the two types is broadly accepted, the surrounding architecture of both is sometimes similar, and there is no evidence for significantly different religious use.

Previously, ritual and cultic actions were traced almost exclusively in specific burial monuments. Deceased persons of the Nuragic culture were buried in so-called giant's tombs (*tombe dei giganti*) close to villages as well as the eponymous *nuraghi*, the monumental, truncated conical towers, standing up to several stories high with corbelled ceilings. The *tombe dei giganti* are collective burial monuments with funerary chambers and concave stone fronts (*exedrae*). Both the *nuraghi* and the *tombe dei gigantic* are imposing monuments, both seem to display a collective or communal effort, and together they appear to have been centers of social activities and widely visible symbols of land tenure and shared ideologies over several centuries.

In the Recent Bronze Age (hereafter RBA), *megaron* temples—the first traceable places dedicated to religious activities, apart from the burial-site centered ancestor-worship—occur. They differ from the Greek

Eneolithic		...			
	Late	Final			2500–2100 BC
	Early (EBA)				2300–1700 BC
		Initial		Nuragic I	1700–1600 BC
	Middle (MBA)				1600–1350 BC
Bronze Age		Full		Nuragic II	
	Late (LBA)	Recent (RBA)		Nuragic III	1350–1200 BC
		Final (FBA)			1200–1000 BC
		I	Geometric	Nuragic IV	1000–730 BC
	Early (EIA)		Orientalizing	Nuragic IV Phoenician	730–580 BC
Iron Age	II		Archaic		580–500 BC
	Late (LIA)		Punic	Nuragic V	525–238 BC
			Roman	Republican	238–1 BC
Roman			Roman	Imperial	AD 1–476

Table 8.1. Chronology of Sardinian archaeology from the Eneolithic to the Late Iron Age based on calibrated radiocarbon dates provided by Depalmas and Melis 2011. The subdivision of the Nuragic culture is based on Lilliu 1999.

namesakes in their general appearance and by their great variety, and seem to be exclusive to the northern and central uplands of Sardinia. They have a rectilinear ground plan and antes that create a vestibule entrance. Some of the *megaron* temples were built in remote places (e.g., Domu de Orgia, Eszterli) and others were included in settlement structures (e.g., Serra Orios, Dorgali). Small groups of huts have been identified around the temples, and they probably served as part of the ritual and festive activities.

It is widely assumed that the emergence of the Nuragic sanctuaries is a response to further structural developments, such as a decline and restructuring of settlements in the FBA and EIA. Some sanctuaries represent the reinterpretation, and partly invention, of ritual spaces within the settlements, such as shrines, rotundas, or *nuraghi*, reused as sanctuaries (Webster 2015).

Concerning social and political structures, Lilliu (1988) pointed out for the first time that within and after the decline of an earlier cohesion, exemplified in the erection of communal monumental construction (*nuraghi*, *tombe dei giganti*), the new sanctuaries appeared to be the most visible reinforcement of unifying activities among communities. Some scholarly interpretation assumes a collapse of the former Nuragic culture in the Late Bronze Age (hereafter LBA) and a later attempt to reinstall older values in the EIA (Depalmas 2012). Others emphasize a reformation phase where people assumed new, and different, social stability when the prevailing elites appropriated influence and power. Webster (1996) first recognized the role of the emergence of the water-

temples as a new element in the social transformation toward a hierarchical system that he later refined to a three-level organization, best observed in settlement hierarchy. In this, the water-temples were the religious, commercial, and social centers of supralocal or regional entities. This model is widely assumed to have been related to the formation of 'confederations' of independent compounds, involving an underlying social concept of a chiefdom organization (Usai 2006; Webster 2015). The sanctuaries most likely also played a role in the economy of the island—as Depalmas (2001) argues, they appear to have been a key element in the redistribution practices of the Nuragic chiefdoms. They would have provided a framework and setting to mediate between individuals and political and economic entities. Ialongo (2013) further highlights their economic function by analyzing and quantifying the contents of ritual depositions within the sanctuaries' compounds.

While the accumulation of metal goods is merely recognizable in the Middle Bronze Age (hereafter MBA), and documented only in domestic contexts, hoards radically increased in both number and size in the EIA, coinciding with the construction of water-temples. Ialongo (2013: 201) interprets this new demonstration of wealth as being extracted by emerging regional-level hierarchies who utilized the whole process of construction and maintenance of water-temples in a communal effort as an institutionalized space fostering their 'claims for hegemony.'

Increasing evidence of pan-Mediterranean contacts during FBA and EIA on Sardinia are believed to have been related to the instability in cultural expression of these periods. New alliances might be observable in elaborate economic networks, as suggests the massive distribution of oxhide ingots on the island (Lo Schiavo *et al.* 2009). On the other hand, there is also reason to presume that civil conflicts, or even natural catastrophes, might have been responsible for the instability (for a summary, see Webster 2015: 216–221). The assumed decimation of the Nuragic population, evident in the abandonment of rural *nuraghe*-settlements, the concentration of population in strongly defensive nucleated centers, represented by core areas fortified with cyclopean walls and bastions, and the newly defined ritual performances, displayed in many domestic and public sanctuaries, seem to demonstrate a drastic transformation. The new settlements often were established by using the older *nuraghi* as nuclei. Ritual performances, on the other hand, appear to be highly developed in their expression, making scholars assume longer religious traditions than evident in the archaeological record.

The preceding highlights the structural role of sanctuaries within the (re)composition of communities coinciding with settlement nucleation. In contrast, the vast number of previously built settlements of single *nuraghi* were scattered in the landscape. Though the majority of the *nuraghe* locations have not been investigated, the current state of research indicates that a high percentage would have been out of use and deserted by the Final Bronze Age (FBA). Nevertheless, *nuraghi* towering over the landscape would have been perceived as beacons of the ancestors' doings. Two religious ideas, among other possible influences, drove the realignment of Nuragic societies in the EIA: 1) ancestors worship, performed in *nuraghe* monuments (as well as using *nuraghe*-idols) and 2) the water-temples specified above. On the one hand, both types of monuments could have drawn reciprocal importance from each other. On the other hand, the proximity of an important inhabited village might have enhanced the status of a sanctuary, while a highly symbolic sanctuary would have affected the surrounding settlements similarly.

This paper examines the location, temporal sequence, and reciprocal impact of LBA/EIA sanctuaries within the settlement organization, and interprets their role in community organization and the crystallization of settlement nuclei. We compare the different clusters of *nuraghi* and temples in their locales through time. (Inter)visibility defines territories of social action (Mubi Brighenti 2010: 186f), and thus is a strong criterion for the aggregation of settlement activity in specific locations. We hypothesize that (in)visibility might have been constitutional criteria for possible locations of sacral monuments as well as for settlement nucleation in some cases. Representation and communication appear to be important for a subset of the sanctuaries,

while other locations were chosen because of their remoteness.

Archaeological Background of the Nuragic Culture

Although this study focuses on the later period of the Nuragic culture, the importance and impact of the water-temples need to be considered as part of the background of broader cultural developments. Archaeologists describe the Nuragic culture as a phenomenon that was limited to the island of Sardinia and occurred from broadly the MBA to the EIA (Ialongo 2011; for references to partly different dating approaches, see Depalmas and Melis 2011). About 6000 *nuraghi* are still visible in the Sardinian landscape, but only a small percentage of them have been investigated in detail. The emergence of the towers appears to have been an endogenous development by the local population, adopted as a unique type of 'residential' building on the island. Despite their highly fortified appearance, so far the evidence rather indicates their domestic use (Depalmas 2006). Settlement activities in the *nuraghi* have been identified at sites dating from MBA to LBA. The limited archaeological record implies that the towers themselves were abandoned as residential buildings in subsequent periods, while settlement activities still took place in the areas around some of the Nuragic villages. Several abandoned *nuraghi* later were reused as sanctuaries, most evident in votive depositions.

The basic type of the towers is the '*tholos*' *nuraghi*, subdivided into single *nuraghi* (single tower) and complex *nuraghi* (multiple towers), the latter being a later development. *Tholos nuraghi* can be found in nearly all landscape types (Depalmas and Melis 2011: 169–170). From later MBA to RBA, the number of *tholos nuraghi* increased markedly, with Contu (1997) suggesting a peak of about 9000 units. Because of their density within the landscape, they have often been related to communication networks (de Montis and Caschili 2012; for details, see below). A social model for the earlier phase of the Nuragic culture is that the 'evenly distributed monumentality' might be evidence of a widely egalitarian society that spent monumental communal effort on local-scale living and afterlife (see below) conditions (Lilliu 1988). As early as the MBA, people started to build circular huts adjacent to several of the *nuraghi*. From smaller numbers of huts at the beginning, they evolved to nucleated and dense settlements during the LBA, some growing to the size and functionality of local and supralocal centers during the FBA and EIA. The famous Nuragic settlement and World Heritage Site of Su Nuraxi in Barumini is described as one of these supralocal centers. Additionally, villages appeared during the LBA without any *nuraghe* to act as the nucleus of development. Blake (2002: 149) estimates about 400 to 500 of those villages on the whole island.

Monument type	Sardinia	Marmilla/Sarcidano/Trextena
	macroregion	mesoregion
nuraghi	5491	715
tombe dei giganti	623	53
water-temples	98 (well 62, font 36)	21 (well 14, font 7)
megaron-temples	18	1

Table 8.2. Number of monuments utilized in the analysis.

While the complexity of several of the villages increased, the original use of the *nuraghi* ceased, and no further *nuraghi* were built later than the RBA. The variety of hut ground plans grew—along with the traditional circular ones, there are trapezoid, rectangular, elliptical, and other shapes. Additionally, the sizes of huts became more varied and larger houses were endowed with a courtyard. A large circular hut with seats around the inside walls was found in several of the new central villages. These are interpreted as 'meeting huts' and stone models of *nuraghi* have frequently been found inside them. This phenomenon is generally seen as ancestor worship since the *nuraghi* during this late phase already were abandoned, as mentioned above, although the surrounding settlements were still occupied. The variation of house types and sizes might indicate both an increasing social differentiation within the Nuragic societies as well as functional diversification. For the LBA, Webster (2015) delineates a three-fold classification. Class 1 is small hamlets, up to 20–40 huts grouped around a central *nuraghe* (size about 0.25–0.5 ha) and occasionally single *nuraghe*-dwellings without adjacent villages. Class 2 generally refers to as complex *nuraghi*, and they were built forward from older *nuraghe* settlements. To the original main tower were added further subsidiary towers, joined together with encasing walls. Class 3 is described as regional centers, organizing larger communities and facilitating communication within larger groups. Criteria for this classification were the size of these places and the presence of different craft shops, meeting places, etc.

During the MBA and FBA, places used for religious, and possibly communal, ceremonies seem to have coincided with burial places. They can be found in various kinds of landscapes and are closely related to the surrounding settlements (Blake 2001, 2002). The presence of conic stones (*betils*) near several of the tombs suggests that ancestor worship may have been practiced. There are several other burial forms documented apart from the *tombe dei giganti*, including burials in caves as well as individual burials in trench or pit tombs (see Depalmas and Melis 2011: 176), but evidence is sparse. Secondary burials placed in the so-called *domos de janas* monuments of the Neolithic Ozieri culture are also known (Webster 2015). Nevertheless,

the *tombe dei giganti* are the most visible and the best-documented burial category. Several of them were used up to the latest phase of Nuragic culture and were rebuilt or newly built in this time.

Apart from burial monuments, there is only vague traceable evidence for dedicated religious or sacred sites in the earlier phases of the Nuragic culture, but older ceramic material at some of the later *megaron*s and water-temples may indicate continuity of place use in some of them. While the *megaron* temples are comparatively rare, water-temples can be identified all over the island (Table 8.2). Currently, the ratio of wells and fonts on the island might be roughly 60:40. For the later water-temples, Ialongo (2011), applying a sociopolitical concept regarding the invention of new ritual water-temples in the Nuragic EIA, emphasized the intentional political use of the buildings of sacred places that became particularly manifest in the supralocal sanctuaries. Following other scholars, he proposed the identification of at least five 'cantonal' groupings in the close vicinity of the supralocal water-temple S. Vittoria in Serri (Ialongo 2011: Vol. II: 479, Figure 3.3). Webster (2015) and Ialongo (2013) both stress the emergence of central sanctuaries as a key feature in the model of social differentiation in the late Nuragic culture, as sanctuaries are assumed to have provided both the ideological framework and the physical space to mediate between individual concepts and a political and economic superstructure. Nevertheless, others have argued for a more egalitarian interpretation of the same evidence (e.g., Araque Gonzales 2014).

From the later phase of the Nuragic culture, other forms of ritual and cult have been observed that suggest domestic and settlement contexts. They include intramural ritual bath cabins, or the abandoned *nuraghi* reused for ritual purposes. Shrines were built inside or nearby some of the *nuraghi* in the FBA and EIA. Moreover, the meeting huts, with the frequently observed *nuraghi* models, can be mentioned within this context and might be linked to an ancestry cult (Depalmas and Melis 2011: 176). Yet these observations are too rare to be subjected to robust quantitative analyses since less than 5% of the Nuragic monuments have received detailed research.

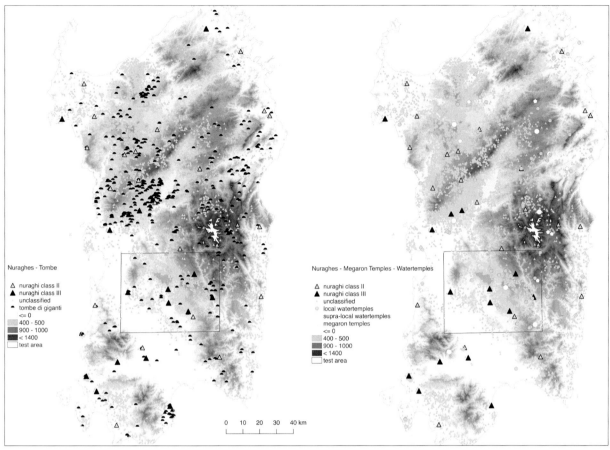

Figure 8.1. Distribution of *nuraghi–tombe dei giganti* and *nuraghi–*water-temples
in Sardinia (figure by the author).

Landscape and Data

As demonstrated above, Nuragic ritual practices and sanctuaries have long been a matter of debate. The present study focuses on the spatial aspect of the sacred monuments within a time-span of about 1000 years, starting with the ritual activities around the *tombe dei giganti* in the MBA (*c.* 1700 BC) and ending with the latest organized ritual use of some of the water-temples in the 6th/5th century BC (as proposed by Ialongo 2013). It examines in detail three previously discussed ritual monument types of different quality and preferences, including *tombe dei giganti*, *megaron* temples, and water-temples, and investigates the importance of the spatial aspects of the different ritual monument types—in particular, the impact of intervisibility of different monument types and their built surroundings. Thereby, this paper seeks to explore if and how the choice of site location of sacred places changed with the modified social significance of the sites as described above. The study moves from a large-scale perspective on the entire island to a mesoscale investigation of a test area in Central Sardinia in the west-central part of the island (Figure 8.1). Though several common developments can be deduced from the island-wide archaeological record, the local setting has

to be considered for each region and can vary strongly (Stiglitz 2007; van Dommelen 1998). Thus, the mesoscale analysis researches the water-temples as they relate to their possible intentional implementation, role, and development in crucial places, to be used as a means of communication and networking in a changing society, as described above for the latest phase of the Nuragic culture. By evaluating the reference of the monument types within the landscapes, this study also explores the communities providing maintenance, orchestration, and an audience for these ritual spaces.

Topography and Landscape Characterization

Sardinia can be subdivided into four main geological units (Carmignani *et al.* 2015; Depalmas and Melis 2011). The mesoregion study area covers 2710 km² in the hilly uplands of Central Sardinia, rising from 47 m above sea level on the Campidano Plain in the south-southwest to 1050 m close to the mountainous region of the Barbagia in the northeast. To the east, the artificially dammed Lago del Flumendosa and the Flumendosa River roughly confine the study area. The volcano massif of the Montiferru, whose main peak is the Monte Urtigu (1050 m), delimits the western boundary. Its eponymous name refers to its wealth of natural resources, exploited for metal ore as well as obsidian and other raw materials. To the west follows the coastal plain of Medio Campidano. The environment is diverse, with mountains, hills, and plains. A further prominent natural feature is the Giara de Gesturi, a wide basaltic plain of 42 km², rising to an average height of 550 m. Certain locations within the Giara di Serri provide a range of vision from the massif of the Gennargentu to the lowlands of the Campidano as well as the Marmilla with its characteristic gentle hills—it is said that on clear days there would be free vision to the sea in the distance.

Archaeological Data

Data was examined at two scales of analysis: the whole island of Sardinia, hitherto also referred to as macroregion, and a mesoregion located in the territory of the Sardinian subregions of Marmilla, Sarcidano, and Trextena, with the Monte Arci in Campidano as a western marker and the Flumendosa River as the eastern boundary. Three major types of archaeological sites have been distinguished: settlements, sanctuaries, and burials. For a further division of *nuraghi*/settlements, Webster's (2015: 87) classification was used. The overall dataset for Sardinia comprises 5492 *nuraghi* that have been surveyed but have not been further studied. Webster (2015) estimates that only about 1% of Sardinia's *nuraghi* have been investigated, and points out that several ideas about these monuments are still widely hypothetical. It can be assumed that most of the *nuraghi* were present as landmarks during the later phases of the Nuragic culture, though a larger quantity might have been abandoned in the course of the later LBA and EIA. The data also includes 623 *tombe dei gigantic* and 18 *megaron* temples, the distributions of which are mostly restricted to the northern part of the island, as well as 98 water-temples cataloged from 91 sites (see Table 8.2). Seven sites present more than one water-temple, and a font and a well appear in the same place in Is Clamoris (Table 8.3).

There is no particular distribution pattern of the two different types, except that the fonts do not seem to be present in the southwestern part of the island. This implies that also in the western part of the selected mesoregion, in Marmilla, Sardicano, and Trextena, there are no fonts, while there are six of them in the eastern part. Ten Sardinian water-temples have been identified as being supralocal (or 'federal') by Webster (2015) and Ialongo (2011), listed in Table 8.4.

The selected mesoregion is located near the supralocal sanctuary of Santa Vittoria, positioned on the southwestern end of a basaltic highland and characterized by very steep escarpments, today called Giara di Serri. This is one of the more intensively investigated water-temples in Sardinia, summarized

Name	Community	Type (number)
Gremannu	Fonni	font 2
Corongiu Murvonis	Calasetta	well 2
Matzanni	Vallermosa	well 3
Sant 'Anastasia	Sardara	well 3
Mont 'e Nuxi	Esterzili	font 3
Is Clamoris	Escalaplano	well 1, font 1
Funtana Crobetta	Ballao	well 2

Table 8.3. Sanctuaries with more than one water-temples.

Name	Community	Type (number)
Serra Niedda	Sorso	well 1
Su Tempiesu	Orune	font 1
Gremanu	Fonni	well 1, font 2
Santa Cristina	Paulilatino	well 1
Santa Vittoria	Serri	well 1
Sant 'Anastasia	Sardara	well 3
Funtana Coberta	Silius	well 1
Matzanni I-III	Vallermosa	well 3
Su Romanzesu	Bitti	well 1
Monte S. Antonio	Siligo	well 1

Table 8.4. Supralocal or 'federal' sanctuaries
(adapted from Webster 2015).

and contextualized lately by Ialongo (2011: 430, 2013) and Webster (2015). The sanctuary covers 3 ha and includes buildings of various functions. The complex contains two 'temples' (a well and an open layout), a large, circular hut with annexes, and a set of enclosures. One of the most representative features is the so-called 'enclosure of reunions'—a large, enclosed, elliptical area about 75 m long on its longest side, with stalls in its outer layout. Finds and shape might identify these enclosures as craft shops and vendors' units, suggesting that the site might have served market and distributional functions, in addition to its religious and communal use. Another well claimed to be of supralocal importance is Sant'Anastasia, although the size and the nearby environment of the sacred area are unclear because most of the Nuragic horizon is obstructed by a medieval church and the modern village of Sardara. Nevertheless, Cypriot bronzes and other metal finds were uncovered as well as a large hut containing circular benches and a *nuraghe* model, as found in several of the 'meeting huts' in other villages, that promoted the site to a supralocal classification.

The mesoregion holds 715 *nuraghi*, including six Class 3 *nuraghi*, 52 *tombe dei gigantic*, two *megaron* temples, a rotunda, and 21 water-temples three of which are of supralocal character (Santa Vittoria, Funtana Coberta,

Sant'Anastasia). The remains of 23 *nuraghi* have been preserved along the slope and perimeter of Giara di Gesturi, but no monument can be found on top of the basaltic plain. The Nuragic complex and World Heritage Site of Su Nuraxi in Barumini is 1.5 km to the south. The slopes of Monte Arci, renowned for its obsidian deposits that were utilized until the Iron Age, likewise contain about 109 *nuraghi*, but again none are located in the upper zones of the mountain. A lot of settlement activity has been identified in the southern lowlands, flattening towards the Campidano Plain.

For this project, data acquisition was conducted by a semi-automated parsing of web content, including tharros.info and wikimapia.org. Tharros.info is a touristic information website, with a database on *nuraghi* and other heritage sites on Sardinia, and wikimapia. org is a public mapping tool that encourages users to create map entries characterizing their environment. The datasets were verified and complemented by consulting satellite imagery and published literature as well as further enriched with site characterization, site contexts, and chronology from other published site catalogs (Cattari 2006; Moravetti 1998; van Dommelen 1998).

Method and Technical Specifications

GIS work and analytics were conducted with GRASS GIS (7.2) and QGIS (2.18, mainly employing the Viewshed plugin). General overviews of Sardinia are mapped to the 30-m NASA SRTM, while the detailed area analyses are based on 10-m ALOS-PALSAR data (Alaska Satellite Facility 2017; Watkins 2017). GIS analyses were applied to the complete Sardinian dataset as well as to the mesoregion in Central Sardinia.

The study is based on geographical intervisibility analyses, a methodological tool that enables archaeologists to limit the complexity of the sets of affordances of the landscape, in order to study how they might have affected and structured human behavior. Lines or areas of sight have been addressed as communication networks as well as spaces of immediate control and power (Brughmans *et al.* 2017; Llobera *et al.* 2004). If a site or landmark can be seen from several other places, it is considered always present and available to users of the land. Viewsheds shed light on observation points and points of concealment, being used as visual communication networks, observable routes, overseeing the characteristics of landforms, like peaks and depressions, and the use of visibility for navigation. Fraser (1983) and more recently Gillings (2015) addressed the study of invisibility as a rewarding path to follow in other contexts.

In the present study, cumulative binary and intervisibility viewsheds were applied. The analyses follow the approach of Mattioli (2006), taking into account the human perception of landscape and the visual decay distance as described in previous literature (Brughmans and Brandes 2017; Gillings 2015; Llobera *et al.* 2004; Mattioli 2006; Wheatley 1995). This work compliments previous studies of Cattari (2006; Cattari *et al.* 2011) and others (Cadeddu 2012; de Montis and Caschili 2012) who have linked the distribution of *nuraghi* with the control of territory and movement (for a similar scenario in a different context, see Minkevičius, this volume).

Due to the density of *Nuragic* monuments on Sardinia, there was no need to interpolate further observation positions. Thus, the overall analysis concentrated on the intervisibility between observer points and target points (respectively monuments). The *nuraghi*, with their two- to three-story heights, were conservatively estimated to rise to about 15 m above the ground. This height was therefore taken as the value for these monuments since if one wanted to control an area or be a part of a signaling system, they would presumably access the most suitable position for that task, that is, the highest observation point possible (Ruiz-Gálvez Priego 2005). As already pointed out by de Montis and Caschili (2012), the *nuraghi*, in particular, fulfill, and even enhance, the criteria supporting observation points.

None of the sanctuary types rises as high as the *nuraghi*, although several of them (e.g., Santa Vittoria) were erected close to previously abandoned *nuraghi*. Nevertheless, the actual sanctuary buildings were estimated to be 5 m above ground level, and the *tombe dei giganti* to approximately 3 m. In addition, the search radius was chosen conservatively, keeping in mind that even target objects of a height of 6 m (e.g., tree crowns) are only discernible at a middle-distance range of no more than 3120 m. Greater distances are described as far distances not suitable to maintain territorial control but only to broadly observe the horizon (Mattioli 2006). Since the monumental *nuraghi* were larger than average tree crowns, the radius sometimes was extended to 5000 m.

Spatial Organization and Religious Monuments

Research on the spatial relationship between the Nuragic *tombe dei giganti* and settlements revealed basic patterns in their positioning, orientation, and clustering, and suggested that they were deliberately constructed in excess of the requirements of pure functionality or environmental necessity (Blake 2001). Analyzing a strategic location of *tombe dei giganti*, Blake concluded that Nuragic groups or societies might have conceived of space as an artifact, to be shaped by the arrangement of monuments and objects in it, thus leading to the unique composition of the Nuragic sites. Based on her studies, the intervisibility of *tombe dei giganti* and *nuraghi* was tested. Blake revisited the interrelation between *tombe dei giganti* and *nuraghi* with spatial statistics. De Montis and Caschili (2012) applied viewshed analysis when researching the intervisibility of *nuraghi*. They hypothesized the existence of a communication network through visibility paths between the *nuraghi*, implying that they were organized and erected to suit the purpose of passing information by visual signaling. Those networks were built to maintain and shape community organization and the identity of clustered settlements. Visibility patterns thus are considered an approach to understanding one aspect of the social networks that defined and connected communities in the past.

The Island-Wide Perspective

As elaborated earlier, community structures seem to have been reorganized during the FBA and EIA, and therefore, it seemed fruitful to check whether these highly organized building patterns were sustained and how they changed with respect to the newly built sanctuaries and the nucleated Nuragic villages (i.e., Class 3 Nuragic development) for the later phases.

Considering the relation of the *tombe dei giganti* and *nuraghi* as a first step, statistically, 8.8 *nuraghi* would 'serve' one *tomba*, but this ratio does not consider the chronological or chorological aspect of both monument groups. The cumulated viewshed of the macroregion shows relatively high overall visibility for most of the *tombe* within a 4000-m radius. Of the 17,114 possible matches within the perimeters of the *tombe* 8073 (47%) are true matches, the other 9040 are false ones. Only 17 (2.7%) of the 623 *tombe* do not have intervisibility with any *nuraghe*.

The intervisibility of *megaron* temples and *nuraghi* shows a similar overall proportion of 112 (42%) true matches out of 265. Intervisibility between *megaron* temples and *nuraghi* is inconsistent throughout the macroregion. This is exemplified by the temple of Serra de Porchileddos (Chiaramonti) and the sacred area with a temple adjacent to the *nuraghe* of Oes in Giave. While Serra de Porchileddos would have 47 *nuraghi* within a radius of 4 km, true reciprocal visibility is given with only seven of them due to the hilly terrain. Within the same radius, the *megaron* temple at Oes would be surrounded by 92 *nuraghi*, 38 of which are in direct line of sight. The majority of the temples, like those facing the coast (e.g., Appiu, Villanova Monteleone, Malchittu, Arzachena) or in the high mountains (e.g., Sos Nurattolos, Alà dei Sardi, Is Clamoris, Perdasdeoggiu) do not seem to follow any dictate of a priori visibility at all, and only draw lines of sight with very few or no settlement in their surroundings. Thus, reciprocal visibility with *nuraghi* does not seem to supply a major

criterion for the location of *megaron* temples but rather their remoteness and invisibility. There is evidence for some of them that the intervisibility with *tombe dei giganti* might have been more distinct (e.g., S'Arcu'e is Forros, Talana, Sa Carcaredda, Villagrande Strisaili). This might not be surprising at all since, as far as it is known today, several of the *tombe* were still in use and others would be valued as ancestral monuments.

Examining the island-wide investigation of water-temples, there is an obvious diversity of visibility/invisibility options (Figure 8.2). Looking at the raw data, the relation of known temples to *nuraghi* is 1:60. Nevertheless, the spatial distribution of the *nuraghi* obscures such reasoning, as does the chronological depth of the data that cannot be fully investigated for the mass of *nuraghi*. From 45 *nuraghi* in a 4000-m perimeter around the *fonte* of Puntanarcu in S'Adde, Sedilo, only one is within direct intervisibility. The *pozzo* of Calegastea positioned on the Abbasante basalt plateau about 3 km west of the Class 3 *nuraghe* Losa is surrounded by 43 *nuraghi*, with 30 intervisibility matches (69.8%) with the sanctuary within the perimeter. Additional matches can be observed for the well of Camboni in Perdaxius with 27 true matches (of 37; 72.9%) of reciprocal visibility. The well of Predio Canopoli in Perfugas in the northwestern part of the isle follows with 42 true matches of 58 *nuraghi* (72.4%). On the other hand, the supralocal well of Monte S. Antonio in Siligo, positioned at a height of 610 m above sea level, would have 27 surrounding *nuraghi*, with only two of them (7.4%) in direct sight in the hilly karst landscape of the Longudoro. *Pozzo Su Trambuccone* in Olbia, in the northeastern section of the island, is surrounded by 17 *nuraghi*, only one of which does not have a line of sight (93.1%), but *pozzo* Sa Testa in Olbia, only 10 km to the northeast at the gulf of Olbia, has intervisibility with just one *nuraghe* (Fumosa Olbia) out of five potential ones. Among the false matches is Class 2 *nuraghe* Belveghile, 4 km to the southeast. The overall intervisibility between water-temples and *nuraghi* is 43.5% of true matches, 566 out of 1299 possible matches within a 4000-m radius (see Figure 8.2). Thus, intervisibility does not seem to have been a mandatory criterion for the erection of sanctuaries in specific locations.

There are only seven cases where water-temples were constructed in the perimeter of Class 2 and 3 *nuraghi*, and only four of these would have been intervisible (i.e., true matches) (Table 8.5). This result suggests that settlement centrality and sanctuary centrality would not necessarily coincide.

The water-temples also do not exhibit particular affinity to the *tombe dei gigantic* because only 34% of 112 possible matches are true. This result would support the idea that the new water-temples were not meant

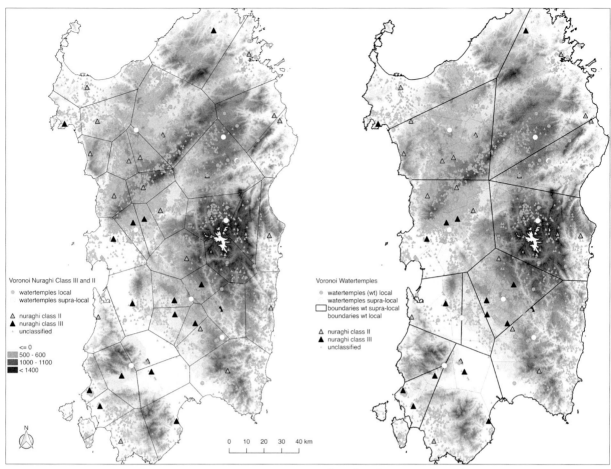

Figure 8.2. Voronoi-partitioning into regions based on distance to points between
Class 3 and Class 2 *nuraghi* and surrounding *nuraghi* (figure by the author).

Table 8.5. Intervisibility
matches *nuraghi* Class 3 and
Class 2 with water-temples.
Search radius: 4000 m.

Source: Nuraghe	Target: Water-temple	Visibility
Losa, Abbasante	Calegastea, Abbasante	True
Arrubiu, Orroli	Su Puzzu, Orroli	True
Nurdole, Nuoro	Nurdole, Orani	True
Seruci, Gonnesa	Is Arenas a Nuraxi Figus, Gonnesa	True
Funtana, Ittireddu	Funtana 'e Baule, Ittireddu	False
Su Sonadori, Villasor	Funtana Corbetta, Ballao	False
Belveghile, Belveghile	Sa Testa, Olbia	False

to express traditional beliefs in just a new facet of ancestral worship but were inventions of a completely new religious tradition. The water-temples were bound to the presence of water in the form of local wells, proximate wells, or rivers that could be channeled and bypassed according to requirements. This primary coercive constraint was more important than cultural stipulation for their construction. Other natural confinements, such as suitable space size or building material, did not seem to have played an important role since material sometimes was acquired from distant places and some of the water-temples were constructed in remote and inaccessible places.

The availability of a vast database with Nuragic monuments also encourages the assessment of territorial boundaries. A particular interest was set in the *nuraghi* of Class 3 and Class 2 and the sanctuaries of local and supralocal character. Since the information content of the data has its constraints, the classification of *nuraghi* types, as well as of the sanctuaries, has been practiced mostly on a limited sample and the majority, especially for the *nuraghi*, was not sufficiently studied to provide a comprehensive view. For this reason, analysis has been carried out using simplified Voronoi diagrams (Figure 8.3), being aware that these do not take into account cultural or landscape characteristics.

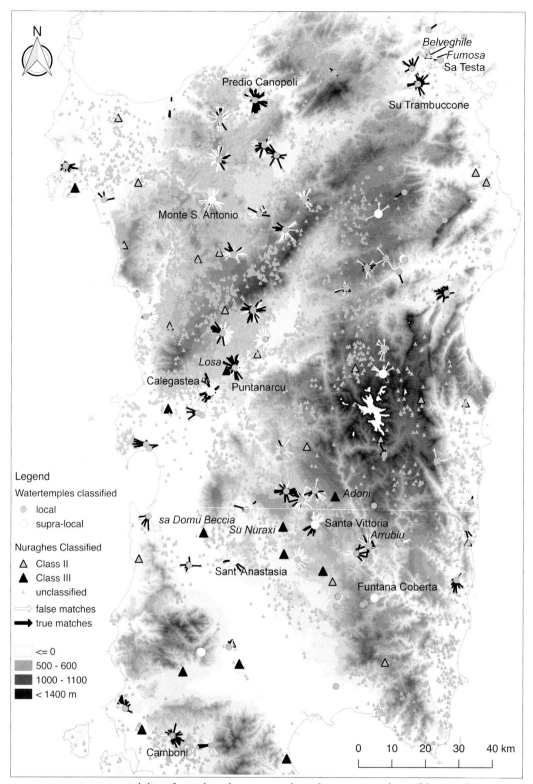

Figure 8.3. Intervisibility of *nuraghi* and water-temples. White arrows indicate false matches, black arrows indicate true matches (figure by the author).

The calculated ideal boundaries for the Class 3 and Class 2 *nuraghi* show a quite regular distribution pattern, with larger areas in the north and the south, and the smaller but denser inhabited allotments in the central regions. The distribution of supralocal sanctuaries appears to exhibit several quite reasonable territorial patterns, though the calculated boundaries are entirely artificial. The supposed 'cantonal' segmentation cannot be verified within the *nuraghi* pattern for all areas, but most of it would not contradict the coarser sanctuaries' distribution, a pattern that might benefit from further, more detailed regional analyses. The mappings suggest a 'cantonal' division of the Nuragic regions, opposed to 'federally' maintained supralocal sanctuaries for the FBA and EIA. In a more detailed analysis, both diagrams could be merged into a territorial model of the supralocal sanctuary, Class 3 Nuragic village, several Class 2 and Class 1 *nuraghi*, as well as a sufficient number of local sanctuaries and burial places. Below, these parameters will be more closely addressed.

Mesoregion: Marmilla/Sarcidano/Trextena

Turning toward the mesoregion, the simple ratio between the *tombe dei giganti* and *nuraghi* is 13:7, slightly higher than the overall ratio (see above). The line of sight toward the *nuraghi* in a radius of 4000 m is similar to the overall observation for this relation, and 47% of the *nuraghi* in the test area would be within the visual field of a *tombe*. The only *megaron* temple close to the selected area is Domu de Orxia in Esterzili, in the high mountains east of the Flumendosa River (Figure 8.4). Though it is surrounded by several monuments, there is no visibility match toward any of them.

Water-temple distribution in the mesoregion is relatively dense: on average, 39.7 *nuraghi* would be matched to one temple, in comparison to the island ratio of 60:1. Distances of the surrounding five Class 3 *nuraghi* toward Santa Vittoria are quite similar,

generally ranging from 9300 m (Su Nuraxi) to 12,300 m (Adoni), with one outlier in the southeast being Arriubiu at 17,000 m (Figure 8.4; Ialongo 2011: Vol. II:479). The western part of the mesoregion might already align to the next nucleus of supralocal sanctuary of Sant'Anastasia in Sardara and Class 3 *nuraghe* of Sa Domu Beccia in Uras. The examples of Sant'Anastasia and Santa Vittoria show that centrality might not always have had a predominant role. If Santa Vittoria was central to the five *nuraghi* mentioned above, in the same scheme, Sant'Anastasia would be regarded as peripheral either to the 'federation' of the five or to a new set of Nuragic centers, such as Sa Domu Beccia. This might indicate a differing pattern and needs further investigation. Moreover, while Santa Vittoria does indeed have high visibility toward the southern perimeter, Sant'Anastasia is definitely out of sight for nearly all of the surrounding *nuraghi* as well as the water-temple at Gutturu Caddi in Villanovafranco (Figure 8.5, upper). In both cases, intervisibility with *nuraghi* does not seem to have been important. The cumulative viewshed indicates that despite a relatively open landscape, the supralocal monuments (*nuraghi* and temples) would not particularly use those areas (i.e., Su Mulinu, Arrubiu, also several of the local sanctuaries and Sant'Anastasia). The intervisibility

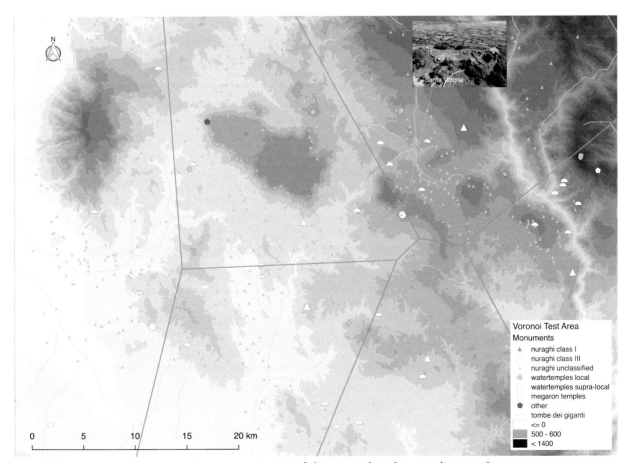

Figure 8.4. Voronoi-partitioning of Class 3 *nuraghi* and surrounding *nuraghi* in the test area (figure by the author).

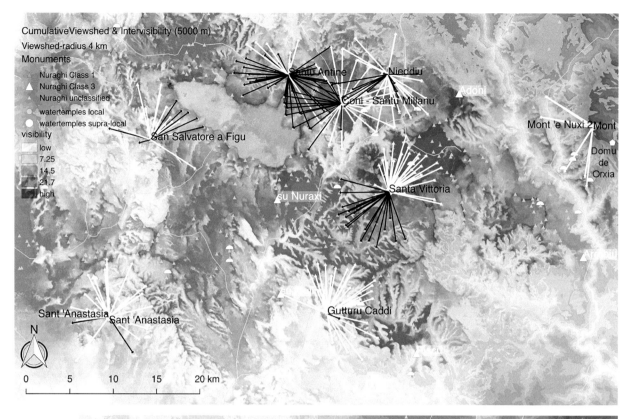

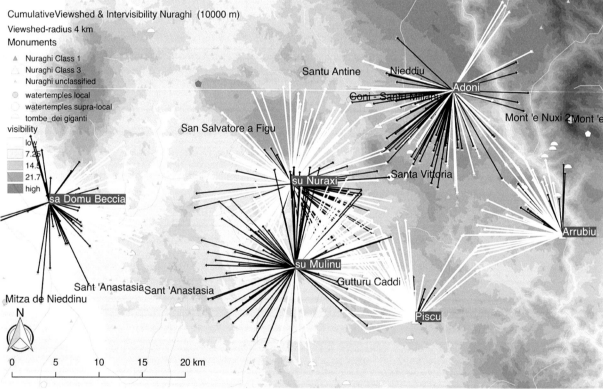

Figure 8.5. Cumulative viewshed and intervisibility of water-temples and *nuraghi* (5000 m in radius, upper) and Class 3 *nuraghi* and surrounding *nuraghi* (10,000 m in radius, lower). White arrows indicate false matches, black arrows indicate true matches (figure by the author).

map of the *nuraghi* and water-temples shows only one match (a false match) between the *nuraghe* Su Mulinu and the sanctuary Gutturu Caddi.

Figure 8.5 shows the intervisibility between the 'central' Class 3 *nuraghi* and other *nuraghi*. Since both headpoints of the matches are *nuraghi* and are supposed to have high visibility within the region, the intervisibility distance was put up to 10,000 m to test if true matches would change significantly by using a wider range. The underlying idea was that by using signaling mechanisms, such as fire or smoke signals, the visibility would increase independently from a real intervisibility between the actual monuments. The matching of the *nuraghi* (Figure 8.5, lower) shows that although a large number of *nuraghi* would be positioned in the perimeter of Class 3 *nuraghi*, they would not necessarily be more visible, but of 589 possible matches, counted for the entire test area, only 249 are unobstructed. The hilly and partly mountainous terrain of the test area would certainly account for a lack of intervisibility, as has been stated in previous literature (Brughmans and Brandes 2017: 11). On the other hand, we can observe that even in the 'lowland' area of the Class 3 *nuraghi*, like Sa Domu Beccia on the Campidano Plain, intervisibility does not increase. Moreover, hills might provide particular observer points that enable control over an area, as can be noticed in the case of the water-temple of Santa Vittoria on the western slope of the Giada Plain, overseeing its hinterland to the southwest. For a scenario of 'signaling,' however, parameters of intervisibility need to be further tuned. Along with the possibility of long-distance communication, network strategies would have to be considered to check on second-order visibility within communication chains because chains of communication utilizing different *nuraghi* as a mediator would be impossible using communication techniques available to the Nuragic culture. As was previously mentioned, a particular function of the *nuraghi* is understood to have been beacons of local power within the network structure they provided. Therefore, even if a direct intervisibility from a sanctuary toward the surrounding *nuraghi* was not always given, it might still have been more possible to communicate within a larger region than the simple intervisibility might suggest.

Social Implications of Catchment and (In)Visibilities of the Sanctuaries

Intervisibility is a basic means of social connectivity and, at least as refers to the built environment and monuments, shared commemoration. The act of seeing, in this case seeing the monuments, is intimately related to shared histories and social cohesion in communities. The density of monuments on Sardinia suggests that there might have been a common (communal) decision on the parameters for the spatial units where the effort of construction was undertaken. Hence, there might also be a chance to develop ideas on the initial *why* of this study. Ideas on the mechanisms of social landscaping through monumental placement in Nuragic Sardinia have been previously expressed by Blake (1999, 2001, 2002), de Montis and Caschili (2012), and Webster (2015).

There appears to be no unique mechanism for the intervisibility with sanctuaries applicable to the entire island, but that there are regional and local stipulations that might have been demanding visibility or invisibility. The parameters of this aspect of Nuragic space syntax are still poorly understood. Yet we can see that they followed different regulations than the previous *nuraghi–tombe dei giganti* dialectic. It is possible to hypothesize group entities and their sets of requirements and options within a spatial pattern. The sanctuaries appear to have been markers that delineated centers in some cases but also boundaries and peripheries in others. The example of Santa Vittoria suggests a ritual center for the surrounding 'cantonal' territories, with those territories developing around nucleated supralocal *nuraghe*/village centers and incorporating smaller *nuraghi*, smaller (local?) sanctuaries, and burials. On the other hand, the data shows Santa Vittoria's topographic openness toward the southwestern landscape and compartmentalization toward the northeast. Moreover, it appears to have been positioned in the boundary area between the influential supralocal Class 3 nucleated settlements of Su Nuraxi, Su Mulinu, Adoni, Piscu, and Arrubiu. The proximity to five large settlement aggregations represents its status. More visually secluded are the sanctuaries of Sant'Anastasia and Gutturu Caddi. The restriction of water-temples to wells/water would have placed them in remote locations, but the centrality or remoteness would not influence their advancement to supralocal level, as can be seen in the case of Sant'Anastasia.

Not only would the monuments themselves (that is, their common construction and the religious and profane rituals executed under their custody) create communal cohesion but also their perpetual presence, verified through visibility, could be utilized for the empowerment of groups and individuals as means of control as well as cohesion. Thus, sightlines and intervisibility, and their effects, can be ambiguous according to social places and subjects. Recognition and control can be understood as two opposing outcomes of visibility (Brighenti 2007; Mubi Brighenti 2010)—the particularity of social visibility of individuals or group visibility through monuments.

Nevertheless, this study would also encourage the idea that empowerment and/or cohesion cannot be accredited unilaterally to either visibility (i.e., traditions of recognition) or invisibility (e.g., similar to that assumed by the *arcana imperii* tradition where certain power is established behind closed doors and in the seclusion of a restricted group). Thus, we might find one of the possible solutions for the invisibility of certain sites, such as Sant'Anastasia or Monte S. Antonio, in deliberate secrecy of a (religious or ruling?) group. This again creates cohesion for the group privileged to share this secrecy.

This study employed parameters such as monument types, scale, estimated height, and waterways to draw conclusions about social behavior. In order to sufficiently investigate and understand the social implementations of monuments for communities, more parameters need to be identified, recorded, and analyzed. Though the archaeological data is coarse and requires refinement to resolve Ialongo's (2011: Vol. II: 477) desiderate for an appropriate encounter of the 'palimpsestic' character of the Nuragic landscape, it demonstrates the potential of zooming in and out from large-scale comparison to local-scale analyses of intervisibility. Thus, the statistical assessment of the rich evidence supports the interpretation of settlement patterns and the structuring of landscape through monumental architecture.

Conclusions

Visibility is a social dimension and often an important factor in the location of sacral architecture within the landscape. Social and economic parameters, such as centrality or proximity to boundaries or surrounding monuments, have been taken into account in this study.

The effort made, as displayed in the monumental architecture of the sanctuaries, is commonly seen not only as a ritual requirement but also as a means for solidifying political hegemony or promoting social cohesion within and/or between communities and therefore served an integrative function. The older nuraghe-towers might have been territorial markers and expressed kinship-based corporate group control over the key resource of grazing land, when cattle herding was the main focus of pastoral tribes. At that time, these towers could have been the centers of scattered, small communities.

Over time, their meaning shifted: most of them were abandoned while others formed the nuclei of larger settlements with more complex divisions. The nucleation of these settlements might have served both to meet new economic necessities and to build a defensive space, with both aspects welding the community together. The interaction of sanctuary and settlement communities on different aggregation-levels probably represents the new complexity of Nuragic societal ideals. Traditional resources (i.e., cattle, agriculture) were now complemented by others, such as the exploitation of copper, silver, and other commodities, all of which required centralized marketplaces.

New contacts on the cusp to colonization brought not just economic but also religious impulses. We can observe that religious inventions were not simply copied but adapted and transformed, as suited to the local situation. Similar adaptations were observed in early colonial contexts in Mediterranean France (Dietler 2010: 227–232).

Visibility analysis highlights the importance of maintaining the strategic influence on landscapes and natural routes by positioning several of the nuraghi and sanctuaries in highly visible locations. The case study of Santa Vittoria suggests that the distinctive location of the monument was based on a need to control territory and routes through visibility. This was particularly important, as many scholars believe that elites created and maintained positions of social dominance by controlling the population and the supply of prestige goods and metal (Kristiansen 1999; Kristiansen and Larsson 2005). The need to control these territories and access to them, as well as to be seen from afar, may have been a significant factor in choosing these locations. Understanding intervisibility as social action, Nuragic sanctuaries served as markers of communal rather than individual expression, and might have contributed to a complex but not necessarily hierarchical society (Araque Gonzales 2014). The factors presented here contribute to the idea of communities sharing a sense of identity with reference to and commemoration of local monuments, as well as to a larger collective through the knowledge of similar monuments on the island. It is more difficult, however, to substantiate assumptions of a site's prominence and strategic positioning when the intervisibility is not explicit or even missing. Studying the intervisibility of Nuragic monuments covers a limited view to their societal significance. Further analyses should explore the natural and social parameters of these sites as well as search for answers to questions such as how earlier societies used the construction of sanctuaries as a means of controlling competition, trade, and exchange in FBA and EIA Sardinia. Moreover, the data needs to be enriched with qualitative contextualizing information, such as chronology and chorology, to be retrieved in analysis. Additionally, more pragmatic concerns, such as general accessibility, ceremonial appropriation (e.g., pilgrimage), or its opposite, such as the remoteness of hermitages, could have played a role regarding the utilization of places of different character.

The highly conservative treatment of long-distant visibility should probably be reassessed. The large nuraghi monument, already highly visible, is an excellent platform for observation. Enhancements to visibility, such as removal of vegetation or use of signaling, have to be taken into account. These constructed landmarks, along with other natural features, such as rivers and mountains, would have been essential for long-distance travel and augmentation by communities may have signaled their ability to trade or manufacture high-status goods in the hope of attracting traders. Thus, sanctuaries might have functioned as symbolic points of reference for travelers and acted as locales for embarkation and destination.

References Cited

Alaska Satellite Facility 2017. Vertex: ASF's Data Portal. Electronic document: https://vertex.daac.asf.alaska.edu/, accessed August 1, 2021.

Araque Gonzales, R. 2014. Social Organization in Nuragic Sardinia. Cultural Progress Without 'Elites'? *Cambridge Archaeological Journal* 24(1): 141–161.

Blake, E. 1999. Identity-Mapping in the Sardinian Bronze Age. *European Journal of Archaeology* 2(1): 35–55.

Blake, E. 2001. Constructing a Nuragic Locale: The Spatial Relationship between Tombs and Towers in Bronze Age Sardinia. *American Journal of Archaeology* 105(2): 145–161.

Blake, E. 2002. Situating Sardinia's Giant's Tombs in Their Spatial, Social and Temporal Context. *Archaeological Papers of the American Anthropological Society* 11: 119–127.

Brighenti, A. 2007. Visibility: A Category for the Social Sciences. *Current Sociology* 55(3): 323–342.

Brughmans, T. and U. Brandes 2017. Visibility Network Patterns and Methods for Studying Visual Relational Phenomena in Archeology. *Frontiers in Digital Humanities* 4: 17, doi:10.3389/fdigh.2017.00017

Brughmans, T., M.S. De Waal, C.L. Hofman and U. Brandes 2017. Exploring Transformations in Caribbean Indigenous Social Networks through Visibility Studies: The Case of Late Pre-Colonial Landscapes in East-Guadeloupe (French West Indies). *Journal of Archaeological Method and Theory* 25: 475–519.

Cadeddu, F. 2012. Aspetti della religiosità Nuragica tra archeologia, lettera ed etnografia. *ArcheoArte 1 Supplemento* 12: 47–65.

Carmignani, L., G. Oggiano, A. Funedda, P. Conti and S. Pasci 2015. The Geological Map of Sardinia (Italy) at 1:250,000 Scale. *Journal of Maps* 12(5): 826–835.

Cattari, G. 2006. La Regione Del Marghine-Planargia in Sardegna: Modello Digitale Del Terreno, Studio Di Visibilita' E Analisi Spaziale Delle Evidenze Archeologiche Attraverso Software GIS. Unpublished Masters thesis, Università di Pisa.

Cattari, G., C. Tozzi and M. Bisson 2011. The region of Marghine-Planargia in Sardinia (Italy): Digital terrain modelling and spatial analysis in archaeology using GIS software. Hidden landscapes from the Late Neolithic to the Early Iron Age, in M. van Leusen, G. Pizziolo and L. Sarti (eds) *Hidden Landscapes of Mediterranean Europe Cultural and Methodological Biases* (BAR International Series 2320): 271–273. Oxford: Archaeopress.

Chapman, R. 1981. The emergence of formal disposal areas and the 'problem' of megalithic tombs in prehistoric Europe, in R. Chapman, I. Kinnes and K. Randsborg (eds) *The Archaeology of Death*: 71-82. Cambridge: Cambridge University Press.

Contu, E. 1997. *La Sardegna preistorica e nuragica*. Sassari: Chiarella.

de Montis, A. and S. Caschili 2012. Nuraghes and Landscape Planning: Coupling Viewshed with Complex Network Analysis. *Landscape and Urban Planning* 105(3): 315–324.

Depalmas, A. 2001. I Monumenti Megalitici Nello Spazio Delle Comunita Dei Metalli in Sardegna, in G. Serreli and D. Vacca (eds) *Aspetti del megalitismo preistorico*: 99–106. Dolianovo: Grafiche del Parteolla.

Depalmas, A. 2006. Guerra E Pace Nell'interpretazione Dell'architettura Nuragica, in *Studi Di Protostoria in Onore Di Renato Peroni*: 567–572. Firenze: All'Insegna del Giglio.

Depalmas, A. 2012. Memories as a Social Force: Transformation, Innovation and Refoundation in Protohistorical Sardinia. Paper presented at the conference entitled 'Gardening Time: Reflections on Memory, Monuments and History in Sardinia and Scotland,' 21st–23rd September, 2012, Magdalene College and the McDonald Institute, Cambridge.

Depalmas, A. and R.T. Melis 2011. The Nuragic People: Their Settlements, Economic Activities and Use of the Land, Sardinia, Italy, in I.P. Martini and W. Chesworth (eds) *Landscapes and Societies. Selected Cases*: 167–186. Dordrecht: Springer.

Dietler, M. 2010. *Archaeologies of Colonialism. Consumption, Entanglement, and Violence in Ancient Mediterranean France*. Berkeley: University of California Press.

Fraser, D. 1983. *Land and Society in Neolithic Orkney* (BAR British Series 117). Oxford: British Archaeological Reports.

Gillings, M. 2015. Mapping Invisibility: GIS Approaches to the Analysis of Hiding and Seclusion. *Journal of Archaeological Science* 62: 1–14.

Ialongo, N. 2011. *Il Santuario Nuragico Di Monte S. Antonio Die Siligo (SS)*. Roma: Sapienzia Università di Roma.

Ialongo, N. 2013. Sanctuaries and the Emergence of Elites in Nuragic Sardinia during the Early Iron Age (ca. 950-720 BC): The Actualization of a 'Ritual Strategy'. *Journal of Mediterranean Archaeology* 26(2): 187–209.

Kristiansen, K. 1999. The Emergence of Warrior Aristocracies, in J. Carman and A. Harding (eds) *Ancient Warfare: Archaeological Perspectives*: 175–190. Stroud: Sutton.

Kristiansen, K. and T.B. Larsson (eds) 2005. *The Rise of Bronze Age Society: Travels, Transmissions and Transformations*. Cambridge: Cambridge University Press.

Lilliu, G. 1988. La Crescita Delle Aristocrazie: L'età Del Ferro, in M. Guidetti (ed.) *Storia Dei Sardi E Della Sardegna I*: 111–127. Milan: Jaca Books.

Lilliu, G. 1999. *La civiltà nuragica*. Sassari: Carlo Delfino.

Llobera, M., D. Wheatley, J. Steele, S. Cox and O. Parchment 2004. Calculating the Inherent Visual Structure of a Landscape ('total Viewshed') Using High-Throughput Computing, in F. Nicolucci and S.

Hermon (eds) *Beyond the Artifact: Digital Interpretation of the Past. Proceedings of CAA2004:* 146–151. Budapest: Archaeolingua.

Lo Schiavo, F., J.D. Muhly, R. Maddin and A. Giumlia-Mair (eds) 2009. *Oxhide Ingots in the Central Mediterranean* (Biblioteca de Antichità Cipriote 8). Rome and Nicosia: Leventis Foundation, Istituto di Studi sulle Civiltà dell'Egeo e del Vicino Oriente del Consiglio Nazionale delle Ricerche.

Mattioli, T. 2006. Landscape Analysis of a Sample of Rock-Art Sites in Central Italy, in A. Posluschny, K. Lambers and I. Herzog (eds) *Modelling Movement and Perception:* 1–6. Bonn: Dr. Rudolf Habelt.

Moravetti, A. 1998. *Ricerche Archeologiche nel Marghine-Planargia. Parte Seconda, La Planargia - analisi e monumenti.* Sassari: Delfino.

Mubi Brighenti, A. 2010. *Visibility in social theory and social research.* Basingstoke (NY): Palgrave Macmillan.

Renfrew, A.C. 1976. Megaliths, territories and populations, in S.J. De Laet (ed.) *Acculturation and Continuity in Atlantic Europe:* 198-220. Bruges: De Tempe.

Ruiz-Gálvez Priego, M. 2005. Nuragic Territory and Ancient Landscape. The Pranemuru Plateau (Sardinia) during the Bronze Age. *Complutum* 10: 19–26.

Stiglitz, A. 2007. Paesaggi della Prima età del Ferro, in S. Angiolillo, M. Giuman and A. Pasolini (eds) *Ricerca e Confronti 2006, Giornate di Studio di Archeologia e Storia dell'Arte:* 267–281. Cagliari: Edizioni AV.

Usai, L. 2006. Osservazioni Sul Popolamento E Sulle Forme Di Organizzazione Comunitaria Nella Sardegna Nuragica, in *Studi Di Protostoria in Onore Di Renato Peroni:* 557–566. Firenze: All'Insegna del Giglio.

van Dommelen, P. 1998. *On Colonial Grounds. A Comparative Study of Colonialism and Rural Settlement in First Millennium BC West Central Sardinia.* Leiden: Leiden University Press.

Watkins, D. 2017. 30-Meter SRTM Elevation Data Downloader. Electronic document: http://dwtkns.com/srtm30m/, accessed August 1, 2021.

Webster, G.S. 1996. *A Prehistory of Sardinia 2300–500 BC.* Sheffield: Sheffield Academic Press.

Webster, G.S. 2015. *The Archaeology of Nuragic Sardinia.* Sheffield: Equinox.

Webster, M. 2014. Watertemples of Sardinia: Identification, Inventory and Interpretation. Masters thesis. University Uppsala Publications, urn:nbn:se:uu:diva-235468, accessed March 13, 2022.

Wheatley, D. 1995. Cumulative Viewshed Analysis: A GIS-Based Method for Investigating Intervisibility, and Its Archaeological Application, in G. Lock and Z. Stančič (eds) *Archaeology and Geographic Information Systems:* 171–186. London: Routledge.

Chapter 9

Settlement Mounds, Identity, and Continuity in the Settlement Organization of Iron Age Jutland

Niels Haue

Abstract

In the northern parts of Jutland, Denmark, some Early Iron Age settlements (500 BC to AD 175) are characterized by thick cultural layers that are interpreted as resulting from long-term settlement continuity combined with the use of turf as a building material. These settlement mounds have a height of up to two meters, and the cultural layers have protected the prehistoric houses from destruction by later agricultural practices. The excavated houses within the mounds are some of the best-preserved structures from this period in northern Europe, enabling their detailed architectural and constructional analyses. This paper will present a case study from northern Jutland to discuss how spatial divisions observed within nucleated settlement mounds could have regulated the socioeconomic patterns and dynamics of prehistoric villages. In particular, the paper focuses on how the 'best addresses' of the village were able to maintain their dominance for several centuries, and how architecture was used to express and manipulate identity within the villages.

Introduction

Early Iron Age societies in Denmark usually are described as egalitarian (Rindel 2001: 87; Webley 2008: 14), an interpretation based mainly on the burial record where wealth, imports, and weapons are absent until the later part of the pre-Roman Iron Age. The first large-scale settlement excavations seemed to confirm an egalitarian structure: most of the early houses were of modest size, and the longhouses showed no significant clustering (Becker 1969, 1971; Rindel 1999). In contrast, clear settlement hierarchy was visible at Hodde (Hvass 1985) and other nucleated villages dating to the late pre-Roman Iron Age (Ethelberg 1995; Mikkelsen 1999), thereby supposedly confirming the then-dominant interpretation of a single, linear development of societies and settlements from small, scattered longhouses to nucleated villages in chiefly social contexts (Hedeager 1990; Jensen 1979). This study presents a comparative analysis of two newly excavated sites—Nørre Hedegård and Nørre Tranders—and two previously excavated sites in northern Jutland. The results indicate a more complex interplay between organizational principles over the *longue durée* (see also Ejstrud and Jensen 2000; Holst 2010).

The excavated contexts of Iron Age houses in Denmark can be divided into two groups. The first is characterized by the presence of substantial numbers of postholes and house plans revealed by large-scale excavations, while the second includes settlement mounds with preserved cultural layers, floors, and pavements. The well-preserved houses mainly are located in the Limfjord area of northern Jutland (Figure 9.1). These differences between the two groups can be explained by two factors: long-lived settlement continuity and the use of turf as building material, which together generated artificial settlement mounds. While the rest of Jutland is characterized by 'wandering villages,' the northern settlements show a remarkable continuity, often spanning more than 500 years. At these sites, the individual farm is placed on or very close to the same location as its predecessors, thereby forming an artificial rise in the landscape that is visible to the trained eye. These hills usually are labeled as settlement mounds, and parallels are drawn to the *terps* in the Frisian region or to the *tells* in Southeast Europe and the Middle East. In northern Jutland, the vertical growth of settlement mounds commonly is explained by the use of turf as a building material, due to the lack of timber in the deforested and highly populated areas of the Limfjord.

Excavations of settlement mounds not only offer detailed insights into the architecture of houses but also allow us to analyze long-term developments within settlements and to raise questions of how differences in construction can be indicators of sociopolitical and ideological trends. The main issues addressed in this paper include how changes in social relations are reflected in the development of the built environment, and how the built environment was used to express or manipulate identity.

The Iron Age Longhouses in Denmark

Iron Age houses in Denmark are three-aisled, timber-built longhouses oriented roughly east–west. They represent a long-lived tradition that began in the Early Bronze Age and lasted, with minor variations, until the end of the Viking Age. In the Early Iron Age (500 BC to AD 175), these structures were typically 5 m wide and 12–20 m long, with the western section containing the dwelling room and the eastern part the animal stall. The houses had one fireplace and two opposing entrances placed in the middle of the structures, one facing north and the other south. The southern entrance was the main entrance, with the largest and finest stone pavement, while the northern entrance could be classified as the back entrance. These characteristics apply to most of the houses from the Early Iron Age (e.g., Webley 2008). On rare occasions, however, the alignment and the interior design were fundamentally different. This paper will address whether these differences should be explained by functional or economic patterns, or rather as a deliberate discriminator in a sociocultural and ideological context. Some of the largest longhouses could be interpreted as chieftain's farms, but the common interpretation is that each longhouse should be considered as a separate and self-sufficient household.

In many ways, the earliest phase of the pre-Roman Iron Age can be described as a prolonged ending of the Nordic Bronze Age, although the few metal objects are made of iron. The houses, settlements, and grave customs derive from the Bronze Age. In the 3rd century BC, a shift can be seen in the material culture, and ceramics, as well as metal objects, show resemblances to the so-called Jastorf culture and other North European cultures of the pre-Roman Iron Age. This development gained further momentum during the last century BC, when metal objects and other influences from the Celtic world emerged (Martens 2010).

One of the characteristic features of northern Jutland is the Limfjord, which separates the Jutland Peninsula from the area of Thy and Vendsyssel to the north. In the Stone Age, the area consisted of many small islands surrounded by water, but it has radically been transformed by a post-glacial isostatic rebound, which is still ongoing. In the Iron Age, most of the islands were connected by wetlands, while the Limfjord formed a saltwater passage between the North Sea to the west and Kattegat to the east (see Figure 9.1; Kristiansen *et*

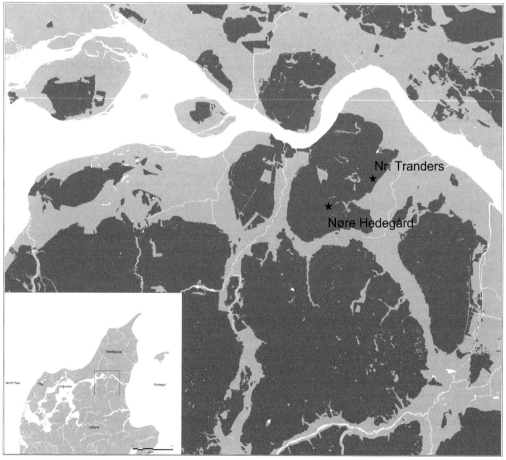

Figure 9.1. Jutland and the Limfjord region, with emphasis on the former hills around present-day Aalborg. Wetlands are marked light gray and arable land is marked dark gray. The division is based on cadastral maps from the late 18th and early 19th century. Note that the Nørre Hedegård and Nørre Tranders settlements are situated on a former island, Tranders, and the island had been surrounded by fertile meadows since the Neolithic (figure by the author).

al. 2020). In prehistoric times, the Limfjord functioned as a communication and trade route from the North Sea to East Scandinavia, allowing people to avoid the dangerous sea route north of Jutland. The two sites presented here are located in the eastern part of the Limfjord area, close to the modern town of Aalborg.

Settlement Mounds in the Eastern Limfjord Area

During the last twenty years, the Historical Museum of Northern Jutland has conducted several settlement excavations on the former island of Tranders that today is surrounded by wetlands. Most of these settlements can be dated to the Early Iron Age, which in Denmark corresponds to the pre-Roman Iron Age (500 to 1 BC) and early Roman Period (AD 1 to approximately AD 175). A majority of the sites have partially been excavated prior to construction works, and more than 400 longhouses have been recovered during these projects.

The temporary Iron Age villages were located close to each other, at a distance of less than 1 km. This shows a densely populated landscape during the Early Iron Age that exceeded even the seventeenth-century rural communities in the area. The Iron Age villages at Nørre Hedegård and Nørre Tranders were both occupied already at the end of the Bronze Age, thereby being among the oldest excavated settlements in southern Scandinavia.

Nørre Hedegård

Nørre Hedegård was excavated in 1998 prior to the construction of a sports arena, in the southeastern part of Aalborg. Approximately 0.8 ha of the 1.2 ha settlement was exposed, revealing a village that had been in use during most of the Early Iron Age. It had repeatedly been subject to sand drift and the excavated houses were extremely well preserved. The village was founded at the end of the Bronze Age and was finally abandoned shortly into the Roman Period, perhaps because of encroachment by the massive sand dunes (Runge 2009).

The excavated 97 houses can be grouped into 10 phases of village development. In the oldest phases, the settlement consisted of around 10 houses, while it incorporated substantially fewer houses in the youngest phases. At the beginning of the Roman Iron Age, the excavated part of the final phase of the village contained only two longhouses. The youngest houses were dug into the village mound. These houses with sunken floors are known exclusively from northern Jutland, and will briefly be touched upon later in this paper. It is difficult to determine whether the village was a planned and founded settlement, or whether it represents a gradual clustering of houses, but the process could barely have taken more than 50 years.

Either way, the village marks a fundamental break in settlement structure compared to the dispersed houses that dominated in the Bronze Age (Runge 2009).

The sand dunes resulted in excellent preservation, and the excavations revealed many details regarding the internal use of the longhouses and the activities of the households. Some architectural details and features that have been destroyed at other Iron Age sites can be studied in detail at Nørre Hedegård. Given the geological conditions in the Aalborg area, chalk, rather than clay, was used as a building material for floors, and in some cases, the walls were daubed with chalk. The use of chalk made stratigraphic observations much easier and resulted in optimal conditions for the preservation of bones.

Analysis of the animal bone assemblage from Nørre Hedegård shows that sheep played an important role in the subsistence economy of the village, with nearly 60% of the identified specimens belonging to sheep/goat (*Caprinae*), while 33% deriving from cattle (*Bos taurus*). Given differences in meat weight, cattle should still be regarded as the most important domesticated animal in this part of Jutland during the Early Iron Age. Only 2% of the bones come from pigs (*Sus scrofa*), which can be explained by the deforestation that occurred in the Limfjord region (Hesel 2009). Flounder (*Pleuronectes flesus*), and to a lesser degree weever (*Trachinus draco*), dominate the fishbone material, suggesting that net fishing was practiced (Enghoff 2009). As in other Iron Age settlements in Denmark, there is no evidence in the faunal assemblage for hunting, so perhaps game was sacred or only selected individuals were permitted to hunt in the society.

Nørre Tranders

Two years after the excavation at Nørre Hedegård, another settlement mound was exposed only 3 km away. The Nørre Tranders settlement mound is located in the eastern part of Aalborg, surrounded by buildings from the 1970s. In 2016 and 2017, these buildings were renovated and small-scale archaeological excavations were carried out, identifying the outline of the Iron Age village. In contrast to Nørre Hedegård, sand drift did not occur at this site. The cultural layer is up to 2 m thick in some places and must be ascribed to accumulated waste through hundreds of years.

The oldest houses at Nørre Tranders date to the transition between the Bronze and Iron Ages, while the youngest phase belongs to the later part of the early Roman Period. The village thereby shows a continuity of 600 years. More than 150 houses were excavated and up to 12 successive phases of settlement development were recorded. The excavated eastern part of the site contained 6–12 contemporary longhouses, and the total number of farms within the village is estimated at 10–15 during the early pre-Roman Iron Age and 18–25 in the late pre-Roman Iron Age and early Roman Period (Haue 2012). Thus, village continuity provides a great opportunity for the study of long-term societal changes.

During the first 400 years at the site, the longhouses typically exhibit some differences in their length and indicate a change in building practices, with the introduction of turf as a building material. Nevertheless, the overall structural organization was retained, with house alignments and interior design remaining more or less the same. As seen in Figure 9.2, the longhouses at Nørre Tranders can be divided into two major groups according to their length: smaller longhouses (less than 14 m) and regular longhouses (more than 14 m). A third and fourth group representing outliers may also be discerned (longer than 20 m and shorter than 10 m, respectively). This division should be considered as a regional phenomenon, and cannot be transferred to other parts of Jutland without modification. The regular longhouses at Nørre Tranders are interpreted as inhabited by leading farmers, or rather farmers who controlled more land and/or livestock than others, while the smaller longhouses had smaller stabling areas, indicating that the economic wealth of these farms was more limited. No clear evidence for an upper elite or chieftain's farm was found at Nørre Tranders. It cannot be ruled out, however, that the chieftain's farm was located in the unexcavated part of the village, but for now, the length of the longhouses indicates a division of the community into two, almost equal-sized groups of farmers: those living in smaller longhouses and those living in regular longhouses.

At the end of the pre-Roman Iron Age, this division in the village became more obvious, and the two groups of longhouses became more standardized. Smaller longhouses contained four sets of roof-bearing posts, while regular longhouses had six sets of posts (e.g., House A288; Figure 9.3). The smaller type makes up 17 excavated houses, while 21 houses belong to the larger type at Nørre Tranders. Some of the smaller longhouses depart from the norm, and thereby show a wide-ranging break in the architectural tradition. Of these, most are characterized by only one entrance, and in some cases, this only remaining entrance was placed to the north, which is regarded typically as the back entrance. The smaller longhouses also had stalls for livestock, but contrary to the spatial organization of regular longhouses, these were often positioned in the western part of the structures, instead of the eastern section. In one case, the alignment of a smaller longhouse is north–south (see House A104; Figure 9.3). Taken together, several architectural practices were used to differentiate the two groups. This raises some significant questions, such as whether these differences can be explained by functional or economic reasons, or if they were intended to differentiate social or ideological status, and whether individual households or the entire community made decisions about the placement and design of longhouses.

These architectural differences might seem insignificant, but they imply a deliberate use of architecture in the alteration of the interior design. The alignment of House A104 is north–south, and the only entrance is facing east. Like the other small longhouses having the stall in the 'incorrect' partition, the stall is placed to the left and not to the right as one enters this house.

Several burned structures were excavated and one of these stands out (Figure 9.4). This house can be dated to the middle of the 1st century BC, and similar to the other longhouses, it was separated into a dwelling room with chalk floor and fireplace in the west and a stabling area in the east. The animals within the structure had been killed by the fire, and their remains were meticulously excavated.

The skeletons of three horses, seven cattle, and four sheep were exposed, and the remains of a suckling pig next to a trial trench indicate that a sow and other suckling pigs were most likely also kept. The sheep were gestated near the lambing date, which indicates that the house burnt down in early spring. The zooarchaeological material therefore provides interesting insights into which animals were kept within Iron Age houses (Kveiborg 2009a; Nielsen 2007). Prior to this study, the most common interpretation of stabling areas was that they provided shelter for the cattle, but this unique find illustrates that a wider

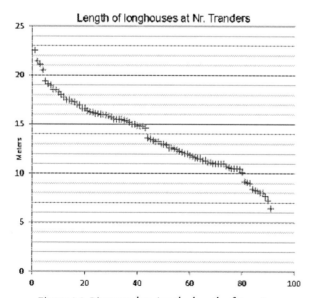

Figure 9.2. Diagram showing the length of Iron Age longhouses at Nørre Tranders. Ninety-one longhouses are included in the diagram, of which length cannot be determined for 45 (figure by the author).

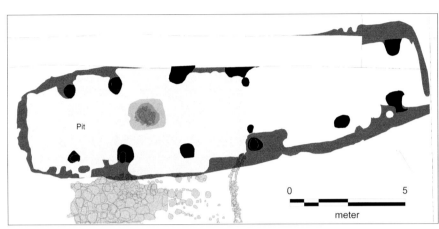
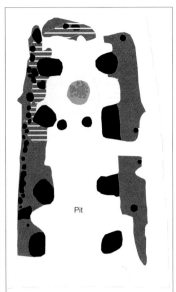

Figure 9.3. Simplified ground plans of two longhouses at Nørre Tranders. To the left is House A288, to the right is House A104. Chalk floor is marked light gray, postholes black, and fireplaces and wall ditch gray (figure by the author).

Figure 9.4. Burned House A371 seen from the east. A test trench separates the chalk floor in the dwelling room in the western part and the byre in the eastern part. The fireplace of the house is positioned in the middle of the dwelling room. The burned livestock lies in the eastern part of the house (photo by the Historical Museum of Northern Jutland).

range of livestock was kept in the houses. Most likely, the vulnerable animals, like the gestated sheep, riding horses, and milking cattle, were kept indoors, while other animals may have lived outside all year round. The variety of livestock in the structure at Nørre Tranders would probably have been different if the fire had started during summer. Among the burned animals, the remains of five people also were uncovered. They probably died while trying to rescue the livestock from the fire (Harvig *et al.* 2015). No byres or stabling boxes were evident at the site, and the longhouses of that time and region probably used a loose housing system, where some of the animals were most likely hitched to a post or stake (Kveiborg 2009b).

The excavation at Nørre Tranders yielded a large number of animal bones within the waste. Analysis of these nearly 5000 pieces of bones shows some similarities with the results from Nørre Hedegård, but also some differences. As at Nørre Hedegård, sheep (43%) and cattle (36%) dominate the assemblage, though the ratio is more comparable. At Nørre Tranders, 12% of the animal bone materials derive from horses, which is a fairly high value compared to other Iron Age settlements (Kveiborg 2008). The significance of cattle and horses at Nørre Tranders can be explained by the topographical placement of the settlement close to fertile meadows (see Figure 9.1). As was the case at Nørre Hedegård, wild game remains were almost absent.

Building Practices

In terms of construction techniques, Iron Age longhouses can be separated into two, chronologically dependent groups. The oldest group has significant parallels to the wattle-and-daub structures found at the large settlement of Grøntoft, western Jutland, excavated in the 1960s (Becker 1971; Rindel 2010), while the youngest group consists of turf houses and a variant of those with sunken floors. The older wattle-and-daub structures must have lasted for no more than 20–35 years, while the turf houses tend to exhibit several repairs and they would have lasted up to 50 or 70 years before being abandoned. At Nørre Hedegård and Nørre Tranders, all these house types were in use, the oldest being the wattle-and-daub ones. At approximately 250 BC, turf houses replaced wattle-and-daub structures in this region, and the sunken-floored turf longhouses occurred somewhat later.

It is possible to estimate the height of longhouse walls based on the walls that collapsed into several structures during fire. They suggest a wall height of approximately 1.25 m. It is furthermore evident that the walls had been plastered with a mixture of chalk, signifying the exploitation of local substrate.

During the pre-Roman Iron Age, turf houses became common in many parts of the Limfjord area; the oldest ones have been recovered in the western part of the region. After use, the turf walls were leveled, thereby contributing to the growth of settlement mounds, although only in rare cases can the turf be recorded during excavations. At the best-preserved sites, turf walls were exposed to a height of 40–70 cm and a width of 1 m (Hatt 1938; Kann Rasmussen 1968), but in most cases, turf structures can no longer be identified.

The introduction of turf longhouses in northern Jutland generally is explained by the lack of usable timber (Kaul 1999: 64). Although the lack of timber, as known from historical times, is a logical explanation in some areas, recent excavations call this interpretation into question for the eastern part of the Limfjord region where an inner wooden wall often accompanies the turf walls. In some cases, the inner wall bears traces of a palisade, consisting of closely placed, vertical wooden posts with a diameter of approximately 20 cm. Thus, these buildings still consumed a lot of timber, perhaps even more than the wattle-and-daub houses. This suggests that an alternative explanation for the use of turf, for instance for climatic, cultural, or architectural reasons, is required for the eastern Limfjord.

Some years ago, students from Copenhagen carried out an interesting experiment at Lejre, Denmark. In a cold February, they lived in a reconstructed Early Iron Age house for two weeks. They concluded that while it was most comfortable to settle near the fireplace, even there they were subjected to draft, and the draft within the wattle-and-daub house was probably more annoying than just being cold (Beck et al. 2007). Wattle-and-daub buildings were still common in historical times in places of Jutland, but during winter, the walls were reinforced with an outer, low turf wall. In the spring, this turf wall was removed to the dunghill, mixed with manure, and used as fertilizer in the agricultural fields (Runge 2009).

Turf houses are part of the North Atlantic building tradition that in historical times, and even up until recent years, still was practiced in several regions, such as Iceland, Greenland, and Scotland. The famous Danish archaeologist J.J.A. Worsaae received a two-year travel scholarship paid by the Danish king and in the years of 1846 and 1847 he visited Britain and the highlands of Scotland. Here, Worsaae described one of the farms in less flattering terms:

> 'The farm consisted of several miserable huts, out of which only the dwelling house was a bit superior to the rest, though still constructed much in the same way using stones and turf with a roof of straw and turf. I was welcomed in the dwelling room, however, where I at first hardly could see a hand in front of me, due to the smoke that only slowly could draw through the smoke hole or lyre in the roof. In the middle of the clay floor, a fireplace was kindled with small twigs and sods that smelled awful. After a while, I could spot some miserable furniture, among them beds made of raw wood. Meanwhile my host was fetched and he gave me a warm welcome and a large glass of whisky, from which I respectfully sipped. It tasted terribly of peaty smoke.' (1934: 152–153, author's translation)

Therefore, even if the use of turf provided some insulation and protection against the wind, the description given by Worsaae might properly reflect the living conditions in Iron Age turf houses.

The insulation of an outer turf wall could also explain the introduction of the sunken-floored longhouses in northern Jutland. These semi-subterranean structures are regular longhouses constructed in a large house pit dug into the subsoil. They have the same shape, dimensions, and spatial divisions as the surface longhouses, with a living area in the western half of the building and a byre in the eastern half. Some of these house pits with sunken-floored structures are almost 1.5 m deep, but most are no more than 1 m. Within the house pit, a timber wall was placed in a trench, and the gap between the wall and the pit was filled with turf, sand, or earth. All sunken-floored longhouses date to the second part of the pre-Roman Iron Age or early Roman Period, and are therefore contemporary with the turf houses. Tacitus (*Germania*, Chapter 16) mentions that some people in Germania were living in dwellings beneath the surface. This could perhaps be a reference to the sunken-floored longhouses in northern Jutland or the cellars in the same region (Lund 1984).

The sunken-floored longhouses are easy to spot on aerial photos. They are most common on sandy and dry hills, but surprisingly they also occur in lowlands where rain- and groundwater must have been a problem. It is possible that these structures were a variant of the regular turf houses, and that people living in areas with easy access to turf constructed their buildings using this material, but it was easier to create house pits in sandy territories. In some cases, more than 100 m³ of sand and gravel were removed, and the pit walls were held in place with wooden walls.

The change from wattle-and-daub to turf houses was almost contemporaneous with other changes in the layout of the longhouse, the curved walls being one of them. Moreover, while the wattle-and-daub structures seldom show signs of repair, the turf houses tend to exhibit several rearrangements of the posts, indicating that the buildings were occupied through generations before being abandoned. While the older structures had stabling boxes, this is not the case in the turf buildings, and house orientation also changed slightly over time. The introduction of turf walls served to insulate and thereby improve living conditions in the pre-Roman Iron Age. These changes could be explained by a shift in the population, but the settlement mounds show continuity that makes explanations based on population replacement or changing ethnicity difficult. Therefore, other possible reasons must be considered. One of those could be a slow decline in timber resources. Another possibility is that the turf houses signify ethnic or regional bonds. There are indications that the northern parts of Jutland remained a local group for a longer period of time (Ringtved 1988), and

even in the Merovingian Period, the houses and other archaeological remains still differed from the rest of the peninsula. Thus, perhaps the use of turf was motivated by regional traditions or adopted by a specific ethnic group in Jutland.

Analysis of the Long-Term Development at Nørre Tranders

The settlement mound at Nørre Tranders offers the opportunity for a detailed analysis of long-term developments within an Iron Age village. In the central parts of the settlement mound, a rigid continuity of farms can be observed. The longhouses were placed in a restricted and structured pattern, and up to 12 phases, the same farm occupied this central area. This fixed settlement structure suggests a direct inheritance system wherein the ownership of or the right to each farm could have been passed on to the next generation.

A strong correlation can be noted between the length of the stabling area and the length of the dwelling room, and therefore, larger houses contained larger stabling areas, however, each house contained only one fireplace. The length of the longhouse is therefore tentatively interpreted as a representation of the wealth of the individual farm and not as a reflection of the size of the household itself.

The locations of the short (less than 14 m) and the regular longhouses (more than 14 m) within Nørre Tranders are seen in Figure 9.5. One particular area of the village stands out, situated in the southwestern portion of the excavated area. In 12 consecutive phases, larger longhouses in this zone represent a regular farm. In contrast, the neighboring areas were dominated by short longhouses. In my opinion, the centrally placed farm should not be interpreted as a chieftain's farm, as it was perhaps not even the largest farm in the village. More likely, it was but one of several leading farms. In either case, this farm seems to have maintained its role throughout the village's history. These observations strengthen the interpretation that house size symbolizes the social status and economic wealth of the farm, rather than representing the size of the household.

Perhaps it was just a matter of having the 'best address in town,' like Tringham suggests in the case of Neolithic tells in southeastern Europe, where the oldest 'addresses' within the villages were most desirable to '*maintain a continuity of place*' (2000: 115). These 'addresses' could perhaps have provided the best access to arable land, meadows, or other resources simply because of the specific history of the individual farms. The history of the farms would thereby determine their future yield and opportunities. The houses at Nørre Tranders indicate a social division at the local scale,

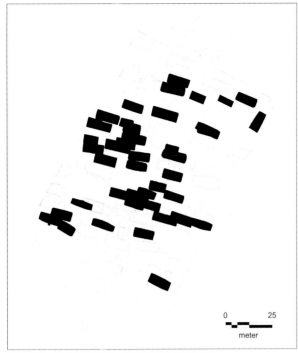

Figure 9.5. The excavated area at Nørre Tranders, with the distribution of the 50 short longhouses (top) and the 41 regular longhouses (below). Forty-five longhouses are marked with a light gray line, indicating that their length could not be measured (figure by the author).

is difficult to establish whether the village was founded throughout a period of 1, 20, or perhaps 50 years. Furthermore, with the formation of a village society, there must have been some rules for the layout of the village as well as access to agricultural areas, livestock, and fresh water. It appears that even though the number of farms at the village doubled over the next 400 years, the settlement organization remained stable.

Settlement Hierarchy in Northern Jutland

Similar observations at other settlements enable a comparative analysis of the relationship between spatial organization and social organization in northern Jutland and permit to address the question of whether the observed variability was intended to set apart certain individual households from their neighbors. In southern Jutland, village formation dates to the late pre-Roman Iron Age. One of the best-known examples is the large, nucleated village of Hodde located in the southwestern part of the peninsula (Hvass 1985). At Hodde, the largest and oldest farm has been interpreted as the founder farm of the village as well as the chieftain's farm. The farm retained this role throughout the life of the village, a period of three to five generations. The layout at Hodde indicates that a fence had surrounded this farm, then this fence was extended to enclose the entire village. The chieftain's farm at Hodde has parallels to Baunehøj, a site located in the northern part of Jutland. The enclosed farm at Baunehøj measures 500 m², exactly the same as the chieftain's farm at Hodde. Despite several similarities, and although this farm was in use for at least two phases, it did not evolve into a village community. The Baunehøj farm thus may represent an unsuccessful attempt to form a village or settlement cluster (Haue 2011).

In a historical context, people in rural Denmark (excluding the landed gentry) were divided into farmers and *husmænd*, which can be translated as smallholders or crofters. In the 18th century, farmers who farmed a croft of fewer than 5 ac were known as *husmænd*, and to survive they worked on regular farms within villages or the larger estates. While two or three horses were common on the farms, the *husmænd* could not afford to feed any horses. The division between the two social groups was fluent and allowed intermarriage. Young people waiting for the right farm could have worked as *husmænd* for some years, and retired farmers could have become *husmænd*. Perhaps a similar division is visible in the late pre-Roman Iron Age, but at Nørre Tranders, it seems that the gap between the two social groups increased during the last century of the village.

An increase is noticeable in the use of a symbolic expression of inequalities between households at Nørre Tranders in the final pre-Roman Iron Age. The

with a low degree of social mobility. The fixed village organization suggests an inheritance system in which each farm was passed on to the next generation, and this system seems to have been planned and intended from the earliest phases of the settlement. In the oldest phases, the village at Nørre Tranders consisted of 10–15 contemporary farms, and it appears that the settlement was founded as a village. No evidence for a founding farm is available, and like Nørre Hedegård, it alignment of the smaller farms was reversed and the length of the houses was standardized into two groups. The inversion of house alignment marked a powerful statement of difference (Webley 2008: 97). Architecture was thereby used as a means to marginalize the poorest farmers at the settlement. This marginalization could be an indication of a new, landless class within the society, representing an institutionalized stratification, where one group of people had unequal access to land. Tacitus describes a similar process in *Germania* (Chapter 25):

> '*The other slaves are not employed after our manner with distinct domestic duties assigned to them, but each one has the management of a house and home of his own. The master requires from the slave a certain quantity of grain, of cattle, and of clothing, as he would from a tenant, and this is the limit of subjection*' (Church and Brodribb 1942)

Whether the inhabitants of the smaller farms at Nørre Tranders should be considered unfree, slaves, landless, or tenants is uncertain.

Other 'inverted' structures from the early Roman Iron Age have been recovered at Hurup, Ginnerup, and Nørre Rødeklit in the western part of the Limfjord area (Webley 2008: 97). All of these longhouses had a modest size, measuring less than 10 m in length, and, like the ones at Nørre Tranders, had only a single entrance. The settlement at Nørre Rødklit was located close to the former coastline and 26 excavated net sinkers indicate that fishing was important (Hatt 1954). Differences in the line of work could perhaps explain the modest size of the longhouse. At Ginnerup, a hoard of 25 Roman coins was buried beneath the floor (Hatt 1935: 47). Even though it was found in 1934, this hoard is still unique in Danish settlement archaeology, and contradicts the interpretation of poor farmers living in smaller longhouses.

The analysis of settlement structure of some Iron Age villages does testify to hierarchy that is seldom visible in the archaeological record outside of burials (Haue 2012: 308–309). At Nørre Hedegård, the village seems to have undergone an opposite development, where the youngest phases of the settlement comprised only a few contemporary farms. The rigid structure at Nørre Tranders is not visible at Nørre Hedegård. Perhaps the smaller number of farms resulted in a different settlement structure, or perhaps the sand dunes played a role in the depopulation at Nørre Hedegård, leading to a final abandonment in the early Roman Period.

During the 2nd century AD, the settlement mound at Nørre Tranders was abandoned after more than 600 years of continuity. It is tempting to correlate this event with a socioeconomic shift, where the dependency of the poorest farmers increased until finally, in the later part of the Iron Age, they were incorporated into larger farms that, during the 3rd century AD, often were comprised of three to eight buildings, instead of one longhouse. In such a development, the poorest farmers eventually became tenants or slaves (Hamerow 2002; Hedeager 1990: 201).

Concluding Remarks

The Early Iron Age society in Denmark is usually described as egalitarian (Rindel 2001: 87; Webley 2008: 14), an interpretation mainly based on the absence of imported materials, weapons, and other obvious signs of wealth in burials until the later part of the pre-Roman Iron Age. Early settlement excavations seemingly confirmed this scenario. The early houses were of relatively modest size and significant clustering of houses was lacking (Becker 1969, 1971; Rindel 1999). A distinct hierarchy within settlements was first visible at the late pre-Roman Iron Age Hodde (Hvass 1985) and other nucleated villages (Ethelberg 1995; Mikkelsen 1999).

The comparative analysis of four examples—Hodde, Baunehøj, Nørre Hedegård, and Nørre Tranders—shows variability in community organization and identity in Early Iron Age Jutland. Each community developed according to local responses to sociopolitical, economic, or environmental stress. A fundamental change in settlement organization can be observed in northern Jutland at the end of the Bronze Age—a shift from dispersed, single-farm settlements to clustered settlements with five to ten longhouses. Each longhouse should still be considered as a household unit, but the shift had a dynamic impact on community organization.

Village formation and development in Jutland followed different courses. At both Hodde and Baunehøj, a large, fenced farm was established during the late pre-Roman Iron Age, but while the farm at Hodde became the focal point for a larger settlement aggregation, the farm at Baunehøj never evolved into a village community. Early villages have been excavated at Nørre Hedegård and Nørre Tranders, both located in the Aalborg area. The village at Nørre Tranders developed into a larger community with more than 18 contemporary farms. A fixed settlement structure from the early pre-Roman Iron Age is visible at this site, showing a remarkable continuity of each farm. The farms that appear to have been the 'best address in town' might have maintained their role for centuries. The continuity of the individual farms at Nørre Tranders represents a community where socioeconomic status could be passed on to future generations. Whether this socioeconomic inheritance was based upon ownership of land or unequal access to village resources is uncertain, but it reflects an institutionalization within the village society, wherein power and wealth were limited to a few farms. It is likely that some of the smaller farms were obligated to supply labor or products to the leading families of the village.

The analysis of the longhouses at Nørre Tranders indicates that the poorest farmers became even poorer over the course of the last phases of the settlement. The short longhouses became smaller and the stalls were placed in the western part of the structures. This could be a sign of limited equalization in the society and the rise of a landless class or a class with limited access to land. It might be that this development gains further momentum at the end of the early Roman Period, where the farms in other areas of Jutland show a significant increase in the numbers and sizes of buildings. This process may have caused the abandonment of Nørre Tranders because the rather small farms did not enable the extensive changes in the spatial organization, leading to a larger household and including a landless class.

Finally, these changes coincided with several changes in the material culture and practices, including the introduction of weapons and Roman imports as grave goods as well as inhumation burials at the beginning of the Roman Iron Age. These shifts occurred at the same time as the Roman influence in northern Europe increased. Changes in the late pre-Roman Iron Age/ early Roman Iron Age led to a shift in settlement structure as well, and from that point, a poor class of inhabitants is recognizable in the settlement record.

References Cited

Beck, A.S., L.M. Christensen, J. Ebsen, R.B. Larsen, D. Larsen, N.A. Møller, T. Rasmussen, L. Sørensen and L. Thofte 2007. Reconstruction and the what? Climatic experiments in reconstructed Iron Age houses during winter, in M. Rasmussen (ed.) *Iron Age houses in flames: testing house reconstructions at Lejre* (Studies in Technology and Culture 3): 134–173. Lejre: Historical-Archaeological Experimental Centre.

Becker, C.J. 1969. Das zweite früheisenzeitliche Dorf bei Grøntoft, Westjütland. *Acta Archaeologica* 39: 235–255.

Becker, C.J. 1971. Früheisenzeitliche Dörfer bei Grøntoft, Westjütland. 3. Vorbericht: Die Ausgrabungen 1967–68. *Acta Archaeologica* 42: 79–110.

Church, A.J. and W.J. Brodribb 1942. *Complete Works of Tacitus*. Electronic document: http://data.perseus.org/citations/urn:cts:latinLit:phi1351.phi002.perseus-eng1:25

Ejstrud, B. and C.K. Jensen 2000. *Vendehøj – landsby og gravplads* (Jysk Arkæologisk Selskabs skrifter 35). Højbjerg: Jysk Arkæologisk Selskab.

Enghoff, I.B. 2009. Fiskeri fra Nr. Hedegård, in M. Runge (ed.) *Nørre Hedegård: En nordjysk byhøj fra ældre jernalder*: 241–246. Højbjerg: Nordjyllands Historiske Museum & Jysk Arkæologisk Selskab.

Ethelberg, P. 1995. The chieftains' farms of the Over Jerstal group. *Journal of Danish Archaeology* 11: 111–135.

Hamerow, H. 2002. *Early Medieval Settlements: The Archaeology of Rural Communities in North-West Europe 400-900*. Oxford: Oxford University Press.

Harvig, L., J. Kveiborg and N. Lynnerup 2015. Death in flames. Human remains from a domestic house fire from early Iron Age, Denmark. *International Journal of Osteoarchaeology* 25(5): 701–710.

Hatt, G. 1935. Jernalderbopladsen ved Ginderup I Thy. *Nationalmuseets Arbejdsmark* 1935: 37–51.

Hatt, G. 1938. Jernalderens bopladser i Himmerland. *Aarbøger for Nordisk Oldkyndighed Og Historie* 1938: 119–266.

Hatt, G. 1954. An early Roman Iron Age dwelling site in Holmsland. *Acta Archaeologica* 24: 1–25.

Haue, N. 2011. Social stratifikation og den 'sociale arv' i ældre jernalder - med udgangspunkt i bopladsstudier fra Nordjylland, in N.A. Møller, S.S. Qvistgaard and S.F. Jensen (eds) *Nyt fra Vestfronten - Nord- og Vestjyske bebyggelser fra ældre jernalder* (Arkæologiske Skrifter 10): 87–98. København: Saxo-instituttet.

Haue, N. 2012. Jernalderens samfund i Nordjylland: Belyst med udgangspunkt i byhøjen Nr. Tranders, Aalborg. Unpublished PhD dissertation, Aarhus Universitet.

Hedeager, L. 1990. *Danmarks jernalder: Mellem stamme og stat*. Aarhus: Aarhus universitetsforlag.

Hesel, A. 2009. Husdyr og vildt fra Nr. Hedegård, in M. Runge (ed.) *Nørre Hedegård: En nordjysk byhøj fra ældre jernalder*: 209–240. Højbjerg: Nordjyllands Historiske Museum & Jysk Arkæologisk Selskab.

Holst, M.K. 2010. Inconstancy and stability: Large and small farmsteads in the village of Nørre Snede (Central Jutland) in the first millennium AD. *Settlement and Coastal Research in the Southern North Sea Region* 33: 155–179.

Hvass, S. 1985. *Hodde: Et vestjysk landsbysamfund fra ældre jernalder*. København: Akademisk Forlag.

Jensen, J. 1979. *Dansk socialhistorie. Oldtidens samfund: tiden indtil år 800*. København: Gyldendal.

Kann Rasmussen, A. 1968. En byhøj i thyland. *Fra Nationalmuseets Arbejdsmark* 1968: 137–144.

Kaul, F. 1999. Vestervig – an Iron Age village mound in thy, NW Jutland, in C. Fabech and J. Ringtved (eds) *Settlement and Landscape*: 53–67. Aarhus: Jutland Archaeological Society.

Kristiansen, S.M., T.E. Ljungberg, T.T. Christiansen, K. Dalsgaard, N. Haue, M.H. Greve and B.H. Nielsen 2020. Meadow, marsh and lagoon: Late Holocene coastal changes and human–environment interactions in northern Denmark. *Boreas* 50: 279–293.

Kveiborg, J. 2008. Fårehyrder, kvægbønder eller svineavlere: En vurdering af jernalderens dyrehold. *Kuml* 2008: 59–100.

Kveiborg, J. 2009a. *Bondens dyr: husdyrhold i ældre jernalder belyst ved fund af indebrændte dyr. Delrapport I.* Nørre Tranders: Moesgård Museum.

Kveiborg, J. 2009b. *Bondens dyr: husdyrhold i ældre jernalder belyst ved fund af indebrændte dyr. Diskussion af staldbrug i ældre jernalder.* Nørre Tranders: Moesgård Museum.

Lund, J. 1984. Nedgravede huse og kældre i ældre jernalder. *Hikuin* 10: 57–82.

Martens, J. 2010. Pre-Roman Iron Age Settlements in Southern Scandinavia, in M. Meyer (ed.) *Haus, Gehöft, Weiler, Dorf: Siedlungen der vorrömischen Eisenzeit im nördlichen Mitteleuropa:* 229–250. Rahden/Westfalen: Marie Leidorf.

Mikkelsen, D.K. 1999. Single farm or village? Reflections on the settlement structure of the Iron Age and the Viking Period, in C. Fabech and J. Ringtved (eds) *Settlement and Landscape:* 177–193. Aarhus: Jutland Archaeological Society.

Nielsen, J.N. 2007. The burnt remains of a house from the Pre-Roman Iron Age at Nørre Tranders, Aalborg, in M. Rasmussen (ed.) *Iron Age houses in flames: testing house reconstructions at Lejre* (Studies in Technology and Culture 3): 16–31. Lejre: Historical-Archaeological Experimental Centre.

Rindel, P.O. 1999. Development of the village community, 500 BC–100 AD in West Jutland, Denmark, in C. Fabech and J. Ringtved (eds) *Settlement and Landscape:* 79–99. Aarhus: Jutland Archaeological Society.

Rindel, P.O. 2001. Building typology as a tool for describing the development of early village communities in the fifth-third century B.C. at Grøntoft, Western Jutland, Denmark, in J.R. Brandt and L. Karlsson (eds) *From Huts to Houses. Transformations of Ancient Societies* (Skrifter utgivna av svenska institutet i Rom, 4°, Vol. 56): 73–87. Stockholm: Paul Astroms Förlag.

Rindel, P.O. 2010. Grøntoft Revisited: New Interpretations of the Iron Age Settlement, in M. Meyer (ed.) *Haus, Gehöft, Weiler, Dorf: Siedlungen der vorrömischen Eisenzeit im nördlichen Mitteleuropa:* 251–262. Rahden/Westfalen: Marie Leidorf.

Ringtved, J. 1988. Jyske gravfund fra yngre romertid og ældre germanertid. Tendenser i samfundsudviklingen. *Kuml* 1986: 95–231.

Runge, M. 2009. *Nørre Hedegård: En nordjysk byhøj fra ældre jernalder.* Højbjerg: Nordjyllands Historiske Museum & Jysk Arkæologisk Selskab.

Tringham, R. 2000. The Continuous House. A View from the Deep Past, in R.A. Joyce and S.D. Gillespie (eds) *Beyond Kinship: Social and Material Reproduction in House Societies:* 115–134. Philadelphia: University of Pennsylvania Press.

Webley, L. 2008. *Iron Age Households: Structure and Practice in Western Denmark, 500 BC – AD 200.* Højbjerg: Jutland Archaeological Society.

Worsaae, J.J.A. 1934. *En Oldgrandskers Erindringer 1821-1847.* København: Gyldendal.

Chapter 10

Multilinear Settlement Development and Nucleation during the Early Iron Age in Southwestern Jutland, Denmark

Niels Algreen Møller and Scott Robert Dollar

Abstract

This paper analyzes variations in settlement dynamics and structure during the Early Iron Age (500 BC to AD 200) in southwestern Jutland, Denmark, focusing on the development of nucleated settlements or villages. The process toward nucleation has traditionally been explained through a unilinear evolutionary model based on a few extensively investigated sites in western and central Jutland, excavated in the 1960s and 1970s. However, the available settlement data for the Early Iron Age has expanded significantly in recent years, owing particularly to development-led excavations, showing that settlement development was far more complex and dynamic than traditionally considered. Using distributional analysis and detailed microregional studies from southern Jutland, this paper demonstrates that settlement development was a multilinear process. Furthermore, the study illustrates how variations in settlement layout during the Early Iron Age reflect differences in the social configuration of local communities and possibly differences in the organization of land tenure.

Introduction

Research into Iron Age settlements is a long-established and substantial part of Danish archaeology. The earliest investigations were undertaken during the first half of the 20th century, with small-scale excavations of individual longhouses on well-preserved sites in western and northern Jutland (e.g., Hatt 1928: 219ff; Hvass 1988: 53). Significant developments occurred in the 1960s and 1970s, when a series of ambitious, large-scale investigations undertook the complete excavation of a few select settlement sites in western Jutland through mechanical soil stripping (e.g., Becker 1965; Hvass 1988). These settlements have subsequently become type-sites that have dominated the models of both development and morphology of Danish Iron Age settlements (Løvschal and Holst 2015: 95ff; Møller et al. 2011: 7). Yet, with an ever-increasing amount of settlement data being generated, especially through development-led archaeology, and the growing complexity of prehistoric settlement materials, it has become increasingly apparent that the rather simplistic model of settlement development must be re-evaluated and qualified. Analyzing data from development-led excavations, this paper illustrates how settlement development during the Early Iron Age was both more complex and more dynamic than the traditional unilinear models had considered.

The first part of this study briefly presents background information concerning Danish Iron Age settlements. This is followed by the distribution analysis of sites from southwestern Jutland that demonstrates how overall settlement development was both dynamic and diverse, with pronounced differences between different microregions. In the final part, a detailed presentation of settlement development from two microregions with contrasting trajectories addresses how the morphology and development of individual settlement units are closely interrelated with settlement dynamics on a large scale. We intend to demonstrate that settlement development and nucleation was a complex, nonlinear process, and that variations in settlement layout during the Iron Age reflected and enforced differences in the social configuration of local communities and land tenure.

Background

Excavation and Preservation of Danish Prehistoric Settlements

Denmark over the last two centuries has been under intensive cultivation, and as a result, plowing has destroyed stratified deposits and floor layers at most settlement sites, with the only settlement remains being postholes, trenches, and pits that were dug down into the subsoil (see also Haue, this volume). The first systematic settlement investigations in the 1920s and 1930s included the excavations of some of the few well-preserved Iron Age houses on what was then rapidly disappearing heathlands.

For the most part, systematic, large-scale excavations of settlements from the 1960s onward in Denmark have uncovered only sporadically preserved cultural layers (e.g., Hvass 1985: 12; Nielsen 1999: 176). This lack of cultural layers in most sites makes it difficult to interpret functional zones within farms as well as to reconstruct relative chronological sequences at multiphase settlements.

The Early Iron Age settlements from southwestern Jutland can roughly be divided into two preservation categories. On coastal sites, cultural layers and hence stratigraphic relations are more often preserved due to the use of cobbled pavements in the byres and farmyards (e.g., Frandsen 2011: 21; Thomsen 1965: 15ff) and the occasional aeolian sand cover (Hatt 1957). By contrast, sites in the interior are more often completely without cultural layers and very hard to sequence (e.g., Dollar and Krøtel 2017). Additionally, although development-led excavations often uncover large areas, complete excavation of a settlement site is rare. Parts of a settlement site not directly threatened by development will most likely remain unexcavated, as funding is restricted to areas directly under threat (for further information on legislation about development-led archaeology in the Danish Museums Act 2002, see Mikkelsen 2012). Therefore, when considering the aspects of archaeological preservation and excavation scale, more often than not, we are dealing with partial and two-dimensional plans of settlements.

Farmsteads and Households

Danish Iron Age societies were rural agrarian societies characterized by independent farmsteads. Each farmstead was comprised of at least one central building in the form of a post-built, three-aisled longhouse. The layout of these longhouses was strictly standardized. They were east–west oriented, rectangular buildings, with two opposing doors placed centrally on the long walls leading into a central entrance area. From here, there was access to the dwelling room identified by the fireplace and cooking utensils in well-preserved houses. A byre was located in the other end of the house, often identified by stall partitions and a cobbled dung channel in well-preserved structures (Hvass 1993: 189). The longhouse is thus the incarnation of the individual household as basic socioeconomic unit, with evidence of both living quarters and an independent subsistence economy based on livestock throughout the Early Iron Age (Webley 2008: 62ff).

This paper focuses primarily on three periods of the Danish Early Iron Age: 1) the early pre-Roman Iron Age (hereafter EPRIA) from approximately 500 to 250 BC; 2) the late pre-Roman Iron Age (hereafter LPRIA) from approximately 250 to 1 BC; and 3) the early Roman Iron Age (hereafter ERIA) from AD 1 to 150/160. The subdivision of the pre-Roman Iron Age is based on Martens (1997) and Jensen (1997), and the chronology for the ERIA is based on Lund Hansen (1987). For further information concerning chronological research for the Early Iron Age, see Oldenburger (2016: 10–11).

In the EPRIA, the vast majority of farmsteads consisted of a single, rather small longhouse, without any nearby outbuildings. During the LPRIA and ERIA, farmsteads became increasingly more complex. Outbuildings and fences were more common and were eventually situated physically close to the longhouses (Løvschal 2014: 725ff; Webley 2008: 114). The size of longhouses and outbuildings, as well as the number of additional outbuildings, increased considerably, enlarging the roofed area within the farmsteads (Ejstrud and Jensen 2000: 93ff; Webley 2008: 110–111). Despite these developments, the longhouse remained the most important physical element of the farmstead throughout the Iron Age, with minor buildings and fences adhering to a strict spatial structure around the longhouse.

Settlements and Local Communities

With the first large-scale excavations took place during the 1970s, Danish archaeological settlement research started to investigate the formation of entire settlements and local communities (Figure 10.1). An interpretative model in two interrelated parts was formulated based on newly excavated type-sites, including Grøntoft (Becker 1965, 1971) and Hodde (Hvass 1975, 1985) for the Early Iron Age, and Vorbasse (Hvass 1975) for the Late Iron Age. One part of the model was the establishment of a socio-evolutionary model for long-term settlement development. This model explained settlement development as a linear process that began in the Late Bronze Age and the EPRIA with a dispersed, variable settlement pattern of single farmsteads that developed into a more stationary nucleated pattern comprised of communally fenced villages in the LPRIA (Figure 10.2; Becker 1965, 1968; Rindel 1999), and eventually culminated with clustered villages comprised of individually fenced farmsteads (Hvass 1988: 70ff). With the availability of completely excavated settlements, much attention was given to this settlement evolution from single farms to villages (Becker 1982: 64; Ethelberg 2003: 131; Hvass 1988, 1993, 1995:23ff; Jensen 1982: 151; Mikkelsen 1999; Rindel 1999, 2001). Meanwhile, the household as the basic social and economic unit received relatively little attention.

The second part of the model was the concept of the 'wandering village,' as the eventual abandonment of large settlement sites called for an explanation. In particular, the settlement of Grøntoft was crucial in the development of this explanation. With the careful examination of house typology (Becker 1971: 99ff; Rindel 1999: 82ff), it was possible to establish how the farmsteads at Grøntoft moved around within a larger settlement cell, defined here as a topographically

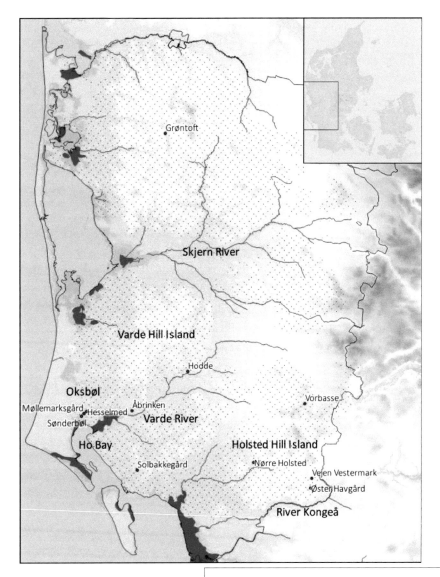

Figure 10.1. Map of southwestern Jutland, with the sites mentioned in the text. Moraine deposits marked in raster pattern, marshlands marked in dark blue (figure by N.A. Møller).

Figure 10.2. Nucleated common-fenced villages from Jutland (adapted from Rindel 1999).

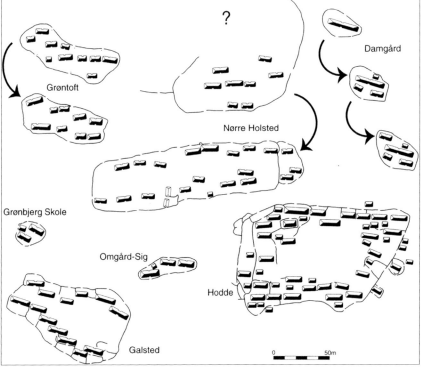

delimited microregion with evidence of an extensive settlement from a given period. Together with later observations from the Hodde and Vorbasse sites, this helped define the traditional model for Early Iron Age settlement dynamics for much of Jutland (Hvass 1985: 204ff; Rindel 2011: 99–100). The concept of 'the wandering village' was thus formulated as a settlement, at first individual farmsteads and eventually entire villages, that moved within a given settlement territory.

The identification of a large 'chieftain's farm' at Hodde led to an emphasis on social inequality in settlement materials (see Haue, this volume). A social hierarchy with asymmetric relations between individual households helped explain the relocation and reorganization of large settlements. The 'chieftain's farm' was interpreted as the first farmstead built within a large, pre-planned, common-fence settlement (Hvass 1985: 179), with the enclosing fence supposedly constructed prior to the arrival of many of the smaller farmsteads (Hvass 1985: 134).

Even though our settlement data has grown in recent years, parts of this model have stood the test of time. In most regions of Jutland, there is discernible nucleation and stabilization of individual farmsteads into larger settlement units throughout the Early Iron Age. However, it has also become evident that there was a greater degree of regional variation in settlement dynamics and structure (cf. Lund 2009; Rindel 2011: 99–100; see also Haue, this volume).

A growing research emphasis on Iron Age households (Webley 2008: 10ff) and the equal rights and obligations between households within local communities (Holst 2010: 157ff, 2014: 184ff) question the impact of asymmetrical relations between households in the formation of local settlements. Indeed, a reanalysis of Hodde has led to the conclusion that some scattered farmsteads had existed before the common-fenced village, and that large parts of the fence enclosure were constructed by individual farmsteads after their establishment (Møller 2013: 86ff).

Finally, while the concept of the 'wandering village' does help explain local settlement displacement within some settlement cells, it cannot explain large-scale settlement displacements identified in some regions of southwestern Jutland (Møller 2013: 188; Rindel 1992: 137ff).

The Area of Southwestern Jutland and the Regional Settlement Development in the Early Iron Age

In a recent study of Early Iron Age settlement systems in southwestern Jutland, an integrated analysis of landscape, land tenure, and settlement development was undertaken on a dataset of some 2867 sites in order to analyze large-scale settlement patterns (Møller 2013: 168ff).

Landscape Development in Southwestern Jutland

The landscape of southwestern Jutland is characterized by three major landforms, each having different soils. The oldest landforms are the gently sloping hill islands of old moraine deposits from the Riss-Saale glaciation. They have variable soils consisting of sand, clayey sand, and gravel. These are often intersected by large outwash plains formed by glacial rivers from the Würm-Weichsel glaciation, with very light, sandy, and gravely deposits. On the coast, the landscape is characterized by continuous development, with the formation of sandy barrier islands, dune formations in the coastal zone, and formations of clay marshland deposits on the sheltered coastline behind the barrier islands. These formations have taken place since approximately 6000 BC due to a decline in the rate of marine transgression (Behre 2007: 84ff; Pedersen et al. 2009: Figure 3.3), with the stabilization of the present-day coastline as a result. At least some of the barrier islands have been under formation since 4100 BC (Madsen et al. 2010: 1254). Because of shifting wind patterns, sand drift has been occurring intermittently, especially in the coastal region, throughout the last 5000 years (Clemmesen et al. 2009: 311; Møller 2013: 33, Figure 3.8). The formation of Danish marshlands has not yet been studied in detail, but the available dates show that the marshes began to form in sheltered positions at least as early as 2500 BC (Pedersen et al. 2009: 77), while more widespread marshes have been forming since the 2nd millennium BC (Jacobsen 1993: 724; Møller 2013: 32).

For the majority of southwestern Jutland, the soils are poor for crop farming, as illustrated by the very low yields of agricultural production in historical times (Dam 2008: 107). The light, clayey sand soils of the moraine can be used for arable farming, but they suffer from soil degradation due to leaching, especially of lime. The very light, sandy deposits of the outwash plains are the least attractive soils for traditional agriculture. They have even less available nutrients and almost no capacity to retain water for plants, with the result that crops are easily susceptible to periodic droughts (Madsen et al. 1992). Traditional agriculture in southwestern Jutland thus depended heavily on animal husbandry, with grazing in extensive heathlands and hay production in the broad meadows along the rivers and sheltered coasts (e.g., Rømer and Stenak 2009: 225ff). The marshlands, by far the most fertile lands of southwestern Jutland, could not be used for crop production due to the risk of occasional flooding before the construction of dikes. They were instead used as very productive grazing lands and/or for hay production through much of prehistory and into modern times. Available pollen diagrams show evidence for tenure of both heathlands and grasslands, the former by occasional burning, which was practiced throughout later prehistory (Odgaard 1985: 51, 2006: 347). Dependence on animal husbandry in the Iron Age is evidenced by both the byres in the longhouses and the occasional find of animal bones despite poor general preservation conditions (Kveiborg 2011: 123).

Regional Settlement Development

The region of southwestern Jutland has witnessed pronounced dynamics in overall settlement development throughout large parts of prehistory. Several studies of settlement dynamics have been undertaken on both microregional (Jensen *et al.* 1998) and regional (Møller 2011, 2013; Rindel 1997, 1999) scales.

The EPRIA sites are widespread across the moraine deposits in both the interior and coastal areas, while the infertile outwash plains were almost completely avoided, as was the case throughout later prehistory (Figure 10.3). In comparison to the Late Bronze Age, however, there was a decline in the number of sites in the interior and along stretches of the open coast, and an increase in the number of sites situated near marshlands. This tendency toward the contraction of sites in coastal areas close to marshlands was even more pronounced in the LPRIA, while the interior moraines were nearly completely abandoned during this period. Abandonment is most evident on the moraine deposits in the interior of Varde Hill Island and on Holsted Hill Island just north of the River Kongeå, but the abandonment of the interior is also apparent on the moraines south of River Kongeå (Rindel 1992: 138ff).

During the ERIA, settlements continued to occupy the coastal areas close to marshlands (see Figure 10.3). An increasing

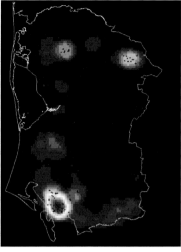

EPRIA

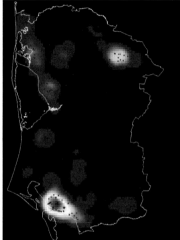

LPRIA

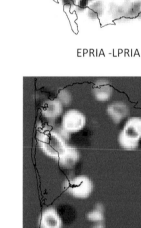

EPRIA -LPRIA

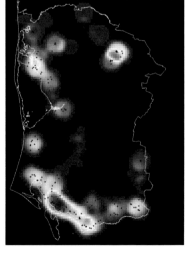

ERIA

LPRIA-ERIA

Figure 10.3. Result of point-pattern analysis. Point distributions are on the left. Yellow and red indicate the highest concentration of sites, blue indicates lower concentrations. On the right, the differences between two consecutive periods are highlighted by subtracting the result of the point distributions from each other. Red and yellow indicate an increase in site concentration, dark green and blue indicate a decrease in site concentration (figure by N.A. Møller).

number of sites within coastal areas show an even more pronounced connection between the location of ERIA sites and the marshlands. At the same time, settlements began to reoccupy the interior moraine that had been nearly devoid of sites in the LPRIA. Holsted Hill Island, nearly completely devoid of LPRIA sites, witnessed a pronounced concentration of sites both along the rivers and in areas with more favorable soils. Both the intensification of occupation in long-established settlement areas and expansion into the interior are mirrored in territories south of our study area as well (Rindel 1992: 140).

Thus, on a regional scale, there was a trend toward the nucleation of sites into smaller areas throughout the Early Iron Age. The favorable areas, particularly along the marshlands, witnessed continuous occupation and gradual development of more densely settled areas, while some areas in the interior of southwestern Jutland witnessed very dynamic developments with pronounced displacements of settlements in the middle of the pre-Roman Iron Age and a major influx of settlements again at the beginning of the ERIA.

Iron Age Settlements in the Area North of Ho Bay

The pronounced nucleation of settlements in the coastal area of the Wadden Sea is evident on a microregional scale in the coastal part of the Varde Hill Island, just north of Ho Bay. Here, numerous excavations have been undertaken in advance of gravel extraction, destructive military activities, and urban development. The following account focuses on the topographically limited microregion (settlement cell) of Oksbøl (Figure 10.4). Large-scale development-led excavations have uncovered two settlement sites from the EPRIA/LPRIA, three from the EPRIA to the ERIA, and nine other sites with settlement remains from the Early Iron Age within an area of some 8 km².[1] Although none of these settlements has been completely excavated, five excavations have exposed sufficiently large areas to make this one of the most informative microregions for the analysis of settlement development in the coastal region of southwestern Jutland.

Early Pre-Roman Iron Age

EPRIA settlements are widespread north of Ho Bay, with multiple sites extending from 5 km inland to

[1] Sites include VAM1179 Hesselmed, VAM1340 Hesselmed Nord, VAM1392 Oksbøl Øst, VAM1463 Industrivej 18, VAM1498 Okbøl Industri, VAM1302 Møllemarksgård, VAM1232 Møllemarksgård Vest, VAM 1385 Oksbøl Flyveplads, VAM1386 Rastepladsen, VAM 1397 Skødstrup, VAM1469 Møllemarksgård SV, VAM1551 Møllemarksgård Nord, VAM1677 Møllemarksgård Øst, VAM1685 Sønderbøl, VAM 1762 Testbanen. Danish sites and monuments register (Fund og Fortidsminder): Aal Parish, sb. no. 133, 156, 157, 159, 183, 211, 213, 216. All sites were excavated by the Varde Museum.

sites overlooking the fertile marshlands. Most of the farmsteads consist of a single longhouse, while additional structures, such as a fence, an additional outbuilding, or a four-post granary, have only been found on a few sites and at a distance typically ranging between 10 and 50 m from the contemporaneous longhouses (Møller 2013: 48ff). Most longhouses dating to the EPRIA are small, with a floor area below 55 m², while a small group of large houses has an average floor area of approximately 110 m².

Regardless of their size, longhouses were built with rather small posts, seldom show evidence of repair, and were never rebuilt on the same spot. When postpipes are visible in the larger postholes in the two lines of roof-supporting posts in the interior of the house, these are only approximately 10 cm in diameter, indicating that these longhouses had a short life span of perhaps a single generation (Møller 2013: 59; for a discussion and further references on the life span of post-built houses, see also Webley 2008: 39).

Since these short-lived houses seldom have a clear stratigraphic relationship with each other, it is difficult to ascertain the overall development of EPRIA settlement sites and the number of potentially contemporaneous farmsteads within a particular site. This is especially problematic with the current state of scientific dating, where only a very limited number of EPRIA houses have been radiocarbon dated. At the sites of Sønderbøl and Testbanen, containing many EPRIA houses, the gradual typological development of longhouses suggests a continuous settlement throughout the Late Bronze Age to the LPRIA. This continuity allows for a rough estimation of the potential number of contemporaneous farmsteads on these sites. At Sønderbøl (Møller 2012: 200ff), one or two farmsteads could have been in use at the same time in an area of 5.8 ha, while the number of houses from Testbanen suggests that this area would not have supported more than a single farmstead within approximately 5.7 ha.

Late Pre-Roman and Early Roman Iron Age

In the LPRIA, many of the EPRIA sites were abandoned and the farmsteads in the settlement cell began to nucleate into loose clusters at five sites in the area North of Ho Bay, three of which have been extensively excavated. The contraction of farmsteads into dense clusters was a gradual process. The site of Sønderbøl had a single farmstead dating to the LPRIA about 500 m away from the nearest contracted settlement, and at the settlement area of Testbanen, some seven farmsteads were in use during the LPRIA.

All the sites that eventually developed into clustered settlements had farmsteads originating from the EPRIA. One of these, the site of Hesselmed, had two,

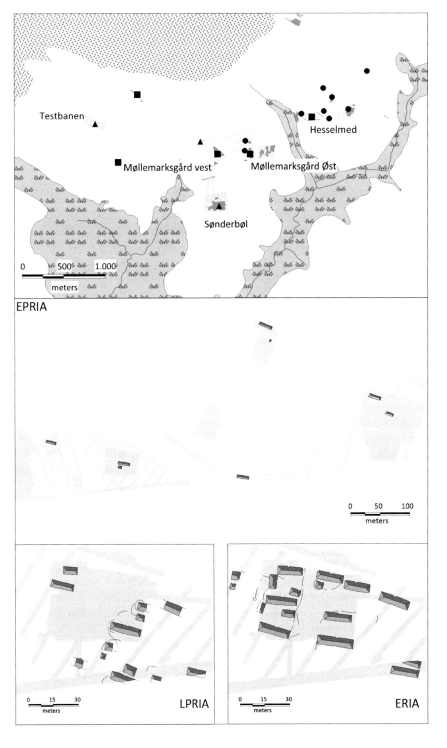

Figure 10.4. Development of clustered villages in the Oksbøl settlement cell. Overall settlement development between sand dunes and marshlands are indicated on the top. Triangles indicate sites with Late Bronze Age and EPRIA farmsteads, circles indicate sites with EPRIA farmsteads, and squares indicate sites with EPRIA farmsteads and LPRIA/ERIA clustered settlements (figure by N.A. Møller).

very large EPRIA farmsteads, but there is nothing to suggest that clustered settlements, as a rule, aggregated around a pre-existing, high-status pre-Roman Iron Age farmstead. In the three excavated clustered settlements, this aggregation process seems to have culminated during the transition from the LPRIA to ERIA. In the nucleated settlements from the LPRIA/RIA, on average, five to eight contemporary farmsteads were uncovered across the excavated areas.

During the LPRIA, the farmsteads began to develop into larger units, as reflected in the increasing size of the longhouses and additional outbuildings. These farmsteads occupied a small area of 170–300 m², though their size and the roofed area within them varied considerably (Møller 2013: 145ff). An average farmstead was limited to one outbuilding, whereas the large farmsteads had two. Fences were added to some farmsteads to delineate a small private farmyard in front of the longhouse. This farmyard was often almost triangular, with a fence running between the corner of the outbuilding and the corner of the longhouse, occupying as little space as possible.

In the ERIA, the farmsteads continued to increase in size and, on average, had two or three outbuildings; the larger farmsteads had as many as five outbuildings. The dimensions of the longhouses of these large farms also increased with the addition of more space in the byre. The total roofed area in the ERIA varied between 90 and 250 m², with the size of the plots ranging from 170 to 500 m². With the increased number of outbuildings, most ERIA farmsteads developed a more rectilinear layout, and as the settlements contracted into more densely structured settlements, fences were used as means of restricting access to the more private spaces within the farmyards (Møller 2013: 151).

Throughout the LPRIA and ERIA, these farmsteads tended to become more stationary and settlements to become more densely occupied. The larger of these dense settlements gradually developed into more structured sites (see Figure 10.4). In the Oksbøl settlement cell, the ERIA farmsteads at all three excavated clustered settlement sites were eventually arranged in a U-shape or oblong form around an open common space, a development also found on the site of Åbrinken further up the Varde River Valley (Møller 2013: 134) and possibly also at Solbakkegård south of the Varde River (Christiansen 1985: 217).

There was pronounced stability of the individual farms from the later part of the LPRIA onward. Houses were built to last, with sturdier posts reaching diameters of as much as 25 cm. Regular repairs and replacements of roof-bearing posts occurred, and the longhouses of the larger farmsteads, in particular, were rebuilt on the same spot several times. Thus, the life spans of these longhouses and farmsteads, especially from the ERIA, were much longer than normally expected of Iron Age houses (Møller 2013: 55ff).

The development of social space within these densely occupied settlements provides insight into the organizational principles of villages. The boundaries between neighboring farmsteads were negotiable, and continuous rebuilding episodes led to slight changes to the plots of the individual farms through time. Yet the farms never expanded into the shared interior space, which was respected throughout the life span of these densely clustered settlements. Additionally, the farmstead fences facing the interior space were more often rigorously maintained than those facing outwards toward the surrounding landscape.

Eventually, some households established themselves as the dominant households in these clustered settlements. The larger farmsteads were more elaborately fenced off than the smaller farms, and they were placed at significant positions on high ground at the end of the interior open common space. On sites such as Møllemarksgård Øst, where communal burial grounds dating to the ERIA have been found, these were situated close to the largest farmstead of the settlement cluster. As a rare discovery of a high-status artifact in a settlement context, a riding spur was found encapsulated in the clay hearth of the largest farmstead from Møllemarksgård Øst. The large farmsteads at all these sites conspicuously displayed differences in their socioeconomic capabilities through the construction of large and elaborately built byres, and in some settlements, the largest farmsteads continuously occupied the same plot throughout the LPRIA and ERIA, while smaller farmsteads were more changeable (Møller 2013: 145ff).

On a microregional scale, these clustered and long-lived settlements of the LPRIA and ERIA Oksbøl settlement cells show a hitherto unsurpassed settlement density. Five clustered settlements from the ERIA, spaced between 250 and 1000 m in a topographically limited microregion, suggest regulation of land tenure at a level above the individual settlement and local community. Considering the numbers of farmsteads at each of these five settlements, the number of farmsteads easily exceeded any of the contemporary but organized villages of the LPRIA and ERIA, such as the approximated 27 farms at Hodde (Hvass 1985: 175–176) and the villages on Holsted Hill Island.

Iron Age Settlements on Holsted Hill Island

In comparison to other regions of Jutland, it is only relatively recently that we have begun to understand prehistoric settlement development within the inland microregion of Holsted Hill Island. With the exception of the excavations undertaken as part of a natural gas line project in the early 1980s, almost no large-scale excavations had been conducted prior to a new motorway-related project in 1992. Over the last two decades, the towns and villages situated on Holsted Hill Island north of the River Kongeå experienced steady urban expansion, and as a result, development-led excavations have made this microregion one of the most intensively investigated areas in the interior of Jutland. The collected data have provided insight into an Early Iron Age settlement development that is remarkably different from the development observed at Oksbøl on the west coast.

Early Pre-Roman Iron Age

A detailed analysis of the EPRIA settlements on Holsted Hill Island has thus far not been conducted, but some general observations can be made about the characteristics of these sites. The most obvious difference in comparison to Ho Bay and other parts of southwestern Jutland is an almost complete absence of houses or other structures in the archaeological record. Only a few investigations have thus far yielded evidence for buildings that may date to the EPRIA. This, however, does not mean that there is a lack of evidence for EPRIA settlement activities. Rubbish pits, usually backfilled with EPRIA pottery, have frequently been documented during both trial excavations and large-scale investigations.

The lack of house remains from sites with rubbish pits cannot be explained simply as a matter of poor preservation. In comparison, evidence for buildings dating to the Late Neolithic, Early Bronze Age, and even Late Bronze Age is relatively common (e.g., for the Late Neolithic, see Dollar 2013). The clusters of rubbish pits are possible indicators of short-term, occasional or seasonal, occupations related to more extensive land use, where permanent structures were simply unnecessary.

Late Pre-Roman Iron Age

In contrast to the coastal areas of southwestern Jutland, evidence for LPRIA settlement in the interior of central-southern Jutland is extremely limited. This already was demonstrated in a study of Early Iron Age settlement patterns in southern Jutland (Rindel 1992: 138). Moreover, despite a dramatic increase in the number of development-led excavations since the early 1990s, Rindel's observations have further been corroborated by the recent studies presented above.

On Holsted Hill Island, Nørre Holsted is currently the only site with extensive settlement remains that can securely be dated to the LPRIA. Excavated by Rindel (1993, 1999: 87) in the 1990s, the LPRIA phase of this site consisted of a two-phase village enclosed by a fence (see Figure 10.2). The settlement was organized differently in each phase. In its earliest stage, it consisted of approximately eight to ten longhouses surrounded by a rounded, pear-shaped fence. The structures, each representing an individual farmstead, concentrated in the southern half of the enclosed area. The northern half of the site seems to have been unoccupied by buildings, though a small part has not yet been excavated.

In its later phase, the entire settlement was completely reorganized into a more regular layout where the fence enclosure had an east–west oriented, oblong form that contained 16 to 19 longhouses. Most of these longhouses were laid out in two rows that ran along the long sides of the enclosure, each with its own entrance through the fence, opposite the longhouses' entrances. An additional fenced enclosure was added to the eastern end of the common fence. This addition comprised three more longhouses, reflecting the growth of the local community. Even though both settlement phases had common fences, Nørre Holsted's later phase consisted of significantly more houses laid out in a more regular settlement structure in comparison to its earliest phase.

The common-fence settlement at Nørre Holsted shares many morphological characteristics with several other common-fenced settlements in western and central Jutland from this period, such as Grøntoft and Hodde (see Figure 10.2; Rindel 1999). Yet it remains the only settlement site from the LPRIA on Holsted Hill Island and in its immediate surroundings. Despite the increase in the number of large-scale investigations since Nørre Holsted was excavated, the number of sites with archaeological remains that can be dated to the LPRIA has barely increased. Excluding Nørre Holsted, LPRIA features have only been found on seven sites. These include two sites with urn burials and five sites with a single or few, pottery-filled rubbish pits, without any definite evidence for buildings. Based on our current settlement data for the LPRIA, we can conclude that Holsted Hill Island and the surrounding areas witnessed a significant decrease in land use that resulted in the extensive abandonment of large tracts of land.

Early Roman Iron Age

With the advent of the ERIA, settlement sites became relatively common. These settlements, however, were fundamentally different from both the common-fenced settlements of the LPRIA and the clustered settlements on the coast. Several of these sites have been excavated extensively enough to demonstrate that they were structured around similar basic principles. Each was comprised of multiple, uniform farmsteads organized in rows in an east–west linear layout, and each seems to have emerged rather suddenly at the transition from the LPRIA to the ERIA.

The most extensively investigated ERIA settlement from Holsted Hill Island is the site of Vejen Vestermark (Figure 10.5), which was excavated during development-led excavations west of the town of Vejen (Dollar and Krøtel 2017; Dollar and Petersen 2010; Krøtel 2015; Terp 2015). Dispersed rubbish pits from the EPRIA indicate the only activities at the site prior to the ERIA, and settlement activities in the Late Roman and Early Germanic Iron Age occurred north of the ERIA settlement. Due to both good preservation and the relative absence of earlier or later settlement phases, Vejen Vestermark has yielded exceptional data for our understanding of ERIA farmstead layout and settlement organization in the interior of southern Jutland.

Vejen Vestermark consisted of nearly 200 post-built houses divided among at least 25 individually fenced farmsteads. Twenty-one of the farmsteads were organized into two parallel, east–west oriented rows approximately 130 m apart. The southern farmsteads, 14 in all, were established earlier than the northern row

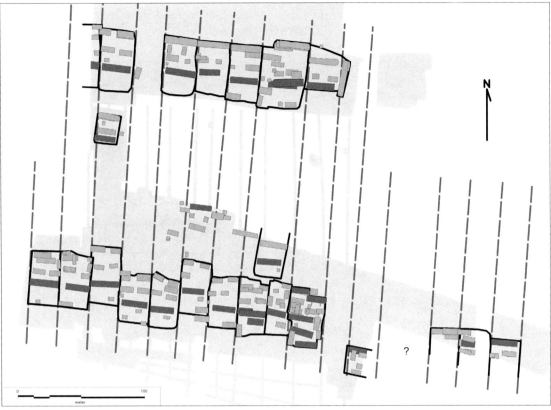

Figure 10.5. ERIA row-village at Vejen Vestermark. Two rows of farmsteads
were laid out according to a pre-defined parcel structure (figure by S. Dollar).

of seven farmsteads, though there was likely a certain amount of overlap in the occupation of the individual farmsteads within each row.

Between these two rows, evidence for four to five farmsteads is available. A large part of this area of the settlement remains unexcavated, but there is much to suggest that these farms could be associated with the pioneer settlement in the area. They were generally smaller, had a different layout with fewer outbuildings, and do not adhere to structural principles behind the two rows of farms at the site. Unfortunately, radiocarbon dating, as well as ceramic and house typology, failed to produce a more precise chronological sorting of these farms in relation to those within the row structure. An unusual curvature of the fences on some farms in the southern row respect the southern entrance of the farm in the interior. This suggests that some of the farms in the southern row were established later than, and partly contemporary with, at least one farm in the interior.

The internal layout of the farmsteads in the two rows, on the other hand, had a relatively uniform character. They were rectilinear in shape and at least partly enclosed by fences. The southern farmsteads range in size between 725 and 1075 m², whereas the chronologically later northern farmsteads were slightly larger, between 1000 and 1200 m², with the largest being 1700 m². Each

farmstead was composed of a longhouse, three to five outbuildings, and one or more four-post structures. The plan of these buildings is architecturally uniform and typologically similar to other buildings from the ERIA in southern Jutland (Hvass 1985: 116).

Each farmstead was arranged around a centrally placed longhouse. The space to the south of the longhouse was generally open, though sometimes with one or two outbuildings and/or four-post structures. Most of the outbuildings were situated to the north of the longhouses and were often laid out in two parallel rows that divided the area into two, smaller farmyards. The northernmost pair of outbuildings delineated the limits of the farmstead. In the northern row of farmsteads, these northernmost outbuildings were replaced by a single, large, robust outbuilding that extended the entire width of the farmstead. It is uncertain whether all the outbuildings were built at the same time or were constructed gradually over the life span of a farmstead.

The life span of individual farmsteads seems to have varied considerably. As with the ERIA houses in the coastal area, many longhouses and outbuildings showed evidence for post-replacement that would have lengthened their life span. In some cases, structures were eventually replaced, either in the same location or in another part of the farmstead. For the most part, the farmsteads had one or two phases, although a few had evidence of three or more phases and could have existed throughout the ERIA. Based on the architectural features of the longhouses and ceramic data, the three easternmost farmsteads in the northern row continued to be occupied into the beginning of the Late Roman Iron Age (Terp 2015).

These two rows of fairly uniform and equally sized farmsteads seem to adhere to a strict principle of structuration in the form of parcels (Dollar and Krøtel 2017). The boundaries between neighboring farmyards from both farmstead rows were in alignment with each other (see Figure 10.5). Most of these north–south parcels were of the same approximate width of 22 to 26 m, while one parcel with a width between 36 and 39 m was occupied by a single farmstead in the northern row, whereas in the southern row, it was divided between farmsteads of 22 and 17 m in width.

Despite variations in the longevity of individual farmsteads in the rows, they all remained within a fixed farmyard area and never expanded into a neighboring farmyard. This might be an indication that the settlement had been parceled at least from the establishment of the southern row, and that this parceling structured the placing of farmsteads throughout the period. However, the farmsteads situated between these two rows do not fit into this parceled structure, and there seems to have been a slight change in the orientation of the farmyards between the central farms and the farms in the two rows.

An additional three sites within a 15-km radius of Vejen Vestermark were organized into a row structure comprised of individual rectangular farmsteads laid out in east–west oriented rows. The site of Øster Havgård is located only 2 km south of Vejen Vestermark (Eisenschmidt 2007: 59–62; Eisenschmidt 2014), and shares many of the same elements in farmstead layout and village organization. The ERIA settlement was made up of at least 23, relatively uniform farmsteads, 15 of which have been excavated completely. Ranging in size from 640 to 1050 m², they were arranged into two parallel, east–west oriented rows approximately 20 m apart. The layout of these farmsteads was similar to those at Vejen Vestermark. They were structured around a centrally placed longhouse, associated with a series of smaller outbuildings and four-post structures mostly located north of the longhouse. Despite these similarities, there were also differences between these two settlements. The farmsteads at Øster Havgård generally showed more rebuilding phases and the boundaries between farmsteads were often, but not always, respected. Additionally, the rigid parceling seen at Vejen Vestermark was not apparent at Øster Havgård.

Though far less extensively excavated, the ERIA settlements at Havgård and Sønder Holsted both exhibit an organized row structure. The site of Havgård consisted of at least eight rectilinear farmsteads in an east–west oriented row, and limited excavations at Sønder Holsted have uncovered a settlement with at least two rows of farmsteads.

Discussion

The different developments documented in the extensively excavated microregions presented above manifest the need for a re-evaluation of the traditional model for settlement trajectories in the Early Iron Age of southwestern Jutland. Broadly speaking, dispersed farmsteads began to nucleate into more densely comprised settlement entities over the course of the Early Iron Age. However, depending on the overall settlement development, nucleation could have led to a variety of settlement forms, such as clusters of farmsteads or regulated villages.

Within both clustered settlements and regulated villages, the individual farmsteads retained their economic autonomy, as indicated by the similar layout of longhouses with a byre present in all size ranges of farmsteads (Hvass 1985: 175ff). As a result of this nucleation, social space in the majority of these settlements became regulated through the use of fences that demonstrated rights and mediated relationships between individual farmsteads and households in these dense settlements (Løvschal and Holst 2015: 10ff; Webley 2008: 114). Nucleation created the need for local communities to clarify rights and obligations among economically independent households (Holst 2010: 158ff).

In southwestern Jutland, the emergence of larger settlement entities is also identifiable on a regional level, with most sites concentrating in rather limited areas that contained favorable resources and particularly areas situated near marshlands. The overall dynamics across the landscape are also clearly reflected in the development of individual sites in different microregions. In the interior of southwestern Jutland, the common-fenced settlement of Nørre Holsted of the LPRIA was completely isolated from other contemporary settlements, while the number of farmsteads in clustered settlements in the Oksbøl area was booming in the same period. The situation of Nørre Holsted is comparable to the LPRIA settlement of Hodde. They were situated in isolated, well-defined, topographically limited settlement cells, and a degree of collective action is indicated by the establishment of common fences enclosing the villages. The common fences underlined the cohesion of the local community (Løvschal and Holst 2015), while, at the same time, limiting the possibilities of actions by individual households. In Nørre Holsted, collective action was further manifested by a major reorganization of the entire settlement, including both the surrounding fence and, apparently, all the farmsteads. This emphasis on collective actions and community at Nørre Holsted, Hodde, and several other communally fenced settlements may be a result of their relative isolation, with the sturdy common fences functioning both as a symbol of the cohesion and unity of the local community and perhaps a rudimentary defensive precaution (Møller 2013: 218–219).

With a resurgence of settlements in the interior of southwestern Jutland during the ERIA, a new type of settlement layout emerged in the form of row settlements. Vejen Vestermark, and to a varying degree all other ERIA settlements in the region, show the strict organization of villages into rows of farmsteads in almost identical plots. At Vejen Vestermark, these plots were laid out according to a more extensive division into parcels. This standardized division of land suggests that the local community largely consisted of households with equal rights, implying that no household could have upheld a pre-established claim of extraordinary rights to land in the area. Claim of equality between households is implied by the very standardized layout and equal size of the majority of farmsteads, once the initial division of land into parcels and plots had been established. Apart from the many row villages on Holsted Hill Island and its immediate surroundings, the same type of settlement, regulated by fences, is found at contemporaneous sites in other parts of Jutland (Webley 2008: 23ff, 107ff).

In the continuously inhabited settlement cell of Oksbøl, sites developed gradually from the dispersed EPRIA farmsteads into clusters of farmsteads by the LPRIA and more neatly organized settlements during the ERIA. However, the ERIA communities never regulated settlements into equally sized plots, as has been observed in the interior of Jutland, and there was a pronounced emphasis on socioeconomic capability, particularly of the larger farmsteads.

Considering the close proximity of clustered settlements in the Oksbøl area, land tenure, especially for the grazing of animals, must have been regulated on a scale above the individual settlement. At the same time, these clusters, with their longevity and demonstration of relatedness to the place through their own burial grounds, very actively manifested land rights in a very tightly nucleated settlement area next to favorable grazing areas in the marshes.

Thus, in the ERIA, there seems to have been two slightly differing principles behind the regulation of rights and social space between the spatially close but still independent farmsteads. In the long-established settlements on the coast, farmsteads are found in fairly small clusters, they are of different sizes, and one or two households in each cluster excelled in the emphasis on longevity, privacy, and size, especially in the size of the byres (Møller 2013: 145ff). Differences in farmstead size suggest an asymmetric relationship between farms within the same cluster in a landscape where competition for favorable resources and a gradual development of both local communities and rights to land may have aided in the development of inequality. This situation is comparable with that of in northeastern Jutland, where long-established settlements show clear indications of social stratification between households (Haue 2011: 87ff; see also Haue, this volume).

On the contrary, in the pioneering settlements from Holsted Hill Island, emphasis was placed on equality between identical farmsteads on plots of equal size in highly regulated settlement forms and in a strictly divided landscape. The governing principle of equality between households and a strictly regulated system of land rights are most likely the results of a community organizing itself in a landscape with a more or less even distribution of resources between individual households and without previously established land rights.

The Multilinear Path from Single Farms to Nucleated Settlements

Differences in settlement forms suggest that the social matrix of local communities may differ as a result of differences in overall developments in settlements and land tenure. In the settlements of Holsted Hill Island, we find cohesion in communal actions and an emphasis on equality amongst households. In the coastal settlements, there was greater variation in farmstead size and a pronounced emphasis on the individuality, longevity, and identity of individual households. The emphasis on the longevity of households in the coastal area might reflect long-established land rights in an area with significant competition for the most favorable resources. The standard plots in ERIA settlements in the interior of southwestern Jutland, on the other hand, may imply that these communities re-established themselves in areas where previous land claims were not as firmly established. This standardized division of land, to a certain degree, anticipates the Late Iron Age settlement organization (Holst 2010: 160ff), while the long-established communities along the west coast were more conservative in the organization of their settlements.

Acknowledgments

A significant part of this work was undertaken as a PhD research supervised by Klavs Randsborg (University of Copenhagen) and Claus Kjeld Jensen (Varde Museum), funded by the Faculty of Humanities at the University of Copenhagen. Niels Algreen Møller would like to thank both his supervisors and former colleagues at the Varde Museum for insightful discussions and support. Scott Dollar would like to thank the Sønderskov Museum for making it possible to partake in the EAA Annual Meeting in Vilnius, and Janne Krøtel, Lars Grundvad, and Martin Egelund Poulsen for their suggestions and support while writing this paper.

References Cited

Becker, C.J. 1965. Ein früheizenzeitliches Dorf bei Grøntoft, Westjütland. *Acta Archaeologica* 36: 209–222.

Becker, C.J. 1968. Das zweite früheizenzeitlische Dorf bei Grøntoft, Westjütland. 2. Vorbericht über die Ausgrabungen 1961–63. *Acta Archaeologica* 39: 235–255.

Becker, C.J. 1971. Früheisenzetliche Dörfer bei Grøntoft, Westjütland. 3. Vorbericht: Die Ausgrabungen 1967–68. *Acta Archaeologica* 42: 79–110.

Becker, C.J. 1982. Siedlungen der Bronzezeit und der vorrömischen Eisenzeit in Dänemark. *Offa* 39: 53–71.

Behre, K.E. 2007. A new sea-level curve for the southern North Sea. *Boreas* 36: 82–102.

Christiansen, H. 1985. Kjærsing. *Journal of Danish Archaeology* 4: 217–218.

Clemmesen, L.B., A.S. Murray, J. Heinemeier and R.D. Jong 2009. The evolution of Holocene coastal dunefields, Denmark: A record of climate change over the past 5000 years. *Geomorphology* 105(3–4): 303–313.

Dam, P. 2008. Historisk geografiske kortlægninger og studier på nationalt plan, in P. Dam and J.G.G. Jacobsen (eds) *Historisk geografisk atlas*: 66–129. København: Geografforlaget.

Dollar, S.R. 2013. Hustomter fra senneolitikum og tidligste bronzealder i Vejen kommunen. *Arkæologi i Slesvig* 14: 39–49.

Dollar, S.R. and J. Krøtel 2017. Vejen Vestermark – A row settlement from the Early Roman Iron Age in Southern Jutland. *Arkæologi i Slesvig* 16: 115–129.

Dollar, S.R. and B. Petersen 2010. Bygherrerapport for HBV 1340 Lille Skovgård I–III. Unpublished excavation report, Museet på Sønderskov.

Eisenschmidt, S. 2007. Die Ergebnisse einer grösseren Siedlungsgrabung in Askov bei Vejen. *Arkæologi i Slesvig* 11: 59–66.

Eisenschmidt, S. 2014. Arkæologisk Rapport for HBV 1142 Øster Havgård. Unpublished excavation report, Museet på Sønderskov.

Ejstrud, B. and C.K. Jensen 2000. *Vendehøj – landsby og gravplads* (Jysk Arkæologisk Selskabs skrifter 35). Højbjerg: Jysk Arkæologisk Selskab.

Ethelberg, P. 2003. Gården og landsbyen i jernalder og vikingetid (500 f.Kr – 1000 e.Kr.), in P. Ethelberg, N. Hardt, B. Poulsen and A.B. Sørensen (eds) *Det sønderjyske landbrugs historie. Jernalder, Vikingetid og Middelalder* (Skifter udgivet af Historisk Samfund for Sønderjylland 8): 123–374. Haderslev: Harderslev Museum.

Frandsen, L.B. 2011. Stenlægning på stenlægning, in N.A. Møller, S.S. Qvistgaard and S.F. Jensen (eds) *Nyt fra Vestfronten - Nord- og Vestjyske bebyggelser fra ældre jernalder* (Arkæologiske Skrifter 10): 27–34. København: Saxo-instituttet.

Hatt, G. 1928. To bopladsfund fra ældre jernalder, fra Mors og Himmerland. *Aarbøger for Nordisk Oldkyndighed og Historie* 18: 219–260.

Hatt, G. 1957. *Nørre Fjand: An Early Iron-Age village Site in West Jutland*. København: Det kongelige danske vidneskabernes selskab.

Haue, N. 2011. Social stratifikation og den 'sociale arv' i ældre jernalder - med udgangspunkt i bopladsstudier fra Nordjylland, in N.A. Møller, S.S. Qvistgaard and S.F. Jensen (eds) *Nyt fra Vestfronten - Nord- og Vestjyske bebyggelser fra ældre jernalder* (Arkæologiske Skrifter 10): 87–98. København: Saxo-instituttet.

Holst, M.K. 2010. Inconstancy and stability: Large and small farmsteads in the village of Nørre Snede (Central Jutland) in the first millennium AD. *Settlement and Coastal Research in the Southern North Sea Region* 33: 155–179.

Holst, M.K. 2014. Warrior aristocracy and village community – Two fundamental forms of social organisation in the Late Iron Age and Viking Age, in E. Stidsing, K. Høilund and R. Fiedel (eds) *Wealth and Complexity - Economically specialised sites in the Late Iron Age Denmark*: 175–197. Aarhus: Aarhus University Press.

Hvass, S. 1975. Hodde – et 2000-årigt landsbysamfund i Vestjylland. *Nationalmuseets Arbejdsmark* 1975: 75–85.

Hvass, S. 1985. *Hodde: En vestjysk jernaldersamfund fra ældre jernalder*. København: Akademisk Forlag.

Hvass, S. 1988. Jernalders bebyggelse, in P. Mortensen and B.M. Rasmussen (eds) *Fra stamme til stat I Danmark 1. Jernalderes stammesamfund* (Jysk Arkæologisk Selskabs skrifter 22): 53–92. Aarhus: Aarhus Universitetsforlag.

Hvass, S. 1993. Settlement, in S. Hvass and B. Storgård (eds) *Digging into the Past: 25 Years of Archaeology in Denmark*: 187–194. Aarhus: Aarhus Universitetsforlag.

Hvass, S. 1995. Oldtidens bebyggelse og kulturlandskabet I dag. In Etting, V. (ed.) *På opdagelse i kulturlandskabet*: 13–31. Copenhagen: Gyldendal.

Jacobsen, N. 1993. Shoreline Development and Sea-Level Rise in the Danish Wadden Sea. *Journal of Coastal Research* 9(3): 721–729.

Jensen, J. 1982. *The Prehistory of Denmark*. London: Routledge.

Jensen, C.K. 1997. Kronologiske problemer og deres betydning for forståelsen af førromersk jernalder i Syd- og Midtjylland, in J. Martens (ed.) *Chronological Problems of the Pre-Roman Iron Age in Northern Europe*

(Arkæologiske Skrifter 7): 91–106. Copenhagen: Danish University Press.

Jensen, S., P. Asing and L. Feveile (eds) 1998. *Marsk, land og bebyggelse. Ribeegnen gennem 10.000 år.* Århus: Jysk Arkæologisk Selskab.

Krøtel, J. 2015. Beretning for HBV 1340 Lille Skovgård IV. Unpublished excavation report, Museet på Sønderskov.

Kveiborg, J. 2011. Indsamling og registrering af brændte dyreknogler fra bopladser – er det besværet værd? En diskussion af materialets muligheder og begrænsninger, in N.A. Møller, S.S. Qvistgaard and S.F. Jensen (eds) *Nyt fra Vestfronten - Nord- og Vestjyske bebyggelser fra ældre jernalder* (Arkæologiske Skrifter 10): 123–127. København: Saxo-instituttet.

Løvschal, M. 2014. Emerging Boundaries: Social Embedment of Landscape and Settlement Divisions in Northwestern Europe during the First Millennium BC. *Current Anthropology* 55(6): 725–750.

Løvschal, M. and M.K. Holst 2015. Repeating boundaries – repertoires of landscape regulations in southern Scandinavia in the Late Bronze Age and Pre-Roman Iron Age. *Danish Journal of Archaeology* 3: 95–118.

Lund, J. 2009. Byhøje og andre stedbundne bebyggelser, in M. Rung (ed.) *Nørre Hedegård - En nordjysk byhøj fra ældre jernalder*: 183–196. Højbjerg: Nordjylland Historisk Museum and Jysk Arkæologisk Selskab.

Lund Hansen, U. 1987. *Römischer Import im Norden: Warenaustausch zwischen dem Römischen Reich und dem freien Germanien während der Kaiserzeit unter besonderer Berücksichtigung Nordeuropas* (Nordisk Fortidsminder Series C 5). København: Den Kongelige Nordiske Oldskriftselskab.

Madsen, A.T., A.S.Murray, T.J. Andersen and M. Pejrup 2010. Luminescence dating of holocene sedimentary deposits on Rømø, a barrier island in the Wadden sea, Denmark. *Holocene* 20(8): 1247–1256.

Madsen, H.B., A.H. Nørr and K.Aa. Holst 1992. *The Danish Soil Classification. Atlas of Danmark I,3.* Copenhagen: Reitzels Forlag.

Martens, J. 1997. The Pre-Roman Iron Age in Northern Jutland, in J. Martens (ed.) *Chronological Problems of the Pre-Roman Iron Age in Northern Europe* (Arkæologiske Skrifter 7): 107–136. Copenhagen: Danish University Press.

Mikkelsen, D.K. 1999. Single farm or village? Reflections on the settlement structure of the Iron Age and the Viking Period, in C. Fabech and J. Ringtved (eds) *Settlement and Landscape:* 177–193. Aarhus: Jutland Archaeological Society.

Mikkelsen, M. 2012. Development-led archaeology in Denmark, in L. Webley, M. Vander Linden, C. Haselgrove and R. Bradley (eds) *Development-led Archaeology in Northwest Europe:* 117–127. Oxford: Oxbow Books.

Møller, N.A. 2011. Dynamiske bebyggelsesmønstre? Ældre jernalders bebyggelser i landskabet, in N.A. Møller, S.S. Qvistgaard and S.F. Jensen (eds) *Nyt*

fra Vestfronten - Nord- og Vestjyske bebyggelser fra ældre jernalder (Arkæologiske Skrifter 10): 155–171. København: Saxo-instituttet.

Møller, N.A. 2012. På kanten af marsken. Gårde fra yngre bronzealder og ældre jernalder ved Sønderbøl, in C. Ringskou, P. Carstensen, K. Clausen, C.K. Jensen and T. Lorangepp (eds) *Opdatering: Årbog for Museet for Varde By og Omegn & Ringkøbing-Skjern Museum 2011*: 199–208. Varde: Museet for Varde By og Omegn.

Møller, N.A. 2013. Dynamiske bebyggelser. Vestjylland i ældre jernalder. Unpublished PhD dissertation, University of Copenhagen.

Møller, N.A., S.S. Qvistgaard and S.F. Jensen 2011. Bebyggelsesarkæologi Anno 2010, in N.A. Møller, S.S. Qvistgaard and S.F. Jensen (eds) *Nyt fra Vestfronten - Nord- og Vestjyske bebyggelser fra ældre jernalder* (Arkæologiske Skrifter 10): 7–12. København: Saxo-instituttet.

Nielsen, S. 1999. *The Domestic Mode of Production - and Beyond. An archaeological inquiry into urban trends in Denmark, Iceland and Predynastic Egypt* (Nordiske Fortidsminder Serie B 18). København: Det Kongelige Nordiske Oldskriftselskab.

Odgaard, B. 1985. Kulturlandskabets historie I Vestjylland. Foreløbige resultater af nye pollenbotaniske undersøgelser. *Antikvariske studier* 7: 48–83.

Odgaard, B. 2006. Fra bondestenalder til nutid, in G. Larsen and K.S. Jensen (eds) *Naturen i Danmark - Geologien:* 333–359. København: Gyldendals Forlag.

Oldenburger, F. 2016. *Højgård - Iron Age Graves in Southern Jutland.* Haderslev: Museum Sønderjylland – Arkæologi Haderslev.

Pedersen, J.B.T., S. Svinth and J. Bartholdy 2009. Holocene evolution of a drowned melt-water valley in the Danish Wadden Sea. *Quaternary Research* 72(1): 68–79.

Rindel, P.O. 1992. Ældre jernalders bebyggelse i Sønderjylland. Bebyggelsesmønstre ressourceud-nyttelse og center dannelser i ældre jernalder, in U. Lund Hansen and I. Nielsen (eds) *Sjællands Jernalder* (Arkæologiske Skrifter 6): 133–158. København: Arkæologisk Institut.

Rindel, P.O. 1993. Bønder fra stenalder til middelalder ved Nørre Holsted. *Mark and Montre*: 19–27.

Rindel, P.O. 1997. Den keramiske udvikling i sen førromersk og ældre romersk jernalder i Sønderjylland, in J. Martens (ed.) *Chronological Problems of the Pre-Roman Iron Age in Northern Europe* (Arkæologiske Skrifter 7): 159–167. Copenhagen: Danish University Press.

Rindel, P.O. 1999. Development of the village community 500 BC–100 AD in west Jutland, Denmark, in C. Fabech and J. Ringtved (eds) *Settlement and Landscape:* 79–99. Aarhus: Jutland Archaeological Society.

Rindel, P.O. 2001. Building typology as a tool for describing the development of early village communities in the fifth-third century B.C. at Grøntoft, Western Jutland, Denmark, in J.R. Brandt and L. Karlsson (eds) *From Huts to Houses. Transformations of Ancient Societies* (Skrifter utgivna av svenska institutet i Rom, 4°, Vol. 56): 73–87. Stockholm: Paul Aströms Förlag.

Rindel, P.O. 2011. Jernalderbebyggelsen ved Grøntoft i forskningshistorik perspektiv, in N.A. Møller, S.S. Qvistgaard and S.F. Jensen (eds) *Nyt fra Vestfronten - Nord- og Vestjyske bebyggelser fra ældre jernalder* (Arkæologiske Skrifter 10): 99–110. København: Saxo-instituttet.

Rømer, J.R. and M. Stenak 2009. Landbrugssystemer i AGRAR 2000 søområderne i perioden ca. 1600–1900, in B.V. Odgaard and J.R. Rømer (eds) *Danke landbrusglandskaber gennem 2000 år. Fra digevoldinger til støtteordninger:* 205–252. Aarhus: Aarhus Universitetsforlag.

Terp, A. 2015. Beretning for HBV 274 Solar II. Unpublished excavation report, Museet på Sønderskov.

Thomsen, N. 1965. Myrtue, Et gårdsanlæg fra jernalder. *Kuml* 1964: 15–30.

Webley, L. 2008. *Iron Age Households: Structure and Practice in Western Denmark, 500 BC – AD 200.* Højbjerg: Jutland Archaeological Society.

Chapter 11

Nucleated Settlements as Assemblages:
A Regional Network Approach to Built Environments

Francesca Fulminante

Abstract

A long tradition of studies has greatly advanced our knowledge of urbanization processes in southern Etruria and *Latium vetus* from the Final Bronze Age to the Archaic Period. What happened and when is well established. How and why still await answers. By studying nucleated settlements and their communities as assemblages and by adopting a network perspective to analyze cultural interactions and transportation infrastructures in Central Italy between the end of the Final Bronze Age and the end of the Archaic Period, it is possible to answer long-standing historical questions, such as how the Latin and Etruscan polities actually worked and possibly why a smaller but more hierarchical and internally well-connected *Latium vetus* prevailed over a larger but less efficiently connected and more heterarchical Etruria.

Introduction

Knowledge of urbanization processes in southern Etruria and *Latium vetus* from the end of the Bronze Age to the end of the Archaic Period is rather advanced, thanks to a long tradition of research (Figure 11.1). Within this time frame, mainly during the Iron Age and the Orientalizing Age, the Italian Peninsula underwent major changes that led to the differentiation of the rather homogeneous Apennine culture on the whole peninsula into various regional material cultures, possibly corresponding to various ethnic groups (for a traditional approach, see Pallottino 1991; for a more recent discussion, see Fulminante 2012a). These were organized as independent polities, mainly consisting of a religious league and/or confederations of city-states, in accordance with the model of peer-polity interactions elaborated by Renfrew and Cherry (1986).

During this time, the modern region of Lazio, north of the Tiber River, was inhabited by people identified by Villanovan material culture, who later became the Etruscans, while the region to the south of the Tiber was inhabited by the Latins (Latin culture subdivided in Latial Period I to IVB), who later became the Romans. The two regions had very similar beginnings and parallel development, but with very different outcomes. Rome and the Latins prevailed over the Etruscans, the reasons for which remain unresolved.

By focusing on nucleated settlements as assemblages and by adopting a systemic network approach to analyze transportation and communication routes and the cultural relations that connected the inhabitants of these settlements, this paper will shed new light on the power dynamics that regulated interactions among the Latin and Etruscan communities. The outcome is a better understanding of how they operated and why in the end they had such different and contrasting trajectories, with Rome and *Latium vetus* prevailing over Etruria. In this way, this study illustrates the benefit of regional-scale, diachronic analyses in the exploration of changes in sociopolitical configurations over time.

Current Knowledge on Latin and Etruscan Iron Age Communities and Identity through Settlement and Funerary Evidence

Regarding settlement dynamics, our understanding of the process of nucleation and centralization of settlements between the end of the Bronze Age and the beginning of the Early Iron Age in southern Etruria and *Latium vetus*, on the large plateaus later occupied by the cities of the Orientalizing Age and the Archaic Period, is now well established (Table 11.1; Bietti Sestieri 1997; Bonghi Jovino 2005; di Gennaro and Guidi 2000, 2009; di Gennaro and Peroni 1986; Fulminante 2014: 44–47; Guidi 2006, 2008; Pacciarelli 2001: 119–136; Peroni 1989, 2000; Vanzetti 2002, 2004).

This process is generally considered more rapid and revolutionary in southern Etruria, where small, dispersed villages of the previous Bronze Age (average of 5–6 ha and sometimes up to 20–25 ha) were abandoned during Final Bronze Age 3, between the second half of the 11th and the first half of the 10th centuries BC. At the same time, the big plateaus of usually 100 to 200 ha, that later became historical cities (Veio, Tarquinia, Caere, Vulci, Bisenzio, and Orvieto), were extensively occupied in a patchwork pattern, with hut compounds interspersed with gardens and allotments. It has been calculated that on average 15–20 villages were

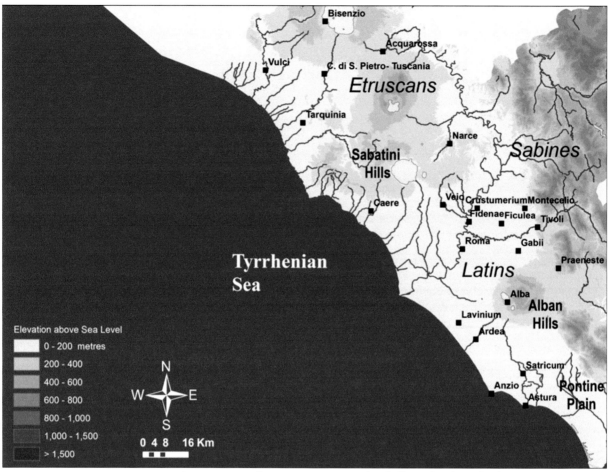

Figure 11.1. Southern Etruria and *Latium vetus* in Central Italy (figure by the author).

abandoned for the formation of each large, proto-urban center (di Gennaro and Guidi 2000; di Gennaro and Peroni 1986; Guidi 2008: 176–177; Pacciarelli 2001: 128–136).

In *Latium vetus*, the nucleation process was more gradual and slightly delayed. Occupation of large plateaus occurred during Latial phases IIA and IIB, between the second half of the 10th and the first half of the 9th centuries BC, and oftentimes plateaus on the side of small *acropoleis* already were occupied during the previous Bronze Age (di Gennaro and Guidi 2000; Guidi 2008; Pacciarelli 2001: 119–128). Recent studies, however, have emphasized that in both regions, there were more specific cases and exceptions to the general trends than previously thought, and therefore, the two regions were probably more similar than previously assumed (Fulminante and Stoddart 2013). Later, during an advanced stage of the Early Iron Age (Early Iron Age 1 Late, around the first half of the 9th century BC), secondary centers were founded by the proto-urban centers both in southern Etruria and in *Latium vetus*. This process created a settlement hierarchy of two–three tiers, with the primary settlements generally larger than 100 ha in Etruria and typically larger than 40–50 ha in *Latium vetus*, but sometimes also between 25

and 50 ha, and smaller, secondary settlements always smaller than 15–20 ha (Fulminante 2014; Pacciarelli 2001: 115–136).

Following this, during Early Iron Age 2, between the second half of the 9th and the first half of the 8th centuries BC, a series of changes occurred that concerns a better definition of the spatial extent and internal organization of large proto-urban centers progressing toward urbanization. In particular, around the middle of the 8th century BC, it is possible to detect: 1) a demographic growth of emerging urban centers testified by an increased intensity of settlement sites on plateaus (for example, Cerveteri: Iaia and Mandolesi 2010); 2) a progressive definition of the spatial extents of emerging urban centers, with a) the concentration of sites within the limits of plateaus and the abandonment of sites on external slopes (for example, Gabii: Guaitoli 1981); and b) the realization of symbolic (for example, Rome: Carandini and Carafa 2000) or more functional fortifications (Baratti *et al.* 2008; Boitani *et al.* 2008; Fontaine 2002–2003; Moretti Sgubini 2006); 3) the internal organization of these emerging urban centers, with the creation of communal spaces for assemblies and communal foci of cult activity as well as the construction of special, larger residencies probably occupied by royal families or aristocratic elites (for Tarquinia, see Bonghi Jovino 2008; for Rome, see Carandini 2007).

At this time, around the middle of the 8th century BC, there is also a more dense and diffuse occupation of the territory by urban elites, with small aristocratic settlements dispersed across the countryside that led to a settlement hierarchy of three–four tiers. In this settlement hierarchy, the primary settlements of various orders were generally larger than 100 ha, but sometimes between 25 and 100 ha, the secondary settlements always were smaller than 15–20 ha, and there were small, high-status settlements in the countryside commonly indicated by small burial grounds (De Santis 1997; Fulminante 2014: 47; Iaia and Mandolesi 2010). By the end of the 8th century BC, the urban centers are fully defined, and they will be consolidated and monumentalized only during the later Orientalizing Age and Archaic Period, between the 8th and the 6th centuries BC (Carandini 2003, 2007; Cifani 2014; Fulminante 2014: 249–260; Hopkins 2014).

When considering the development of social hierarchies and the construction of community identity as mirrored in the funerary evidence (Table 11.2), it is generally agreed that the princely burials of the late 8th and early 7th centuries BC had an important precedent in the warrior burials and rich female burials interred during the entire 8th century BC. Furthermore, the emergence of princely burials represents only the final point of a long process of social differentiation, the early stages of which might have occurred as early as the Final Bronze Age (FBA; De Santis 2005; Fulminante 2003; Fulminante and Stoddart 2013; Guidi and Santoro 2008; Seubern 2005).

In fact, important studies by De Santis and Bietti Sestieri have identified religious and political leaders in a few male burials of the Latial Period I unearthed in the territory of Rome (for example, Quadrato di Torre Spaccata and Santa Palomba; Bietti Sestieri and De Santis 2003; De Santis 2011). These individuals had a full suit of armor, including double shields, greaves, spears, and swords, and numerous pottery items as well as cult and prestige objects, such as a knife, an incense burner, possibly a holmos, and a cart.

Similarly, it is now widely agreed that the low degree of funerary variability in Latin burials dating to Latial periods IIA and IIB, or in earlier Villanovan cemeteries, is probably due to an egalitarian ideology rather than an actual absence of social stratification (Fulminante 2003; Pacciarelli 2001; Vanzetti 1996: 175). A new discovery in this regard comes again from the work of De Santis (2011: 44–51), who excavated and published Tomb 6 from Tenuta Cancelliera at Santa Palomba. Dated to Latial Period IIB, Tomb 6 was equipped with spectacular objects, such as a complete suit of armor, including double shields, greaves, spears, and swords, an axe, working tools, a cart, small human figures, and a gold nail. Similarly, the populist and egalitarian ideology of the city, fully developed under the tyrannical regime of the Tarquins, imposed the reduction to the complete absence of grave goods in Latin burials during the Recent Orientalizing Age and the Archaic Period (Bartoloni *et al.* 2009; Colonna 1977).

Methodology I: A Regional Network Approach to Settlements and Built Environments as Assemblages

The study of the relations between material culture, interactions, movement, and space at nucleated settlements, both within and between sites, is a long-standing problem in archaeology that is frequently addressed by discussing issues of scale (for example, see Lock and Molyneaux 2006). Conventionally, this problem is approached by incorporating two or more distinct levels (micro vs. macro, or a series of nested scales). However, the ontological turn and the introduction of the concept of assemblages (De Landa 2006) suggest that the property of the whole emerges from interactions between the constituent parts at each scale. Moreover, while the simplest entities can be conceived as assemblages of some sort, conversely, assemblages can be considered as entities.

Building on these concepts, Marston, Jones, and Woodward suggest a redefinition of the concept of 'site' as an '*emergent property of its interacting human and non-human inhabitants*' (2005: 425). They argue that sites are entities that do not precede the connectivity that brings them into reality, either internally (intrasite) or across networks (intersite). This, in turn, is consistent with recent conceptualizations of networks as self-organizing systems (for an overview of complex networks and their properties, see Newman 2003).

Following these perspectives, this paper adopts a systemic approach to study nucleated settlements as emerging properties of interaction and utilizes a regional perspective to analyze cultural interactions as well as transportation and communication infrastructures in southern Etruria and *Latium vetus*. The goal is to explore transformations in sociopolitical settings and to understand why these two regions had so similar trajectories but also so different outputs.

The networks of communication infrastructures and cultural/commercial relations have been considered as global systems and the settlements as assemblages that are produced by interactions among their inhabitants within their built environments, but that can also represent entities themselves within the wider network at the global macroregional level. These global, regional networks have been studied by characterization

Pre-Urban	Proto-Urban			Urban		
Final Bronze Age 1–2 (Proto-Villanovan)	Final Bronze Age 3 (Latial Period I)	Early Iron Age 1 Early (Latial Period IIA)	Early Iron Age 1 Late (Latial Period IIB)	Early Iron Age 2 (Latial Period IIIA-IIIB)	Early and Middle Orientalizing Age (Latial Period IVA)	Recent Orientalizing Age (Latial Period IVB) & Archaic Period
1325/1300–1050/1025 BC	1050/1025–950/925 BC	950/925–900 BC	900–850/825 BC	850/825–750/725 BC	750/725–640/630 BC	640/630–509 BC
Dispersed villages	Nucleation and centralization of settlements	Large proto-urban centres		Definition of limits or emerging urban centers and internal organization	Urban realization	Urban monumentalization
			Foundation of secondary centers	Capillary colonization of the countryside		
Settlement hierarchy of 1-2 tiers	Settlement hierarchy of 1-2 or 2-3 tiers	Settlement hierarchy of 2-3 or 3-4 tiers		Settlement hierarchy of 3-4 or 4-5 tiers		

Table 11.1. Settlement dynamics in Central Italy between the end of the Final Bronze Age and the end of the Archaic Period.

Pre-Urban	Proto-Urban			Urban		
Final Bronze Age 1–2 (Proto-Villanovan)	Final Bronze Age 3 (Latial Period I)	Early Iron Age 1 Early (Latial Period IIA)	Early Iron Age 1 Late (Latial Period IIB)	Early Iron Age 2 (Latial Period IIIA-IIIB)	Early and Middle Orientalizing Age (Latial Period IVA)	Recent Orientalizing Age (Latial Period IVB) & Archaic Period
1325/1300–1050/1025 BC	1050/1025–950/925 BC	950/925–900 BC	900–850/825 BC	850/825–750/725 BC	750/725–640/630 BC	640/630–509 BC
Incineration egalitarian ritual	Emerging burials	Shared symbols of power		Warriors and rich female burials	Princely burials	Reduction and disappearance of grave goods
Generally small groups of burials with scarce differentiation (e.g., Tolfa-Allumiere) and only rarely with vertical roles (Ardea, Campo del Fico)	Political and religious leaders (Latium) (complete suit of armor, knife, cart, incense-burner, holmos?). Rich infant burial (Le Caprine Tomb 5, *Latium vetus*) with spinning and weaving instruments and knife	Prestige and power symbols for male burials, spinning and weaving tools for female burials, hut-urn, statuettes, knife distributed among various individuals (Osteria dell'Osa). Exceptional Tomb 6 Tenuta Cancelliera (Santa Palomba): offensive and defensive weapons, cart, statuettes, working tools, knife, gold, many vases		Warrior graves with complete suit of armor and prestige goods (flabellum, incense-burner, metal vases, etc.). Rich female burials with many ornaments, bronze cist, spinning and weaving tools (Etruria and Latium)	Princely burials with hundreds of pottery vases, precious material vases and ornaments (gold, silver, amber, ivory), drinking sets, oriental power symbols (flabellum, footrest, and sceptre) (Etruria and Latium)	Drastic reduction until complete absence of grave goods; family chamber tombs (especially Latium and progressively also in Etruria)

Table 11.2. Social dynamics as mirrored by the funerary evidence in Central Italy between the end of the Final Bronze Age and the end of the Archaic Period.

by means of indices or metrics as well as measures that evaluate specific behaviors or properties of the networks and allow quantitative-comparative studies (for an example of a review article that compares networks, including different disciplines, from a structural point of view, see Boccaletti *et al.* 2006).

More specifically, a number of common and basic (network) metrics have been utilized to characterize networks and study cultural interactions: 1) *Average distance* measures the average path length among all reachable sites in terms of the number of links (not geographical distance); 2) *Average degree* measures the average number of links of each node, that is, the average number of its neighbors; 3) *Network density* is the ratio of the number of links in the networks to the maximum number of connections that can be built on the same set of nodes, that is, the number of node pairs; 4) *Degree centralization*; and 5) *Betweenness centralization* indicate the variation in the degree centrality (defined above) and betweenness centrality (the proportion of all geodesic that is the shortest paths—number of links in an unweighted network or smallest sum of weights of the links in a weighted network—between pairs of other vertices that include that vertex) of the vertices divided by the maximum degree centrality and betweenness centrality that is possible in a network of the same size, respectively (De Nooy *et al.* 2012).

The present analysis aimed to compare the mode of circulation of goods and crafts in two regions to find similarities and/or differences in their behavior as systems. This first stage of this part of the research was an exploratory investigation, and therefore, simple and basic measures have been chosen for the analysis. Some of those measures were linked to one another, and in general, depended upon the density of the networks, which differed in the two regions (see below).

The communication and transportation infrastructure networks have already been discussed in previous works (Fulminante 2012b; Fulminante *et al.* 2016) and a few, more refined measures have been adopted in collaboration with other colleagues to characterize the different properties and behaviors of geographical networks. Most of these measures described briefly in Table 11.3, including average node strength <s>, average edge length <le>, average clustering coefficient <c>, global efficiency (Eg), local efficiency (El), and smallest positive value of the eigenvalue or algebraic connectivity (Lw), have been more extensively illustrated also from a mathematical point of view in another paper (Fulminante *et al.* 2017: for the Laplacian eigenvalue, we refer directly to Van Mieghem 2012). Based on these measures, terrestrial and fluvial communication networks have been characterized and compared in Etruria and *Latium vetus* to evaluate both the efficiency and the resilience of these two transportation and communication systems.

Finally, some network modeling of the terrestrial connection routes between settlements was performed to investigate the power dynamics behind the creation and maintenance of this particular aspect of the interaction between people and their environment. Terrestrial infrastructure communication routes were influenced by the natural environment, and their creation and maintenance required a certain degree of cooperation and agreement among the settlements; therefore, they can provide information regarding political and social interaction.

First, network analysis techniques were used to characterize the terrestrial communication and transportation systems of Etruria and *Latium vetus* between the beginning of the Early Iron Age and the end of the Archaic Period by utilizing the measures described above. Then, based on different hypotheses, models were devised, and finally, it was verified which model would reproduce better the empirical networks. In this way, it was possible to get an understanding of the principles and mechanisms of the origin of their

1	Average node strength <s>	Average of the sum of the length of the links connected to a site.
2	Average edge length <le>	The mean value of the weights of all the links that are present in the system.
3	Average clustering coefficient <c>	Among all the potential links between the neighbors of a node, the clustering coefficient indicates the proportion of them that actually exists. By averaging this ratio over the whole set of sites, we obtain a global indicator of the density of closed triangles in the network.
4	Global efficiency (Eg)	The efficiency of communication between two sites is defined by the length of the shortest path (in the network) between them divided by the geodesic distance between their location. The global efficiency is calculated as an average on all pair of nodes.
5	Local efficiency (El)	The capacity of the network to react to a damage at the local level. In particular, the local efficiency of a node defines how efficiently information is shared and moved among neighbors if that node is eliminated.
6	Smallest positive value of the eigen-value or algebraic connectivity (Lw)	The capacity of the network to react to a damage at the global level. Its resilience.

Table 11.3. Measures selected to characterize the empirical networks.

evolution. The principles adopted for the construction of the models are illustrated also from a mathematical point of view in another work to which we refer for details (Prignano *et al.* 2019).

By measuring, quantifying, and comparing the characteristics and behaviors of the cultural networks (based on trade and circulation of objects), the geographical networks (based on fluvial and terrestrial communication routes), and the results of the modeling that provides clues to the political and social organization of the two regions, it is possible to evaluate whether Latin and Etruscan communities behaved similarly or differently within their own regions. Furthermore, it is possible to evaluate whether any one of them had a cultural, economic, or infrastructural advantage over the other, and to start discussing on a quantitative basis which of these factors might have been more influential in the final success of Rome and the Latin communities over the rival Etruria.

Methodology II: How the Networks Were Constructed and Which Data Were Used

Settlements

For this study, settlements in southern Etruria and *Latium vetus* dating from the beginning of the Early Iron Age to the end of the Archaic Period have been considered. *Latium vetus* settlements had already been discussed in another work by Fulminante (2014) and in important publications by Alessandri (2007, 2013). For southern Etruria, the *Repertorio dei Siti Preistorici e Protostorici della Regione Lazio* (Belardelli *et al.* 2007), the *Dictionary of the Etruscans* (Stoddart 2009), and the work by Rendeli (1993) on the territorial organization of southern Etruria in the Orientalizing Age and in the Archaic Period are fundamental. In addition, for this study, the list of settlements has been updated based on more recent publications in *Studi Etruschi*, some comprehensive conference proceedings (e.g., *Preistoria e Protostoria in Etruria, Annali della Fondazione per il Museo 'C. Faina'*), and exhibition catalogs (e.g., Della Fina and Pellegrini 2013).

The settlements incorporated in this research are primarily known from either excavations or surveys, and geophysical prospection has been used in recent years by teams led by the British School at Rome and the University of Siena. However, the geophysical data, which provide new information especially about the built environment and the organization of space within nucleated settlements as well as open up new perspectives for multiscalar analyses, are partially unpublished and have not been considered at this stage of research.

Regarding settlements documented by excavations or surveys, some specific assumptions have been made,

following a long tradition of research in Central Italy. According to these assumptions, settlements are hypothesized in the case of coherent orographical units even if only a few sherds were found. This applies mainly to Bronze Age and Early Iron Age sites, for which evidence is scarcer. In addition, some other sites identified by using literary sources but for which archaeological evidence is not available have also been included in this study. This particularly applies to the Latin region, rather than the Etruscan one, for which literary sources are available.

We have considered the maximum period during which settlements co-existed without major changes and distinguished five time-slices, including Early Iron Age 1 Early (EIA1E; 950/925–900 BC), Early Iron Age 1 Late (EIA1L; 900–850/825 BC), Early Iron Age 2 (EIA2; 850/825–730/720 BC), Orientalizing Age (OA; 730/720–580 BC), and Archaic Period (AA; 580–500 BC).

Geographical Links

Both terrestrial and fluvial communications have been considered in this study. To reconstruct the terrestrial and the fluvial routes, a bidirectional link has been established between two settlements directly adjacent to a terrestrial or a fluvial route without any settlement in between. The fluvial routes are based on digital data of modern rivers provided by Regione Lazio and published on the Ministero dell'Ambiente website (http://www.pcn.minambiente.it/viewer/). While some studies are available on the changes of the Tiber River route through time (for a reconstruction of the paleoriver of the Tiber with references to the modern and ancient coastline, see Alessandri 2007, 2013), to our knowledge, studies have not been published in respect to the regional level. To eliminate recent channels and irrigation works and to obtain the network most likely to have been present in Antiquity, the modern rivers were selected with a query performed in GIS regarding the superimposition of modern rivers and alluvial deposits because these are the channels that were most likely present in ancient times.

The terrestrial communication and transportation routes were reconstructed based on hypotheses advanced by various scholars. For *Latium vetus*, the reconstruction by Quilici and Quilici Gigli elaborated at the regional level for the Archaic Period by Colonna (1977) was used. For the Etruscan region, similar comprehensive studies are still lacking, although important work on road cuts was carried out by Tuppi (2014). Various studies have therefore been considered (Bonghi Jovino 2008; Brocato 2000; Enei 2001; Potter 1985; Schiappelli 2008; Tartara 1999; Zifferero 1995). The different interpretations were also tested by considering their alignment with settlement sites discovered more recently, after the publication of those investigations.

Both settlements and communication routes have been considered constant within each time-slice. In this sense, the analysis concerned five static networks rather than an evolving system. However, this does not mean that the system was actually constant during the five distinguished periods. Some sites were abandoned and others were founded, and therefore, not only did the routes change but also the settlements. Finally, in order to consider the geography of the territory, links between settlements have been weighted based on the linear distance between each pair of settlements. We chose this simple but reasonable approach because the studied region is spatially limited and relatively homogeneous, with scarce orographic variability.

Artifacts

Similarly, the spatial distributions of ceramic and metal products from the end of the Bronze Age to the end of the Archaic Period, as well as luxury items and architectural decoration types for the later Orientalizing Age and Archaic Period, were used to reconstruct cultural interactions in the two regions during the considered periods. In particular, several comprehensive typological studies concerning various classes of materials, detailed in Tables 11.4 and 11.5, were fundamental sources to establish cultural and economic links among settlements.

During this study, only materials published in these sources have been considered, thus the distribution patterns could be biased by unpublished materials. Even in the cases of published materials, biases could occur due to uneven density of study or excavation among sites. However, these biases are relatively less important when looking for general trends between the two studied regions because both would be similarly affected by them.

Table 11.4. Pottery production from the Final Bronze Age to the end of the Archaic Period, and luxury items and architectural decorations of the Orientalizing Age and Archaic Period considered in this study.

Period	Class of material	Reference
Final Bronze Age	Pottery	Barbaro 2010
Early Iron Age	Pottery	Ampolo *et al.* 1980
Final Bronze Age, Early Iron Age	Pottery	Bartoloni *et al.* 1987
Orientalizing Age	Pottery	Ten Kortenaar 2011
Orientalizing Age	Pottery	Neri 2010
Orientalizing Age	Pottery	Biella 2014
Orientalizing Age	Pottery	Micozzi 1994
Orientalizing Age, Archaic Period	Luxury goods	Giovannelli 2015
Orientalizing Age, Archaic Period	Pottery	Szilágyi 1992–1998
Orientalizing Age, Archaic Period	Architectural decorations	Winter 2009
Archaic Period	Architectural decorations	Shoe Meritt and Edlund-Berry 2000

Period	Class of material	Reference
Final Bronze Age	Fibulae	Savella 2015
Final Bronze Age, Early Iron Age, Orientalizing Age	Razors	Bianco Peroni 1979
Final Bronze Age, Early Iron Age, Orientalizing Age	Swords	Bianco Peroni 1970
Final Bronze Age, Early Iron Age, Orientalizing Age	Knives	Bianco Peroni 1976
Final Bronze Age, Early Iron Age, Orientalizing Age	Pins	Carancini 1975
Final Bronze Age, Early Iron Age, Orientalizing Age	Axes	Carancini 1984
Early Iron Age	Various objects	Iaia 2005
Early Iron Age, Orientalizing Age	Various objects	Ampolo *et al.* 1980
Orientalizing Age	Ribbed bowls	Sciacca 2005
Orientalizing Age	Shields	Geiger 1994
Orientalizing Age	Breast plates	Tomedi 2000
Orientalizing Age	Flasks	Marzoli 1989
Early Iron Age, Orientalizing Age	Horse bits	von Hase 1969
Final Bronze Age, Early Iron Age, Orientalizing Age, Archaic Period	Wheeled vehicles	Woytowitsch 1978

Table 11.5. Metal production from the Final Bronze Age to the end of the Archaic Period considered in this study.

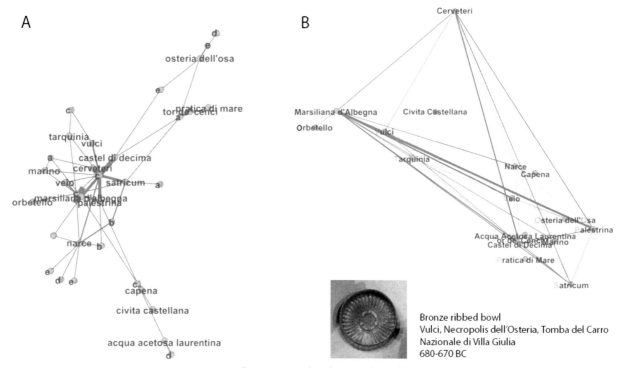

Figure 11.2. Etruscan and Latin networks of Orientalizing bronze ribbed bowls.
A: Bimodal; B: Unimodal derived from bimodal and georeferenced (figure by the author).

Cultural-Economical Links

To obtain the Latin and Etruscan cultural networks, in the first instance, bimodal networks of sites and types of objects were created for the Etruscan and Latin regions together. In bimodal networks, each type is linked by a line to the site in which it has been attested (Figure 11.2A). Secondly, bimodal networks of object types and sites were reduced to unimodal networks using the function NET>TRANSFORM>2-MODES to 1-MODES in Pajek (Figure 11.2B; De Nooy *et al.* 2012: 122). This function produces a link among those settlements that have in common the same type of pot or other object. This methodology might seem simplistic and reductive by assuming contact or cultural transmission in the presence of simple common behaviors, that is, adoption of the same object and/or way of producing an object. In a paper on cultural transmission and identity creation, Da Vela (2014–2015) used the similarity coefficient of Jaccard to create unimodal networks of settlements from bimodal networks of settlements and objects/cultural behaviors.

The focus of this exploratory analysis of cultural networks is not on cultural transmission but on defining measures that allow the comparisons of systems of circulations at the global scale. Therefore, the traditional assumption that two places that have the same object/style/technology must have been in contact somehow, even if the mean and possible model points of these contacts cannot be identified, is still valid and sufficient for the purpose of this paper. By reducing the network from bimodal to unimodal, it was possible to measure and classify them according to different characterizing indexes and measures detailed above.

The time-slices considered for the cultural networks (i.e., FBA, EIA, OA, and AA) are less detailed chronologically than the ones used for the transportation networks, and the EIA is considered as a single phase because we did not want to fragment the evidence too much; however, a more refined distinction between EIA1 and EIA2 would also be possible. To compare the two studied regions through time, all types of objects related to each of these time-slice periods were grouped for each region separately, so that for each period we had, respectively, an Etruscan and a Latin network based on all different types of objects considered (Figure 11.3).

Analysis and Discussion of the Results

Cultural Interactions

As discussed in the previous section, networks were created both for the Latin and Etruscan regions based on the commonality of a number of different pottery and metal products, luxury items, and architectural decorations to characterize them for comparisons of how they worked in different periods. Unfortunately, a sufficient dataset concerning the Archaic Period (AA) is lacking for the Latin region, but a comparison is still possible in regard to the other periods.

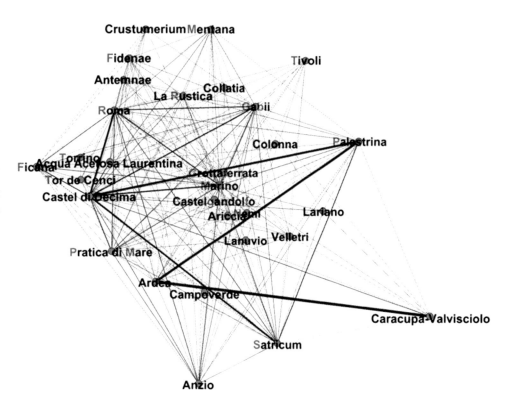

Figure 11.3. Orientalizing Age Latin network. Unimodal georeferenced network derived from a bimodal network of sites and all types of objects combined (figure by the author).

The average distance is usually very small. The maximum value is just above two in the Final Bronze Age (FBA) in both regions and tends to decrease with time, although there is a small relative increase in the Orientalizing Age (OA). The average degree tends to increase steadily in both regions. In Etruria, the increase is more gradual and becomes substantial only in the AA. In *Latium vetus*, the increase was already more dramatic from the Early Iron Age (EIA). The density of the networks also tends to increase but in a less homogeneous way. In both regions, it seems to be slightly lower in the OA than in the EIA, and increases again in the AA at least for Etruria, where we have data available. In absolute terms, the density of the Latin networks is always higher than the Etruscan networks.

Degree centralization increases constantly in both regions. In absolute terms, it is higher in Etruria than in Latium during the EIA, and slightly higher in Latium than in Etruria in the OA. Betweenness centralization decreases drastically in both regions from the FBA to the following periods. It is generally remarkably higher in Etruria than in *Latium vetus*.

These analyses seem to indicate that the circulation of goods in the two regions was similar. Both regions appear to have become increasingly more connected over time, with sites connected to more distant sites (i.e., a decrease of average distance), and with an increased degree of connectivity for each site (i.e., increase of average degree). Variation in the number of

links for each site (i.e., degree centralization) increases through time, which possibly indicates a more uneven number of sites with many connections or with very few connections in the later period. Variation in betweenness centrality decreases drastically from the FBA to the following period, possibly indicating that there are fewer bottleneck sites; that is, sites with high betweenness that are passed by frequently by an ideal traveler moving through the system. In general, connectedness seems to have increased steadily over time for both regions, although the intensity of connections seems to have been higher in *Latium vetus* (i.e., density; Figure 11.4).

Fluvial and Terrestrial Transportation Networks: Efficiency Measures

To compare the efficiency and functionality of the communication and transportation networks of southern Etruria and *Latium vetus*, a few classifying measures, such as global efficiency, the smaller positive eigenvalue or algebraic connectivity, local efficiency, and average weighted degree, were calculated for the fluvial and terrestrial route networks of the two regions and were compared to one another. In all these measures, a weight was also introduced to the links, based on the geodesic distance between sites.

At the macroregional level, global efficiency shows a clear advantage of the fluvial route system and a small advantage of the terrestrial route system of *Latium vetus*

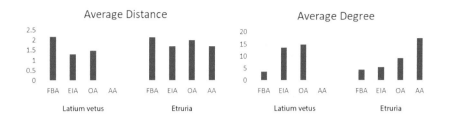

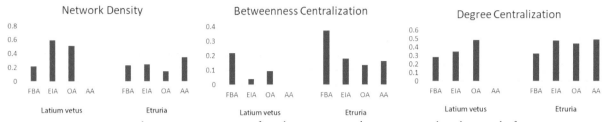

Figure 11.4. Characteristic measures of southern Etruria and *Latium vetus* cultural networks from the Final Bronze Age to the Archaic Period: average distance, average degree, network density, betweenness centralization, and degree centralization (figure by the author).

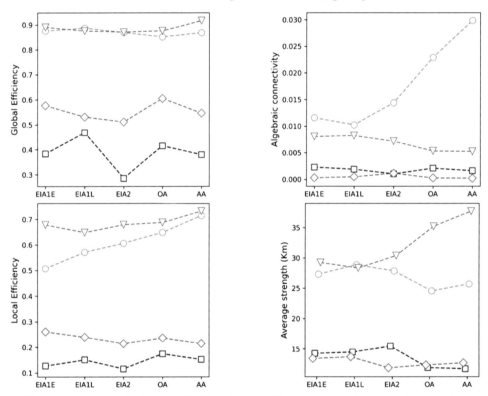

Figure 11.5. Efficiency measures calculated on fluvial and terrestrial routes networks in Etruria and *Latium vetus*: global efficiency, algebraic connectivity, local efficiency, and average weighted degree (figure by I. Morer and L. Prignano).

over Etruria; on the opposite, the algebraic connectivity clearly shows a better performance of the terrestrial route system and only a little advantage of the fluvial system of *Latium vetus* in comparison to Etruria.

At the local level, the efficiency of the fluvial communication system in *Latium vetus* is higher, while the small advantage of the terrestrial route system in this region declines during later periods; on the contrary, the average weighted degree shows a clear advantage of the terrestrial communication and transportation system in *Latium vetus* (Figure 11.5).

Terrestrial Routes Transportation Networks: Modeling

To identify the principles behind the creation and maintenance of terrestrial communication routes in Etruria and *Latium vetus* and better understand the sociopolitical organization behind them, the networks have been characterized through the measures outlined in the methodology section. Then, three different types of mechanistic network models have been built according to specifically defined principles and the same characterizing measures have been calculated on the resulting networks to see which ones would fit better the empirical networks and explain the principles behind them.

In the construction of the models, the settlements and their locations are fixed starting points. The models are built by a series of commands/rules that starting from a certain number of disconnected sites (i.e., the settlements of the empirical networks) that defined which links would be created or not. Model LL (local-local) implies that every node tries to connect to the highest number of nearest nodes possible, with no specific strategy, but in a sort of blind competition, until its resources—the total length of the terrestrial routes in the system, which is a fixed point in the empirical network—is exhausted. In this model, the nodes, which can be considered as agents, are aware only of their direct neighbors.

In Model GL (global-local), the nodes-agents are slightly smarter and prefer to connect to those neighbors that are relatively more difficult to reach, and for which there does not already exist another reasonable route. In this way, the nodes-agents are aware of routes that exist and also had a greater distance than a neighboring node; that is, routes that are passing through a third node (and possibly fourth, fifth, etc.). The mechanism (i.e., basic competition) is the same as in Model One, but the principle is different because each node selects the new node to connect to based on geodesic distance as well as knowledge of the entire system.

Model EE (equitable efficiency) adopts the same criteria as Model GL, but the decision about which new connection to create is a global one. In other words, a level of 'cooperation' is introduced in the basic principle of coordinated prioritization of new connection creation: each node-agent has its individual needs and priorities, but the new links are created where they are most needed at the global level. The new connections are those that exist between very distant nodes in comparison to their geographical distance. The information available to the nodes-agents is the same as in Model Two, but their use is different. A global priority is negotiated that does not pursue local or individual interests.

As long as it concerns southern Etruria, Models LL and GL capture some of the characteristics of the empirical networks, but miss some others. Model Three, in contrast, can reproduce with good accuracy all relevant characteristics for all periods considered, a part with a small difference in the clustering coefficient: 1) decrease of average length; 2) non-monotonous increase of clustering coefficient; 3) constant global efficiency; 4) monotonous increase of local efficiency.[1] Differently from Etruria, in *Latium*

vetus, each model reproduces some of the trends of the figures of the empirical networks, but misses, always, some others. Therefore, Model GL, in which the nodes-agents pursued personal interests of improving connectivity, seems to work better in *Latium vetus* than in Etruria.

However, Models GL and EE, which work for southern Etruria, are not able to predict the situation existing in *Latium vetus* of some sites with many distant links, such as Rome. Nonetheless, when Model EE is slightly modified with the addition of the preferential attachment (EE-PA), according to which the 'rich gets richer,' that is, the sites that have more and longer links, grow more and, in turn, attract more links in a feedback loop, then the model can reproduce the empirical situation with Rome and its numerous links to neighboring sites (Figure 11.6; for a more detailed explanation of the models and a comparison between Etruria and Latium, see also Fulminante *et al.* 2020).

Comparison and Discussion of the Results

The analysis of cultural interactions among Latin and Etruscan communities is still at a preliminary stage. Some specific aspects of the methodology must still be improved, and specific trends associated with different characterizing measures have not been fully evaluated yet. However, for the comparison of different levels of interactions among communities and their built environment, which is the scope of this paper, it is possible and important to notice that both regions show a very similar pattern of circulations, and therefore, the way in which they interacted in terms of trade and exchange of goods is very similar. This similarity is not surprising given the markedly analogous developments of these communities based on settlement patterns and material culture associated with funerary ideology and identity. It is more striking though if we consider that the results might be skewed by the uneven intensity of research and study at the different sites.

The analysis of the terrestrial and fluvial transportation and communication routes showed that the two regions were also very similar at the infrastructural level. Local efficiency, global efficiency, and average weighted degree are all very similar, probably indicating that the two regions, very similar also morphologically, had probably similar infrastructure systems too. Interestingly, the resilience of the Latin system seems to have been much better than that of the Etruscan system.

This result appears to be consistent with the modeling results, according to which balanced coordinated decision-making processes were shaping the route

---

[1] Note that the average weighted degree remains the same both for empirical networks and those created by the models because it is based on the total length of all links divided by the number of settlements that are both fixed input points in each model.

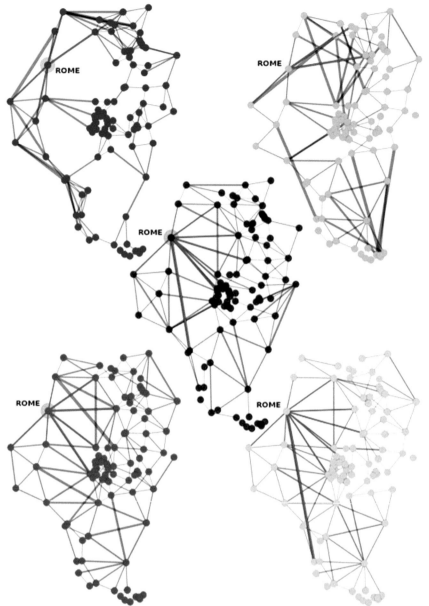

Figure 11.6. Comparison between the Latin empirical network (black) with Model LL (blue), Model GL (green), and Model EE (red) and the modification of Model EE-PA (yellow) (adapted from Fulminante *et al.* 2017, where Models LL, GL, and EE are referred as 1, 2, and 3).

network in Etruria, whereas in *Latium vetus*, an unbalanced dynamics of power constituted the most likely underlying mechanism. As shown by previous analyses based on rank-size calculations, while Etruria was featured by a few important and competing centers with equal power, none of which was able to dominate the others, in *Latium vetus*, the dramatic growth of Rome by the end of Latial Period IIA and the beginning of Latial Period IIB dramatically changed the dynamics in the region, with Rome as a more densely populated urban site, richer of interactions both within and outside, and therefore, probably much stronger than other settlements (Fulminante 2014).

Recent comparative work on urbanism in the modern and ancient world has shown that a clear relationship exists between the dimension of a site, the density of its internal interaction and exchanges, and its economic outputs (Ortman *et al.* 2016). The results of this paper

suggest that this model might successfully be applied to the case of Rome and the surrounding regions as well both at the beginning of its history and during later times. This hypothesis will be tested in the future.

Conclusions

Between the end of the Final Bronze Age and the end of the Archaic Period, southern Etruria and *Latium vetus*—together with some other regions in Early Iron Age Italy, including northern Etruria, Veneto, Campania, and some areas in southern Italy— underwent similar developments and transformations in their settlement, social, economic, and political organizations that led to the formation of the first city-states in southern Europe (for an overview of urbanization processes in pre-Roman Italy, see Attema 2004; Fulminante 2014; Guidi 1998, 2006, 2008, 2010; Pacciarelli 2001; Rendeli 2015).

This process has long been considered more sudden, revolutionary, and slightly earlier in Etruria than in *Latium vetus*, where changes might have occurred somewhat later and more gradually (e.g., Pacciarelli 2001). However, recent research has suggested that the two regions had more in common than previously thought (Cangemi 2016; Fulminante and Stoddart 2013; Marino 2015). To better understand these sociopolitical settings and their development over time, this paper explored and compared changes in regional settlement networks and interaction patterns through the analyses of fluvial communication routes, circulation of artifacts, and architectural decoration types.

Research into cultural interactions, based on the circulation of artifact types and objects, indicated that the two regions, taken separately, had very similar modes of circulation. The analyses of communication and transportation networks implied that *Latium vetus* might have had a relative advantage due to a more connected and more resilient infrastructural system. However, the most significant difference between the two regions seems to have developed in the contrasting dynamics of power revealed by the modeling of transportation and communication network systems. Therefore, it seems plausible that a more compact region with a single dominant center, much more densely populated, and thus internally richer in exchange and interactions, but also with a slightly more efficient and more resilient system of infrastructural connections externally, such as *Latium vetus*, had a greater advantage than a larger but more dispersed and heterarchical region, such as Etruria (see also Stoddart, this volume).

The analysis and comparison of different levels of interactions, based on the circulation of objects (i.e., cultural networks), fluvial communication routes, and terrestrial infrastructures (i.e., geographical networks), suggest that the specific built environment of Rome, as a very densely populated and connected nucleated settlement, together with its particular political organization, also reflected in the physical space, contributed largely to its final success over Etruria.

Acknowledgments

I would like to thank Attila and Roderick for inviting me to contribute to their stimulating session at the EAA 2016 annual meetings in Vilnius and to contribute to this volume. They have been most professional and friendly. Research for this paper was conducted during a Marie Sklodowska Curie Fellowship by the author at the University of Roma Tre (Italy) between 2014 and 2016 (Grant N 628818). The analyses of fluvial and terrestrial transportation networks were conducted in collaboration with Sergi Lozano, Luce Prignano, and Ignacio Morer. The paper was developed, written, and revised thanks to fellowships at the Institute of Advanced Studies at Durham (UK, Lent Term 2017) and the Christian-Albrechts-Universität zu Kiel (Germany, Autumn Term 2018). Discussions at those institutions with Rob Witcher and Oliver Nakoinz, respectively, were most fruitful. All errors remain the responsibility of the author.

References Cited

Alessandri, L. 2007. *L'occupazione costiera protostorica del Lazio centromeridionale*. Oxford: Archaeopress.

Alessandri, L. 2013. *Latium Vetus in the Bronze Age and Early Iron Age/Il Latium vetus nell'età del Bronzo e nella prima età del Ferro* (BAR International Series 2565). Oxford: Archaeopress.

Ampolo, C., A.M. Bietti Sestieri, G. Bartoloni and M. Cataldi Dini 1980. *La Formazione della città nel Lazio: Seminario tenuto a Roma, 24-26 giugno 1977*. Roma: Alpha Print.

Attema, P. (ed.) 2004. *Centralization, Early Urbanization and Colonization in First Millennium BC Greece and Italy. Part 1: Italy* (Babesch Supplementa 9). Leuven: Peeters.

Baratti, G., M. Cataldi and L. Mordeglia 2008. La cinta fortificata di Tarquinia alla luce della nuova documentazione, in G. Camporeale (ed.) *La città murata in Etruria*: 155–169. Pisa and Roma: Fabrizio Serra Editore.

Barbaro, B. 2010. *Insediamenti, aree funerarie ed entità territoriali in Etruria meridionale nel Bronzo finale* (Grandi contesti e problemi della Protostoria Italiana 14). Firenze: All'Insegna del Giglio.

Bartoloni, F., V. Nizzo and M. Taloni 2009. Dall'esibizione al rigore: analisi dei sepolcreti laziali tra VII e VI sec. a.C., in R. Bonaudo, L. Cerchiai and C. Pellegrino (eds) *Tra Etruria, Lazio e Magna Grecia: indagini sulle necropoli*: 65–86. Salerno: Pandemos.

Bartoloni, G., F. Buranelli, V. D'Atri and A. De Santis 1987. *Le urne a capanna rinvenute in Italia* (Tyrrhenica I, Archaeologica 68). Roma: Giorgio Bretschneider.

Belardelli, C., M. Angle, F. di Gennaro and F. Trucco 2007. *Repertorio dei siti Protostorici del Lazio. Province di Roma, Viterbo e Frosinone*. Firenze: All'Insegna del Giglio.

Bianco Peroni, V. 1970. *Le spade nell'Italia continentale*. München: C.H. Beck.

Bianco Peroni, V. 1976. *I coltelli nell'Italia continentale*. München: C.H. Beck.

Bianco Peroni, V. 1979. *I rasoi nell'Italia continentale*. München: C.H. Beck.

Biella, M.C. 2014. *Impasti Orientalizzanti con Decorazioni incise in Agro Falisco*. Trento: Tangram.

Bietti Sestieri, A.M. 1997. Italy in Europe in the Early Iron Age. *Proceedings of the Prehistoric Society* 63: 371–402.

Bietti Sestieri, A.M. and A. De Santis 2003. Il processo formativo della cultura Laziale, in *Atti della XXXV riunione scientifica. Le comunità della preistoria italiana:*

studi e ricerche sul neolitico e le età dei metalli. Castello di Lipari 2-7 giugno 2000, in memoria di Luigi Bernabò Brea: 745–763. Firenze: Instituto de Italiano di Preistoria.

Boccaletti, S., V. Latora, Y. Moreno, M. Chavez and D.-U. Hwang 2006. Complex networks: structure and dynamics. *Physics Reports* 424(4–5): 175–308.

Boitani, F., S. Neri and F. Biagi 2008. Nuove indagini sulle mura di Veio nei pressi di porta Nord-Ovest, in G. Camporeale (ed.) *La città murata in Etruria:* 135–154. Pisa and Roma: Fabrizio Serra Editore.

Bonghi Jovino, M. 2005. Citta' e territorio. Veio, Caerae, Tarquinia, Vulci: appunti e riconsiderazioni, in O. Paoletti and G. Camporeale (eds) *Dinamiche di sviluppo delle citta' nell'Etruria meridionale: Veio, Caere, Tarquinia, Vulci:* 27–58. Pisa and Roma: Istituti Editoriali e Poligrafici Internazionali.

Bonghi Jovino, M. 2008. *Tarquinia etrusca. Tarconte e il primato della citta'.* Roma: L'Erma di Bretschneider.

Brocato, P. 2000. *La necropoli etrusca della Riserva del Ferrone.* Roma: Edizioni Quasar.

Cangemi, I. 2016. A Scale-Free, Relational Approach to Social Development in Late-Prehistoric Tyrrhenian Central Italy. Unpublished Masters thesis, University of Michigan.

Carancini, G.L. 1975. *Gli spilloni nell'Italia continentale.* München: C.H. Beck.

Carancini, G.L. 1984. *Le asce nell'Italia continentale.* München: C.H. Beck.

Carandini, A. 2003. *La nascita di Roma. Dei, Lari eroi e uomini all'alba di una civiltà.* 2nd edition. Torino: Giulio Einaudi.

Carandini, A. 2007. *Roma, il primo giorno.* Roma and Bari: Laterza.

Carandini, A. and P. Carafa (eds) 2000. *Palatium e Sacra Via, I.* (Bollettino di Archeologia 31–34). Roma: Istituti Poligrafico e Zecca dello Stato.

Cifani, G. 2014. Aspects of urbanism and political ideology in Archaic Rome, in E.C. Robinson (ed.) *Papers on Italian urbanism in the first millennium B.C.:* 15–28. Portsmouth (RI): Journal of Roman Archaeology.

Colonna, G. 1977. Un aspetto oscuro del Lazio antico. Le tombe di VI-V secolo a.C. *La Parola del Passato* 32: 131–165.

Da Vela, R. 2014–2015. Applicazione della social network analysis per lo studio della trasmissione culturale e dell'evoluzione delle identità culturali locali durante la tarda età Ellenistica. *Atti e Memorie dell'Accademia Toscana di Scienze e Lettere la Colombaria* 79–80, n.s. 75–76: 207–229.

De Landa, M. 2006. *A New Philosophy of Society: Assemblage Theory and Social Complexity.* London: Continuum.

Della Fina, G.M. and E. Pellegrini 2013. *Da Orvieto a Bolsena. Un percorso tra Etruschi e Romani.* Roma: Pacini Editore.

De Nooy, W., A. Mrvar and V. Batagelj 2012. *Exploratory Social Network Analysis with Pajek.* Cambridge: Cambridge University Press.

De Santis, A. 1997. Alcune considerazioni sul territorio veiente in età Orientalizzante e arcaica, in G. Bartolonim (ed.) *Le necropoli arcaiche di Veio. Giornata di studio in memoria di Massimo Pallottino:* 101–104. Roma: L'Erma di Bretschneider.

De Santis, A. 2005. Da capi guerrieri a principi: la strutturazione del potere politico nell'Etruria protourbana, in O. Paoletti and G. Camporeale (eds) *Dinamiche di sviluppo delle città nell'Etruria Meridionale: Veio, Caere, Tarquinia, Vulci:* 615–631. Pisa and Roma: Istituti Editoriali e Poligrafici Internazionali.

De Santis, A. (ed.) 2011. *Politica e leader nel Lazio ai tempi di Enea.* Roma: Soprintendenza speciale per i beni archeologici di Roma.

di Gennaro, F. and A. Guidi 2000. Il bronzo finale dell'Italia centrale. Considerazioni e prospettive di indagine, in M. Harari and M. Pearce (eds) *Il protovillanoviano al di qua e al di là dell'Appennino* (Biblioteca di Athenaeum 18): 99–132. Como: New Press.

di Gennaro, F. and A. Guidi 2009. Ragioni e regioni di un cambiamento culturale: modi e tempi della formazione dei centri protourbani nella valle del Tevere e nel Lazio meridionale. *Scienze dell'Antichità. Storia, Archeologia, Antropologia* 15: 429–445.

di Gennaro, F. and R. Peroni 1986. Aspetti regionali dello sviluppo dell'insediamento protostorico nell'Italia centro-meridionale alla luce dei dati archeologici e ambientali. *Dialoghi di Archeologia* 3: 193–200.

Enei, F. 2001. *Progetto Ager Caeretanus. Il litorale di Alsium: ricognizioni archeologiche nel territorio di Ladispoli, Cerveteri e Fiumicino (Alsium-Caere-Ad Turres-Ceri).* Regione Lazio e Comune di Ladispoli.

Fontaine, P. 2002–2003. Le Fortificazioni Etrusche. Nuove Scoperte Archeologiche (1997–2003). *Etruscan Studies* 9: 77–84.

Fulminante, F. 2003. *Le sepolture principesche nel Latium Vetus fra la fine della prima eta' del Ferro e l'inizio dell'età Orientalizzante.* Roma: L'Erma di Bretschneider.

Fulminante, F. 2012a. Ethnicity, Identity and State Formation in the Latin Landscape. Problems and Approaches, in S. Stoddart and G. Cifani (eds) *Landscape and Ethnicity in the Archaic Mediterranean Area:* 89–107. Oxford: Oxbow Books.

Fulminante, F. 2012b. Social Network Analysis and the Emergence of Central Places: A Case Study from Central Italy (Latium Vetus). *BaBesch* 87: 1–27.

Fulminante, F. 2014. *The Urbanization of Rome and Latium vetus from the Bronze Age to the Archaic Era.* Cambridge: Cambridge University Press.

Fulminante, F., A. Guidi, S. Lozano, I. Morer and L. Prignano 2020. Terrestrial Transportation Networks and Power Balance in Etruria and Latium Vetus between the Beginning of the Early Iron Age and the End of the Archaic Period, in H. Dawson and F. Iacono (eds) *Bridging Social and Physical Space through Networks:* 31–46. Leiden: Sidestone Press.

Fulminante, F., S. Lozano and L. Prignano 2016. Social network analysis and early Latin cities (central Italy), in P. Attema, J. Seubers and S. Willemsen (eds) *Early states, territories and settlements in protohistoric Central Italy:* 101–110. Groningen: Groningen University Press.

Fulminante, F., L. Prignano, I. Morer and S. Lozano 2017. Coordinated and Unbalanced Powers. How Latin Cities Shaped Their Terrestrial Transportation Network. *Frontiers in Digital Humanities* 4, https://doi.org/10.3389/fdigh.2017.00004

Fulminante, F. and S. Stoddart 2013. Indigenous political dynamics and identity from a comparative perspective: Etruria and Latium Vetus, in M.E. Alberti and S. Sabatini (eds) *Exchange Networks and Local Transformations: Interactions and Local Changes in Europe and the Mediterranean between Bronze and Iron Age:* 117–133. Oxford: Oxbow Books.

Geiger, A. 1994. *Treibverzierte Bronzerundschilde der italischen Eisenzeit aus Italien und Griechenland.* Stuttgart: F. Steiner.

Giovannelli, E. 2015. *Scarabei e scaraboidi in Etruria, Agro Falisco e Lazio Arcaico dall'VIII al V sec. a.C.* Trento: Tangram.

Guaitoli, M. 1981. Gabii: osservazioni sulle fasi di sviluppo dell'abitato. *Quaderni dell'Istituto di Topografia Antica dell'Università di Roma* 9: 23–57.

Guidi, A. 1998. The Emergence of the State in Central and Northern Italy. *Acta Archaeologica* 69: 139–161.

Guidi, A. 2006. The Archaeology of the Early State in Italy. *Social Evolution and History* 5(2): 55–90.

Guidi, A. 2008. Archeologia dell'Early State: Il caso di studio Italiano. *Ocnus* 16: 175–192.

Guidi, A. 2010. Archaeology of the Early State in Italy: New Data and Acquisition. *Social Evolution and History* 9(2): 1–26.

Guidi, A. and P. Santoro 2008. The Role of the Greeks in the Formation of the New Urban Aristocratic Ideology, in F. Fulminante and A. Guidi (eds) *Urbanization and State Formation in Italy during the 1st Millennium BC.* Roma: FAO.

Hopkins, J.N. 2014. The creation of the Forum and the making of monumental Rome, in E.C. Robinson (ed.) *Papers on Italian urbanism in the first millennium B.C.:* 29–61. Portsmouth (RI): Journal of Roman Archaeology.

Iaia, C. 2005. *Produzioni toreutiche della prima età del ferro in Italia centro-settentrionale: stili decorativi, circolazioni, significato.* Pisa: Istituti Editoriali e Poligrafici Internazionali.

Iaia, C. and A. Mandolesi 2010. Comunita' e Territori nel Villanoviano evoluto dell'Etruria meridionale, in N. Negroni Catacchio (ed.) *L'Alba dell'Etruria Fenomeni di continuita' e trasformazione tra XII e VIII secolo. Ricerche e Scavi:* 61–78. Milano: Centro Studi di Preistoria e Archeologia.

Lock, G. and B. Molyneaux 2006. *Confronting Scale in Archaeology: Issues of Theory and Practice.* New York: Springer.

Marino, T. 2015. Aspetti e fasi del processo formativo delle città in Etruria meridionale costiera, in M. Rendeli (ed.) *Le città visibili. Archeologia dei processi di formazione urbana I. Penisola Italiana e Sardegna:* 97–141. Roma: Officina Etruscologia.

Marston, S.A., J.P. Jones and K. Woodward 2005. Human geography without scale. *Transactions of the Institute of British Geographers* 30: 416–432.

Marzoli, D. 1989. *Bronzefeldflaschen in Italien.* München: C.H. Beck.

Micozzi, M. 1994. '*White-on-red': Una produzione vascolare dell'orientalizzante etrusco.* Roma: GEI.

Moretti Sgubini, A.M. 2006. Alle origini di Vulci, in M. Moretti and M. Pandolfini Angeletti (eds) *Archeologia in Etruria meridionale:* 317–360. Roma: L'Erma di Bretschneider.

Neri, S. 2010. *Il Tornio e il pennello. Ceramica depurata di tradizione geometrica di epoca Orientalizzante in Etruria meridionale.* Roma: Officina.

Newman, M.E.J. 2003. The Structure and Function of Complex Networks. *SIAM Review* 45(2): 167–256.

Ortman, S., K.E. Davis, J. Lobo, M.E. Smith, L.M.A. Bettencourt and A. Trumbo 2016. Settlement scaling and economic change in the Central Andes. *Journal of Archaeological Science* 73: 94–106.

Pacciarelli, M. 2001. *Dal villaggio alla citta'. La svolta proto-urbana del 1000 a.C. nell'Italia Tirrenica.* Firenze: All'Insegna del Giglio.

Pallottino, M. 1991. *A History of Earliest Italy.* Ann Arbor: University of Michigan Press.

Peroni, R. 1989. *Protostoria dell'Italia continentale. La penisola Italiana nelle età del Bronzo e del Ferro* (Popoli e civiltà dell'Italia antica 9). Roma: Ente per la Diffusione e l'Educazione Storica.

Peroni, R. 2000. Formazione e sviluppi dei centri protourbani medio-tirrenici, in A. Carandini and R. Cappelli (eds) *Roma, Romolo, Remo e la fondazione della città (Exhibition catalogue):* 26–30. Milano: Electa.

Potter, T.W. 1985. *Storia del paesaggio dell'Etruria meridionale.* Roma: La Nuova Italia Scientifica.

Prignano, L., I. Morer, F. Fulminante and S. Lozano 2019. Modelling terrestrial route networks to understand inter-polity interactions (southern Etruria, 950–500 BC). *Journal of Archaeological Science* 105: 46–58.

Rendeli, M. 1993. *Città aperte. Ambiente e paesaggio rurale organizzato nell'Etruria meridionale costiera durante l'età orientalizzante e arcaica.* Roma: GEI.

Rendeli, M. (ed.) 2015. *Le città visibili – I. Archeologia dei processi di formazione urbana I. Penisola Italiana e Sardegna.* Roma: Officina.

Renfrew, C. and J.F. Cherry (eds) 1986. *Peer polity interaction and socio-political change.* Cambridge: Cambridge University Press.

Savella, D. 2015. *Le fibule dell'età del Bronzo dell'Italia centrale: definizione dei tipi e della loro cronologia e* distribuzione tra Italia, Sicilia ed Egeo. Bonn: Dr. Rudolf Habelt.

Schiapelli, A. 2008. *Sviluppo storico della Teverina*. Firenze: All'Insegna del Giglio.

Sciacca, F. 2005. *Patere baccellate in bronzo: Oriente, Grecia, Italia in età orientalizzante*. Roma: L'Erma di Bretschneider.

Seubern, J. 2005. The Dead and the Wealthy. Unpublished Masters thesis, University of Groningen.

Shoe Meritt, L. and I.E.M. Edlund-Berry 2000 (1965). *Etruscan and Republican Roman Mouldings*. Philadelphia: University Museum, University of Pennsylvania.

Stoddart, S. 2009. *Historical Dictionary of the Etruscans*. Plymouth: Scarecrow Press.

Szilágyi, J.Gy. 1992–1998. *Ceramica Etrusco-Corinzia Figurata, I–II*. Firenze: L.S. Olschki.

Tartara, P. 1999. *Torrimpietra*. Firenze: L.S. Olschki.

Ten Kortenaar, S. 2011. *Il colore e la materia. Tra tradizione e innovazione nella produzione dell'impasto rosso nell'Italia medio-tirrenica*. Roma: Officina.

Tomedi, G. 2000. *Italische Panzerplatten und Panzerscheiben*. Stuttgart: F. Steiner.

Tuppi, J. 2014. Approaching road-cutting as instruments of early urbanization in central Tyrrhenian Italy. *Papers of the British School at Rome* 82: 41–74.

Van Mieghem, P. 2012. *Graph Spectra for Complex Networks*. Cambridge: Cambridge University Press.

Vanzetti, A. 1996. Evidenze Funerarie e figure sociali nel bronzo e primo ferro italiani. Unpublished PhD dissertation, University La Sapienza.

Vanzetti, A. 2002. Some Current Approaches to Protohistoric Centralization and Urbanization in Italy, in P. Attema, G.-J. Burgers, E. Van Joolen, M. Van Leusen and B. Mater (eds) *New Developments in Italian Landscape Archaeology: Theory and methodology of field survey land evaluation and landscape perception, pottery production and distribution* (BAR International Series 1091): 36–51. Oxford: Archaeopress.

Vanzetti, A. 2004. Risultati e problemi di alcune attuali prospettive di studio della centralizzazione e urbanizzazione di fase protostorica in Italia, in P. Attema (ed.) *Centralization, Early Urbanization and Colonization in First Millennium BC Greece and Italy. Part 1: Italy* (Babesch Supplementa 9): 1–28. Leuven: Peeters.

von Hase, F.W. 1969. *Die Trensen der Früheisenzeit in Italien*. München: C.H. Beck.

Winter, N.A. 2009. *Symbols of Wealth and Power: Architectural Terracotta Decoration in Etruria and Central Italy, 640-510 B.C.* Ann Arbor: University of Michigan Press.

Woytowitsch, E. 1978. *Die Wagen der Bronze- und frühen Eisenzeit in Italien*. München: C.H. Beck.

Zifferero, A. 1995. Economia divinita' e frontiere: sul ruolo di alcuni santuari di confine in Etruria meridionale. *Ostraka* 4: 333–350.

Chapter 12

Landscape as Metaphor:
Burial Monuments and 'Landscapes of Power' in Late Iron Age Britain

Karolis Minkevičius

Abstract

This paper explores the landscape context of Late Iron Age cremation burial monuments in East and Southeast Britain. Several authors previously have argued that such monuments were used to create 'landscapes of power' at the *oppida*. This project employed viewshed and spatial analyses in GIS to test whether it was possible to view these monuments from contemporary nearby roads and certain earthworks. The state of research on Late Iron Age landscapes in Britain is reviewed, alongside former attempts to utilize GIS to study archaeological visibility. I argue that burial monuments with surrounding landscape features were constructed to serve as identity markers for the local communities. Moreover, they were used to emphasize the continuity of tradition to legitimize the political power of the ruling elites. The analyses and interpretations led to the conclusion that these monuments played a vital role in settlement nucleation that followed the Claudian conquest.

Introduction

Over the last several decades, Iron Age studies in Britain have undergone a series of important transformations. Among others, these transformations included a detailed and largely successful critique of the central place, hierarchical, chiefdom model of Iron Age society as well as the increasing recognition of cosmological references for the symbolic structuring of domestic space in Iron Age households and communities (Moore 2007: 79). The critique presented by post-processualists highlighted that society was far from being the central focus of Iron Age studies in Britain. There have been relatively few attempts to describe, let alone understand or explain, how Iron Age societies were organized (Hill 2006: 170). These critiques also acknowledged the importance of such factors as variability and agency of both individuals and societies. Nevertheless, despite the light cast by these studies on how Iron Age communities experienced and structured their social spaces at the local, household scale, there has been surprisingly little discussion of how Iron Age societies were organized at the broader scale (Moore 2007: 79).

More recently, studies exploring the complex relations between cultural landscapes and Iron Age communities have begun to emerge. However, to this date, they remain relatively scarce. This significantly hinders our attempts to understand the Iron Age. Cultural landscapes convey information about the skills and intentions of their creators, and also their effects on the society. Thus, neglecting the context of social transformations often has reduced the study of landscapes to a mere analysis of the physical space. The general lack of interest in the social aspects of

the built environment played a major role in Iron Age becoming 'boring,' especially when compared to the earlier periods of prehistory (Hill 1989). While major developments have taken place in the fields of contextual studies, artifact analyses, and site-based spatial or architectural research (Parker Pearson and Richards 1997), landscape studies did not advance all that much. Despite a long tradition of survey-based archaeology in Britain, relatively few studies have assessed the role of landscapes within the wider spatial context of social practices. British Iron Age archaeology has developed as a highly empirical school, in which increasingly sophisticated surveys using non-site and/or off-site strategies were utilized to map settlements, fields, enclosures, and agricultural facilities (Taylor 1997: 192). For a long time, this caused a failure to acknowledge the complexity, immeasurable nature, and constantly changing meanings of landscapes.

Landscapes and Communities: Approaches and Debates

This 'depopulation' of landscapes has been a major problem. Early archaeological phenomenologists (i.e., Tilley 1994) have argued that landscapes are the geographical time-space context of human activities, and that they influence, and are influenced by, social interactions and social structures. In addition, as has been argued elsewhere (Hodder 1982), the meaning of an object is not fixed but is constantly changing. Similarly, landscapes are neither homogeneous nor static and it is not possible to determine 'the meaning' of any landscape. It is also subject to regional and chronological variation (Ingold 1993). Furthermore, relationships with landscapes can differ even within the same society, depending on the experience—routine or unusual—that any individual has of a particular location (Bevan 1997: 181).

Only some of the multitudes of human activities have left any archaeological traces in the landscape. Cultural landscapes, when discussed at all in the archaeological literature of the Iron Age and Roman Period, have tended to be considered as a technical term for the visual environment. In this context, landscapes were studied with a 'measured and detached gaze,' and the investigations were reduced to the study of land rather than landscape, geometric space rather than geographical and symbolic one (Taylor 1997: 192). However, ideas forged by the post-processualists during the end of the 20th century have since found their way into studies of the British Iron Age. In particular, some of the more recent works have emphasized the idea that place and space play a principal role in the organization of communities (i.e., Bryant 2007; Creighton 2006; Moore 2007). Landscape features related to the division and demarcation of land must be understood within the context of long-term social transformations in concepts on continuity, tenure, and inheritance (Giles 2007: 247). Some parts of the cultural landscapes were essential to land management, while others likely resulted from such practices. Considering this, landscape investigations unveil some of the social processes that were taking place within a society, alongside the ways particular places were perceived and how they functioned. In other words, how their foundation and presence shaped the society.

While recent theoretical advances in landscape theory significantly improved our appreciation of Iron Age landscape studies (i.e., Giles 2007; Moore 2007; Rennell 2008), the methodological side of this field has not received much, if any, attention. In most cases, this resulted in post-processual landscape archeology being overtly subjective and hyper-interpretive. This was not limited to Iron Age studies. It was a fundamental weakness of the post-processual approaches to landscape studies. Unsurprisingly, it did not take long before this field received notorious criticism. As summarized by Fleming (2006), post-processual theorists have sought to supplant conventional landscape archaeology by the production of 'experimental' forms of fieldwork and writing, which explicitly seek to go 'beyond the evidence.' Critics concluded that the suspension of critical judgment was not a price worth paying for making illusory progress with 'the people agenda.' Post-processual landscape archaeology was never overly obsessed with objectivity. While fieldwork began shortly after clearing the theoretical ground, a firm methodological grounding was never established, let alone polished. As a result, the post-processual landscape approaches are still to a large extent experimental, speculative, and detached from scientific testing.

Landscape as Metaphor

In addition to the previous critique, it is essential to note that another major pitfall lies within what is usually considered a major strength of the post-processual landscape approaches. This is the tendency to focus on the ever-changing meanings of landscape. Associated with this is an emphasis on the influence of perception and meanings on prehistoric communities. This emphasis, however, undermines the fundamental characteristics of cultural landscapes. Every man-made object, including landscapes, is part of a behavioral chain, the sequence of all activities in which an element participates during its 'life' within a cultural system (Schiffer 1975: 106). In this paper, it is useful to view each of these activities as belonging to one of two distinct stages. The first stage comprises production, from various pre-planning activities to the manufacturing of an object. Aspects such as the economic, social, and political need for the object, previous experience, required skills, and means of manufacturing all fall into this category. The second stage encompasses everything that happens after the manufacture. Repairs, alterations, and adaptations of the object belong to this category, alongside possible changes in its importance, meaning, and role in the society.

Most post-processual landscape approaches tend to overstate the importance of this second stage. Unfortunately, this ought to be considered as a significant drawback. Transformations of an object's meaning during its life cycle are an exciting topic allowing for theoretical exploration. However, the most characteristic trait of the second stage is that it is *reactive*. Meanings of a cultural landscape change and alterations are made as reactive responses to the changing environment. Whether by changes in climate, political system, spiritual culture, or any other variable, objects are altered to meet ever-changing social and/ or cultural needs. Yet, it is all too often forgotten that the first stage is a *proactive* one. It provides a window into the world before the manufacture of the object. As has been argued by cognitive archaeologists, ideas are born before physical objects are created (Renfrew 1990; Renfrew and Zubrow 1994). This is also true when dealing with cultural landscapes.

The creation of landscape monuments informs us about the original intentions of its creators and tells us more about the communities that constructed them than it does about the ones that used them. A good example comes from Witcher (1998), who illustrates the relations between Roman settlements in Britain, such as Colchester, and road networks constructed to link them. As discussed in Witcher's article, there is little doubt that Rome considered these roads and landscapes to be Roman. To build from this point, they also reveal the experience and skill set, alongside knowledge, worldviews, and possibly numerous other cultural traits required to construct such networks. In this sense, landscapes act as metaphors, and they serve as a gateway to the metaphysical. Rather than attempting to grasp this from the phenomenological perspective—so often adopted by post-processual landscape archeologists—starting from the planning stage allows exploration of such ideas in a way that is susceptible to scientific analyses. Conclusions from the *proactive* stage can be drawn with much more certainty than, for example, trying to determine how Roman roads might have been perceived by British Iron Age communities.

Burial Monuments in Late Iron Age Britain

The Late Iron Age in Britain is marked by the abundance of archaeologically visible material, especially when compared to earlier periods. This covers a range of characteristics, from its increasingly enclosed nature to the emergence and abrupt increase in earthworks and changes in ritual life. A characteristic trait of the period is the emergence of the *oppida*. In British Iron Age archaeology, this label is usually given to a variety of large, enclosed sites that date to the 1st centuries BC and AD. These sites are supposed to correspond to the *oppida* found in parts of contemporary temperate Europe, which are often seen as urban settlements (Hill 1995b; see also Fernández-Götz, this volume). However, few of them have evidence amounting to the dense nucleated sites of La Tène and Augustan Gaul (Creighton 2006: 70). Whatever changes are visible in the archaeological record, they reflect (some) advances in (some) social, political, economic, and ritual aspects of life. These practices abruptly began leaving more traces in the archaeological record. Were such changes already taking place before and during the Late Iron Age, and if so, why? Alternatively, did they happen under the new conditions that pertained after the Roman conquest (Gwilt and Haselgrove 1997: 6)? The transitional phase of the period is arguably the most revealing as it indicates the close interaction of two distant worlds.

Another characteristic feature of the Late Iron Age is the re-emergence of cremation burials. In the late 1st millennium BC, cremations became widespread in northern France (Haselgrove 2007) as well as other parts of the La Tène cultural zone. This burial rite, broadly similar to that of northern France, was also introduced to parts of southern and southeastern Britain (Carr 2007: 445), where cremation burial monuments were usually situated in highly visible locations (Gwilt and Haselgrove 1997; Hill 1995b). This

placement implies that visibility was an important factor when planning their location. Since such burial rites require constructing a monument and elaborate planning of the rite itself, it is unlikely that places for these acts could have been chosen by chance. Moreover, similar monuments in different parts of the region appeal to the rule that this might have been a relatively standardized practice in East and Southeast England, the regional focus of this paper. Burial rites are much more closely related to the living than to the dead. Planned and performed by living individuals for a particular purpose, whether functional and/or symbolic, these rites typically include little that can be directly attributed to the deceased. It is also possible that such rites were directly linked to traditions. Even so, traditions are maintained by the living for a specific purpose or set of purposes, and this suggests that a similar tradition across the region indicates similarities in social organization.

Due to the history and nature of Iron Age studies in Britain, East and Southeast England have received more attention than have other parts of the country. As mentioned above, the amount of archaeological material dated to the Late Iron Age is substantial. Unfortunately, such a relative abundance of data is misleading since it does not necessarily reflect the proportion of information obtained about Iron Age societies (Hill 1995a). In the archaeological literature, this region is usually defined as the 'Southern and Eastern kingdoms' (Creighton 2000; Haselgrove 1987). The region is typically presented as to some extent homogeneous, or at least that it functioned in relatively similar ways (Creighton 2000: 10). Creighton (2000, 2006) has argued that some of the strategies employed, such as legitimizing the rule of a particular individual or group of individuals via the claims of ancestral kingship, were extremely similar throughout the region in the Late Iron Age. However, most of his suggestion comes from interpreting coin evidence, which is not unbiased.

This paper draws from Creighton's ideas about the use of burial monuments in the establishment and maintenance of social and political power. In his monographs, Creighton (2000, 2006) presented the idea that the burial monuments of Folly Lane, Stanway, and Lexden had all been employed in very similar landscape control strategies, namely that these monuments might have been constructed to dominate the entrances to the *oppida* of Verulamium and Camulodunum. This hypothesis relies on the assumption that the individuals and/or communities involved in the construction process had an excellent understanding of how such landscape features worked. This would not be possible without knowledge of the local landscape, which, in turn, suggests that at least some of the architects were indigenous people. It is also highly unlikely that anyone could have constructed them by accident. This means that whoever was involved in the process must have known exactly how such strategies functioned and how to apply them in each situation. Therefore, to support the hypothesis that such strategies were being employed, the process must have been far from coincidental and thus reflect the existence of close social and political networks across the region.

Visibility in Archaeology

To bridge the divide between the theoretical and methodological aspects of Iron Age landscape studies, and drawing from earlier attempts (i.e., Creighton 2000, 2006) to link visibility of landscape features with creation and maintenance of 'landscapes of power' at the *oppida*, this study utilizes GIS-based visibility analysis to examine and evaluate visual relations of landscape features. Surprisingly, GIS-based visibility studies have attracted little attention in the field of Iron Age and Roman studies in Britain (with some notable exceptions, e.g., Eckardt *et al.* 2009). Such studies ought to be more prevalent since this toolkit is well suited for the manipulation of spatial data. Despite the obvious threats of environmental determinism (Gaffney and van Leusen 1995), GIS offers the potential to collate and integrate various temporal scales and sources of evidence (Witcher 1999: 15). In landscape archaeology today, no other tool can provide comparable results.

Visibility-based approaches have a long pedigree in archaeology, varying from the observations of antiquarians to the rigorous quantitative methodologies proposed by researchers such as Renfrew, Davidson, and Fraser (Wheatley and Gillings 2000). More recently, the importance of vision—in the sense of visual perception—has been brought to the fore within cognitive archaeology and in theoretical debates concerning the relationship between bodily experience and understanding, in which the role of vision has been re-examined in the context of narrative and framing devices (Wheatley and Gillings 2000). Yet the most recent advances in technology enable archaeologists to conduct line-of-sight (*visibility*) and field of view (*viewshed*) analysis using GIS software packages. GIS-based approaches have proved to be a dramatic methodological advancement. They presented a solution to problems such as how to quantify and represent visibility. These possibilities started a trend that resulted in an abundance of studies exploring visibility in prehistory. Perhaps the biggest breakthrough was in making it possible to quantify, capture, and store spatial information, which was then immediately available for a significantly larger audience of scholars in both space and time.

It became increasingly evident, however, that the capabilities of the method overshadowed its real potential (Llobera 2007: 51). In terms of visibility, early GIS-based studies focused primarily on what was visible from particular locations. Inevitably, such approaches invited critique. First, the method was accused of being exclusively quantitative and subject to often narrow and reductionist agendas. It has been suggested that these approaches are unsatisfactory since it is evident that such a research focus lacks the perceptional and humanistic approaches necessary to elucidate an enhanced understanding of the archaeological record (Tschan *et al.* 2000). Secondly, it soon became clear that there are numerous procedural problems with the calculation of viewsheds, ranging from difficulties in reconstructing vegetation, which might have affected visibility, to the overall robustness of the viewshed (Lock and Harris 1996). While some of the critiques were constructive and attempted to account for the complex nature of such analyses and improve on its use (e.g., Wheatley and Gillings 2000), others suggested dismissing it altogether, at least in its current form.

GIS are highly specific to investigations concerning geographical data/space, and this primary functional purpose is reflected in their overall design. This means that geographers and scholars of related earth science disciplines can advance their knowledge using a powerful tool that is tailor-made for their areas of research (Tschan *et al.* 2000: 31). Archaeologists are only borrowers of the technology, which requires that we tweak and adjust the tools to fit our needs. The sophistication of computer equipment, and especially current GIS-based analytical techniques, does not by default result in an increased understanding of the past by simply incorporating the latest 'gadgets' (Tschan 1999: 303). This is especially true when studying archaeological visibility. Viewsheds themselves are unlikely to reveal anything more than what was likely to be visible from a dot on the map. The ability to process a significant amount of data while making 'fancy' analyses contributes little to our understanding of the past. GIS, as well as any other tool, can only help to arrive at meaningful interpretations or conclusions if incorporated into an appropriate theoretical framework. For that reason, this study incorporates some of the recent advances from the theoretical side of British Iron Age studies with GIS viewsheds to investigate three cremation burial monuments dating from the Late Iron Age to the Early Roman Period.

Case Studies

Folly Lane, Hertfordshire

The Folly Lane burial complex is located in the southern part of the modern city of St. Albans. It is sited on the hilltop dominating the view from the Roman town of Verulamium. Archaeologically, Verulamium was founded in the late 1st century BC as a series of sub-

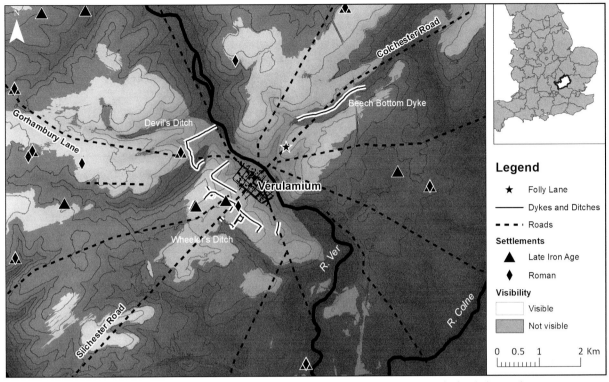

Figure 12.1. Viewshed analysis, with areas intervisible with the Folly Lane marked in lighter colors.
Crown copyright/database right 2012. An Ordnance Survey/EDINA supplied service
(figure by the author).

rectangular enclosures on a plateau edge overlooking a marshy area of the River Ver. Interpretation has usually seen this low-lying area as serving some kind of administrative function in the Late Iron Age (Creighton 2006: 125). The whole complex is now generally considered as a royal ceremonial site, based on evidence summarized by Haselgrove and Millet (1997) and Niblett (1999: 405, 2001). This landscape of multiple enclosures, spread over 2 to 3 km of the valley, contrasts greatly with the compact town that was to emerge over the next two generations. The Folly Lane burial complex was the key element to the design of the new town of Verulamium (Creighton 2006: 124). The massive rectangular enclosure was set on the crest of a hill, on the side of the River Ver, opposite the St. Michael's enclosure. Excavations revealed that an unnamed individual of extremely high status was cremated there in the years shortly after the Claudian annexation, with Niblett (1999) presenting a more precise date of between AD 50 and 55. It has been suggested based on the grave goods that the individual had served in the Roman cavalry (Creighton 2006), and it is highly likely that he represents one of the friendly kings of the Claudian period, or else a very close relative or successor.

The Folly Lane monument is located on a hillside close to the western bank of the River Ver. It is evident that this location was chosen due to its exceptional visibility as the monument visually dominates the valley of the Ver as well as the substantial portion of the surrounding area. In some cases, visibility extended even to more distant sites (e.g., Wheathamstead). The location of the Folly Lane complex on the western hillside, rather than on the hilltop, suggests that visibility from a specific location(s) was more important than visibility from a wider region. An interesting phenomenon results—the monument dominates areas to the west and southwest, while areas to the east (e.g., the valley of the Colne River) remain out of sight.

The significance of this became apparent after analyzing the visibility of surrounding landscape features. Nearby earthworks—dykes and ditches—were investigated first. The distribution of features dating to the Late Iron Age did not reveal any significant patterns when plotted on a map. When combined with the visibility analysis, however, some striking patterns were revealed. All dykes and ditches were oriented in directions that correspond to the orientation of the viewshed (Figure 12.1). In addition, the earthwork system was positioned to cover the entire extent of visible areas and ends immediately after entering areas of obscured visibility. During the Roman Period, several new earthworks were constructed, all following the same pattern. When observed from Folly Lane, this would have created an impression that a considerable portion of the surrounding area was enclosed, even though the actual distribution of ditches and dykes is somewhat sporadic.

Most of the earthworks are clustered near the supposed Late Iron Age road, around Gorhambury Lane, which cuts across the earthwork system of Devil's Ditch, New Dyke, and White Dyke. The existence of a road crossing this feature implies that restricting movement to and from Verulamium, and thus limiting it to a specific direction, was an important part of the overall design. Considering this, the presence of the road would have enhanced the impression of the earthwork system serving as a symbolic boundary marker during the Late Iron Age, which was later transformed into an elaborate entrance during the Roman Period. A similar pattern can be observed to the south, where the Silchester Road crosses the earthwork system named Wheeler's Ditch. This system also covered most of the visibility field's extent and likely controlled movement across most of the visible territory southwest of the burial. The visual impact was probably enhanced by the supposed enclosure further in the Prae Wood.

There are two Late Iron Age roads in the area surrounding Folly Lane. While the monument was visible from all sections of one of them, it was obscured by the hillside while moving along the Beech Bottom Dyke, the ceremonial route suggested by Bryant (2007). The traveler was unlikely to see the monument until the very point where this route meets the valley between the hills. During the Roman Period, evidence suggests that it was not particularly important for the Folly Lane complex to be visible from the roads. The monument was visible from slightly less than half, 45.45%, of the road network. Nevertheless, it appears that some roads, namely Colchester Road, Silchester Road, and Gorhambury Lane, were of major significance with their visibility ranging between 50% and 77.78%. Unsurprisingly, these roads are located within the most visible areas and are oriented toward most visually dominated directions. Finally, even though the burial complex was not visible from remote sections of the roads, the visibility of the monument gradually increased when a traveler was approaching Verulamium (Figure 12.2).

Stanway, Essex

The Stanway burial complex is located on a flat plateau to the southwest of modern Colchester. It lies only 0.25 km west of Gryme's Dyke, the westernmost element of the system of dykes that protected the Late Iron Age and Roman *oppidum* of Camulodunum (Crummy and Bojko 2007). Archaeological research so far has revealed not a dense, nucleated settlement but rather a broad plateau between the Roman and Colne rivers, given coherence by a set of large, linear earthworks (Creighton 2006: 130). The trajectory of urban living here was significantly altered in AD 49 by the foundation of the Colonia Victricensis, westward from Camulodunum (Creighton 2006: 110).

According to Creighton, the result was that the Iron Age settlement did not develop into a Roman town. The Stanway burial complex contained a series of wealthy cremation burials from the period between 50 BC and AD 90 (Crummy and Bojko 2007). Since they represent a small number of individuals buried in a series of related enclosures over several generations, the complex gives the impression of a sustained tradition. Hawkes and Crummy (1995: 169) interpreted this as showing continuity within the ruling class of the area (see also Creighton 2006: 131).

Although situated in a low-lying area, the burial complex features exceptional visibility. Positioned to dominate a considerable portion of the surrounding landscape, it also controlled the southern entrance to Camulodunum—to enter the *oppidum* from the south, one had to pass the monument (Figure 12.3). While valleys of nearby rivers appear not to have been visible, the extent of the viewshed focuses on the territory surrounding the *oppidum*. The orientation of the viewshed suggests that the location of the monument was chosen to dominate the eastern, northern, and southern directions, while territories to the west were largely ignored. If we take into consideration the fact that no significant changes in elevation in this direction are present, in contrast, for example, with the north, it seems likely that the orientation toward particular directions was a result of a deliberate act.

The distribution of dykes and ditches in the area also corresponds with the orientation of visibility from the monument. All were clearly visible from the burial monument and only covered the extent of the visibility field; no such features existed westward from the complex. Thus, the built environment created the illusion of an 'enclosed landscape.' The system of earthworks (i.e., Oliver's Dyke, Gryme's Dyke, Moat Farm Dyke, and Berechurch Dyke), which seems to have enclosed the area of the *oppidum*, is entirely visible from the burial complex. Viewshed analysis revealed that Berechurch Dyke was placed to cover the entire extent of the visibility field to the east when observed from the complex, and the same results apply to the other earthworks, including Oliver's Dyke, Heath Farm Dyke, Moat Farm Dyke, and Gryme's Dyke.

The Roman Period in East and Southeast England was marked by an obvious elaboration of the road network. Visibility analysis revealed that 50.48% of the nearby road system was visible from the Stanway complex. The burial complex was largely not visible from remote sections of the roads so that the visibility of the complex gradually increased as travelers approached the *oppidum* of Camulodunum, and later, Roman Colchester. Some parts of the road network, including Gosbecks Road and Stane Street, even featured exceptional visibility from the burial monument. Unsurprisingly,

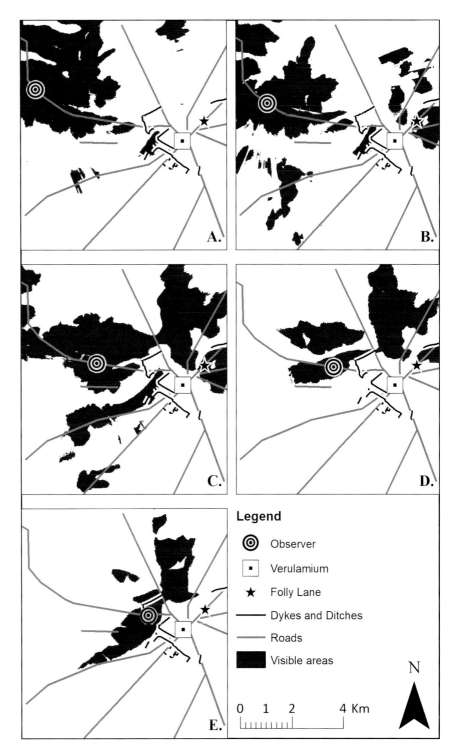

Figure 12.2. Viewshed analysis from five points along the Gorhambury Lane, illustrating changing vistas available to travelers (figure by the author).

all of them were laid in the most visible areas and their orientation corresponded with the visibility fields of the burial complex (see Figure 12.5).

The only entrance from the south was between Oliver's Dyke and Heath Farm Dyke, only several hundred meters away from the Stanway complex. Anyone who intended to enter the *oppidum* must have first passed the burial. In addition, the only identified Late Iron Age road from the area, located north of the complex, seems to have guided travelers to the likely entrance from the north, between Gryme's Dyke and Moat Farm Dyke. This becomes even more evident as we transition to the Roman Period. The major roads—Gosbecks Road and Stane Street—are positioned to reinforce the paths of movement established and enforced by the system of dykes. This is especially evident in the southern part of the *oppidum* where the Stanway complex is located. Here, the new Roman road not only approached the entrance to Camulodunum from the southwest but also passed by the burial complex.

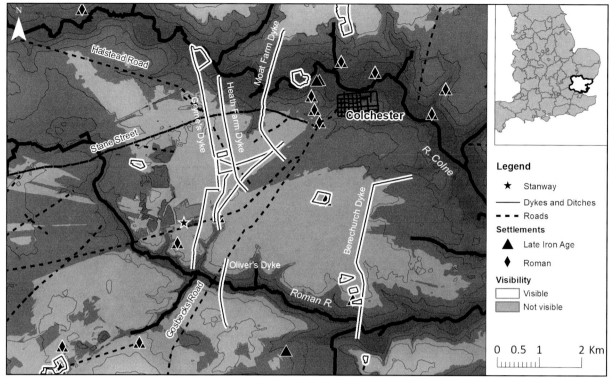

Figure 12.3. Viewshed analysis, with areas intervisible with the Stanway complex marked in lighter colors.
Crown copyright/database right 2012. An Ordnance Survey/EDINA supplied service
(figure by the author).

The Early Roman Period was marked by a clear shift of focus from the *oppidum* to the newly established town. As can be observed from the road network, a considerable portion of it leads to the town, and the elaboration of the earthwork system northward from the Stanway complex is likely to have served the same purpose. The earthworks were extended to cover the entire width of the visual areas to the north and west, creating the impression of an enclosed territory for anyone approaching from these directions. Furthermore, the layout of the road network in these directions (e.g., the Colchester-Halstead Road and Stane Street) also implies that they were built with respect to the established ways of movement. This was further reinforced by the construction of earthworks. The roads cross the earthworks in the same locations where their Roman Period additions and extensions meet the older features, thus restricting and controlling movement across the landscape.

This perceived continuity in the use of ritual landscapes confirms the findings of Creighton (2006). The Stanway complex presents evidence for the use of ritual landscapes being enforced by the Romans who drew upon royal lineages to legitimize the present. However, it is important to note that while in many ways analogous to Verulamium, the *oppidum* lacks urban character. In this case, the Roman town grew some 3 km away to the northeast, on the foundation of the legionary base. If not for the previous Roman

occupation, the town would likely have grown near the ritual complex as has been observed in the case of Verulamium.

Lexden, Essex

The Lexden tumulus lies within the modern boundary of the city of Colchester, just 3 km northeast of the Stanway complex. Archaeologically, it was located outside the Roman town of Colchester but within the system of Late Iron Age dykes that surrounded Camulodunum (Foster 1986). This is the area where two principal groups of Late Iron Age and Early Roman Period burials have been uncovered. The Lexden tumulus was a large mound covering a burial chamber. Much like the Folly Lane example, it contained deliberately broken and fragmented remains of grave goods and pyre goods belonging to a single individual. The ceramics date the assemblage to around 15–10 BC, and the imports included amphorae, a folding chair, and other exotic items, most famously a silver medallion of Augustus himself. This burial is often assumed to be of a friendly king, although which one has always been open to question (Creighton 2006: 131). In addition, the burial was not alone; other cremations, which contained ceramics imported in the Late Iron Age, have been found in the vicinity (Hawkes and Crummy 1995: 85).

Viewshed analysis revealed that the burial monument was intervisible with a significant portion of

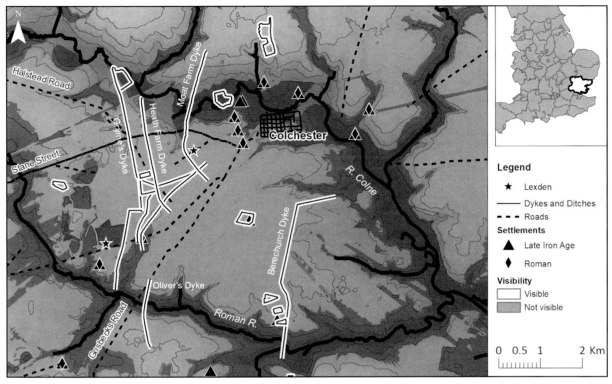

Figure 12.4. Viewshed analysis, with areas intervisible with the Lexden tumulus marked in lighter colors.
Crown copyright/database right 2012. An Ordnance Survey/EDINA supplied service
(figure by the author).

surrounding areas (Figure 12.4). It is evident that this structure was deliberately positioned with little regard to any one particular direction, but instead dominated the entire surrounding landscape. At the Folly Lane and Stanway complexes, we could observe the specific orientation of visibility toward particular areas. In contrast to the Stanway complex, Lexden not only dominated the Late Iron Age *oppidum* but also oversaw the Roman town of Colchester, alongside the entire plateau between the Colne and Roman rivers. Because it was difficult in these lowlands to find a place that could be seen from far away in any direction, the argument for overall visibility at Lexden becomes even more convincing.

The layout of the Roman road network corresponds with the visual dominance of the complex. Lexden was visible from as much as 77.67% of the surrounding roads. All of the roads were laid either westward or eastward from the monument, with only two exceptions. One of these, the Gosbecks Road, is characterized by exceptional intervisibility with the Stanway complex, as discussed above. The fact that it is clearly visible from only one of the monuments, and is relatively obscured from the other, suggests that this placement might have been deliberate. Since the road likely served as a pathway to the *oppidum* from the south, it is unsurprising that the visibility of the southern monument was considered to be more important.

All of the Late Iron Age earthworks in the vicinity were visible. Once again, their positioning implies that they were constructed to cover the entire extent of the visible areas. This is well illustrated by examples of Berechurch Dyke to the east and the system of earthworks to the west (Oliver's Dyke, Gryme's Dyke, etc.). The resulting visual phenomenon and its visibility from both monuments confirm the hypothesis of meticulous planning. This is also reaffirmed by later extensions of the earthwork system during the Early Roman Period. The extensions of Gryme's Dyke and the newly constructed Triple Dyke filled in the missing gaps between the visible and invisible areas. After that, the earthwork system covered the entire extent of the visible territory westward from the monument. As in the other cases described above, the system must have created the perception of an enclosed landscape and resulted in an impression of boundedness. In this regard, a ritual landscape would have constructed and shaped the common discourse for the local community by demarcating the geographical boundary between what was to be considered 'communal' and the 'otherness.'

Finally, a viewshed analysis of the roads laid to the northeast from the burial complex revealed an interesting pattern. This area was obscured from the Stanway complex, yet visible from the Lexden tumulus. These roads not only were intervisible with the tumulus but they also led to a specific place in

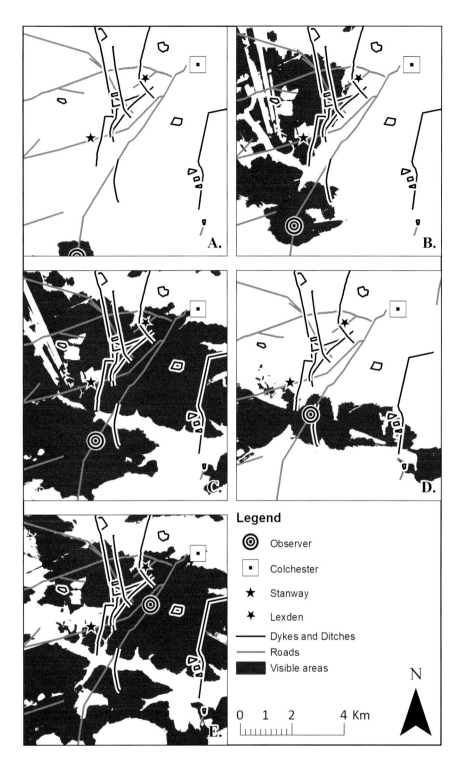

Figure 12.5. Viewshed analysis from five points along the Gosbecks Road, illustrating changing vistas available to travelers (figure by the author).

the landscape, just northeast to Camulodunum. This area was not enclosed by the earthwork system, but it is where Roman Colchester was built. This suggests that while both the Stanway and Lexden complexes dominated the landscape controlled by the Late Iron Age *oppidum*, their importance gradually decreased after the center of power moved to the Roman town. Despite their changing meaning, it is evident that their importance did not disappear completely, as both were left to control movement from the south and west. It is also likely that the Lexden tumulus was superior to

the Stanway complex since it dominated a considerably larger portion of the landscape and might have been visible for most travelers along the roads (Figure 12.5).

Discussion

The case studies discussed above illustrate how different populations were constructing their own version of a 'Roman nucleated community.' As already noted by Creighton (2006), this is the problem (or delight) with people. Everyone is trying to achieve the same perceived aim, but their actions are bound by their knowledge. In the case of Verulamium, the Iron Age *oppidum* was allowed to continue to develop into a 'British' version of a Roman town, less influenced by people of knowledge. By contrast, in Camulodunum, the model of Roman nucleation was coming from the dense settlement of Roman troops—the town of Colchester was assembled on the foundations of the Roman legionary base. Yet, in both cases, burial monuments remained essential to settlement development. The case studies shared similar patterns in their landscape setting across the region of the 'Southern and Eastern kingdoms.' The monuments dominated a significant portion of the surrounding landscapes, with some favoring orientation toward specific directions. This is related to the established ways of movement and construction of systems of dykes and ditches during the Late Iron Age. When plotted on a map, these features seem scattered across the landscape. Visibility analysis, however, revealed that their location and position created the impression of an enclosed landscape. The creation of such features in the region is not known before the Late Iron Age. After the Roman conquest, parts of the earthwork systems were extended and elaborated, though no major alterations were made. The newly constructed road networks only complemented existing ways of movement and, on some occasions, turned some parts of the earthwork systems into elaborate entrances.

What Does It Mean?

It is evident that these landscape features dramatically restricted the ways of movement and thus the possible perception of landscape. Such constructions relied on several factors, including 1) experience in construction; 2) knowledge and understanding of the location; 3) resources and human labor; and 4) political, social, and/or economic necessity. Such landscape alterations in East and Southeast England started during the Late Iron Age, suggesting that the experience and technical skills required must have been obtained from elsewhere. Creighton (2006) has suggested that similar strategies may have been learned from the Romans, via the practice of *obsides*, which started shortly after Caesar's invasion, but evidence for this is limited to historic parallels mentioned in classical texts and interpretation of coins. It also implies the presence of relatively strong and regular communication between the indigenous communities and Rome. Our findings indirectly support this hypothesis. In this light, the modifications to the landscape made after the Roman conquest can be seen as completion rather than alteration. For example, in the case of Verulamium, these features were gradually completed as the *oppidum* evolved into a Roman town. By comparison, in the case of Camulodunum, the landscape was slightly modified because after the conquest the center of political power shifted from the *oppidum* to the newly built Colchester.

Even this case implies some form of continuity. The center of social and political focus migrated, thus, the landscape features were altered to maintain their original purpose. Finally, the intended function and the scale of these constructions indicate a high degree of organization to assemble and manage the required labor.

What Role Did These Landscapes Play?

It is evident that the earthworks were not constructed for a defensive purpose, as indicated by their sporadic distribution in the landscape. It is much more likely that these features were built with the intention of creating an 'imagined community' (Anderson 2006)—a socially constructed community, imagined by the people who perceived themselves as a part of that group. Although this concept is more common when discussing the emergence of the modern nation-state, the findings of this paper suggest that the shaping of Late Iron Age cultural landscapes may have acted in a similar way to the printing press. The concept of 'print capitalism' is characteristic of nineteenth-century Europe (Anderson 2006), and it illustrates how the press was used to create a common discourse for masses of individuals who would otherwise not perceive themselves as a part of a larger group. During the Iron Age, cultural landscapes were likely to be another such vector, providing a ritualized demonstration of a kind of belonging.

These cremation burial monuments and their landscape settings were closely linked to the local communities. The elaborate funerary rites required meticulous planning and were likely to bring a whole community to a specific place. The entire surrounding landscape appeared to have been enclosed when observed from the monuments. This created an impression of an enclosed space—a 'communal territory'—and enforced a sense of belonging. In addition, the construction of features such as dykes and roads was also likely to be a communal event. A gathering of the local population for a specific period of time to conduct communal labor required a high degree of social organization. These events allowed the community to construct and maintain social networks on a scale not limited to a single settlement. Furthermore, after completion, the landscape features served as identity markers for the community.

The monuments also helped to reinforce the ideology of the ruling elites. The road network restricted movement across the landscape, thus determining the ways in which it would be perceived. Any traveler, either local or an outsider, was forced to approach the Late Iron Age *oppida* and Roman towns from a specific direction. They first had to pass the earthwork systems turned into elaborate entrances, which created the impression of entering an enclosed area—a territory controlled by an individual or a group of local elites. Second, the visibility of burial monuments gradually increased when travelers approached these settlements, which served as a signal that one is approaching the center of social, political, and economic power.

Finally, we can observe a clear case of continuity and tradition. For example, Folly Lane contains evidence of a Late Iron Age sanctuary underneath the Roman temple. This suggests that these enclosed landscapes were perceived as communal property, inherited by a community via the rights of ancestral kinship. Moreover, the maintenance of tradition may also have served as one of the means of legitimizing power. The mechanisms of obtaining and maintaining political power during the Late Iron Age in Britain are still debated, but the presented case studies suggest that continuation and tradition were emphasized over change. This can be noted even after the Roman conquest. There is little doubt that after the conquest, Romans considered these landscapes to be Roman. However, there is no evidence of major Roman alterations to the local landscape. Newly constructed features and road networks only reinforced the preexisting ways of moving and perceiving the landscape. These, therefore, should be seen as a form of completion and elaboration rather than transformation. The landscape features were likely intended to serve the very same set of purposes— to shape social identity, maintain communal integrity, emphasize continuity, and legitimize the power of the ruling elite.

Conclusions

The findings of this paper illustrate how burial monuments were used in the construction of physical and social space in Late Iron Age and Early Roman Britain. They suggest that some monuments may have played an important role in the emergence of monumental centers and settlement nucleation, which intensified after the Roman conquest.

The case studies demonstrate how burial monuments could have been employed in the creation of 'landscapes of power.' The location of a monument in relation to natural and man-made landscape features created an impression of an enclosed space, a communal territory, and conveyed a sense of belonging to a particular community. Also, these functioned as symbols of continuity and a maintained tradition, thereby legitimizing the rule of the local elites. Finally, after the conquest, these monuments were incorporated into new road networks, which, in turn, assisted in facilitating Roman ideology.

This evolution of the Iron Age built environment is an example of continuity over time, even with the arrival of outsiders and the subsequent reuse of the same

landscape features. While it is impossible to know for certain how prehistoric communities perceived their environment, essential pieces of evidence are embedded in the cultural landscapes. By examining these as metaphors for the knowledge, skills, and intentions of their architects, we come closer to understanding the organization, lives, and experiences of past societies.

Acknowledgments

Most of this paper stems from my MA dissertation. I would like to thank my mentors, Dr. Tom Moore and Dr. Rob Witcher, for the guidance and supervision during this project. Thanks are due to Dr. Radoslaw Grabowski and the rest of the IMASS research group for valuable ideas and discussions. I would also like to thank the HER offices of Hertfordshire and Kent for providing access to the excavation data. Finally, I would like to thank the editors and anonymous reviewers. If not for your remarks, comments, and suggestions, this paper would have not seen the light of day. Any errors remain my own responsibility.

References Cited

Anderson, B. 2006. *Imagined Communities: Reflections on the Origin and Spread of Nationalism.* London: Verso.

Bevan, B. 1997. Bounding the Landscape: Place and Identity during the Yorkshire Wolds Iron Age, in A. Gwilt and C. Haselgrove (eds) *Reconstructing Iron Age Societies: New Approaches to the British Iron Age:* 181–191. Oxford: Oxbow Books.

Bryant, S. 2007. Central Places or Special Places? The Origins and Development of *'Oppida'* in Hertfordshire, in A. Gwilt and C. Haselgrove (eds) *Reconstructing Iron Age Societies: New Approaches to the British Iron Age:* 62–80. Oxford: Oxbow Books.

Carr, G. 2007. Excarnation to Cremation: Continuity or Change?, in C. Haselgrove and T. Moore (eds) *The Later Iron Age in Britain and Beyond:* 444–554. Oxford: Oxbow Books.

Creighton, J. 2000. *Coins and Power in Late Iron Age Britain.* Cambridge: Cambridge University Press.

Creighton, J. 2006. *Britannia: The Creation of a Roman Province.* London: Routledge.

Crummy, P. and A.-M. Bojko 2007. *Stanway: An Élite Burial Site at Camulodunum.* London: Society for the Promotion of Roman Studies.

Eckardt, H., P. Brewer, S. Hay and S. Poppy 2009. Roman Barrows and their Landscape Context: a GIS Case Study at Bartlow, Cambridgeshire. *Britannia* 40(1): 65–98.

Fleming, A. 2006. Post-processual Landscape Archaeology: a Critique. *Cambridge Archaeological Journal* 16(3): 267–280.

Foster, J. 1986. *The Lexden Tumulus: A re-appraisal of an Iron Age burial from Colchester, Essex* (BAR British Series 156). Oxford: B.A.R.

Gaffney, V. and P.M. van Lusen 1995. Postscript – GIS, environmental determinism and archaeology, in G. Lock and Z. Stančič (eds) *Archaeology and Geographical Information Systems*: 367–382. London: Taylor and Francis.

Giles, M. 2007. Good Fences Make Good Neighbours? Exploring the Ladder Enclosure of Late Iron Age East Yorkshire, in C. Haselgrove and T. Moore (eds) *The Later Iron Age in Britain and Beyond*: 235–249. Oxford: Oxbow Books.

Gwilt, A. and C. Haselgrove 1997. Approaching the Iron Age, in A. Gwilt and C. Haselgrove (eds) *Reconstructing Iron Age Societies: New Approaches to the British Iron Age*: 1–8. Oxford: Oxbow Books.

Haselgrove, C. 1987. *Iron Age Coinage in South-East England: The Archaeological Context* (BAR British Series 174). Oxford: B.A.R.

Haselgrove, C. 2007. The Age of Enclosure: Later Iron Age Settlement and Society in Northern France, in C. Haselgrove and T. Moore (eds) *The Later Iron Age in Britain and Beyond*: 492–522. Oxford: Oxbow Books.

Haselgrove, C.C. and M. Millet 1997. Verlamion Reconsidered, in A. Gwilt and C. Haselgrove (eds) *Reconstructing Iron Age Societies: New Approaches to the British Iron Age*: 282–296. Oxford: Oxbow Books.

Hawkes, C.F.C. and P. Crummy 1995. *Camulodunum 2*. Colchester: Colchester Archaeological Reports.

Hill, J.D. 1989. Re-Thinking the Iron Age. *Scottish Archaeological Review* 6: 16–24.

Hill, J.D. 1995a. *Ritual and Rubbish in the Iron Age of Wessex: A study on the formation of a specific archaeological record*. Oxford: Tempus Reparatum.

Hill, J.D. 1995b. The Pre-Roman Iron Age in Britain and Ireland (ca. 800 B.C. to A.D. 100): An Overview. *Journal of World Prehistory* 9(1): 47–98.

Hill, J.D. 2006. Are we any closer to understanding how later Iron Age societies worked (or did not work)?, in C. Haselgrove (ed.) *Les mutations de la fin de l'âge du Fer: Celtes et Gaulois: l'Archéologie face à l'Histoire*: 169–179. Glux-en-Glenne: Center archéologique européen.

Hodder, I. 1982. *Symbols in action: Ethnoarchaeological studies of material culture*. Cambridge: Cambridge University Press.

Ingold, T. 1993. The Temporality of the Landscape. *World Archaeology* 25(2): 24–174.

Llobera, M. 2007. Reconstructing Visual Landscapes. *World Archaeology* 39(1): 51–69.

Lock, G.R. and T.M. Harris 1996. Danebury Revisited: An English Iron Age Hillfort in a Digital Landscape, in M. Aldenderfer and H.D.G. Maschner (eds) *Anthropology, Space, and Geographic Information Systems*: 214–240. Oxford: Oxford University Press.

Moore, T. 2007. Perceiving communities: Exchange, landscapes and social networks in the Later Iron Age of Western Britain. *Oxford Journal of Archaeology* 26(1): 79–102.

Niblett, R. 1999. *The Excavation of a Ceremonial Site at Folly Lane, Verulamium* (Brittania Monograph Series 14). London: Society for the Promotion of Roman Studies.

Niblett, R. 2001. *Verulamium: The Roman City of St. Albans*. Stroud: Tempus.

Parker Pearson, M. and C. Richards (eds) 1997. *Architecture and Order: Approaches to Social Space*. London: Routledge.

Renfrew, C. 1990. What Song the Sirens Sang, in C. Renfrew (ed.) *Archaeology and Language: The Puzzle of Indo-European Origins*: 1–9. Cambridge: Cambridge University Press.

Renfrew, C. and E.B.W. Zubrow (eds) 1994. *The Ancient Mind: Elements of Cognitive Archaeology*. Cambridge: Cambridge University Press.

Rennell, R. 2008. Exploring 'everyday' places in the Iron Age landscape of the Outer Hebrides, in O. Davis, N. Sharples and K. Waddington (eds) *Changing Perspectives on the First Millennium BC*: 43–60. Oxford: Oxbow Books.

Schiffer, M.B. 1975. Behavioral Chain Analysis: Activities, Organization, and the Use of Space. *Fieldiana, Anthropology* 65: 103–119.

Taylor, J. 1997. Space and place: some thoughts on Iron Age and Romano-British landscapes, in A. Gwilt and C. Haselgrove (eds) *Reconstructing Iron Age Societies: New Approaches to the British Iron Age*: 192–204. Oxford: Oxbow Books.

Tilley, C. 1994. *A phenomenology of landscape: places, paths and monuments*. Oxford: Berg.

Tschan, A.P. 1999. An Introduction to Object-Oriented GIS in Archaeology, in J.A. Barceló, I. Briz and A. Vila (eds) *New Techniques for Old Times: CAA 98 – Computer Applications and Quantitative Methods in Archaeology* (BAR International Series 757): 303–316. Oxford: Archaeopress.

Tschan, A.P., W. Raczkowski and M. Latalowa 2000. Perception and viewsheds: are they mutually inclusive?, in G. Lock (ed.) *Beyond the Map: Archaeology and Spatial Technologies*: 28–48. Amsterdam: IOS Press.

Wheatley, D. and M. Gillings 2000. Vision, perception and GIS: developing enriched approaches to the study of archaeological visibility, in G. Lock (ed.) *Beyond the Map: Archaeology and Spatial Technologies*: 1–27. Amsterdam: IOS Press.

Witcher, R.E. 1998. Roman roads: phenomenological perspectives on roads in the landscape, in C. Forcey, J. Hawthorne and R. Witcher (eds) *TRAC 97: Proceedings of the Seventh Annual Theoretical Roman Archaeology Conference*: 60–70. Oxford: Oxbow Books.

Witcher, R.E. 1999. GIS and Landscapes of Perception, in M. Gillings, D. Mattingly and J. van Dalen (eds) *Geographical Information Systems and Landscape Archaeology*: 13–22. Oxford: Oxbow Books.

Chapter 13

Kernavė Town in the 13th and 14th Centuries: Social and Cultural Patterns of Community

Rokas Vengalis and Gintautas Vėlius

Abstract

Medieval Kernavė was one of the earliest and most important urban centers of Lithuania. Because historical records do not provide any data about the spatial structure of Kernavė in the 13th and 14th centuries AD, archaeological data is the only source of information available for reconstructing the relationship between spatial organization and social dynamics in the town. This paper focuses on the functional and social organization of Kernavė based on the built environment. A detailed analysis of the archaeological data provides insight into how historical events and fluctuations in political relations are reflected in the development of the built environment, how the built environment and locations of functional zones can be used to understand relationships between spatial structure and social organization, and how various social groups can be recognized and the resulting patterns interpreted. The division of Kernavė into distinct structural units—the duke's residence, defensive fortifications, fortified and unfortified parts of the town—indicates social stratification. Comparisons of archaeological data from various parts of the town enable the understanding of Kernavė's spatial structure as it related to status, function, and ethnic–confessional identity.

Introduction

During the Middle Ages, the Southeast Baltic was populated by Baltic tribes, including Prussians, Yatvings, Lithuanians, Curonians, Semigalians, Latgalians, and other smaller tribes, whose social, economic, and political developments were quite isolated, and thus, European trends spread into the region slowly and belatedly (Leciejewicz and Valor 2007: 63–64). Christianity was not dominant, states were not established, and urban settlements did not form until the beginning of the 13th century when the Teutonic Order changed the cultural evolution of a large portion of this region by conquests and colonization. Crusaders immediately brought Christianity and founded Teutonic Order states and towns (Christiansen 1980: 89–104). The lands of a few tribes, primarily Lithuanians and Samogitians, were not conquered, and a pagan state, the Grand Duchy of Lithuania (hereafter GDL), arose in their territory in 1236 (Bumblauskas 2005: 36–37). The newly established state immediately expanded significantly by incorporating the neighboring Christian territories inhabited by Slavs (Rowell 1994: 20–21).

Many administrative, craft, trade, and cultural centers, which had existed for a long time in the eastern Slavic lands, were incorporated into GDL territory during this expansion. Interestingly, the GDL state administration did not take advantage of existing infrastructure and the political center was retained in Lithuania proper, where only small agrarian settlements existed previously. Because such state structure was not logical economically—Lithuania was a small area within the territory of the state, was located in its very outskirts, and did not accommodate developed urban centers—it can be assumed that this was a political decision, most likely also related to religious concerns.

Such historical background surrounded the formation of the first towns in Lithuania proper in the 13th and 14th centuries. Their evolution is divergent because primarily political forces, rather than economic forces, drove their development (Gudavičius 1999: 92; Žulkus and Jarockis 2013: 72). In a political–administrative sense, they had a more prominent position than did other, economically and culturally more developed towns across other regions of the GDL. Such a position, in turn, eventually influenced their economic and cultural development.

Therefore, the political–historical circumstances alone—including the beginning of urbanization processes that occurred *c.* 300–500 years later than in surrounding European countries and the operation of pagan administrative–political centers, which administrated much larger Christian centers—point to the uniqueness of these centers and their importance to understand the history of pre-industrial urbanization in Europe. A major problem is that the results of research in these centers are difficult to access for the wider scientific community—detailed publications are seldom and the few available studies have been published typically in Lithuanian (e.g., Gudavičius 1991; Katalynas 2006; Vaitkevičius 2010; Vėlius 2005).

In this paper, we discuss the spatial and social development of one of the earliest and most important urban centers of Lithuania—Kernavė. We focus on the functional and social organization of Kernavė based on the built environment. The main issues discussed here include how historical events and fluctuations in political settings shaped the development of the built environment, how the built environment and functional zones can be used to comprehend relationships between spatial and social organization, what social groups can be recognized in the town, and how the built environment was used to express social, confessional, and ethnic identity. We believe that this paper can be of interest not merely in the context of GDL history but also for researchers who explore early towns and urbanization processes worldwide as well as for those interested in the spread of Christianity and manifestations of religious syncretism.

Historical Context

The period of Lithuanian state formation was accompanied by significant changes in the social structure of the society. Professional craftspeople and merchants emerged in traditional agrarian communities. They lived in settlements adjacent to hillforts, which were the dukes' residences. Therefore, the rudiments of towns formed from communities that fulfilled the needs of the feudal and military elite (Gudavičius 1999: 90–92; Vėlius 2005: 23).

Researchers are confident that in Lithuania proper, urban communities already existed in Vilnius and Kernavė at the end of the 13th century (Vaitkevičius 2010: 64–65). There were more urban centers within the confines of the GDL, though they all were associated with the historical development of Christian Slavic communities (Figure 13.1; Vėlius 2005: 10).

The circumstances of the evolution of the first towns in Lithuania become clearer in the light of historical processes within this larger territory. The 11th to 13th centuries coincided with the rearrangement of political forces and cultural influences across the Baltic region (Žulkus and Jarockis 2013: 270–290). As was the case throughout its entire history, Lithuania at that time was at the crossroads of the West and East. Sociopolitical processes in the coastal and eastern regions of Lithuania were related to the changing geopolitical settings in Europe (Vėlius 2003: 161–162). Intensive military and commercial activities of Scandinavian Vikings stimulated the appearance of the first proto-towns in coastal Lithuania during the 9th and 10th centuries (e.g., Palanga: Žulkus 2007: 386; Žulkus and Jarockis 2013: 50–72). However, these commercial centers existed only as long as the Scandinavians needed them and they never became larger, political–administrative centers (Žulkus and Jarockis 2013: 72).

Fundamental sociopolitical transformations in eastern Lithuania occurred much later, in the 13th century. Before that, during the 11th and 12th centuries, the region was a target area for the Kievan Rus' expansion policy. In the upper reaches of the Nemunas River, in the former territory of the Baltic Yatvings tribe, Slavic towns—Grodno, Volkovysk, Slonim, and Novogrudok—began to spring up as border outposts (Žulkus and Jarockis 2013: 50). However, as early as the end of the 12th century, troops of Lithuanian dukes started to attack the neighboring eastern Slavic lands and towns (Gudavičius 1999: 35–36). During the 13th century, a whole range of powerful, well-fortified hillforts, such as Vilnius, Kernavė, Maišiagala, and Nemenčinė, developed in eastern Lithuania. Archaeological data from settlements adjacent to these hillforts testify to an increasing population (Vėlius 2003: 162). The hillforts previously functioned as fortified settlements or hideouts for nearby agrarian communities, but during this later period, they became the residences of a new military elite—the dukes and their warriors (Vengalis 2009: 154–162). These processes in eastern Lithuania led to the birth of the Lithuanian state in 1236, which nearly coincided with the devastation of Kievan Rus by a Mongol-Tatar campaign in 1240. These political events detached the above-mentioned Slavic towns from their political and cultural roots, and the first Lithuanian king Mindaugas (1236–1263) took advantage of this opportunity and incorporated them into the GDL (Dubonis 2009b: 169–170). In the first half of the 14th century, as the quality and variety of craft production show, the material culture of Slavic towns of the Upper Nemunas began to decline considerably (Zverugo 1983: 62). Thus, the decline of neighboring Slavic towns, the growth of the GDL's military potential and political power, and the development of the first Lithuanian towns of Vilnius and Kernavė were simultaneous processes with mutual influence (Vėlius 2003: 162).

Some remarks about the earliest urban development and structural model of Vilnius are found in historical sources (Vaitkevičius 2010: 21–23). Concerning the evolution of Kernavė, however, one can rely almost exclusively on archaeological data. In the middle of the 14th century, Vilnius consisted of four main parts: 1) the duke's castle on the fortified hill and the adjacent Lower Town surrounded by a masonry wall; 2) the wooden castle on the other hill and the so-called Crooked Town adjacent to it; 3) the Orthodox district (*civitas Ruthenica*); and 4) the Catholic part of the town (Girlevičius 2016: 370–372). Several Orthodox and Catholic churches were built in various parts of the town during the 14th century (Jonaitis 2011). Thus, the primary structure of Vilnius was largely based on community confession—Orthodox, Catholics, and pagans who were linked to Crooked Town (Girlevičius 2016: 370). Only the central, prominent, and fortified section of the town was not organized by such principles. The high-ranking rulers

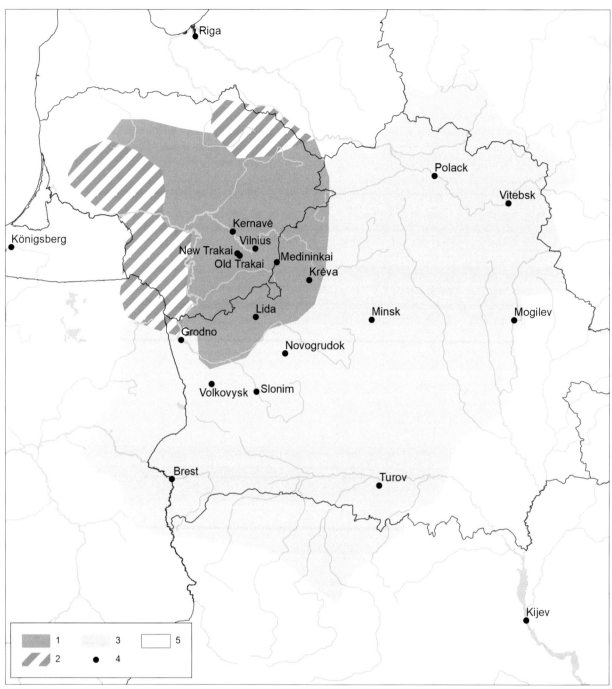

Figure 13.1. The territory of the Grand Duchy of Lithuania (GDL) during the reign of Grand Duke Gediminas (1316–1341). 1: The GDL at the end of the 13th century; 2: The adjacent territories recognizing the authority of the GDL; 3: Expansion of the GDL during the reign of Grand Duke Gediminas; 4: Main urban centers; 5: Modern state boundaries (figure by R. Vengalis).

and grand dukes were pagans, whereas some of their family members were Orthodox (e.g., Grand Duke Algirdas' wives). Moreover, the first Catholic church was erected in this central area at the turn of the 13th and 14th centuries (Vaitkevičius 2010: 61). Therefore, this part of Vilnius was markedly mixed in terms of confession and was organized according to political and economic realities dictated by the elite. When Kernavė's evolution is concerned, such knowledge about the early structure of Vilnius is important because we

can presume that Kernavė's development and earliest spatial organization would be to some extent similar.

Kernavė in the Written Sources

Lithuanian society traditionally and widely regards Kernavė as the cradle of statehood and the first capital of the GDL. Historians do not favor this tradition and presume that there was no a single and constant capital before the establishment of one in Vilnius around 1323

(Rowell 1994: 69–72). Kernavė is rarely mentioned in contemporaneous literary sources, and when it occurs it does in fragmentary terms (Gudavičius 2005), however, the value of these mentions is extremely exalted in historical memory. Moreover, it is not a modern but an old phenomenon, clearly expressed in sources written as early as the 16th century (Gudavičius 2005: 141).

The state chancellery of the GDL was established only at the end of the 14th century. Therefore, the early history of the GDL is documented exclusively in the annals of the neighboring countries and is very fragmentary (Markman 2015). Consequently, sources about Kernavė written in the 13th century are incidental—they only mention that Kernavė belonged to Grand Duke Traidenis in 1279, and some merchants from Kernavė are referred in Riga's debt book (Gudavičius 2005: 140–142). Kernavė occurs in fourteenth-century sources more often, and there is no reason to doubt that the town became an important center by then (Gudavičius 2005: 142–144). At the same time, however, these literary data demonstrate an increasingly growing lag between Kernavė and other leading centers, such as Vilnius and Trakai.

This lag is detectable in many facets. In particular, it is related to the significance of the Kernavė castle as a military fortress. Masonry castles were built in Vilnius and Trakai in the first half of the 14th century and there were even more by the second half of the same century, but Kernavė was not recorded as one of them (Vélius 2003: 161). Therefore, Kernavė's wooden castle, which probably was the most powerful fortification complex in Lithuania at the beginning of the 14th century, clearly lost its strategic importance. This is further indicated by sources about the attacks of Kernavė in 1365 and 1390, which reported that the castle was no longer able to cope with the sieges (Gudavičius 2005: 142–143). The second siege was decisive, as the castle was not rebuilt and Kernavė is no longer mentioned among the important centers in the written sources.

Another indicator of Kernavė's significance is trade. The first Lithuanian merchants were mentioned in 1290 and 1303 and they were from Kernavė (Gudavičius 2005: 142). However, at that time, the merchant class might not have been well established yet and was not weighty; this is testified by the undermining tone of the Grand Duke toward them (Dubonis 2009b: 159–161; Gudavičius 2005: 142). By the 1330s, this situation was certainly different because the Grand Duke gave privileges to the merchants, tried to lure them from distant lands, and built churches specifically for them (Gudavičius 1999: 90–92). From this changed context, however, there is no literary evidence for Kernavė's merchants and the contemporary sources only mention merchants from Vilnius.

Urban centers also are often inseparable from their religious functions (Rowell 1994: 130–132). This is a complicated issue, however, when the early towns in Lithuania are concerned. One could assume that after the establishment of the Lithuanian state, and before the adoption of Christianity, paganism should have transformed into an institutionalized religion with specific religious centers (Vaitkevičienė and Vaitkevičius 2001: 312–318). Despite this assumption, there is no data for such centers, or if they were located in the emerging administrative centers.

In summary, the reliable contemporaneous historical sources do not refer directly to Kernavė as a significant center. From the 1320s and 1330s onward, Vilnius and Trakai were the dominant Lithuanian centers in every sense, and if Kernavė had been the state-level administrative center, it could have lasted only for a relatively short time, from the 1250s to 1310s, during the early stages of its urban development. The more mature urbanization stage in Kernavė throughout the 14th century seems to have coincided with a gradual decay of its political and economic importance. By the 15th century, Kernavė was already one of the ordinary provincial towns. It is noteworthy that Kernavė is not mentioned among the places with the first parishes and churches after the baptism of Lithuania in 1387 (Gudavičius 2005: 144–145).

Structural Components in Kernavė

Kernavė is one of the most important Lithuanian archaeological sites and the Cultural Reserve of Kernavė is in the UNESCO World Heritage list (Figure 13.2). The site contains settlement remains representing virtually all major prehistoric and historic periods, from the withdrawal of the glaciers to the present day. Archaeological excavations in Kernavė have been conducted annually since 1979. As a result, approximately 17,000 m² have been excavated, and features and artifacts associated with the medieval settlement were found across nearly half of this area.

Although Kernavė has been investigated for a long time, current knowledge about the size, structure, and other characteristics of the town is far from comprehensive and changes virtually every year as archaeological research progresses. Interpretations presented in previous publications have shifted significantly. For example, only one actual residential area, the Lower Town, had been assumed in Kernavė, with a small number of homesteads in the Upper Town (Luchtanas and Vitkūnas 2004: 42–46; Vitkūnas 2005: 72–73). Recently collected data indicate that many former interpretations are questionable and should be quite different. Accordingly, interpretations presented here may change in the future as new data will emerge.

Figure 13.2. The hillforts of Kernavė (photo by A. Kuzmickas).

Medieval Kernavė was located in the valley of the Neris River and on its upper terraces. In its heyday, during the 13th and 14th centuries, the town consisted of several structural units, including the castle (the duke's residence and its fortification system of two hillforts), the Fortified Town, the unfortified Lower and Upper Towns, and two cemeteries outside of the settlement (Figure 13.3). Excavations have been carried out across the site and the primary function of each of these sections has been identified.

The residence of the duke was located in the central hillfort (Figure 13.3.1). Situated on a steep, 20-m-high hill surrounded by ditches, the residence covered an area of 0.2 ha. Two defensive hillforts protected the duke's residence (Figure 13.3.2). The Fortified Town is distinguishable right next to the castle with its 1.5 ha-area separated by a formidable rampart and a ditch in the upper terrace (Figure 13.3.3).

The Lower Town was located in the valley of the Neris River. Its size is currently difficult to estimate, but it could have covered 20 to 25 ha. A working hypothesis is that two adjacent zones developed in the Lower Town featured by different paleoenvironmental conditions and, as indicated by the archaeological data, possibly different functions. Lower Town I was situated on the wetter portion of the valley, at the foot of the hillforts, on an abandoned riverbed filled with peat deposits (Figure 13.3.5). Lower Town II was located in the dry portion of the valley, on sandy soils, along the Neris River (Figure 13.3.6).

Lower Town I was discovered in the early stages of research at Kernavė. It attracted much attention because features with well-preserved organic materials, including wooden buildings, fences, and other structures, were unearthed in the waterlogged soil. After these initial excavations, it was thought that the town covered the entire valley between the hillforts and the river (Luchtanas 1988: 142). However, recent test excavations revealed that its extent was bounded by swamps and residual pools in the ancient riverbed (Vėlius and Vengalis 2016: 141–144), and it seems that it was relatively small, about 7-8 ha in size.

The boundaries of Lower Town II are likewise not quite clear, but the currently available data indicates that it covered at least 12 ha. Because the soil in this section is dry, the archaeological horizon is poorly preserved and information comes primarily from subsurface features and finds from the topsoil.

In the Upper Town, the archaeological horizon is much more degraded due to more intensive activities in later historical times. A part of this area is built-up and the rest has been subject to plowing for a long time. Current data indicates that the Upper Town was at least 18 ha, although it may have covered even a larger area (Figure 13.3.4).

The data presented above indicates that during the 13th and 14th centuries the total area of Kernavė was at least 40 ha (excluding slopes). Bearing in mind the known size of individual courtyards (c. 900 m^2; Luchtanas 1990: 149), the population of Kernavė might have been 1500–2500 people. This was a relatively substantial size, but Vilnius and the main Slavic centers were significantly larger in the second half of the 14th century (Vėlius 2003: 162–163). Kernavė differed from these centers

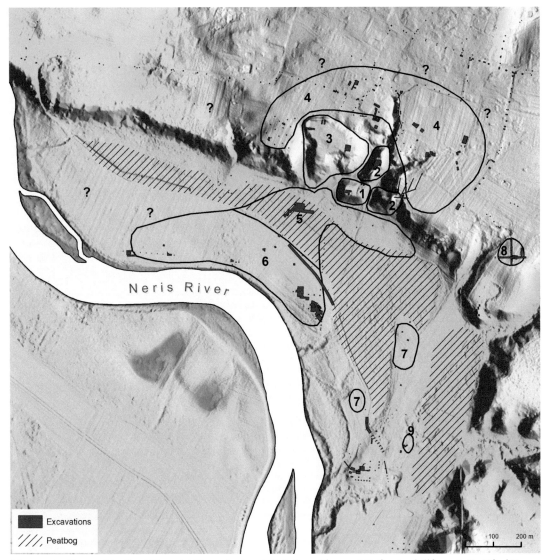

Figure 13.3. Kernavė in the 13th and 14th centuries. 1: Duke's residence; 2: Defensive hillforts; 3: Fortified Town; 4: Upper Town; 5: Lower Town I – craftspeople properties in the peatbog area; 6: Lower Town II – possible location of the marketplace; 7: Isolated farmsteads; 8: Inhumation cemetery; 9: Cremation cemetery; ?: Unexplored locations – possible extensions of the town area (figure by R. Vengalis).

in other respects as well. In this town, there were no masonry buildings, courtyards had relatively large areas, and the buildings in the individual properties were scattered and not arranged along streets. The absence of churches and the lack of evidence for the regular use of writing (e.g., styluses, inscriptions) are particularly noteworthy in thirteenth- and fourteenth-century Kernavė because these were fundamental attributes in contemporary European urban centers.

For the time being, two cemeteries associated with Kernavė and dating to the 13th and 14th centuries are known. Both are located outside of the town, and one of them, the inhumation cemetery of 0.5–0.6 ha in extent has been intensively excavated (Figure 13.3.8; Vėlius 2005, 2012b). This cemetery incorporated approximately 1500 graves. The burials were oriented to the west, interred in a single layer, and contained many grave

goods except weapons. The other cemetery is located in the valley (Figure 13.3.9). A distinctive burial rite was observed here—the cremated bones were mingled with the grave goods and seem to have been poured into the rivulet. This cemetery was identified a few years ago and only small-scale excavations have been conducted here; therefore, its area and the total number of burials have not yet been determined (Vengalis 2011b). Because nobility and warrior graves were not found in either of these two cemeteries, they were possibly interred in a currently unknown cemetery or cemeteries.

In the rest of this paper, the structure of Kernavė is addressed using different perspectives. The first is a chronological approach related to major structural changes over time, followed by the discussion of three spatial aspects, focusing on function, social stratification, and the confessional–ethnic perspective.

Chronological Issues

The absolute chronology of archaeological horizons and structures of Kernavė's medieval town remains one of the most challenging issues. The town flourished for a short time, and therefore, a very precise chronology is necessary to trace its development. However, dendrochronological dating has been applied only on one occasion, AMS 14C dating is complicated due to a plateau on the calibration curve between 1250 and 1400, and typo-chronology has not been developed sufficiently. It is noteworthy that most of Kernavė's development occurred during the pre-monetary GDL period, thus it is impossible to correlate typo-chronology with coins. Consequently, the archaeological horizons and burials in Kernavė have been dated based on written sources. The beginning of the town is considered to have taken place between the formation of the Lithuanian state in 1236 and the first mention of Kernavė in 1279. The town's main developmental phase terminated in 1390 when it was set on fire and afterward never recovered to its previous scale (Vėlius 2005: 22–24). In addition, the castle was burned down in 1365, and this date is considered to be distinctive when two separate stratigraphic layers are found (Luchtanas and Vitkūnas 2004). However, a critical approach to the archaeological data casts doubt on this chronological framework and allows the formulation of a slightly different model, albeit with more unknowns.

The town was not founded in an empty place because a permanent settlement already existed here during the 1st millennium AD (Vengalis 2012). Judging by the theoretical model of the formation of Lithuanian urban centers (Gudavičius 1991: 17–23), the evolution of Kernavė town began with the construction of the duke's residence in the main hillfort, which operated as the administrative center of the region. This hillfort dates back to much earlier, but its function had been different and it became the duke's residence only at the beginning of the 2nd millennium AD (Vengalis and Vėlius 2019).

The beginning of the formation of the urban center at Kernavė should not be linked exclusively with the establishment of the castle. Developments in the town's open parts, with the homesteads of freely employed craftspeople and merchants who served the castle, played an equally important role in Kernavė's evolution (Gudavičius 1991; Moździoch 1994: 137). The earliest townspeople's properties outside the castle supposedly were established at the very foot of the hillforts in Lower Town I and were dendrochronologically dated to the middle of the 13th century. However, this zone was quickly abandoned due to unfavorable natural conditions—the construction of fortifications in the hillforts initiated large-scale erosion processes that

manifested as recurrent landslides from the ravines and slopes (Vengalis et al. 2020).

The stratigraphy of Lower Town I includes some alluvial layers. These layers were previously interpreted as flood deposits from the Neris River, but recent research revealed that they are alluvial deposits related to the erosion processes in the slopes of the hillforts (Vengalis et al. 2020). One thick alluvial layer divides the archaeological stratum into two horizons. Previously, some researchers linked this division to the assault of Kernavė in 1365. They argued that the town was burned down and at least a dozen years had passed before its reoccupation (Luchtanas 1990: 152; Vėlius 2005: 21). These interpretations are unfounded. Evidence for destruction by fire has been recorded in only two of 14 buildings in Lower Town I and both were rebuilt immediately after the burning episodes. Moreover, the alluvial deposits could have developed over the course of a single event, and therefore, it cannot be considered as evidence for a hiatus in inhabitation. After this destruction episode, the network of streets and property boundaries were restored identically as it had been before in Lower Town I. This is not the case regarding individual buildings—some of them were reconstructed identically, others were not rebuilt, and new buildings were erected (Figure 13.4; Vitkūnas 2005: 73). Excavations revealed that there were some empty properties close to the streets both before and after the devastating landslide episode. Therefore, it is argued that Lower Town I was not the most intensively occupied quarter in any stage of Kernavė's development. Likewise, the upper horizon in Lower Town I does not show any traces of fire. Thus, the termination of the quarter's occupation cannot be associated with the assault in 1390. Instead, it seems that Lower Town I was destroyed by another, larger landslide, which probably happened well before 1390.

The Upper Town, in contrast to Lower Town I, shows evidence for fundamental restructuring, during which parcel boundaries and their functions transformed at least once (Vėlius 2006; Vengalis 2007). The date of this shift remains unclear, but it might not represent the degradation stage of the Upper Town because activities only intensified after the restructuring. This implies that different parts of Kernavė experienced quite different development and faced different social and natural challenges.

Recent research also raises serious doubts concerning the year 1390 as the date of the complete abandonment of Kernavė. There is a widely held assumption that the siege and fire in that year destroyed the town, and it was only several decades later that a new, much smaller town was established on the upper terrace of former Kernavė (Luchtanas and Vėlius 1996: 82–84; Vitkūnas 2005: 72–73). However, given that clear burning horizons were

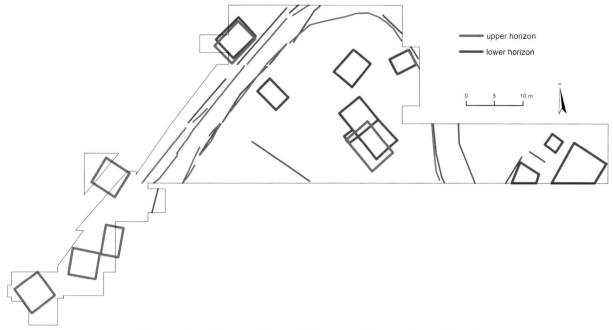

Figure 13.4. Buildings and fences in the excavated area of Lower Town I
(modified from Vitkūnas 2005 by R. Vengalis).

unearthed only in the hillforts of the town, the overall abandonment of Kernavė is hardly likely. The year 1390 was indeed tragic for the castle, and the entire Lower Town I probably had been already abandoned by this time, but no evidence for destruction or abandonment has yet been found in the Upper Town. On the contrary, coins dating back to the beginning of the 15th century have been recovered from that quarter.

In any case, evidence suggests that the entire spatial organization of Kernavė changed after 1390. The duke's manor was built to replace the castle about 1398 (Gudavičius 2005: 144), although it is not clear if the manor was located in the same place as the castle. After the baptism of Lithuania proper, the church was built in the central part of the Upper Town. The first mention of this church is only from 1495, but it might have been constructed earlier (Gudavičius 2005: 147). Archaeological evidence confirms this because graves dating as far back as the beginning of the 15th century were found in the churchyard (Jankauskas and Luchtanas 1990: 139).

Functional Structure

By using various criteria, scholars have proposed many different definitions of 'medieval town' to distinguish them from rural settlements (e.g., Blomkvist 2001; Hodges 1982). Concerning the historical context, the most important functional criteria for the early towns of the East Baltic region are their administrative functions, fortifications as well as craft, trade, and religious activities (Gudavičius 1991; Šešelgis 1996: 24–30).

Administrative functions must have been concentrated in the castle, which also served as the residence of the duke and the focal point of the town. In theory, the key identifier showing that the castle was the administrative and political center should be the presence of monumental architecture. In the Middle Ages of Lithuania, as across Europe, the architectural monumentality of the castle, typically related to the scale of fortification works, was inseparable from its defensive function. In this respect, by the beginning of the 14th century, Kernavė's wooden fortifications were undoubtedly exceptional among all Lithuanian castles. The duke's residence, two separate defensive hillforts, deep ditches, and the Fortified Town together formed a unique system.

Fortification systems in Lithuania radically changed during the reign of Grand Duke Gediminas (1312–1341). Gediminas is associated with the stabilization of administrative state centers in Vilnius and Trakai, where at that time the first Lithuanian masonry castles were constructed (Gudavičius 2005: 141). It can be assumed that these castles were intended to mark the new, exclusive status of these centers. Kernavė persisted with the wooden castle, and this might be viewed as supporting the interpretation that at the time of the building of the first masonry castles Kernavė no longer held real political significance.

In an administrative and political sense, Kernavė's decay must have begun in the first half of the 14th century, but the town itself undoubtedly flourished for a time, with the loss of importance, impacting urban development, a little later. Gradually, however, this impact grew stronger, eventually leading to the radical decline of the town at the end of the 14th century. Thus, it can be concluded that the flourishing of Kernavė in the early period was determined by its state-level administrative functions and not by the city itself, administrating and collecting resources from its hinterland. The capacity of Kernavė's hinterland also remains unknown. Historical sources note a rich and densely populated region (Gudavičius 2005: 140), but the archaeological evidence is contradictory. Recent surveys indicate rather sparse settlements during the 13th and 14th centuries, even sparser than in some previous periods of the 1st millennium AD (Vėlius 2012a; Vengalis 2014, 2015).

With regard to defensive potential, the absence of masonry fortifications in Kernavė does not seem to be a radical flaw—Lithuanian defensive systems throughout the 14th century were based mostly on wooden castles, which were still quite effective during warfare. Their effectiveness is reflected in the fact that the Teutonic Order also built wooden fortifications throughout the war against the GDL (Kuncevičius 2016: 351). In the second half of the 14th century, however, the defensive capability of the Kernavė castle was worn down. As mentioned above, the castle was burned in 1365. This is confirmed by archaeological data, in particular, through the evidence for burnt horizons in Kernavė's hillforts. It is interesting that after this burning episode, the castle was not just rebuilt but efforts were made to strengthen it further (Vengalis et al. 2020). Thus, it can be assumed that resources for the reconstruction of the castle were made available, but it was no longer considered as one of the key castles of the Lithuanian state.

One of the key features of medieval urban settlements is the diversification of production, with some part of its economy centered on craft production. The permanent residence of craftspeople in Kernavė is supported by archaeological evidence. The archaeological record of Lower Town I indicates craft production, with large quantities of craft-related finds (e.g., raw materials, semi-finished products, production waste, tools) recovered from crafting properties (Jarockis 1992; Luchtanas 1988, 1990). A single, specialized craft was practiced in workshops at each of these excavated properties during their entire existence. In Lower Town I, the homesteads of a bone carver, two jewelers, and perhaps a blacksmith have been unearthed.

Excavations in the Fortified Town and Upper Town also testify to the presence of craftspeople. In the Fortified Town, a jeweler's property was discovered (Volkaitė-Kulikauskienė 1984), and in the Upper Town, although specific crafts are not always clearly identifiable due to poorer preservation, an iron smelting area and the properties of blacksmiths and jewelers were found (Vėlius 2006; Vengalis 2007). Though it is evident that

many occupants from various parts of Kernavė were engaged in craftsmanship, it cannot be determined whether it was their main productive activities, or it was only supplementary to farming. Animal husbandry was practiced by these inhabitants, as some buildings in craftspeople's properties were byres and substantial layers of animal dung were unearthed in their yards (Vaičiūnienė 2000: 132; Vitkūnas 2005: 103). The extent of crop cultivation in medieval Kernavė cannot be addressed, in part, because archaeobotanical materials have not yet been sufficiently analyzed.

The presence of craftspeople's properties in various parts of the town, and especially in Lower Town I, raises another question: where did the poor laborers, serfs, servants, and farmers live? The currently available archaeological data do not provide any clue to answer this question, so it can be only hypothetically presumed that they lived somewhere in the unexcavated areas of Kernavė, in the peripheral districts, or even beyond town boundaries (see Figure 13.3.7).

Trade was as important as craft production to the medieval town, and organized trading regularly occurred in a special area as the essential attribute of the town—the marketplace. Unfortunately, marketplaces are difficult to detect archaeologically. To pinpoint its location, one should expect to find an area free of domestic spaces or courtyards, containing an archaeological horizon with features designed for storage, and sporadic finds directly associated with trade (e.g., scales, balance weights). There is no clearly identified marketplace in Kernavė to date. However, it is possible to predict its location based on theoretical considerations and indirect evidence. It is assumed that the rivers were the main communication routes in Lithuania until the middle of the 14th century (Šešelgis 1996: 34–36). Therefore, it would be quite logical to look for the marketplace in Kernavė somewhere by the bank of the Neris River, probably in Lower Town II. Excavations, including quite extensive ones, have been conducted in various locations in Lower Town II, but no traces of domestic divisions of townspeople (e.g., buildings, fences) were discovered here, while such features are present almost everywhere in Lower Town I and the Upper Town. In addition, it is noteworthy that the distribution of other features (e.g., pits, postholes) in Lower Town II is quite different from the other parts of Kernavė. Several large storage pits, which are not typical for townspeople' properties, were unearthed here and the magnetometer survey revealed that there are more such pits in this area (Vengalis 2011a). Nevertheless, the most important information regarding the location of the marketplace is that some balance weights were found in Lower Town II, while these finds are absent in other areas of Kernavė. Thus, although there is a lack of truly undisputable data, the archaeological record indicates that there were no townspeople' properties but rather an urban district with another function in Lower Town II—likely the marketplace.

Places of worship are also important elements of the medieval town. As Kernavė flourished in pagan times, one might expect to find a pagan temple here. However, it is unclear what a pagan place of worship would look like and no features that could be related to a temple have been found so far. Another interesting issue here concerns Christian churches, both Catholic and Orthodox. The only known Catholic church in Kernavė was located in the Upper Town, but the archaeological material dates this structure to the 15th century. Meanwhile, it is evident that masonry churches already existed in Vilnius in the time of Gediminas (Gudavičius 1999: 91). Although at that time Vilnius also was officially pagan, the early appearance of churches demonstrates its significant multiethnic and multiconfessional nature. Various authors have referred to Kernavė's community as multiethnic, as they believed that communities from Christian regions lived here together with indigenous pagans (Dubonis 2009b: 167–168; Vėlius 2003, 2005; Zabiela 1998: 356–357). However, the absence of churches in fourteenth-century Kernavė suggests that the Christian community here was not large or influential at that time.

Spatial Structure of Social Stratification

Regarding the spatial organization of social stratification, special attention should be given to architecture as the most expressive form of status display in the context of Kernavė. Bearing in mind that architecture was entirely of wood, and therefore has been poorly preserved, only the comparative study of building sizes can be utilized to address this matter. The best-preserved buildings in Kernavė are located in Lower Town I, where they are consistently small, 4–5 m wide and 5–8 m long (Luchtanas 1990). Structures identified in the Upper Town were at least four times bigger (Vengalis 2007). All these buildings belonged to craftspeople and their differences indicate that a significant degree of social inequality developed among the craftspeople.

An additional identifier of social inequality is discrete patterns in the distribution of specific finds across the town. For different reasons, objects should not be considered as reliable as architecture when social inequality is concerned, but it is evident that the spatial distribution of precious metal finds, as well as imports and more advanced jewelry, is quite variable in Kernavė. In terms of the relative frequency of luxury objects in the town, the area of the duke's castle stands out. A great amount of imported and luxury items were found here, including glass bracelets, beads, slate spindles from Kievan Rus, lead seals of West European goods, imported pottery, and fragments of glass cups from the

Middle East (Luchtanas 1994: 53). These objects are very rare or completely absent in all other parts of Kernavė, suggesting that they are associated with the status of the duke's castle and its dwellers.

The residents of the Fortified Town and Upper Town might be assigned to the somewhat lower stratum of the social hierarchy in Kernavė. Some luxury finds were discovered in both of these areas, and these data correspond with the previously mentioned architectural observations. Sophisticated jewelry and even gold items were found in the jeweler's property within the large buildings in the Upper Town, which is different from the jewelers' properties featured by smaller buildings in Lower Town I (Vengalis 2007). A silver ingot hoard of almost half a kilogram, recovered from the property of craftspeople living in the Fortified Town, is similarly significant in this context (Luchtanas 1986). This hoard implies that this part of Kernavė was not occupied by the duke's servants or slaves, but self-employed and wealthy craftspeople lived here.

In Lower Town I, craftspeople properties are indicative of a lower social class than those living in the Fortified Town and Upper Town because luxury items were not found in this quarter. Even the products manufactured by these craftspeople may have been intended for a lower social class. For example, a jeweler's courtyard exhibited only copper alloy raw materials and waste, and the excavated jewelry typically was of simplest forms and technologies. The social status of Lower Town I occupants is important for understanding the organization of social space across all of Kernavė. On the one hand, the location of properties right at the foot of the castle should have been prestigious (see Figure 13.3). On the other hand, it must also be considered that this location was very humid and was regularly affected by landslides after the reconstruction of hillfort fortifications (Vengalis et al. 2020). For these reasons, Lower Town I likely became a less favorable area for permanent habitation. The quality of luxury items recovered from the Upper Town indicates that the town center developed there.

Coin finds in Lower Town II suggest that it was abandoned at the end of the 14th century. As mentioned above, Kernavė's role as a political center was constantly diminishing over the course of the 14th century, and this process probably decreased its significance as a trading center. Therefore, the marketplace also might have terminated in the town. If the finds unearthed in Lower Town II are indicative of the location of Kernavė's marketplace, it is possible that it ceased to function after the castle was burned down in 1390. When overland routes gained more importance, a new, small marketplace may have been established closer to the town's center, somewhere in the Upper Town. That is, after the castle and the riverbank marketplace no longer existed, communal activities might primarily have taken place in the Upper Town. In addition, it appears that it no longer made sense to live in the quite disadvantageous natural conditions of Lower Town I, and the inhabitants abandoned this quarter. Such reasoning again supports the notion that 1390 should not be associated with the total abandonment of Kernavė, but rather with a spatial transformation to adapt to a radical decline in the town's status.

Artifacts excavated in craftspeople' courtyards in Lower Town I may also serve to assess more precisely the status of these occupants and determine whether they were independent, self-employed craftspeople, or the servants and slaves of the duke. Some historians argue that only people serving the castle, the duke's slaves or prisoners brought from Slavic towns, lived in Kernavė (Dubonis 2009a, 2009b: 165–168). This interpretation suggests that Kernavė was only a large estate of the monarch and not an actual town. However, the archaeological data indicates that craftspeople in Kernavė produced for the market. Hoards of accumulated valuables of the craftspeople and the existence of monetary relations support this view. Although the first coins of the GDL were minted only at the end of the 14th century, silver ingots or their fragments were used widely as currency before that period and they are markedly common finds in Kernavė (Bagdzevičienė and Vėlius 2010).

Confessional–Ethnic Structure of the Town

As mentioned above, the historical and archaeological data from Vilnius implies the spatial arrangement of communities according to confessions (Girlevičius 2016: 370–372). Below, we will address the questions of how the citizens' religious views, along with their ethnicity, influenced Kernavė's structure and development, and whether the model of Vilnius is valid for Kernavė.

There is no data on the presence of a Catholic community in Kernavė prior to the establishment of the first parish and church at the beginning of the 15th century. An Orthodox community, however, might have occurred in Kernavė already in the 14th century (Vėlius 2017: 225). The brothers of Kernavė's Duke Traidenis were Orthodox (Dubonis 2009b: 64), and the families of Orthodox craftspeople from Slavic towns could have been accommodated in Kernavė as the Grand Duke's service personnel. In addition, historical sources state that Yatvings, a Baltic tribe already familiar with the Orthodox confession, retreated into the GDL due to pressure from the Teutonic Order (Dubonis 2009b: 130).

It would be reasonable to study the locations of communities of different confessions in Kernavė through the spatial distribution of finds with symbolic meanings. The credibility of such an approach may

seem arguable because communities could have exchanged these items. Nevertheless, the regular exchange of objects with symbolic meanings should be characteristic only for highly integrated, largely undifferentiated communities. When separation occurs, the exchange of symbols is expected to be less common, and symbols accentuating membership in a certain group would be of greater use. In Kernavė, the most obvious material symbols of Christianity, the cross-shaped pendants, evidently concentrate in the Upper Town, and only few similar items have been found elsewhere in the settlement. Concerning pagan symbols, the situation is somewhat more complicated— they are more difficult to identify, as many of them were used for a long time even after baptism. Pagan symbols, including swastika and animal nail or fang pendants, are often found together with cross-shaped pendants in Kernavė. The town's inhumation cemetery, used in the 13th and 14th centuries, particularly has many examples of co-occurring, contradictory symbols (Vėlius 2012b: 189). Therefore, the archaeological data from Kernavė indicates that some kind of spatial separation may have existed in the town, although it might not have been very strict.

Additionally, because Orthodox people were nonlocal in Kernavė, greater concentrations of nonlocal artifacts, not merely religious symbols, may be interpreted as indicators of the Orthodox community. Such assumption undoubtedly requires some theoretical and methodological precautions because artifacts that demonstrate a certain identity should be distinguished from those that were exchanged, traded, or copied. Jewelry or other craft products are among the least reliable indicators; nevertheless, these artifacts are common in Kernavė. Jewelry untypical for Balts (e.g., glass bracelets) frequently occurs in the Upper Town (Vaičiūnienė 2000: 133) and is very rare in the Lower Town. The lack of foreign artifacts in Lower Town I suggests that its residents were local pagans, although this deficiency can also be interpreted as the outcome of their low social status. Architecture and pottery may more reliably indicate foreign cultural traditions, but they have yet to be analyzed from this point of view (cf. Baltramiejūnaitė 2016).

The interpretation of burial practices in Kernavė's cemeteries is quite complicated as well. The inhumation cemetery of the 13th and 14th centuries has been excavated extensively (Vėlius 2005, 2012b). The burials were oriented west–east, which is the common orientation in Christian graveyards during the period. However, this cemetery is located several hundred meters away from the town (see Figure 13.3.8), and the majority of graves contained grave goods; these practices are indicative of pagan traditions and are uncharacteristic for the Orthodox burials of that time. Paleodemographic studies revealed that only a part of the town's population was placed here (Vélius 2005: 88). The grave goods suggest that ordinary and poor townspeople were interred in this cemetery and the elite and warrior members were likely buried elsewhere. The location, burial rites, and grave goods imply that the members of a confessionally highly syncretic urban community used this cemetery (Jonaitis *et al.* 2016).

Another burial site in Kernavė is definitely pagan. It is situated beyond the town boundaries in the Neris Valley, in an abandoned, small riverbed (see Figure 13.3.9). A continuous horizon of cremated bones mingled with grave goods has been unearthed here (Vengalis 2011b). This suggests that cremated bones of men, women, and children, as well as various animals, were dumped repeatedly into the water. Sherds of ritually broken pots and small fragments of various burnt objects prevail among the grave goods. The number of people interred here and the duration of site use remain unknown, thus it is unclear whether this burial ground is related to a long-standing tradition or a single historical event (e.g., Teutonic Order assault).

In sum, concerning the cemeteries of Kernavė, the archaeological evidence is quite ambiguous. Whereas discrete cemeteries in the Middle Ages tend to demonstrate the co-existence of multiple confessional-ethnic groups in urban communities, it is difficult to relate the inhumation cemetery in Kernavė to a particular confession or ethnic group. We argue, therefore, that this cemetery was utilized by a syncretic, blended community.

Conclusions

Historical sources do not provide any information about the spatial structure of Kernavė in the 13th and 14th centuries, and therefore, the archaeological data remains the sole source in this regard. At this moment, a nuanced interpretation is still substantially limited by certain issues, such as the lack of high-resolution absolute chronology and the constrained understanding of the function of certain sections in the town. However, it is clear that even an initial analysis of the new archaeological data allows quite different interpretations about the spatial development of Kernavė than presented in previous literature.

The division of Kernavė into discrete structural units—the duke's residence, defensive fortifications, the Fortified, Upper, and Lower Towns—indicates social stratification in the settlement. Furthermore, the comparative study of archaeological data from various parts of the town permitted us to identify Kernavė's spatial organization as it relates to social status, function, and confessional-ethnic identity. The focal point of medieval Kernavė was the duke's castle,

which is considered the main force for the formation, growth, and decline of the town. The importance of the political-administrative function is supported by the fact that the evolution of the town reflects shifts in the castle's political significance, rather than the economic development of the region.

The economic basis of the town came from ordinary townspeople—craftspeople, merchants, farmers, and laborers. Craftspeople are the best represented in the archaeological record because other activities did not produce a considerable amount of archaeologically identifiable features in Kernavė. This could be a reason why no courtyards for merchants, farmers, or laborers have been recovered in the town, and why we have a very limited understanding of the locations of their residences. However, data in this respect is quite explicit regarding craftspeople. The archaeological record indicates that their courtyards were located in several parts of Kernavė: in the Fortified Town, the Upper Town, and Lower Town I. This suggests that major distinctions between the various quarters of the town were not functional in nature but rather social or confessional-ethnic.

The cemeteries of medieval Kernavė imply that at least two confessional-ethnic communities, featured by different mortuary customs, lived in the town. Cremation burials are associated with the pagan community, while the inhumation cemetery demonstrates religious syncretism. Summarizing these observations, one can conclude that Lower Town I was inhabited by residents of lower social status who might have been indigenous pagans. The archaeological record from the Upper Town and the Fortified Town testifies to a higher-status community in those quarters, which might have been associated with, or at least highly influenced by, non-indigenous Orthodox Christians.

References Cited

Bagdzevičienė, J. and G. Vélius 2010. Lietuviški piniginiai sidabro lydiniai Kernavėje. *Archaeologia Lituana* 11: 156–168.

Baltramiejūnaitė, D. 2016. XIII–XIV amžiaus Kernavės keramika. *Archaeologia Lituana* 17: 112–141.

Blomkvist, N. 2001. The Concept of the Town and the Dawn of Urban Life East and West of the Baltic, in M. Auns (ed.) *Lübeck Style? Novgorod Style?: Baltic Rim Central Places as Arenas for Cultural Encounters and Urbanisation 1100-1400 AD*: 11–35. Riga: Nordik.

Bumblauskas, A. 2005. *Senosios Lietuvos istorija 1009-1795.* Vilnius: R. Paknio leidykla.

Christiansen, E. 1980. *The Northern Crusades: The Baltic and the Catholic Frontier 1100-1525.* London: Macmillan.

Dubonis, A. 2009a. Review of *Kernavės miesto bendruomenė XIII-XIV amžiuje*, by G. Vélius. *Lietuvos archeologija* 35: 259–264.

Dubonis, A. 2009b. *Traidenis*. Vilnius: Lietuvos istorijos instituto leidykla.

Girlevičius, L. 2016. Vilnius Old Town: The Key to Learning about the City's Past, in G. Zabiela, Z. Baubonis and E. Marcinkevičiūtė (eds) *A Hundred Years of Archaeological Discoveries in Lithuania*: 370–378. Vilnius: Society of the Lithuanian Archaeology.

Gudavičius, E. 1991. *Miestų atsiradimas Lietuvoje*. Vilnius: Mokslas.

Gudavičius, E. 1999. *Lietuvos istorija, Vol. I. Nuo seniausių laikų iki 1569 metų*. Vilnius: Lietuvos rašytojų sąjungos leidykla.

Gudavičius, E. 2005. Kernavės žemė ir valsčius iki 1564–1566 metų administracinės reformos, in S. Buchaveckas (ed.) *Musninkai. Kernavė. Čiobiškis* (Lietuvos valsčiai 13): 140–148. Vilnius: Versmės leidykla.

Hodges, R. 1982. *Dark Age Economics. The Origins of Towns and Trade, AD 600–1000*. London: Duckworth.

Jankauskas, A. and A. Luchtanas 1990. Senųjų Kernavės bažnyčių tyrinėjimai, in A. Tautavičius (ed.) *Archeologiniai tyrinėjimai Lietuvoje 1988 ir 1989 metais*: 138–140. Vilnius: Lietuvos TSR Mokslų Akademijos Istorijos institutas.

Jarockis, R. 1992. Kaulinių-raginių dirbinių gamyba Kernavėje XIII-XIV a. *Lietuvos archeologija* 9: 168–182.

Jonaitis, R. 2011. Orthodox Churches in the Civitas Rutenica Area of Vilnius: The Question of Location. *Archaeologia Baltica* 16: 110–128.

Jonaitis, R., I. Kaplūnaitė and G. Vėlius 2016. Early Christian Burials, in G. Zabiela, Z. Baubonis and E. Marcinkevičiūtė (eds) *A Hundred Years of Archaeological Discoveries in Lithuania*: 430–441. Vilnius: Society of the Lithuanian Archaeology.

Katalynas, K. 2006. *Vilniaus plėtra XIV-XVII a.* Vilnius: Diemedžio leidykla.

Kuncevičius, A. 2016. Masonry Castles and Forts, in G. Zabiela, Z. Baubonis and E. Marcinkevičiūtė (eds) *A Hundred Years of Archaeological Discoveries in Lithuania*: 350–359. Vilnius: Society of the Lithuanian Archaeology.

Leciejewicz, L. and M. Valor 2007. Peoples and Environments, in J. Graham-Campbell and M. Valor (eds) *The Archaeology of Medieval Europe, Vol. 1*: 46–75. Aarhus: Aarhus University Press.

Luchtanas, A. 1986. Kernavės Pilies kalno tyrinėjimai, in A. Tautavičius (ed.) *Archeologiniai tyrinėjimai Lietuvoje 1984 ir 1985 metais*: 32–35. Vilnius: Lietuvos TSR Mokslų Akademijos Istorijos institutas.

Luchtanas, A. 1988. Tyrimai Kernavėje, in A. Tautavičius (ed.) *Archeologiniai tyrinėjimai Lietuvoje 1986 ir 1987 metais*: 137–142. Vilnius: Lietuvos TSR Mokslų Akademijos Istorijos institutas.

Luchtanas, A. 1990. Tyrinėjimai Pajautos slėnyje Kernavėje, in A. Tautavičius (ed.) *Archeologiniai tyrinėjimai Lietuvoje 1988 ir 1989 metais*: 148–152. Vilnius: Lietuvos TSR Mokslų Akademijos Istorijos institutas.

Luchtanas, A. 1994. 'Aukuro kalno' piliakalnio Kernavėje tyrinėjimai, in V. Kazakevičius (ed.) *Archeologiniai tyrinėjimai Lietuvoje 1992 ir 1993 metais*: 50–53. Vilnius: Diemedžio leidykla.

Luchtanas, A. and G. Vėlius 1996. Laidosena Lietuvoje XIII–XIV a., in A. Astrauskas and M. Bertašius (eds) *Vidurio Lietuvos archeologija. Etnokultūriniai ryšiai*: 80–88. Vilnius: Žalioji Lietuva.

Luchtanas, A. and M. Vitkūnas 2004. Kernavės gynybinis kompleksas. *Karo archyvas* 19: 30–83.

Markman, K. 2015. Between Two Worlds: A Comparative Study of the Representations of Pagan Lithuania in the Chronicles of the Teutonic Order and Rus. Unpublished PhD dissertation, University of California.

Moździoch, S. 1994. The Origins of the Medieval Polish Towns. *Archaeologia Polona* 32: 129–153.

Rowell, S.C. 1994. *Lithuania Ascending: A Pagan Empire Within East-Central Europe, 1295-1345*. Cambridge: Cambridge University Press.

Šešelgis, K. 1996. *Lietuvos urbanistikos istorijos bruožai (Nuo seniausių laikų iki 1918 m.)*. Vilnius: Mokslo ir enciklopedijų leidykla.

Vaičiūnienė, D. 2000. Kernavės viršutinio miesto tyrinėjimai, in A. Girininkas (ed.) *Archeologiniai tyrinėjimai Lietuvoje 1998 ir 1999 metais*: 131–134. Vilnius: Diemedžio leidykla.

Vaitkevičienė, D. and V. Vaitkevičius 2001. XIII a. Lietuvos valstybinės religijos bruožai. *Lietuvos archeologija* 21: 311–334.

Vaitkevičius, G. 2010. *Vilniaus įkūrimas*. Vilnius: Lietuvos nacionalinis muziejus.

Vėlius, G. 2003. Kernavė in the Context of Towns of the Grand Duchy of Lithuania. *Archaeologia Lituana* 4: 161–174.

Vėlius, G. 2005. *Kernavės miesto bendruomenė XIII–XIV amžiuje*. Vilnius: Vilniaus universiteto leidykla.

Vėlius, G. 2006. Kernavės menamos senosios kalvės vietos tyrinėjimai, in G. Zabiela (ed.) *Archeologiniai tyrinėjimai Lietuvoje 2005 metais*: 43–47. Vilnius: Society of the Lithuanian Archaeology.

Vėlius, G. 2012a. Neries pakrantės tarp Karmazinų ir Kernavės (Geležies amžiaus gyvenvietės). *Lietuvos archeologija* 38: 221–252.

Vėlius, G. 2012b. 13th-14th-century Kernavė (Kriveikiškis) Cemetery, in G. Zabiela, Z. Baubonis and E. Marcinkevičiūtė (eds) *Archaeological Investigations in Independent Lithuania (1990-2010)*: 180–189. Vilnius: Society of the Lithuanian Archaeology.

Vėlius, G. 2017. Kernavė viduramžių epochoje, in D. Baltramiejūnaitė, J. Poškienė, R. Vengalis and G. Vėlius (eds) *Atrastoji Kernavė. Kernavės archeologinės vietovės muziejaus katalogas*: 120–231. Kernavė: Valstybinio Kernavės kultūrinio rezervato direkcija.

Vėlius, G. and R. Vengalis 2016. Tyrimai Kernavės archeologinėje vietovėje, in G. Zabiela (ed.) *Archeologiniai tyrinėjimai Lietuvoje 2015 metais*: 141–148. Vilnius: Society of the Lithuanian Archaeology.

Vengalis, R. 2007. Kernavės viršutinis miestas, in G. Zabiela (ed.) *Archeologiniai tyrinėjimai Lietuvoje 2006 metais:* 93–100. Vilnius: Society of the Lithuanian Archaeology.

Vengalis, R. 2009. Rytų Lietuvos gyvenvietės I–XII a. Unpublished PhD dissertation, Vilnius University.

Vengalis, R. 2011a. Kernavės senovės gyvenvietės ir miesto archeologiniai tyrimai magnetinių anomalijų vietose, in G. Zabiela (ed.) *Archeologiniai tyrinėjimai Lietuvoje 2010 metais:* 83–87. Vilnius: Society of the Lithuanian Archaeology.

Vengalis, R. 2011b. Semeniškių kapinynas, in G. Zabiela (ed.) *Archeologiniai tyrinėjimai Lietuvoje 2010 metais:* 124–127. Vilnius: Society of the Lithuanian Archaeology.

Vengalis, R. 2012. Geležies amžiaus gyvenvietė Kernavėje: ilgalaikio apgyvendinimo atspindžiai archeologinėje medžiagoje. *Lietuvos archeologija* 38: 175–220.

Vengalis, R. 2014. Žvalgomieji tyrimai Neries slėnyje, tarp Dūkštų ir Čiobiškio, in G. Zabiela (ed.) *Archeologiniai tyrinėjimai Lietuvoje 2013 metais:* 105–120. Vilnius: Society of the Lithuanian Archaeology.

Vengalis, R. 2015. Žvalgomieji tyrimai Kernavės apylinkėse, in G. Zabiela (ed.) *Archeologiniai tyrinėjimai Lietuvoje 2014 metais:* 105–117. Vilnius: Society of the Lithuanian Archaeology.

Vengalis, R. and G. Vélius 2019. Kernavės piliakalnių funkcinė raida geležies amžiuje: naujos senų duomenų interpretacijos. *Archaeologia Lituana* 20: 75–115.

Vengalis, R., J. Volungevičius, G. Vélius, A. Kuncevičius, J. Poškienė and R. Prapiestienė 2020. Žmogus prieš gamtą: Reljefo transformavimas įrengiant XIII–XIV a. Kernavės pilį ir jo sukelti eroziniais procesai. *Lietuvos archeologija* 46: 207–253.

Vitkūnas, M. 2005. Kernavės miestas XIII–XIV amžiuje, in S. Buchaveckas (ed.) *Musninkai. Kernavė. Čiobiškis* (Lietuvos valsčiai 13): 63–123. Vilnius: Versmės leidykla.

Volkaitė-Kulikauskienė, R. 1984. Kernavės 'Pilies kalno' tyrinėjimai 1983 m, in A. Tautavičius (ed.) *Archeologiniai tyrinėjimai Lietuvoje 1982 ir 1983 metais:* 38–40. Vilnius: Lietuvos TSR Mokslų Akademijos Istorijos institutas.

Zabiela, G. 1998. Laidosena pagoniškoje Lietuvoje. *Lietuvos archeologija* 15: 351–379.

Zverugo, J.G. 1983. K voprosu o rannih etapah istorii gorodov Ponemanja, in L.D. Pobol, M.M. Charnjavski and G.V. Shtyhov (eds) *Drevnerusskoe gosudarstvo i slavjane: Materialy simpoziuma, posvjashchennogo 1500-letiju Kieva:* 42–45. Minsk: Nauka i tekhnika.

Žulkus, V. 2007. *Palanga in the Middle Ages. Ancient Settlements.* Vilnius: Versus aureus.

Žulkus, V. and R. Jarockis 2013. *Lietuvos archeologija, Vol. IV. Vikingų laikai ir ikivalstybinis laikotarpis.* Klaipėda: Klaipėdos universiteto leidykla.

Chapter 14

The Creation and Maintenance of
Powerful Places in Etruria

Simon Stoddart

Abstract

This paper examines the processes underlying the construction of powerful places in Etruria. On the one hand, the landscape of much of Etruria was dominated by what have been defined as primate centers in studies of political geography. On the other hand, burial evidence indicates the retention of counterweighing political genealogies that evidently contrasted with the apparent centralization of power in the large centers. The paper explores the resolution of this tension by matching emerging evidence from the nucleation of settlement (layout and organization) with evidence for succession amongst political elites and their individual participants (the sequence and content of graves). The variation of this pattern at an interregional level will be added to the complex, and often heterarchical, pattern of Etruria.

Key Issues in Nucleation

Why and how should a large human population gather together in a stable social network? How are these actions expressed in the built environment both at the center and in the surrounding countryside? The answers to these questions lie at the heart of urban formation and nucleation, the spatial response to a specific political decision to act together. Other spatial solutions are possible (e.g., Stegmaier 2017), but nucleation appears to prevail especially in conditions of competition. The reasons include expression of identity and integrity, economics and politics, external and internal forces, collective and individualistic actions. However, there is often some controversy over the nature and relative degree of these factors, and how these play out and can be recognized in the built environment. Furthermore, once nucleation is formed, the network also needs to be maintained, and this requires another consolidating step in political development. The following paper will explore these matters, firstly in terms of relevant small-scale political anthropology, and then in terms of the Etruscans, an important political phenomenon of the 1st millennium BC, which is regularly excluded from comparative discourses or relegated to a periphery of the Classical world.

The implementation and stable maintenance of nucleation had a variable success that separated the rapid cycles of urbanism seen, for instance, in parts of first-millennium BC temperate Europe from the solid, long-term constructions of place seen in certain focal points of the Mediterranean. The Mediterranean, of course, includes Etruria as well as more famously Rome and Greece (Stoddart 2016, 2017a, 2020). The Greeks had a word for this process, *synoecism*, which,

simply expressed, entailed the planned formation of a new, larger center from a range of smaller centers (Thucydides ii 15). In mythological terms, this was connected with the great hero figure of Theseus, whose authority gathered small villages into one large community in Athens. The myth of Romulus provides a comparable example in Central Italy. These mythological accounts are closely associated with a centralizing political motivation based on one agent, and Flannery (1999) draws further attention to this phenomenon based on both ethnohistorical and archaeological examples. Thus, historically, credence has been given to the personality of the actor in persuading a community to act collectively, and this is particularly true of the ancient Mediterranean world where such forceful personalities emerge from the literature as *dictatores* who cross their personal political Rubicon.

The consequent underlying stresses between individuals and larger groupings within corporate communities, and their interpretation, have been widely reported. In the Valley of Oaxaca in Central America, Blanton and Flannery have differently interpreted the political choices leading toward the first nucleation (see Stoddart 2010) from the very same evidence. Flannery (1999) prefers centralized leadership dependent ultimately on one charismatic individual, whereas Blanton (1978: 39–40) favors some form of confederacy of the parts that make up the whole. From a very early date (Fustel de Coulanges 1864), Classical scholars have additionally placed great weight on the religious authority for both the original nucleating force and the subsequent maintenance of the community. Another commonly referenced reason for nucleation is military, generally, to gather sufficient force to act against an external threat (Fleisher 2010). As well as these top-down explanations, some scholars have given credence to bottom-up components, such as 'household-level attraction' for economic and administrative reasons (de Montillon 1987), but these can be more difficult to detect in the archaeological record without focused archaeological research on the less visible members of societies.

In the anthropological literature, Fallers (1956) and Goody (1966b) have pointed out the consequent potential tension between the state and the corporate lineage, and this tension profoundly affects the construction of identity within nucleated communities. These issues are particularly marked when it comes to the succession of the political authority that maintains the cohesion of the nucleated population, the 'transfer of scarce resources' (Goody 1966a: 2). Succession to office is a phase of intense political danger since the transition needs to transcend the presence, and then the memory of the charisma of any one individual who, to follow Flannery's (1999) model, had orchestrated the nucleation. The method of transfer of power is also a key issue. To what degree should the succession be elective or appointive? The first can be divisive and uncertain, whereas the second can be unrepresentative of the skills and the will of the community, even if more certain in its outcome. In the case of succession in Medieval Europe (Bloch 1961: 384) or amongst the Ashanti (Goody 1966a: 28), an element of indeterminacy created a constitutional balance between election and appointment, allowing flexibility in the choice of the politically most adept within a descent group or dynasty. Such political choices must also have faced the Etruscans, as we shall see. Similar internal tensions have played themselves out in the political development of any scaling up of political development, starting with the initial decision to form a nucleated population and followed up in the subsequent political trajectory of any given civilization. The outcomes varied according to the nature of the political authority. These same issues also faced the development of Etruscan politics and were probably never fully resolved, leading potentially to weaknesses in the face of other political organizations, such as that of Rome.

The analysis by Boissevain (1964, 1968) of the village communities of modern Malta also has considerable relevance in understanding the internal dynamics of what was involved. His study shows, with great vigor and eloquence, how subgroups continued to exist in both small and increasingly large, nucleated communities. Furthermore, he demonstrated these subgroups had their own internal dissensions, and that all these practices played out in the spatial distribution and organization of portable and built material culture. In essence, the village communities of Malta

contained competing interest groups that played out their intravillage politics in ritual rivalry (Boissevain 1964: 1279, 1968: 552). The origin of these ritualized factions is uninvestigated by Boissevain because of the lack of written records, but, by the time of written records, it is clear that any one constituent individual was either born into, or married into, a ritual faction, and such groups had over time developed strong corporate solidarity, with an ordered succession that goes beyond more temporary factionalism. Through time, differences in occupation and wealth developed for each grouping, but they were not necessarily spatially segregated. Rivalry over the sponsorship of alternative saints ran alongside a common pride in the main parish church where all the community had invested their wealth. Against all predictions, the theatrical play of festa celebrations of the patron saint and Holy Week celebrations has increased in modern times, even after the independence of Malta in 1964, providing social and political foci, in a changing, and sometimes dangerous, political world (Boissevain 1992). This central materialized, monumental focus also provides a pivot, at a higher scale, for intense competition between villages, demonstrating the complexity of the politics involved even in small-scale nucleated communities. Indeed, these ethnographic examples show the intricacy of the internal dynamics of nucleation, demonstrating that nucleation does not indicate the necessary presence of hierarchy, but many competing threads of political cohesion.

An important component of political control is the extent to which territory around the nucleated center can be managed, and how much frontiers are defended tightly and rigorously, if at all. Some scholars have seen this as a function of the degree of enforced political control, measured by the degree to which the total population is gathered in the nucleated center (e.g., de Montmollin 1987). This can vary in both demographically small-scale and large-scale societies, from full to very low degrees of nucleation. A purely political interpretation downplays the fact that the issue of territory also has an important economic component, particularly in terms of procurement of resources. Halstead (1987) points out the costs of nucleation in terms of new scales and distances of food procurement, simply expressed in terms of the greater distance required to bring cultivated and husbanded food into the demographically more demanding community. He also suggests that nucleation 'narrowed the range of available subsistence options,' perhaps focusing on animals as a store of cultivated food (Halstead 1987: 82). These issues again point to the important relationship between the nucleated center and its countryside, and implicitly raise the question of to what extent rural populations share the identity of the nucleated population (Stoddart 2017b; Stoddart et al. 2020). For these reasons, it is critical to consider the spatial disposition of the territory alongside the nucleated center.

The Wider Context of First-Millennium BC Europe

The varied outcomes of political control can be seen in societies contemporary to the Etruscans within first-millennium BC Europe. In these societies of temperate Europe (e.g., the *Fürstensitze* and the *oppida*; Stoddart 2017a; see also Fernández-Götz, this volume), such difficulties led to considerable instability in the development of nucleated populations, preventing their enduring cohesion for more than a few generations. In the case of Rome, a solution to these problems was achieved most radically, to the extent that Rome engaged in a politics of inclusion that incorporated other political groups, leading to a successful expansionist state. In the case of Etruscans, a dynamic equilibrium was achieved at two scales: the nucleated center (that contained competing descent groups) and the cluster of urban centers (that contained competing nucleations of population) (Stoddart 2014). At both scales, for some 500 years, the cluster of nucleated centers was held in

balance until disrupted by disequilibrium from without, namely from that of Rome itself.

Introduction to the Nucleation of Etruria

Etruria is well known for its primate centers (Figure 14.1), in the classical sense of the term 'primate' (Jefferson 1939). The Etruscan city typically stands out from its landscape, head and shoulders above the surrounding countryside, disproportionately larger than the next subsidiary settlement. In this sense, the Etruscan case study offers a classic occurrence of well-developed nucleation, a process whereby population is drawn into a physically defined community and is successfully retained by political action over a considerable period of time. However, a deeper study of the detail of Etruria shows enormous variation in the way in which this apparent stability was achieved. Five points stand out. Firstly, an examination of the internal structure of even the more apparently nucleated Etruscan centers reveals internal tensions, most notably between the descent groups (materialized in tombs) and the centralized authority (materialized

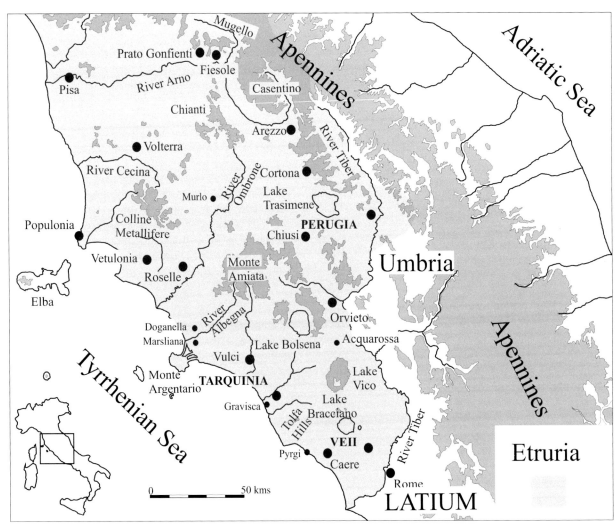

Figure 14.1. Etruria and the major nucleated centers (figure by the author).

in the city walls and the principal, substantially ritual, monuments). Secondly, there was a variation in the degree of nucleation through time, with cycles of centralization and decentralization, perhaps most vividly seen in the countryside but also in the relative density of occupation of the urban center. At some times, centralization appears to have been more effective in gathering the nucleated population than at others. Thirdly, there may easily have been low-density areas within the city, and even open gardens or fields. This interpretation is proposed, even though there is a lack of extensive excavations of all representative areas of the cities, with a tendency to focus on ritual zones. This situation applies even in the case of the most nucleated Etruscan cities in the south, which are in a number of cases open field sites without later occupation. The possibility can be best seen in the case of Veii, a leading example presented below (see Figure 14.4). Fourthly, some centers, notably in the north of Etruria, were much more polyfocal than the rest in the layout of the nucleation, clearly expressing multiple foci of political power. In all cases of Etruscan nucleation, it appears that the internal organization of the city paralleled the distinct layout of the multiple nucleated cemeteries to a greater or lesser degree according to the region and the phase of development, thus leading to an element of polyfocality. Finally, the centers were not uniformly dominant in their landscape, but had varied relationships to their local countryside. Some centers had direct control of their territory, whereas others appear to have had their control mediated through centers of intermediate size. This relationship to the territory also affected how the nucleated center defended its territorial frontiers and most probably how it viewed its own identity. These initial points already indicate the intricacies of the built environment constructed by nucleated populations, well-illustrated by the Etruscan case study.

The Central Issue of the Motivation for Political Nucleation in Etruria

Explanations of Etruscan nucleation tend to be a subset of the Classical tradition, proliferating with terms taken from the Roman world, such as the *gens*. The explanations tend to be untheorized and broadly related to ethnic formation and thus ultimately a new identity of the '*fresh, primitive, malleable, early Etruscan mind*' in a relationship with '*the mature civilizations from across the seas*' (Pallottino 1975: 81). The political force appears to be a '*paterfamilias ... leader of patriarchal social group of medium size, warrior, and priest of family cults that represent the ideological cement of the cell*' (Torelli 1981: 47). A number of these scholars also link the new nucleations with an expansionistic colonizing force associated with the rise of a military elite (d'Agostino 2003: 13–15). Protohistorians, less affected by Classical influence, also emphasize the political force associated

with the military prowess visible in the material record and point to some form of central power above 'mass of warriors of more or less equal rank' (di Gennaro 2000; Pacciarelli 2000: 267–276) as the causative force behind nucleation.

Great controversy surrounds the process of nucleation in Etruria. At the one extreme, there is the strongly heterarchical view, first explicitly proposed by Ward-Perkins (1961), that emphasizes the continued integrity of the individual Bronze Age villages which combined to form the larger community on the Iron Age plateau in the course of the 10th century BC. In some ways, this model has similarity to that already mentioned of Blanton (1978), stressing the confederate decision of the constituent parts of the newly formed community. This suggests an identity expressed at the corporate level, while retaining subidentities at the descent group level. At the other extreme, there is the position of Guidi (1989)—and generally of the whole school of Peroni and his successors (e.g., di Gennaro *et al.* 2004: 159)—which stresses the immediate coherence and integrity of the newly formed community. This requires central authority to be masked in the practices of the burial ritual because at the time of transition there was a lack of evidence of differentiation of access to wealth expressed in the funerary record. This view is more akin to the views of Flannery (1999) which envisages a strong central authority, perhaps even a key individual, behind the decision to form a new community.

What is interesting is that the process of nucleation in Etruria took some 350 years to complete in terms of the full materialization of the urban form, if one generalizes from the examples of the southern Etruscan places of power, where sufficient excavations have been undertaken to recover patterns, including Veii, Tarquinia, and, to a limited extent, Cerveteri (Stoddart 2010). Different rates of change can be followed in different sectors of the emerging urban landscape: the layout of the settlement, the formality of ritual, the type of house form, and the style of burial. The phasing of the construction of different sectors of the built environment informs on the phases in the construction of social identity. The first step was the intensified gathering together of population at about 950 BC. All the major Etruscan centers had a Final Bronze Age origin, but it was only in the First Iron Age that this nucleation gathered strength. Some settlements do show evidence of a focal ritual within these communities of increasing formality (e.g., the *zona monumentale* at Tarquinia and the Piazza d'Armi at Veii), but the general layout of the settlement cannot be defined as laid out formally. The type of house form at this stage was still the wooden posthole and gully oval structure, easily maintained and modified to reflect the changing cycle of life of the household. The best-known cemeteries were clusters of inurned cremations placed in their own

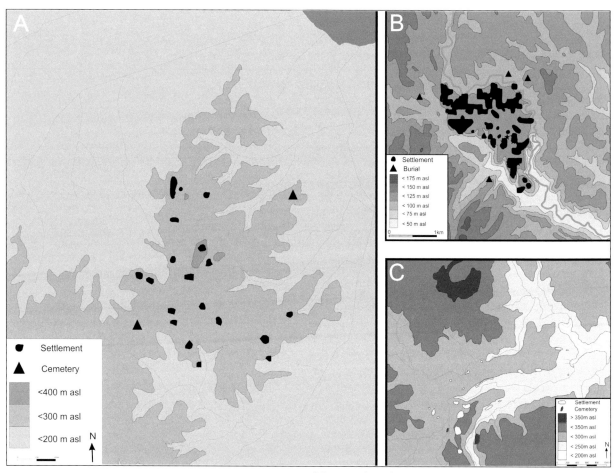

Figure 14.2. A comparison of three nucleated centers.
A: Chiusi; B: Veii; C: Aquarossa (figure by the author).

micronucleations, overlooking the boundaries of the plateau, and this stage showed no visible differentiation of wealth. The formalization of the domestic sphere in terms of rectilinear houses took between 100 and 200 years to achieve, although the evidence remains partial because of the lack of excavations outside the main ritual areas. The formalization of the funerary sphere took up to 300 years to achieve, passing through intermediate stages of increased exhibition of differentiated wealth, the adoption of inhumation and trench tombs, the adoption of tumuli, and finally, rectilinear structures that paralleled, after a period of delay, the patterns of the living. The ritual foci of the city followed a broadly similar pattern, most clearly seen in the *zona monumentale* of Tarquinia, passing from structured deposits in curvilinear structures to massive upstanding monuments with architectural terracottas. The evidence of the built environment suggests that subidentities, most probably descent groups, continued to survive even when population was gathered at a greater scale than before.

Etruscan cities are too frequently represented as being characterized by unitary nucleation, but in fact there is a considerable range from the apparently unitary examples of the south to the distributed power represented by the polyfocal nucleations of the north (Chiusi, Chianciano Terme, and Perugia; Figure 14.2) and the interstices between powerful nucleated centers (Acquarossa and Murlo). The full sequence of Veii will be contrasted with Perugia below (see Figures 14.4 and 14.5), but suffice to state the essentials here. Veii was placed on the massive plateau of 190 ha overlooking the other bank of the Tiber to that of Rome. It was surrounded by cemeteries and had major ritual foci in the temples of Piazza d'Armi, Portonaccio, and Campetti. Cerveteri, Tarquinia, Vulci, and Orvieto in the south of Etruria all essentially followed a similar pattern, where the plateau of broadly similar size in this volcanic landscape were very well defined, contained monumental ritual complexes reaching a climax in the 5th century BC, and were surrounded by cemeteries. The repeated modular pattern, allowing for some variation in size, contrasts with the pattern of Chiusi, a powerful community that was articulated in a very different way. To some extent, the contrast was created by the differences in landscape topography. The distinctive plateau does not exist in the north of Etruria, so that the parallel political pressures of nucleation were mapped very differently onto the available landscape. A further caution must be expressed that many of these northern centers (Chiusi in Figure 14.2A, Perugia in Figure 14.5, and Volterra) are still occupied by modern settlement that militates against surface survey, leading to partial knowledge that is dependent on urban excavations. Nevertheless, the experiential effect of landscape was very different, where different topographic locations had to work together in a manner that was immediately less unitary, raising questions over the substantial figures for surface area that have sometimes been proposed.

The implications of nucleation went well beyond the urban center into the countryside. The degree of central control and the need to fuel the nucleation with human and material resources had major implications on the placing of population within the countryside (Figure 14.3). This effect played itself out in the variability of political landscape of Etruria. Veii was highly dominant in her immediate, landlocked landscape on the lower middle Tiber, not tolerating any rival nucleations in the immediate vicinity. The main nucleated center was also highly expansive (potentially reaching a territorial size of 2500 km²; Redhouse and Stoddart 2011), rivaling Rome, located a mere 15 km away on the other side of the Tiber. The early history of the landscape in c. 1000 BC involved the suction of population from the even distant Bronze Age sites. This political effect on the demography particularly affected the so-called Faliscan territory to the north (Ceccarelli and Stoddart 2007), which lost most of its population at this time of first nucleation. This same area contained its own nucleated centers (Nepi, Civita Castellana, and Narce) from the 8th century BC onward, which, whilst culturally

different, were most probably under the political control of the Veii, the primate center, although this interpretation remains controversial (Ceccarelli and Stoddart 2007). Provided this latter interpretation is accepted, the relationship of Veii to its territory showed a very distinctive profile: direct control of farmsteads in the immediate vicinity of the urban center and control mediated through a culturally distinctive set of secondary centers at a greater distance. Cerveteri was equally dominant in its territory, but—because this territory was hedged in by surrounding rival centers—it was much smaller (c. 800 km²) and led to an absence of larger secondary centers. The lack of terrestrial territory was replaced by a strong relationship to the sea and a spatially close relationship to its surrounding landscape. Tarquinia was a classic case of a city engaged in a balanced relationship with its countryside. The size of the center (150 ha) at the time of foundation was in proportion to the size of its territory (c. 1700 km²), and the relationship to the countryside was achieved through a stepped gradation of settlement size, from the urban center through secondary centers to the farmsteads themselves. Additionally, the primate center had access to maritime space through its port of trade at Gravisca. These last two cities, Cerveteri and Tarquinia, also managed their frontiers with the greatest political energy, in response perhaps to the smaller territorial scale of their territories. Sanctuaries and smaller settlements were located to manage these liminal zones of transition (Riva and Stoddart 1996). Chiusi was the polyfocal center of a much less centralized landscape where a number of relatively large secondary centers

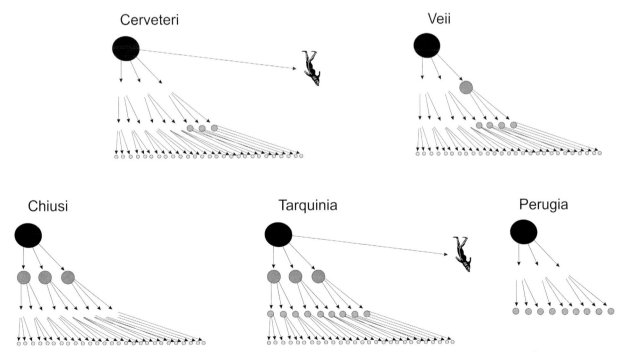

Figure 14.3. A comparison of relationships between five nucleated centers and their countryside.
The sea is represented by an anthropomorphized dolphin, drawing on the artistry of
the Etruscan 'Micali' painter (figure by the author).

(e.g., Pienza, Chianciano Terme) approached Chiusi in size, and these collectively connected directly to the farmsteads in the countryside. Finally, Perugia on the political frontier with a very different world, generically characterized as Umbrian, appears to have been the largest of a local network of nucleated centers, whereas farmsteads appear to have been completely absent from the landscape. Beyond the political frontier in Umbria, this pattern of no rural settlement appears to have continued where the landscape was dominated by smaller nucleated settlements, some upland hillforts, and sanctuaries, but no rural farmsteads, such as encountered in Etruria (Bonomi Ponzi 2014).

These different examples show the variation in the degree to which population was nucleated in the Etruscan and immediately neighboring landscapes. The southern primate centers had immense power of suction of population into their enclosures, but also delegation of production to the rural landscape. The northern centers had much less power of suction of population, but also less delegation of production to the more remote zones of the landscape. The identity of the populations concerned would have reflected these essential differences.

Two More Detailed Examples: Veii and Perugia

The contrasts in nucleation between the two limits of Etruria can be illustrated in greater detail by the political development of two primate centers at the southern and northeasterly extremes of the region: Veii and Perugia. These represent two solutions—temporally, organizationally, and spatially—to the problems and opportunities posed by nucleation. Veii is the more forceful and centralized, such that it was a rival, albeit ultimately unsuccessful, to Rome itself. Perugia was the slower and more distributed example, never reaching its full development because of incorporation within the political territory of Rome.

Veii was the largest primate center of Etruria (190ha; Figure 14.4), hard up against the frontier with the Latin world to the south of the Tiber, with which it paradoxically shared so much, including aspects of material culture (di Gennaro *et al.* 2004: 152–153), formalized ritual production, and an openness to trade. However, no Etruscan nucleation had the capacity to incorporate other groups—in spite of some considerable evidence of mobility in the names of descent groups—to the same level achieved by Rome (cf. Smith 2012: 5–8). The rejuvenation of the volcanic landscape by the tributaries of the Tiber in the area north of Veii created a distinctive inhabited landscape of mainly smaller plateaus separated by canyons (Alvarez 1972) that gave distinctive opportunities for nucleation. It has been suggested that the volcanic soils and the availability of water supported a city largely focused on

agriculture (based on soils in the 490 km^2 catchment) rather than connectivity based on trade, in spite of the 7 km-proximity of the Tiber (Schiappelli 2012: 330). Fortunately, this is a city that has unusually been studied in some detail from all the key perspectives: surface survey (Cascino *et al.* 2012b; Ward-Perkins 1961) and excavation (Bartoloni 2009; Bartoloni and Acconcia 2012) of the city, study of burials (Bartoloni 1997), study of ritual foci (Colonna 2004), and a regional survey (Patterson *et al.* 2004; Potter 1979). The research activity has been facilitated by the fact that the city has remained a green field site, albeit badly damaged by deep plowing. This openness of the urban landscape has permitted the pursuit of some interesting detail, even if great care must be taken not to overinterpret what may ultimately be geomorphological or taphonomic patterns, or simply a product of accessibility for research (see the incomplete coverage achieved by Ward-Perkins: Cascino *et al.* 2012a: 32, Figure 4.1).

Perugia was a different type of smaller frontier city more softly nestling against the much more fuzzy boundary with Umbria (Stoddart *et al.* 2012; Figure 14.5). The topography of the city was a series of hills, probably of fluvio-lacustrine deltaic origin from the paleo-Tiber on a marly sandstone foundation (Bertacchini 2014), raised some 300 m over the modern course of the Tiber some 5 km distant. By contrast with Veii, Perugia developed into an important urban center in the Medieval Ages and the modern period, where research is thus restricted to urban rescue works as well as the study of the surrounding cemeteries (Bratti 2007; Nati 2008) and some study of its territory (Bonomi Ponzi 2014; Cenciaioli 2005; Donnini and Bonci 2008; Malone *et al.* 2014; Stoddart *et al.* 2012). In spite of these issues, recent discoveries have begun to establish more clearly the nature of its urban structure (Cenciaioli 2014). Even if there are some contrasting fortunes in research between the two urban centers, some valid comparisons and contrasts do surface.

The area of Veii was first occupied in the Final Bronze Age, like so many other Etruscan cities, leaving aside one small fragment of Middle Bronze Age material, but occupation was focused on the much smaller plateau of Isola Farnese, a separate and distinct topographical entity to the south of much larger plateau of Veii (Babbi 2005; Figure 14.4A). At least two cemeteries (Casale del Fosso and Quattro Fontanili) that continued into the later Iron Age (di Gennaro *et al.* 2004: 150, 157), as well as a deposit near the Northwest Gate (di Gennaro 1986), had founding phases in the Final Bronze Age. A curious feature of the immediately surrounding human landscape of Veii at the time of the Final Bronze Age is the absence of other contemporary settlement (Schiappelli 2012: 330); assuming that we are not dealing with a problem of survival since Final Bronze Age sites have generally been recognized from their

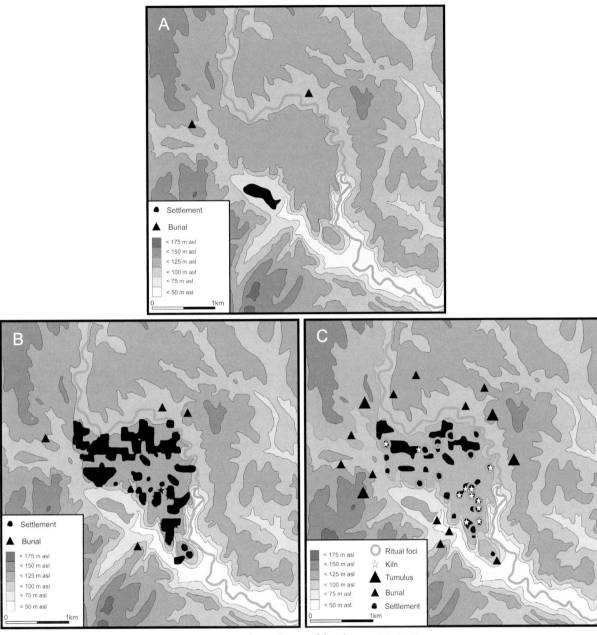

Figure 14.4. Three phases of development in Veii.
A: Bronze Age; B: Iron Age; C: Archaic Period (figure by the author).

topography and only Isola Farnese has that necessary topography in the immediate area. The very nearest known settlement is at a distance of 10 km and more substantial settlement at a distance of 17 km.

The major phase of nucleation took place in the First Iron Age (Figure 14.4B), and the political authority over the new plateau nucleation must have had a distant reach to provide the necessary accumulation of population. Three features are prominent in nucleation that took place on the Veii plateau. Firstly, surface survey from three traditions—one British in the 1950s and two Italian in the 1980s and 1990s—suggests that the occupation was dense but not continuous: 'scattered huts linked by pathways and interspersed with animal enclosures, with open spaces for agriculture and pasture, in an environment that still preserved patches of woodland' (Schiappelli 2012: 336). Secondly, at least four cremation cemeteries, at least two continuing from the Bronze Age, were placed on the bluffs overlooking the main plateau. Thirdly, an important ritual focus developed on the Piazza d'Armi, a partly separated promontory at the extreme southeast end of the plateau. What do these changes suggest about the process of nucleation? Firstly, the distinct cremation cemeteries project statements of distinct burial identities within the community, some of which emerged out of the dispersed Bronze Age landscape. Secondly, the distribution of settlement from surface survey can be read to reflect distinct living communities that match the buried communities across

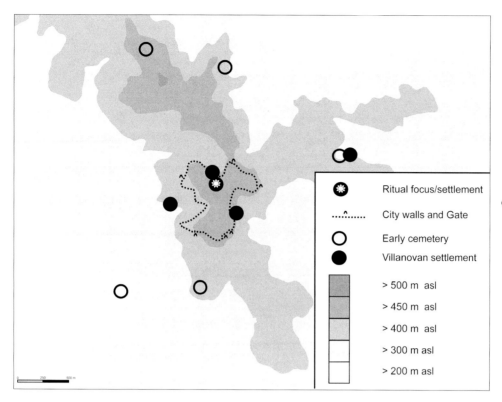

Figure 14.5. The layout of nucleation in Perugia (figure by the author).

the canyons. Water, and the aggressive cost surface of the canyon itself, separates the living and the dead, even though they share an interlocked gaze. Finally, on the Piazza d'Armi, research has uncovered the successive development of a funerary chapel into an oval shrine and finally into a more formal, rectilinear ritual structure (Bartoloni 2002–2003). This process formed a focus of the community, in addition to the multiple heterarchically built environments that characterize the main part of the plateau. Such essential facts seem to suggest that the community retained subdivisions in its earlier years that were perhaps only resolved in the next phase.

By the 6th century BC, the community of Veii offered a different appearance (Figure 14.4C). Firstly, the ring of cemeteries had multiplied over the intervening period, totaling at least 15 locations. In four of these, their conspicuous nature was strengthened by the construction of tumuli to emphasize the visual nature of political power. Some of the first painted tombs were commissioned in Veii (De Agostino 1964), even if this was a practice that did not later retain the popularity seen in Tarquinia and some other Etruscan cities. As might be expected, such as in the Vaccareccia cemetery, a tumulus was matched by equally elaborate internal architecture (e.g., a long *dromos* or entry passage) and elaborate grave goods, such as *bucchero*. Secondly, the internal layout of the settlement appeared to take on a more structured form. In many areas, a transition can be seen between oval structures and rectilinear structures over the course of the 7th century BC, closely

integrated with the presence of drainage channels and wells. The arrangement of these structures appears to have included open spaces as well as the retention of some still dense areas organized in rectilinear patterns, most noted in the Piazza d'Armi excavations (Bartoloni 2009). Some of the internal spaces became the workshops of potters (demonstrated by kiln waste). Other areas became foci for ritual production, demonstrated by the discovery of architectural terracottas. Two prominent examples of these were placed within the city (Macchiagrande and Comunità), whereas two other prominent examples (Portonaccio and Piazza d'Armi) were placed at the limits of the city. It is thought-provoking, in the spirit of Boissevain (1964), how the multiplicity of the burial places of the dead, the resting places of the descent groups, was matched by a multiplicity of ritual foci of the living. The built environment of the nucleated city suggests a more open and formally organized sense of space where rival corporate groups were still at work in the formulation of political power and the consequent identity.

The development of the settlement of Perugia (Figure 14.5) is more difficult to construct because of the technical difficulties of understanding the past in a living city. In some respects, the sequence of political development is similar since the origins of occupation of the general area also dated back to the Final Bronze Age, although with much less conviction than is the case with the southern cities. The nearest settlement of this period was just southwest of the urban area shown in Figure 14.5 (Cenciaioli 1990). In the same way as in

Veii, there was subsequently a detectable Villanovan Iron Age presence and the organization of the later urban structure did seem to be centered on a ritual sequence, now known thanks to recent excavations under the Cathedral (Cenciaioli 2014). Equally as in Veii, the hilltop was also penetrated by a series of drainage tunnels that on current knowledge extended 1.3 km under the city (Bertacchini 2014: 49), running just above the 400-m contour.

In spite of these overall similarities, there are differences. Most notably nucleation was less forceful. While Villanovan settlement has been found in at least three distinct locations within the city limits, other evidence has been found on the more distant outskirts of the city at Monteluce (and Palazzone?), suggesting a less powerful political impetus than in the southern and coastal Etruscan cities. The central ritual focus of the city also seems to have been developed less early than in other Etruscan cities. A foundation ritual of late seventh-century BC *bucchero* feasting vessels was the first deposit, followed only in the late 5th to 4th century BC by more monumental remains indicated by residual wall foundations, including possible column supports and drainage systems, and dated by architectural terracottas (Cenciaioli 2014: 60; Sisani 2014), even if these terracottas derive from a later fill. In general, there is sufficient sixth- to fifth-century BC ceramic material, some with Etruscan graffiti, to show continuous occupation of an area that was considerably modified when the zone was terraced for later ritual activity. The earlier of these terracottas have similarities to those of the Belvedere temple of Orvieto (Cenciaioli 2014: 60; Sisani 2014), and a number of the names of descent groups were shared with more westerly Etruscan cities (Marchesini 2007). A distinctive sarcophagus from the Sperandio necropolis has also often been interpreted as inferring an ideology of incursive descent groups from the west since it seems to depict a raiding party of incoming military forces (Haynes 2000: 186–187). Over the course of this same Archaic Period, cemeteries began to encircle the urban hilltop at locations such as Sperandio and Monteluce, but only with any demographic conviction in the Hellenistic Period (Bratti 2007; Della Fina 2002). This was the same period when the city walls were themselves constructed on the 400-m contour. Indeed, the pace of development was very much slower in all respects. Perugia thus represents an example of much less vigorous nucleation, perhaps dependent on external input from Etruscan cities further west, at a later date than the more dynamic developments in the south.

Conclusions

The unitary nature of Etruscan nucleation has been rewritten in recent years. The situation is much more complex than suggested by the 12 peer polities of the ancient authors. In parallel, this is a lesson for readers of this volume, namely that the apparent size of nucleation masks a complexity of heterarchically expressed social processes that may or may not be matched in the layout of the built environment. The classic primate cities had an external differentiation that marked out multiple trajectories of political development and an internal differentiation of identity that was profoundly demarcated along descent group lines. The more polyfocal centers were divided by geography and identity. The more northerly centers were slower to develop forces of centralization and may have received an injection of population from other communities. The individual cities had profoundly different relationships to their countryside, and this set up divergent patterns of nucleation, with different proportions and distributions of urbanization across space. They also had profoundly different and changing relationships to Rome as this expansionist political force took over the peninsula. In many ways, these observations fit the pattern of variation of power and identity expressed in nucleation that have been detected in other geographical regions (e.g., de Montmollin 1987), but given the relative isolation of research on the Etruscans, these similarities need to be expressed more openly in a comparative framework. This contribution to a comparative volume should make a step toward this goal. In more than a few ways, there were structural similarities in the unequal peer polity interaction and the power of descent groups that have been uncovered amongst both the Maya and the Etruscans (Stoddart 2007–2008). Common processes of nucleation are found in profoundly separate cultural and geographical traditions, and comparisons can aid the understanding of communities that were radically different in cultural terms.

References Cited

Alvarez, W. 1972. The Treia valley north of Rome: volcanic stratigraphy, topographic evolution and geographical influence on human settlement. *Geologia Romana* 11: 153–176.

Babbi, A. 2005. L'insediamento protostorico di Isola Farnese. Considerazioni sull'età del bronzo finale nel distretto Veiente, in O. Paoletti (ed.) *Dinamiche di sviluppo delle città nell'etruria meridionale. Veio, Caere, Tarquinia, Vulci:* 665–673. Pisa and Roma: Istituti editoriali e poligrafici internazionali.

Bartoloni, G. (ed.) 1997. *Le necropoli arcaiche di Veio: giornata di studio in memoria di Massimo Pallottino.* Roma: Università degli studi di Roma, La Sapienza, Dipartimento di scienze storiche archeologiche e antropologiche dell'antichità.

Bartoloni, G. 2002–2003. Una cappella funeraria al centro del pianoro di Piazza d'Armi-Veio. *Annali* dell'Istituto Orientale di Napoli Archeologia e Storia Antica 9–10: 63–78.

Bartoloni, G. (ed.) 2009. L' abitato etrusco di Veio: ricerche dell'Universita di Roma La Sapienza. Vol. 1. Cisterne, pozzi e fosse. Roma: IUNO.

Bartoloni, G. and V. Acconcia (eds) 2012. L' abitato etrusco di Veio: ricerche dell'Universita di Roma La Sapienza. Vol. 2. Un edificio tardo-arcaico e la seguenza stratigrafica. Roma: IUNO.

Bertacchini, M. 2014. Il sottosuolo della cattedrale di Perugia. Una finestra sulla geologia del territorio Perugino, in L. Cenciaioli (ed.) Perugia. La citta antica sotto la Cattedrale di S. Lorenzo. I risultati degli scavi: 31–55. Napoli: Edizioni Scientifiche ed Artistiche.

Blanton, R. 1978. Monte Albán: Settlement Patterns at the Ancient Zapotec Capital. London: Academic Press.

Bloch, M. 1961. Feudal Society. London: Routledge and Kegan Paul.

Boissevain, J. 1964. Factions, Parties and Politics in a Maltese Village. American Anthropologist 66(6): 1275–1287.

Boissevain, J. 1968. The Place of Non-Groups in the Social Sciences. Man 3(4): 542–556.

Boissevain, J. 1992. Play and Identity. Ritual Change in a Maltese Village, in J. Boissevain (ed.) Revitalizing European Rituals: 137–154. London: Routledge.

Bonomi Ponzi, L. 2014. L'evoluzione del sistema insediativo umbro dalle origini all conquista romana, in M.C. Bettini (ed.) Gli Umbri in età preromana: 189–211. Firenze: Istituto di Studi Etruschi.

Bratti, I. 2007. Forma Urbis Perusiae. Città di Castello (Perugia): Edimond.

Cascino, R., F. Di Gennaro, H. Di Giuseppe, M.T. Di Scarcina, H. Patterson, M. Sansoni and A. Schiappelli 2012a. Catalogo topografico: le aree di raccolta del survey, in R. Cascino, H. di Giuseppe and H. Patterson (eds) Veii. The Historical Topography of the Ancient City. A Restudy of John Ward-Perkins's Survey: 31–83. London: British School at Rome.

Cascino, R., H. di Giuseppe and H. Patterson (eds) 2012b. Veii. The Historical Topography of the Ancient City. A Restudy of John Ward-Perkins's Survey. London: British School at Rome.

Ceccarelli, L. and S.K.F. Stoddart 2007. The Faliscans, in C. Riva, G.J. Bradley and E. Isayev (eds) Ancient Italy: Regions without boundaries: 131–160. Exeter: Exeter University Press.

Cenciaioli, L. 1990. Perugia: l'insediamento protovillanoviano di Via Settevalli, in M.P. Corbucci and S. Pettine (eds) Antichità dall'Umbria a Leningrado: 83–92. Perugia: Electa Editori Umbri.

Cenciaioli, L. 2005. Per una carta archeologica della diocesi di Perugia, in A. Bartoli Langeli and E. Menestò (eds) La chiesa di Perugia nel primo millennio: 211–229. Spoleto: Centro italiano di studi sull'alto medioevo.

Cenciaioli, L. (ed.) 2014. Perugia. La citta antica sotto la Cattedrale di S. Lorenzo. I risultati degli scavi. Napoli: Edizioni Scientifiche ed Artistiche.

Colonna, G. 2004. I santuari di Veio: ricerche e scavi su Piano di Comunità, in H. Patterson (ed.) Bridging the Tiber: Approaches to regional archaeology in the Middle Tiber Valley: 205–221. London: British School at Rome.

d'Agostino, B. 2003. Gli Etruschi. Milano: Jaca Book.

De Agostino, A. 1964. La tomba delle anatre. Roma: Villa Giulia.

Della Fina, G.M. (ed.) 2002. Perugia Etrusca. Atti del IX Convegno Internazionale di studi sulla storia e l'Archeologia dell'Etruria. Roma: Quasar.

de Montmollin, O. 1987. Forced settlement and political centralization in a Classic Maya polity. Journal of Anthropological Archaeology 6(3): 220–262.

di Gennaro, F. 1986. Forme di insediamento tra Tevere e Fiora dal Bronzo Finale al principio dell'età del ferro. Firenze: Olschki.

di Gennaro, F. 2000. 'Paesaggi di potere': l'Etruria meridionale in età protostorica, in G. Camassa, A. De Guio and F. Veronese (eds) Paesaggi di potere: problemi e prospettive: 95–119. Roma: Quasar.

di Gennaro, F., A. Amoroso and A. Schiappelli 2004. Un confronto tra gli organismi protostatali delle due sponde del Tevere. Le prime fasi di Veio e di Crustumerio, in H. Patterson (ed.) Bridging the Tiber: Approaches to regional archaeology in the Middle Tiber Valley: 147–178. London: British School at Rome.

Donnini, L. and L.R. Bonci 2008. Civitella d'Arna (Perugia, Italia) e il suo territori: carta archeologica. Oxford: John and Erica Hedges.

Fallers, L.A. 1956. Changing Customary Law in Busoga District of Uganda. Public Administration and Development 8(3): 139–144.

Flannery, K. 1999. Process and agency in early state formation. Cambridge Archaeological Journal 9(1): 3–21.

Fleisher, J.B. 2010. Swahili Synoecism: Rural Settlements and Town Formation on the Central East African Coast, A.D. 750–1500. Journal of Field Archaeology 35(3): 265–282.

Fustel de Coulanges, N.D. 1864. La cité antique: Étude sur le culte, le droit, les institutions de la Grèce et de Rome. 2nd edition. Paris: Durand.

Goody, J. 1966a. Introduction, in J. Goody (ed.) Succession to High Office (Cambridge Papers in Social Anthropology 4): 1–56. Cambridge: Cambridge University Press.

Goody, J. (ed.) 1966b. Succession to High Office (Cambridge Papers in Social Anthropology 4). Cambridge: Cambridge University Press.

Guidi, A. 1989. Alcune osservazioni sull'origine delle città etrusche, in G. Maetzke, M.G. Marzi Costagli, M. Iozzo, O. Paoletti and E.J. Shepherd (eds) Atti del Secondo Congresso Internazionale Etrusco. Firenze

26 maggio – 2 giugno, 1985: 285–292. Roma: Giorgio Bretschneider.

Halstead, P. 1987. Man and Other Animals in Later Greek Prehistory. *The Annual of the British School at Athens* 82: 71–83.

Haynes, S. 2000. *Etruscan Civilisation. A Cultural History.* London: British Museum Press.

Jefferson, M. 1939. The law of the primate city. *Geographical Review* 29: 226–239.

Malone, C., S. Stoddart, L. Ceccarelli, L. Cenciaioli, P. Duff, F. McCormick, J. Morales, S. Armstrong, J. Bates, J. Bennett, J. Cameron, G. Cifani, S. Cohen, T. Foley, F. Fulminante, H. Hill, L. Mattacchoni, S. Neil, A. Rosatelli, D. Redhouse and S. Volhard-Dearman 2014. Beyond feasting: consumption and life style amongst the invisible Etruscans, in K. Boyle, R. Rabett and C. Hunt (eds) *Living in the Landscape: Essays in Honour of Graeme Barker:* 257–266. Cambridge: McDonald Institute.

Marchesini, S. 2007. *Prosopographia Etrusca II, 1: Studia: Gentium Mobilitas.* Roma: L'Erma di Bretschneider.

Nati, D. 2008. *Le necropoli di Perugia 1.* Città di Castello (Perugia): Edimond.

Pacciarelli, M. 2000. *Dal villaggio alla città: la svolta protourbana del 1000 a.C. nell'Italia tirrenica* (Grandi contesti e problemi della protostoria italiana 4). Firenze: All'insegna del Giglio.

Pallottino, M. 1975. *The Etruscans.* London: Allen Lane.

Patterson, H., H. Di Giuseppe and R. Witcher 2004. Three South Etruria 'Crises': First results of the Tiber Valley Project. *Papers of the British School at Rome* 72: 1–36.

Potter, T.W. 1979. *The Changing Landscape of South Etruria.* London: P. Elek.

Redhouse, D.I. and S.K.F. Stoddart 2011. Mapping Etruscan State Formation, in N. Terrenato and D. Haggis (eds) *State Formation in Italy and Greece: Questioning the Neoevolutionist Paradigm:* 161–178. Oxford: Oxbow Books.

Riva, C. and S.K.F. Stoddart 1996. Ritual Landscapes in Archaic Etruria, in J.B. Wilkins (ed.) *Approaches to the Study of Ritual. Italy and the Mediterranean:* 91–109. London: Accordia.

Schiappelli, A. 2012. Veio in epoca protostorica: analisi topografica e territorial, in R. Cascino, H. di Giuseppe and H. Patterson (eds) *Veii. The Historical Topography of the Ancient City. A Restudy of John Ward-Perkins's Survey:* 327–336. London: British School at Rome.

Sisani, S. 2014. La struttura arcaica, in L. Cenciaioli (ed.) *Perugia. La città antica sotto la Cattedrale di S. Lorenzo. I risultati degli scavi:* 121–125. Napoli: Edizioni Scientifiche ed Artistiche.

Smith, C. 2012. Historical Introduction, in R. Cascino, H. di Giuseppe and H. Patterson (eds) *Veii. The Historical Topography of the Ancient City. A Restudy of John Ward-Perkins's Survey:* 1–8. London: British School at Rome.

Stegmaier, G. 2017. Ritual, society and settlement structure: driving forces of urbanisation during the second and first century BC in southwest Germany, in S. Stoddart (ed.) *Delicate urbanism in context: the case of pre-Roman German urbanism:* 41–48. Cambridge: McDonald Institute.

Stoddart, S.K.F. 2007–2008. The Etruscan Body. *Accordia Research Papers* 11: 137–152.

Stoddart, S. 2010. Boundaries of the State in Time and Space: Transitions and Tipping Points. *Social Evolution & History* 9(2): 28–52.

Stoddart, S. 2014. A view from the south(west). Identity in Tyrrhenian Central Italy, in C.N. Popa and S. Stoddart (eds) *Fingerprinting the Iron Age. Approaches to Identity in the European Iron Age. Integrating South-Eastern Europe into the Debate:* 266–282. Oxford: Oxbow Books.

Stoddart, S. 2016. Power and Place in Etruria, in M. Fernández-Götz and D. Krause (eds) *Eurasia at the Dawn of History: Urbanization and Social Change:* 304–318. Cambridge: Cambridge University Press.

Stoddart, S. (ed.) 2017a. *Delicate urbanism in context: the case of pre-Roman German urbanism.* Cambridge: McDonald Institute.

Stoddart, S. 2017b. The Apparent Invisibility of the Non-Elite and Rural Settlement North of the Tiber in the Age of Tarquin, in C.J. Smith and P.S. Lulof (eds) *The Age of Tarquinius Superbus: Central Italy in the Late 6th Century* (Babesch Supplements 29): 187–194. Leuven: Peeters.

Stoddart, S. 2020. *Power and Place in Etruria.* Cambridge: Cambridge University Press.

Stoddart, S.K.F., M. Baroni, L. Ceccarelli, G. Cifani, J. Clackson, F. Ferrara, I. della Giovampaola, F. Fulminante, T. Licence, C. Malone, L. Mattacchioni, A. Mullen, F. Nomi, E. Pettinelli, D. Redhouse and N. Whitehead 2012. Opening the Frontier: the Gubbio–Perugia frontier in the course of history. *Papers of the British School at Rome* 80: 257–294.

Stoddart, S., A. Palmisano, D. Redhouse, G. Barker, G. di Paola, L. Motta, T. Rasmussen, T. Samuels and R. Witcher 2020. Patterns of Etruscan urbanism, in F. Fulminante, J.W. Hanson, S.G. Ortman and L.M.A. Bettencourt (eds) *Where Do Cities Come From and Where Are They Going To? Modelling Past and Present Agglomerations to Understand Urban Ways of Life. Frontiers in Digital Humanities* 7:1, doi: 10.3389/fdigh.2020.00001

Torelli, M. 1981. *Storia degli Etruschi.* Roma and Bari: Editori Laterza.

Ward-Perkins, J.B. 1961. Veii. The historical topography of the ancient city. *Papers of the British School at Rome* 29: 1–123.

Index

A

Aalborg (site), 132-133, 139-141
abandonment, 55, 75, 87, 117, 139-140, 143, 146, 150, 158, 192-193, 196
abundance, 21, 70, 175-176
acculturation, 84, 93, 130
acropolis, 39, 158
activity zones, 2, 8, 14, 43, 45-47, 49-55, 57, 59-61
adaptation, 5, 29, 72, 97, 128, 174
administration, 100, 109, 186
administrative center, 189, 192
Aegean, 29, 57, 59-60, 76-77, 80-81, 94
aeolian, 143
aerial photography, 84, 92, 137
agglomeration, 40, 64, 72, 78, 91, 96
aggrandizing, 92-93
aggregation,
    population aggregation, 8, 43, 46, 50, 54-55, 62-65, 67, 69, 71, 73, 75-77, 79, 81-82; *see also group fissioning*
    settlement aggregation, 8-9, 57, 75, 81, 139
agricultural, 15-16, 19-20, 22, 24-26, 28-29, 46, 50-51, 55, 58, 61, 90-91, 93-94, 107, 111, 128, 131, 136, 138, 143, 145, 173, 186-187, 206-207
Akşehir Settlement, 15-29
Akşehir Plain, 15-16
Albania, 4
Alföld Linear Pottery culture, 73, 76
alluvial, 15-16, 46, 64, 97, 162, 192
American Southwest, 51, 54-56, 75
analogy, 14, 21, 29, 51, 90, 92
Anatolia, 8, 14-16, 19-20, 26-29, 56, 58
ancestor, 37, 89-90, 115, 117-118
ancestral, 37, 39, 55, 75, 122-123, 175, 184
architecture, 9-10, 15, 43-44, 49, 52, 56, 58, 60, 62, 71, 74-75, 77-78, 80, 90, 97, 115, 128, 131, 134, 139, 185, 193, 195-196, 208
Aşıklı Höyük (site), 20-21, 26
Aszód-Papi földek (site), 63, 70
autonomous communities, 72-73
Aztec Sun Stone, 7

B

Baden culture, 82, 84, 87, 92, 97-98
Banat, 48-49, 56, 76, 78, 80
barrier, 48, 56, 79, 145, 155
barrow, 52, 83, 88, 92, 184
behavior, 2, 5, 8, 19, 24, 29, 44, 57, 76, 88, 90, 94, 105, 113, 121, 128, 161
behavioral, 8, 12, 22, 24, 28, 60, 62-63, 72, 174, 185
Berettyóújfalu-Herpály (site), 47-49, 53, 57-58, 77

Bibracte (site), 34, 37-39, 41
bimodal, 164-165
binomial, 108-110
borders, 36, 88, 91
Bordoš (site), 63, 70, 78
Bosnia, 53, 56
boundaries, 6, 23, 32, 45, 51, 70, 80, 83, 89, 91, 106, 123-124, 127-128, 149, 152, 155, 188, 190, 192, 194, 197, 204
boundedness, 50, 181, 190
Britain, 9, 38, 41, 136, 173-176, 184-185
Broadacre City, 2
Bronocice (site), 82-88, 90-93, 95-96
built environment, 1-8, 10, 12, 14, 19-21, 28, 44, 51, 62, 74-75, 80, 90-91, 131, 162, 167, 169, 173, 178, 184, 186-187, 200, 204, 208-209
burial,
    complex, 176-179, 181
    monument, 9, 115, 118, 173, 175-176, 178, 180, 183-184
    practices, 96, 183, 196, 203
Bylany (site), 23
byre, 135, 137, 143, 146, 149, 152-153, 194

C

Cahokia (site), 12, 51, 55, 61, 77
Calvert (site), 45
Camulodunum, 175, 178-180, 182-185
Caribbean, 129
Carpathian Basin, 8, 10, 46-47, 52, 59-60, 75
Carpathians, 57, 60, 76-77, 80-81, 94, 97-98, 101
Çarşamba River, 15
Çatalhöyük (site), 20, 26, 29, 49, 53-54, 56, 60, 76
catchment, 127, 206
cemetery, 50-52, 87-89, 91, 107, 159, 190-191, 196-197, 203-204, 206-209; *see also necropolis*
Central Place Theory, 99-101, 103-104, 106, 109, 111
centrality, 6, 54, 113, 122, 125, 127-128, 161, 165
centralization, 8-10, 32-33, 52, 54, 157, 161, 165-166, 169, 200, 203, 209
ceramics, 12, 58, 70, 73, 76, 79, 82, 84, 88-89, 102, 112, 132, 150, 159, 163-164, 180, 195-196
ceremonial, 26, 32-33, 51, 71, 128, 177-178, 185
    ceremonial route, 178
châine opératoire, 86
chiefdom, 52, 55, 111, 116, 173
chieftain, 132, 134, 137-138, 145
Childe, Vere Gordon, 99, 111
church, 4, 7, 120, 139-140, 187-189, 191, 193, 195-196, 201
climate, 2, 72, 136, 140, 154, 174

Ćmielów (site), 82-84, 86-87, 91-92, 94

coalescence, 50-51, 56, 58

coastal, 34, 58, 120, 140, 143, 145-147, 150-151, 153-154, 187, 209

cohesion, 6, 8, 32, 43-44, 54, 60, 62-63, 73-74, 82, 115-116, 127-128, 152-153, 201-202

Čoka-Kremenjak (site), 63, 70

Colchester (site), 174, 178, 180-185

collapse, 15, 28, 109, 111, 116

collective memories, 40

Colne River, 177-178, 181

colonial, 1, 128-130

colonization, 128, 169, 186

communication, 2, 9-10, 24, 57, 60, 66, 80, 83, 89, 100, 117-119, 121-122, 127, 133, 157, 159, 161-163, 165-167, 169, 183, 194

community organization, 1-3, 9-10, 32, 100, 106, 117, 122, 139

comparison, 2, 8-10, 14-15, 21, 25, 50, 52, 56, 76, 106, 109, 125, 128, 146, 149-150, 164, 166-169, 183, 204-205

complexity, 5, 29, 40, 42, 44, 50-51, 59, 76, 94, 99, 111, 118, 121, 128, 142, 154, 173, 201, 209

conflict, 6, 12, 16, 18, 24, 27-28, 36, 49-50, 56, 59, 72-73, 117; see also violence

consumption, 19-21, 26, 28, 44, 46, 96, 129

cooperation, 2, 21-22, 72, 91, 161, 167

Corded Ware culture, 82, 93

cosmology, 6, 12, 63, 74, 115, 173

courtyard, 17-18, 21, 118, 195

craft production, 26, 34, 53, 60, 91, 187, 194

craftspeople, 187, 191-192, 194-197

cremation, 9, 173, 175-176, 178, 180, 183-184, 191, 197, 203, 207

Crnobrnja (site), 48, 56, 66, 75

Csárdaszállás (site), 46-50, 52, 54, 63, 71

Cucuteni-Tripolye culture, 8, 99, 102, 107; see also Trypillia culture

Çumra Settlement, 15-29

D

Danebury (site), 185

Danmark, 154-155; see also Denmark

Danubian, 95

daub, 48, 85, 136-137

defense, 43, 50-51, 56, 84, 92, 117, 128, 153, 183, 186, 190-191, 193-194, 197

deforestation, 92, 133

demography, 16, 78, 96, 111-113, 205

Denmark, 9, 34, 46, 131, 133, 136, 138-142, 154-156; see also Danmark

Dobrovody (site), 102, 106-107

Draper (site), 56

E

Early Bronze Age, 97, 116, 150

Early Copper Age, 46, 51-52, 54, 57-58, 60-61, 64, 66, 71, 75-77, 94

Early Iron Age, 9, 37, 115-118, 120, 122, 125, 128-129, 131-133, 136, 139-140, 142-143, 145, 147, 149-150, 152, 157-158, 161-165, 168-169

Early Neolithic, 63, 73, 79-80, 90-91, 93, 113

earthworks, 9, 173, 175, 177-178, 180-183

Eaton (site), 45, 50, 60

economic inequality, 9

enclosure, 17, 37, 50-52, 59, 69-72, 74, 79, 87-88, 92, 97, 120, 145, 150, 173, 177-178, 185, 206-207

environmental stress, 9, 139

ethnicity, 5-6, 8, 29, 78, 137, 196

ethnoarchaeology, 8, 14, 29, 45, 56, 58, 60, 185

ethnographic, 9-10, 14, 19, 21, 43, 88, 101, 201

Etruria, 9-10, 157-159, 161-162, 165-169, 200-207, 209

Etruscan, 9-10, 157, 162, 164-165, 167, 200-206, 208-209

exchange, 40, 43-44, 54, 72, 93, 113, 128, 167, 169, 185, 196

F

farmstead, 143, 145, 147-153

Fedorovka (site), 102, 106-107

Final Bronze Age, 9, 116-118, 122, 128, 157, 159-166, 168, 203, 206

flint, 52, 83, 86-87, 91

Folly Lane (site), 175-178, 181, 184-185

fortification, 32, 37, 39, 87, 189-190, 193

frontier, 197, 206

functional zones, 143, 186-187

funerary rites, see burial practices

Funnel Beaker culture, 8, 82-85, 87-89, 91, 93-95, 97; see also TRB

G

Gamla Uppsala (site), 34, 41

Garden Cities, 2

gender, 5-6, 56, 111

general systems theory, 99-100

geoarchaeology, 60-61

Geographic Information Systems (GIS), 9, 58, 62, 78, 121, 129-130, 162, 173, 176, 184-185

geophysical survey, 69; see also magnetic survey

Globular Amphora culture, 82

Glubochek (site), 102, 106-107

Göbekli Tepe (site), 8, 33, 41-42

Grand Duchy of Lithuania, 186-189, 192, 194, 196

grave goods, 87, 89, 159, 177, 180, 191, 196-197, 208

Great Hungarian Plain, 8, 43, 46, 49, 51-59, 61-64, 67, 70-76, 78-80

Gródek Nadbużny (site), 82-83, 85-86, 90, 92, 94-95

group fissioning, 44, 54

Grzegorzewice-Zagaje (site), 82-83

H

hamlet, 45

hillfort, 190, 192, 195

hinterland, 34, 127, 194

hoard, 139, 195

Hódmezővásárhely-Gorzsa (site), 47-49, 57

house cluster, 22, 45, 50, 55

house plan, 17-18
household, 14-15, 17-29, 44-46, 48, 50-58, 60-61, 71-75, 81, 86, 91-92, 96, 132-134, 137-141, 143, 145, 149, 152-153, 156, 173, 201, 203
Hungary, 12, 43, 46-47, 49, 51-52, 54-57, 59-61, 64, 75-81
Huron, 51

I
Iberia, 39
identity,
    collective, 5-8, 90
    ethnic, 7, 187, 197
    group, 6-8, 54, 74, 115
    construction of, 32, 90
infrastructure, 161, 167, 186
ingot, 117, 130, 196
instability, 99, 116-117, 202
integration, 3, 8-9, 27, 40-41, 43-46, 49-52, 54, 56, 59-60, 67, 73, 75, 82, 99
integrative mechanism, 8, 44, 51, 54, 74
intensification, 50, 93, 147
intervisibility, 9, 115, 119, 121-128, 130, 181
intrasite, 88, 159
Iroquoia, 45, 50-54, 56, 60
islands, 89, 132, 145
Italy, 42, 129-130, 157-158, 162, 168-169, 200

J
Jutland, 9-10, 95, 131-147, 149-156

K
karst, 122
Kernavė (site), 9, 186-197
kin group, 20-22
kinship, 6, 20, 52-53, 72, 88, 115, 128, 141, 184
kiva, 51, 58, 60
Kongeå River, 146, 149
Konya Plain, 15
Körös culture, 73, 75
Körös River, 61, 64, 67-68
Körös Valley, 63-64, 66-67, 70-71
København, 140-141, 154-156

L
land tenure, 115, 142, 145, 149, 153
landforms, 1, 121, 145
landmark, 33, 115, 120, 128
landscape, 4-5, 7-12, 14, 23, 32, 40, 44, 46, 55-56, 59-60, 64, 66, 72, 75, 78, 83-84, 89-91, 94, 96, 102, 113, 115, 117-119, 121-123, 125, 127-131, 133, 140-141, 145, 149, 152-153, 155, 173-184, 200, 202-207
Late Bronze Age, 37, 116, 143, 146, 148, 150, 155
Late Iron Age, 8-9, 32, 34-35, 37, 39-42, 116, 143, 154, 173, 175-181, 183-184
Late Neolithic, 8, 43, 45-46, 48-60, 62-81, 96, 129, 150
Latial Period, 157-160, 168
Latium vetus, 9-10, 157-159, 161-162, 165-169

Lazio, 157, 162, 169
LBA, 116-118, 120; *see also Late Bronze Age*
leaders, 8, 38, 82, 88-89, 92-93, 159, 203
Lengyel culture, 70, 77, 79-80, 82, 84, 87, 89
Lesser Poland, 8, 82-83, 85, 87, 89-93, 95-98
Lexden (site), 175, 180-182, 184
Leżnica (site), 85, 97
Limfjord, 131-133, 136, 139
lineage, 10, 19, 23-25, 28, 33, 39, 48, 51, 53-54, 89, 180, 201
Linear Pottery Culture, 73, 76, 82, 84
lithic, 52, 81
Lithuania, 9, 186-189, 193-194
longhouse, 9, 48-52, 81, 131-140, 142-143, 146-152
longue durée, 39, 131
lowland, 33, 42, 56, 83, 88, 95, 120-121, 127, 137, 181

M
macrobotanical analysis, 46-47, 52, 55
magnetic survey, 68
Maidanetske (site), 102-104, 106-107
Mantle (site), 51-52, 55
market, 20, 34, 42, 99-101, 104, 106, 111, 113, 120, 196
marketplace, 34, 44-45, 56, 60, 113, 128, 191, 194-195
marshlands, 144-148, 152; *see also wetlands*
material culture, 70, 74-75, 89, 101, 105, 132, 140, 157, 159, 167, 187, 206
materiality, 29, 59, 79
materialization, 15, 203
MBA, 116-119; *see also Middle Bronze Age*
Medieval Age, 4, 8-9, 33-34, 79, 99, 111, 120, 140, 186, 189-190, 192-195, 197, 201, 206
Mediterranean, 12, 34, 36, 38, 40, 55, 57, 60-61, 79, 116, 128-130, 200
mega-sites, 9, 78, 84, 92, 96, 102, 107, 109, 111, 113
megalithic, 83, 90, 129
megaliths, 115, 130
megaron, 115-116, 118-120, 122, 125
Mesoamerica, 10, 28-32, 34, 37, 42, 46, 56, 61
microremains, 43, 45-46
midden, 21, 26, 45, 49-50, 52
Middle Bronze Age, 9, 115-116, 206
Middle Neolithic, 64-66, 70, 73-74, 79, 84, 90, 93
middle-range societies, 8, 62-63, 65, 67, 69, 71, 73, 75, 77, 79, 81
migration, 7, 12, 16, 27, 55, 96-97, 105, 108, 111
Mikulin (site), 83
Mississippian, 48, 51-52, 55-56, 58-59
mobility, 16, 27-28, 44, 53, 58, 70, 89, 138, 206
monument, 5, 7, 9-10, 69, 75, 79, 88-89, 93, 96, 115, 117-123, 125, 127-129, 147, 173-178, 180-181, 183-184, 203-204
mortuary, 72, 92, 197
Moshurov (site), 104
motherhood, 2, 12
mound, 8-10, 34, 46-47, 49-51, 55, 66, 69, 71, 78, 131, 133, 135-137, 139-141, 180
Mozgawa (site), 82-88, 93, 95

N

Nebelevka (site), 102-107
necropolis, 209
neighborhood, 7, 12, 14, 21-22, 26, 28-29, 71-75
Neris River, 192, 194
networks, 9-10, 12, 16, 21, 58, 60, 66, 72-73, 80, 82, 92, 100, 109, 115, 117, 121-122, 127, 129, 157, 159, 161-169, 174-176, 178, 180-181, 183-184, 192, 200, 206
nuraghi, 9-10, 115-128
Nuragic culture, 9, 115-125, 127-130

O

obsidian, 120-121
Öcsöd-Kováshalom (site), 47, 49-50, 52, 54, 59-60, 63-65, 67-69, 71-74, 76, 79-80
Okolište (site), 53
oppidum, 8, 10, 32, 34-42, 173, 175-176, 178-184, 202
Orientalizing Age, 116, 157, 159-160, 162-163, 165
outbuilding, 50, 143, 148-149, 151-152
oven, 20, 48, 52-54

P

paganism, 4, 9, 186, 195-197
palisade, 47-48, 50-52, 54-55, 69, 84, 136
parish, 147, 189, 196, 201
Parţa (site), 47-49, 53, 56, 76
pastoral, 107, 128
pastures, 16, 23, 25-26, 207
pathways, 42, 50, 55, 73-74, 122, 161, 179, 207
Pawłosiów (site), 83
peer polity, 80, 209
Peregonovka (site), 102, 106-107
Perugia (site), 204, 206, 208-209
phosphate, 50, 52
Pisa, 129, 169, 209
pit, 29, 45, 49-50, 52, 68, 71, 84-85, 87, 137, 142, 150, 194
plateau, 57, 97, 122, 177-178, 181, 192, 203-204, 206-208
plaza, 32, 34, 37, 42, 45, 55-56, 71
ploschchadka, 85-86
Poland, 8, 23, 82-83, 85, 87, 89-93, 95-98
Polgár Island, 64, 66, 70-71, 75
Polgár-Csőszhalom, 47-49, 53, 55, 58-59, 63, 66, 69-76, 78-80
polity, 3, 32, 37, 41, 51, 59, 74, 80, 157, 209
preservation, 133, 142-143, 146, 150, 194
profane, 9, 33, 67, 115, 127
proto-urban, 8, 158
proto-historic, 113
pueblo, 51, 55, 60, 75

Q

quarter, living, 17, 22, 24-25, 82, 92, 192-193, 195-196

R

radiocarbon dating, 39, 46, 61, 68-70, 87-89, 94-95, 97, 109, 116, 147, 151
raiding, 107, 209
reciprocal, 9, 14, 18, 115, 117, 122

reciprocity, 3
reorganization, 23, 72, 122, 145, 150, 152
residence, 6, 20, 64, 70, 73-74, 186, 190-194, 197
resilience, 2, 161, 167
Rhine River, 37, 40-41
riverine, 9
rivers, 102, 123, 128, 145, 147, 162, 178, 181, 194
Roman, 1, 9, 36-41, 68, 99, 116, 131-134, 136-141, 143, 147-150, 152, 154-155, 168, 174-184, 203
Romanovka (site), 104
Rome, 4, 9-10, 37, 42, 130, 157-159, 162, 167-169, 175, 183, 200-202, 204-206, 209

S

sacred, 6, 8, 33-34, 37-40, 44, 48, 51-52, 115, 118-120, 122, 133
San Cibrán de Las (site), 39-40
sanctuary, 5, 8-10, 32-41, 48, 115-129, 184, 205-206
Sant'Anastasia (site), 120-121, 125, 127
Santa Vittoria (site), 115, 120-121, 125, 127-128
Sardinia, 9, 115-121, 127-130
satellite site, 8-9, 54, 64, 99, 106, 109
scalar stress, 5, 55, 75, 77
secondary center, 158, 205
Selinunte (site), 1
Serbia, 47, 70, 78-79, 81
settlement,
    cluster, 54, 64, 103-104, 138, 149
    hierarchy, 131, 138, 158-159
shrine, 48, 51, 71, 116, 118
simulation, 9, 99, 107-111
Skołoszów (site), 83
Slavic, 186-187, 190, 196
social,
    hierarchy, 24, 91-92, 145, 195
    inequality, 55, 60, 145, 195
    reproduction, 40
    status, 137, 195-197
soilscape, 60, 80, 97
specialization, 43-44, 48, 52-53, 78, 100, 194
stabling, 17-18, 20, 25, 46, 134-135, 137
Stanway (site), 175, 178-182, 184
status, 47, 89, 91-93, 117, 127-128, 134, 137, 139, 148-149, 159, 177, 186, 193, 195-197
steppe, 15, 90, 94, 102
storage,
    domestic, 48
    bin, 20
    pit, 49, 194
strategic, 7, 24, 54, 57, 64, 81, 92, 105, 121, 127-128, 173, 175-176, 183, 189
stratification, 9, 93, 139, 153, 159, 186, 191, 195, 197
stratigraphy, 47, 67-69, 80, 133, 143, 147, 192, 209
structuration, 41, 152
Stryczowice (site), 82-83
subsistence, 8, 15, 20, 28-29, 47, 50-51, 54, 58, 96-97, 99-100, 109, 133, 143, 201
surface survey, 44, 67, 94, 205-207

Sushkovka (site), 102, 106-107
Szakálhát culture, 73, 77, 81
Szeghalom-Kovácshalom (site), 47-48, 50, 54-55, 57, 63-65, 67-74, 76, 94

T
Talianki (site), 102, 106-107
Talnoe (site), 104
Tarquinia (site), 203-205, 208
technology, 70, 76-77, 81, 140-141, 164, 176
tell (site type), 20-21, 33, 46-60, 63-64, 66-72, 74-81, 131, 137
temple, 9-10, 32-34, 37-39, 48, 58, 115-120, 122-127, 184, 195, 204, 209
territoriality, 14, 23-24, 28-29
Thessaly, 63, 80
Tiber River, 157, 162, 204-206
Tisza culture, 64, 68, 70-74
Tisza River, 63-64, 69
Tiszazug, 47, 63-64, 68, 70, 75
Titelberg (site), 34, 36-37, 42
Tomashovka (site), 102, 106-107
tombe dei giganti, 115-116, 118-119, 121-122, 125, 127
tomb, 9, 83, 90, 115, 118, 129, 202, 204, 208
topography, 15, 18, 29, 64, 80, 119, 136, 204, 206-207
Trakai, 189, 193
transegalitarian, 8, 82, 92-93
transportation, 9, 27, 100-101, 157, 159, 161-162, 164-167, 169
TRB, 10, 82-93, 95-96
tribal, 18-19, 29, 37-38, 41, 44, 53, 55, 59, 75
tribe, 16, 187, 196
Trypillia culture, 84-85, 92, 94, 96, 101, 111-114
tumulus, 37, 180-182, 184, 204, 208
typology, 46, 75, 81, 88, 115, 141, 143, 151, 155

U
Uivar (site), 47, 49, 53, 56, 76, 80

Ukraine, 82, 85, 95, 99, 101-102
UNESCO, 189
uplands, 19, 83-84, 90-91, 102, 116, 119, 206
Uppåkra (site), 33, 41-42
urbanization, 2, 8, 32, 40-42, 56, 73, 75-79, 81, 99, 157-158, 168-169, 186-187, 189, 209

V
Varde River, 146-147, 149, 153-155
Veii (site), 203-208
Ver River, 177
Vésztő-Mágor (site), 47-48, 57, 60, 63-64, 76-77, 94
viewshed, 9, 121-122, 125-126, 129-130, 173, 176-182
Villanova culture, 157, 159, 209
Vilnius, 187-190, 193, 195
Vinča culture, 56, 75
violence, 44, 51-52, 58, 129
visibility analysis, 128, 177-178, 183
Vladimirovka (site), 102, 106-107
votive offering, 37, 117

W
wandering village, 143, 145
water-temple, 10, 115-120, 122-123, 125-127
wealth indicators, 9
well, 15, 22-25, 28-29, 48, 50, 52, 68, 71, 115, 118-120, 122-123, 127, 208
wetlands, 78, 132-133
woodlands, 50, 75
workshop, 42, 194, 208
worldview, 6, 8, 75, 175
worship, 25, 37, 89, 115, 117-118, 123, 195
Wright, Frank Lloyd, 2

Z
Zimno (site), 82-83, 85, 87
Zuni, 51